THE STRATEGIC MANAGEMENT PROCESS

Third Edition

THE STRATEGIC MANAGEMENT PROCESS

Third Edition

Samuel C. Certo
Crummer Graduate School of Business at Rollins College

J. Paul Peter
University of Wisconsin—Madison

With Special Assistance of:
Edward Ottensmeyer
Clark University

AUSTEN
PRESS

IRWIN

Chicago • Bogotá • Boston • Buenos Aires • Caracas
London • Madrid • Mexico City • Sydney • Toronto

To our daughters, Sarah and Angela.
We love them dearly.
— SAMUEL C. CERTO —
— J. PAUL PETER —

Publisher: William Schoof
Acquisitions Editor: John R. Weimeister
Production Manager: Bob Lange
Marketing Manager: Kurt Messersmith

Development, design, and project management provided by Elm Street Publishing Services, Inc.

Compositor: G&S Typesetters, Inc.
Typeface: 10/12 New Baskerville
Printer: Von Hoffmann Press, Inc.

Library of Congress Cataloging-in-Publication Data
Certo, Samuel C.
    The strategic management process / Samuel C. Certo, J. Paul Peter. — 3rd ed.
        p.   cm.
    Previous ed. published under title: Strategic management : a focus on process.
    2nd ed. Irwin. 1993.
    Includes index.
    ISBN 0-256-18149-7
    1. Strategic planning.   I. Peter, J. Paul.
HD30.28.C42   1995
658.4'012—dc20   94-24725

Printed in the United States of America
1 2 3 4 5 6 7 8 9 0   V H   9   8   7   6   5   4

Address editorial correspondence:
Austen Press
18141 Dixie Highway
Suite 105
Homewood, IL 60430

Address orders:
Richard D. Irwin, Inc.
1333 Burr Ridge Parkway
Burr Ridge, IL 60521

Austen Press
Richard D. Irwin, Inc.

Preface

The continued acceptance of our hardback text, *Strategic Management: Concepts and Applications,* by strategic management instructors throughout the United States and several foreign countries has been very gratifying. That book is a comprehensive text designed for strategic management or business policy courses at either the undergraduate or graduate level. The hardback text focuses on strategic management theory and contains a set of 36 comprehensive strategic management cases.

Publication of this separate paperback text, *The Strategic Management Process,* third edition, is a result of feedback primarily from colleagues who have reviewed our hardback text with cases but would like to use the strategic management theory section without the case portion. Thus, this paperback, designed to meet the educational needs of these instructors, is the strategic management theory portion of our hardback text.

Although this third edition includes several improvements, its goal remains the same as prior editions: to provide students with an integrative learning experience that helps them develop strategic management knowledge and skills. We believe that for students to become effective strategic managers, they need to learn strategic management concepts and to practice applications of these concepts.

A strategic management text should do more than simply discuss theoretical concepts and their applications, leaving students to relate the former to the latter. We believe that a strategic management text should actually help students bridge the gap between theoretical concepts and their applications. The following sections discuss how *The Strategic Management Process* bridges this gap through the combination of a clear, pragmatic presentation of strategic management theory and a unique array of related student learning activities that stresses how they should be applied.

TEXT CONTENT: AN EMPHASIS ON CLARITY AND PRAGMATISM

This text includes five parts devoted to concepts of strategic management. These parts and related chapters are organized around the strategic management model shown on page vi.

Part I: An Overview of Strategic Management

This part provides a survey of strategic management and a framework for the remainder of the textual material. After reading Chapter 1, students should have a clear understanding of the nature and scope of strategic management and the strategic management process.

Strategic Management Model Used in Chapters 1 to 13

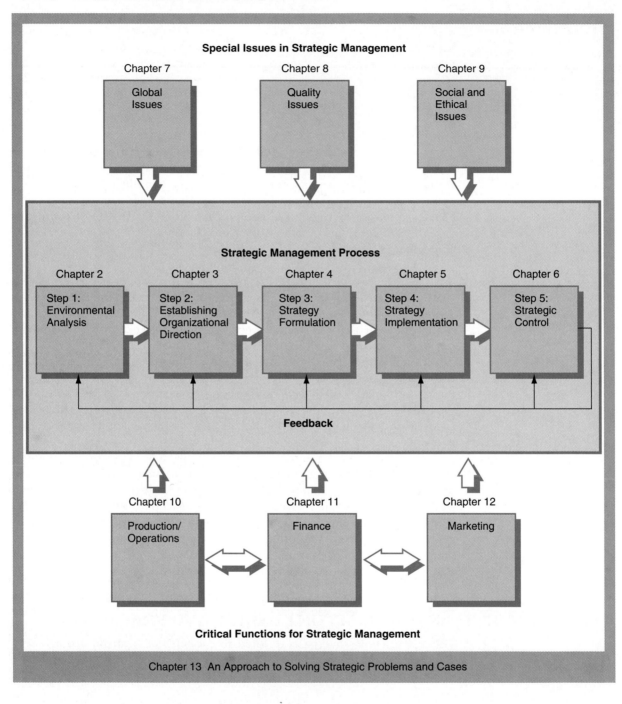

Part II: Strategic Management Process

In this part we discuss the five major steps in the strategic management process. These steps include environmental analysis (Chapter 2), establishing organizational direction (Chapter 3), strategy formulation (Chapter 4), strategy implementation (Chapter 5), and strategic control (Chapter 6).

Part III: Special Issues in Strategic Management

Although the previous sections include the major topics commonly discussed in strategic management courses, we believe at least three other areas require special consideration. These areas are international operations (Chapter 7), total quality management (Chapter 8), and social responsibility and ethics (Chapter 9). We devote an entire chapter to each of these topics because of their important influence on strategic management decision making and the need for specialized knowledge of these topics in a variety of strategic management problems and cases.

Part IV: Critical Functions for Strategic Management

Successful strategic management efforts involve the application of the major business functions both individually and collectively or cross-functionally. This part covers the fundamentals of three important business functions to help students focus on cross-functional strategic management issues. The functional issues are discussed through individual chapters on operations (Chapter 10), finance (Chapter 11), and marketing (Chapter 12). In addition, information on these and other business functions is also integrated throughout the text.

Part V: A Framework for Strategic Analysis

We recognize that no single approach can be universally applied to all strategic management cases and problems; however, we are also mindful that students often need a framework for approaching case and problem analysis. A sound framework is particularly important when students first begin analyzing major strategic management cases and problems. For this reason we have included an extended discussion of a general approach to case and problem analysis in Chapter 13. This chapter on the process of case and problem analysis is designed to provide another bridge between concepts and applications. Even if students are not asked to analyze cases in a strategic management course, this chapter can be extremely useful in helping them to solve actual strategic management problems in the future.

APPLYING STRATEGIC MANAGEMENT THEORY: SPECIAL LEARNING EXERCISES

Each chapter in our text contains a variety of pedagogical features designed to enhance student learning and to facilitate the transfer of concepts to applications. Each chapter contains the following features:

- *Company Examples* that extend text material and provide illustrations of the application of strategic management concepts to well-known organizations.
- *Skills Modules* that challenge students to apply strategic management concepts to real organizational situations. These short exercises follow selected topics in the chapters, thus affording students directed activities for increasing their understanding and ability to apply strategic management concepts.
- *Checklists* that itemize major issues to be addressed in analyzing strategic management problems and cases. These checklists are keyed to the topics covered in each chapter and offer students a starting point for applying strategic management concepts to case situations.

- *Cases* (at the end of each chapter) that provide a brief scenario focusing on one or more topics covered in the chapter. They include specific questions for analysis, thus offering students an opportunity to apply chapter material in a directed way. The cases help students reach a better understanding of strategic management concepts and their applications and prepare them for longer, more involved strategic management cases.

CHANGES IN THE THIRD EDITION

We have made several changes in the third edition to better meet the needs of strategic management educators and students:

1. Recognizing the importance of the quality movement in strategic management, we have included a new chapter on total quality management.
2. Recognizing the integrative and cross-functional nature of strategic management, we have added new material throughout the text emphasizing these issues.
3. Recognizing the importance of timeliness for enhancing student interest in text material, we have provided a variety of new examples, illustrations, activities, additional readings, and applications throughout the text.
4. Recognizing the importance of key terms and concepts, we have added a list of key terms with page references at the end of each chapter.

INSTRUCTOR'S RESOURCE PACKAGE

This text is supported by a comprehensive instructor's resource package. Carefully developed to meet the unique demands of strategic management educators, the package consists of the following items:

- *Instructor's Manual.* The instructor's manual for this text was designed to provide exceptional support for anyone teaching a course in strategic management or business policy. The following is a discussion of the major sections of the instructor's manual:
  - *Suggestions for Teaching Strategic Management.* This introductory section provides insight about how the strategic management (or business policy) course can be taught. Discussion focuses on various teaching tools such as cases, lectures, exams, films, speakers, simulations, projects, and readings. A special section on how to use student study teams discusses team assignments, progress reporting, peer group evaluations, presentation evaluations, and suggestions on using team cases or projects. This section ends with discussion of course design and grading.
  - *Materials Supporting Text Chapters.* The second section of the instructor's manual presents several ingredients to support each text chapter. These ingredients include an author's overview or summary of a chapter, a chapter outline, key concepts and issues for classroom discussion, and detailed suggestions on how to use chapter Company Examples, Skills Modules, and Cases at the end of each chapter.
  - *Transparency Program.* Transparency masters are available to adopters of *The Strategic Management Process.* These masters focus on key theoretical concepts and issues in strategic management. Most are reproductions of selected graphics in the text.
  - *Test Item File.* The fourth section of the instructor's manual is a comprehensive test bank of about 350 true/false and multiple-choice items. It is also available on Irwin's Computerized Testing Software.

- *Selected Cases in Strategic Management, third edition,* also by Certo and Peter, is available as a set of comprehensive strategic management cases that can be used to supplement this text. The casebook offers an array of 36 cases divided into nine parts. In essence, the casebook and this theory-oriented text were carefully designed for efficient and effective use within the same course. A comprehensive *Case Enrichment Portfolio* provides exceptional instructional support for professors using the casebook.

ACKNOWLEDGMENTS

The positive feedback we have received relating to this project has been extremely satisfying. As with any project of this magnitude, however, the end product is actually the result of the efforts of several people, not simply the authors.

In particular, we would like to recognize the valuable role that our reviewers played in this project. Their dedication to high teaching standards and professionalism provided us with many worthwhile ideas that helped to make our text a more efficient and effective learning instrument. The reviewers who made significant contributions to the initiation and evaluation of this project are:

Bruce Charnov
Hofstra University
V. C. Doherty
Wayne State University
James H. Donnelly, Jr.
University of Kentucky
Bruce Fisher
Northeastern Illinois University
Robert Goldberg
Northeastern University
James R. Harris
Florida State University
Alan N. Hoffman
Bentley College
Janice Jackson
Virginia State University
Calvin Kellogg
Illinois State University
Rose Knotts
North Texas State University
Daniel Kopp
Southwest Missouri State University

Edwin C. Leonard, Jr.
*Indiana University, Purdue University
   at Fort Wayne*
William Litzinger
University of Texas at San Antonio
Martin K. Marsh
California State University, Bakersfield
Bob McGowan
University of Denver
Hugh O'Neil
University of North Carolina
Shiv Sawhney
Quinnipiac College
Marilyn Taylor
University of Kansas
Robert Vichas
Old Dominion University
Wendy Vittori
Northeastern University
Stanley Willing
St. Francis College

We would like to thank David Flynn of Hofstra University for writing the *Instructor's Manual* for this text. Finally, we extend thanks to our colleagues and students for all they have taught us, as well as the many strategic management educators who responded to our research surveys and provided excellent ideas for designing this project. In particular, we thank Ed Ottensmeyer of Clark University and Rajan Kamath of the University of Cincinnati for their insights and efforts, which greatly improved our text. We thank Bill Schoof, John Weimeister, and the staff at Elm Street Publishing Services for their patience and persistence throughout this project. And, of course, we thank our families and friends for their encouragement and tolerance during the preparation of this work.

Samuel C. Certo
J. Paul Peter
November 1994

About the Authors

Samuel C. Certo is Professor of Management and former dean at the Roy E. Crummer Graduate School of Business, Rollins College, Winter Park, Florida. His current teaching responsibilities include an array of management courses with special emphasis on business strategy as well as a strategy-focused computer simulation course. He has been actively involved in management education at the college and university levels for over fifteen years and recently received the Charles A. Welsh Memorial Award for outstanding teaching at the Crummer School. Dr. Certo's numerous publications include articles for such journals as the *Academy of Management Review, The Journal of Experiential Learning and Simulation,* and *Training.* He has also written several successful textbooks, including *Modern Management: Diversity, Quality, Ethics, and the Global Environment; Supervision: Quality and Diversity Through Leadership;* and *Human Relations Today: Concepts and Skills.* A past chairman of the Management Education and Development Division of the Academy of Management, he has been honored by that group with its Excellence of Leadership Award. Dr. Certo has also served as president of the Association for Business Simulation and Experiential Learning, as associate editor for *Simulation and Games,* and as a review board member of the *Academy of Management Review.* His consulting experience has been extensive with notable experience on boards of directors.

J. Paul Peter is James R. McManus-Bascom Professor in Marketing at the University of Wisconsin—Madison. He taught at Indiana State University, Washington University, and Ohio State University before joining the faculty at Wisconsin in 1980. He has taught a variety of courses and has won several teaching awards, including the John R. Larson School of Business Teaching Award in 1990. His articles on consumer behavior, marketing theory, and research methodology are frequently cited in the marketing literature. He was awarded the prestigious William O'Dell Award from the *Journal of Marketing Research* in 1986. Dr. Peter has coauthored several books, including *A Preface to Marketing Management, Marketing Management: Knowledge and Skills,* and *Consumer Behavior and Marketing Strategy;* he is coeditor of *Measurement Readings for Marketing Research* and *Marketing Theory and Practice.* He has served as editor of AMA Professional Publications and as editor of *JMR*'s Measurement Section. He has served on the Editorial Review Boards of the *Journal of Marketing, Journal of Marketing Research, Journal of Consumer Research,* and *Journal of Business Research* and has been a consultant and executive teacher for a variety of corporations as well as the Federal Trade Commission.

Brief Contents

Detailed Contents

NOTE TO THE INSTRUCTOR

Austen Press texts are marketed and distributed by Richard D. Irwin, Inc. For assistance in obtaining supplementary material for this and other Austen Press titles, please contact your Irwin sales representative or the customer service division of Richard D. Irwin at (800) 323-4560.

PART I

Overview of Strategic Management

This section provides an overview of strategic management and builds a framework for the remainder of the text. Its major purpose is to acquaint you with the nature and scope of strategic management and its development as a critical area of management education. In carefully studying this section, you should develop a basic understanding of the cross-functional process of strategic management and an appreciation for the importance of strategic management in running a successful organization.

Introduction to Strategic Management

Sega Takes Aim at Disney's World

The Profit Machine: NordicTrack Is the Muscle behind Top-Ranked CML

Losing Altitude: Once-Solid Delta Air is Burdened by Cost of European Foray

After Initial Fuzziness, AT&T Clears Up Signal to Asia

Footwear Fad Makes Nike, Reebok Run for Their Money: Doc Martens Shoes and Boots are Popular among Trend Setting Teenagers

Headlines like these from the business press capture the drama, excitement, and dynamism of strategic management in action.[1] The adventure you are about to begin with this text will help you to understand the strategies and analyses behind the headlines, and carefully selected cases will put you in the manager's chair to let you practice strategic management techniques and experience the qualities of leadership needed to translate analysis into effective action.

As in any field, a beginner must do a great deal of work, especially in the early stages, to learn the basics. The student must speak and understand a new language and view the world from a new perspective. For example, analysis of the cases in this text must extend beyond the limits of one discipline's viewpoint (marketing, finance, operations, or organizational behavior); strategic management cases address all of these topics at the same time, in the way that real managers must address them. Thus, the cases will require you to draw on what you have learned about these functions and to use the cross-functional tools of the general manager, whose responsibilities reach throughout an entire firm, or a significant part of one.

When they see that a strategic management course focuses on the general manager's perspective, some students view the course narrowly, as something they will not need for several years, or until they become general managers or high-ranking business executives themselves. We strongly encourage you to begin the study of strategic management with a wider view! Never before have business firms shown more interest in the contributions of employees and managers at all levels to the overall good of the firm. Even the smallest actions might reduce costs or improve quality—both primary focuses of strategic management. Entry-level workers may reap valuable rewards if they approach their early corporate experiences well-versed in strategic management techniques and thinking more broadly about their firms than their first specialized jobs might require. The strategic management course may not get you your first job, but it may get you promoted out of that job faster. We hope this will be your experience.

The fundamental reality is this: mastering strategic management is a career-long endeavor for the successful general manager. At its most basic, strategic management requires careful, creative thought about the future and effective action that places the organization in a better position in that future. Leaders of businesses, armies, churches, and governments have faced these challenges since humans first organized their activities.

Clearly, some strategic management efforts have been less successful than others—the Roman Empire crumbled, Napoleon lost at Waterloo, and IBM is struggling in the mid-1990s to regain its lost leadership position. Successes as well as failures dot the strategic management landscape, underscoring the dynamic and risky nature of the endeavor. However, thinking and acting strategically is vital for the modern leader who hopes to guide any enterprise to success. No one masters strategic management once and for all—it is a lifelong journey for the successful leader. We trust that this text will serve you well as a starting point and as a road map on your own journey.

Chapter 1 provides some background and an overview of the strategic management field. First, we outline the evolution of strategic management as a field of study, then we formally define the subject and describe how to apply its concepts and what benefits accrue to organizations that practice it. Next, we suggest the phases through which an organization passes in developing its strategic management process. We briefly trace the steps in the process of strategic management and consider several contemporary challenges in the field. We examine how the strategic management process relates to three major business functions, and finally we review the case analysis approach to learning the subject.

EVOLUTION OF STRATEGIC MANAGEMENT AS A FIELD OF STUDY

The study of strategic management first took shape after the Ford Foundation and the Carnegie Corporation sponsored research into the curriculum at business schools in the 1950s. A synopsis of this research, the Gordon-Howell report, recommended expanding business education to include a capstone course in an area called *business policy*.[2]

By design, the business policy course was meant to integrate other areas of study, teaching students to apply analytical techniques learned in earlier courses in marketing, finance, organizational behavior, or operations management to problems that would confront a business firm as a whole. The course would thus give students the opportunity to exercise qualities of judgment that did not arise explicitly in any earlier courses.

The Gordon-Howell report gained widespread acceptance. By the early 1970s, most schools of business included business policy courses within their curriculum requirements. As time passed, however, the focus of the course became wider. The business policy course began to consider the total organization and its environment. For example, it addressed issues such as social responsibility and ethics, as well as the potential impacts of political, legislative, and economic events on the successful operation of an organization.

In the 1980s, an impressive outpouring of research supplemented the growing literature on competitive strategy. Over time, this research effort refined a new tool kit of techniques such as industry analysis, that sharpened the traditional focus to establish the business policy course as the place in a business curriculum where students would examine the big picture of business decision making. This newer, broader emphasis prompted leaders in the field to change the name of the course from *business policy* to *strategic management*.[3]

Recent curricular innovations in business schools may affect the strategic management courses of the future. Instead of presenting a capstone course to integrate material learned earlier in function-focused courses, some business schools are now integrating functional learning from the beginning. This development reflects a conscious attempt to spread the benefits of integrative learning—long the goal of business policy and strategic management courses—across the business curriculum. It is difficult to predict the impact of such changes on strategic management courses as we have come to know them in the last decade. However, we suspect that, while some of the core material of strategic management may appear earlier in an undergraduate or MBA curriculum, students will continue to need a single, challenging, integrative experience.

This text has been carefully designed to reflect the most current research and to serve as a foundation for students to learn concepts that are both pragmatic and theoretically up to date. In addition, we expect a strong strategic management course to help students refine their communications skills through written and oral presentations. Table 1.1 presents a list of the specific skills you can expect to develop in this course.

NATURE OF STRATEGIC MANAGEMENT

Strategy and strategic management are concepts that evolve over time.[4] These ideas defy universally accepted definitions because scholars develop them and

---

TABLE 1.1

Strategic Management Course Skills

1. Identification of core problems or issues in a business situation or case
2. Wide-ranging assessment of opportunities and threats in the environment and the strengths and weaknesses of an organization and its managers
3. Analysis of strategic alternatives appropriate to a variety of situations and from the perspectives of a variety of stakeholders
4. Formulation and selection of specific courses of action to implement chosen strategies
5. Focused application of analytical skills from functional courses—production, finance, marketing, operations research, personnel, and so forth—to effectively develop, select, and implement competitive strategies
6. Oral and written communication of analyses and recommendations for action

---

managers practice them in diverse ways.[5] This lack of consensus, however, does not keep most contemporary organizations from trying to reap the benefits of strategic management by developing innovative strategies to out-maneuver their competitors.

Definition of *Strategy*

In this text, following James Brian Quinn, **strategy** will be defined as "the pattern or plan that integrates an organization's major goals, policies, and action sequences into a cohesive whole."[6] Quinn also suggests that a strategy helps a firm to allocate its resources, to capitalize on its relative strengths and mitigate its weaknesses, to exploit projected shifts in the environment, and to counter possible actions of competitors.

This definition helps students to understand and appreciate what a strategy looks like, what its key elements are, and what it is supposed to accomplish for the organization that implements it well. Thus, a firm with a well-articulated strategy should:

- Set a clear direction
- Know its strengths and weaknesses compared with its competitors
- Devote its hard-won resources to projects that employ its set of core competencies, the primary skills within the organization
- Identify factors in the political and social environment that require careful monitoring
- Recognize which competitor actions need critical attention

In short, managers in such a firm should have a rational, clear-headed notion, purged of wishful thinking, of (1) its mission, (2) its external competitive environment, and (3) its internal capabilities. Keeping this notion fresh and current, and orchestrating the changes and adaptations that updates inevitably require, is the essential task of the strategic management process. All departments and functions must contribute to complete this enormous task effectively.

We would point out, however, that a firm without a carefully articulated, written strategy statement might still have a strategy. Quinn's definition of strategy encompasses both formal plans and informal patterns of activity. This is consistent with Henry Mintzberg's notion of strategy as a "pattern in a stream of decisions."[7] Thus, even if a firm's managers cannot name or label its own strategy, the pattern of their decisions over time would define its real strategy. However, the enormous attention that corporate strategy and strategic management have received in the past 20 years, from best-selling books to regular coverage in the popular press, has increased the probability that managers in even the smallest start-up firms will discuss their competitive strategies explicitly.

Understanding a manager's comments about a firm's strategy is often tricky work. First, one must separate real strategy from competitive ploys. A firm may announce a change in its strategy or a new strategic initiative in an attempt to confuse or slow down a key competitor. The computer software industry has developed a specific term—*vaporware*—to describe a new software product that an industry competitor has announced but not yet completed. Announcements about vaporware send messages to a firm's customers (i.e., don't buy from our competitors; our product will be out soon) as well as its competitors (i.e., don't even think about trying to compete with us; we've got the new and improved version).

A manager's comments about strategy, even if a firm has a stated strategic plan, may reflect wishful thinking more than careful analysis of the competitive environment. For example, start-ups or small businesses often load strategy statements with heavy doses of wishful thinking to attract early-stage financing from banks or venture capitalists.

Answering Basic Questions to Develop Strategy

If a strategy says so much about a firm, what key questions must managers answer to develop one? Table 1.2 summarizes these questions. First, developing a strategy forces the manager to focus on the very basic question about the business in which the firm really competes, or would like to compete. *What good or service do we really sell?* What do we, as a firm, do best? For example, does an athletic shoe company sell high performance or style?

Second, *how will we produce our goods or deliver our services?* For example, in our industry at this point in time, can we succeed with an upscale entry or would a stripped-down, low-cost version be more successful? Answering these

---

TABLE 1.2

Some Key Questions in Strategy Development

1. What good or service do we really sell?
2. How will we produce our goods or deliver our services?
3. Who will buy our goods or services?
4. How will we finance the operation?
5. How much risk are we willing to take?
6. How will we implement our strategy?

first two questions forces managers to look carefully at their core competencies, which, in turn, shape product characteristics as well as manufacturing requirements.[8]

The third question asks *who will buy our goods or services?* This brings the customer and the existing industry structure squarely into the middle of the strategy equation. An answer to this question requires industry and competitor analyses, marketing research, and distribution channel and logistics analyses.

The fourth question asks *how will we finance the operation?* A new strategy can be quite costly, as the firm gears up to design new products, enter new channels, challenge competitors in new market segments, purchase new manufacturing equipment, hire new workers, etc. Finding the funds to implement a new strategy is not a trivial concern.

The fifth question is closely related to the fourth. *How much risk are we willing to take?* A new strategy may require management to bet the business on its success. If the strategy is a winner, the firm wins; if it fails, the firm collapses. These risk assessments are often among the most difficult judgments that business leaders make. Delta Airlines' expansion into the European air travel market has been unsuccessful (as the headlines at the start of this chapter hinted). This is an example of a strategic decision gone awry, with potentially serious implications for the long-term survival of the company.

The first five questions are all concerned with analysis and judgment to define a strategy for an organization. The sixth question asks *how will we implement our strategy?* How will we revise it along the way? What changes in structure, systems, or staffing will we need to make to improve an intended strategy's chance to succeed? Mintzberg and Waters remind us that intended strategies often do not survive in their initial states.[9] For example, Steve Jobs's venture, NeXT Computer, had to shift its strategy toward innovative computer software and away from new hardware because of dramatic changes in the market.[10] Thus, NeXT's intended and realized strategies differed markedly.

The six basic questions guide the analyses that underlie the firm's effort to formulate and implement a competitive strategy. From these questions flow the critical decisions that shape an organization's future. The overarching methodology or process that brings these questions into clear focus is called *strategic management.*

Definition of *Strategic Management*

Strategic management is a continuous, iterative, cross-functional process aimed at keeping an organization as a whole appropriately matched to its environment. This definition emphasizes the series of steps that a manager must take. These steps, which we will discuss individually in the following pages, include performing an environmental analysis, establishing organizational direction, formulating organizational strategy, implementing organizational strategy, and exercising strategic control. Additional information on each of these steps will appear throughout this text.

The definition also suggests that the strategic management process is continuous; the organization never finishes its strategic work. Although different strategic management activities may receive more or less emphasis and require effort of varying intensity at different times, managers should virtually always be focusing or reflecting on some aspect of strategic management.

The term *iterative* in the definition reinforces this idea. The process of strategic management starts with the first step, carries on to the last step, and then begins again with the first step. Strategic management consists of a series of steps repeated cyclically.

The term *cross-functional* signifies that the strategic management process integrates organizational human resources and expertise from critical functions such as marketing, operations, and finance in a comprehensive effort. This helps the process, and the plan it generates, to deal more effectively with potential conflicts in recommendations of individual functions operating in isolation. A cross-functional approach allows no one, not marketing nor manufacturing nor finance, to control or dominate the process; each contributes simultaneously to create a better plan and result. Working as a cross-functional team, members of the management group can more clearly visualize the overall picture of where the firm is and what it needs to do in the future to achieve a sustainable competitive advantage. This method can encourage commitment of key executives to a strategic plan.[11]

The last part of the definition of *strategic management* identifies its purpose as ensuring that an organization as a whole appropriately matches its environment, that is, its competitive surroundings. Business environments change constantly, and organizations must modify their strategies accordingly to achieve organizational goals. New legislation may affect the organization, its labor supply may change, and competitors may launch new initiatives. These are examples of changes within the organization's environment that often require the attention of top managers.

Although the definition of *strategic management* seems clear and straightforward, actually performing the task is not. Carrying out this process in an organization usually becomes a very complex job that consumes much top management time. Increasingly, the involvement of managers and employees has spread throughout organizations.

ROLES IN STRATEGIC MANAGEMENT

A firm's top management, board of directors, and planning staff tend to be most involved in and to have the most influence on its strategic management process.[12] The following sections discuss, in more detail, the roles of these participants in the strategic management process.

Top Management's Role in Strategic Management

Traditionally, top managers have made strategic decisions for organizations. The term *top management* refers to the relatively small group of people at the uppermost levels of the organization hierarchy. Titles that are generally considered to be top management positions include president, chief executive officer (CEO), chief operating officer (COO), vice president, and executive vice president.

The strategic management process of today tends to be shaped primarily by the CEO, the executive who is responsible for the performance of the organization as a whole. Although this strategic role is generally apparent in organizations of all sizes, it is most prominent in smaller organizations, where the CEO might also be an owner/entrepreneur. The CEO's central role may be somewhat diluted in medium-sized companies, and even further reduced in large companies, because CEOs of larger organizations tend to carry broader and more comprehensive duties, and the work involved in strategic management for these firms demands a larger staff.

The CEO is usually responsible and accountable for the success of the strategic management process. This does not necessarily mean, however, that the CEO carries it out alone. Instead, a successful CEO generally designs a cross-functional strategic management process that involves members from many different organizational areas and levels. For example, in addition to the CEO, organizations commonly enlist production specialists, marketing personnel, finance experts, and division managers in identifying strategic issues and making strategic decisions.

According to George Grune, chairman of the board and CEO of Reader's Digest Association, recruiting others to participate in the strategic management process generally results in more realistic goals, objectives, and strategies. In this situation, other managers often suggest to top management how to integrate their areas within the strategic management of the organization as a whole.[13] Grune maintains that such participation and involvement builds organizational commitment to achieve the goals and implement strategies that the process develops.[14]

Board of Directors' Role in Strategic Management

In a corporation, a board of directors, elected by stockholders, exercises ultimate authority and responsibility for the organization. The board guides the affairs of the corporation and protects stockholder interests.[15] Inside board members are people who already work for the organization in some other capacity; outside board members work for other organizations. Board members typically elect a chairperson to oversee board business, and they form standing committees that meet regularly to conduct their business. A list of standing committees and their responsibilities within a typical board of directors is presented in Table 1.3.

TABLE 1.3

Committees and Their Responsibilities within a Typical Board of Directors

---

EXECUTIVE COMMITTEE
1. To act within specified bounds for the board of directors between board meetings
2. To serve as a sounding board for the CEO's ideas before they are presented to the full board
3. To monitor extended negotiations
4. To oversee activities not specifically delegated to other committees

AUDIT COMMITTEE
1. To assure that company policies and practices remain within the bounds of accepted conduct
2. To select (or recommend) auditors and determine the scope of audits
3. To review financial reports to gain full insight into the company's current and likely future financial condition
4. To review internal accounting procedures
5. To assure the integrity of the company's operations

TABLE 1.3

Continued

COMPENSATION COMMITTEE

1. To assure that compensation (including stock options, benefits, bonuses, and salaries) attracts, holds, and motivates key personnel
2. To see that compensation and benefit plans throughout the organization are competitive, equitable, and well-executed
3. To oversee the development and implementation of human resource plans

FINANCIAL COMMITTEE

1. To review and advise the board on the financial structure and needs of the organization
2. To recommend to management and the full board the timing and types of financing that the firm needs (both long-term and short-term financing)
3. To assist top management in establishing good working relationships with the financial community
4. To provide advice about various investment, expenditure, and funding alternatives

NOMINATING COMMITTEE

1. To recommend candidates for membership on the board
2. To recommend candidates for management or officer positions in the company
3. To advise management on human resource planning

SOURCE: Adapted from J. K. Louden, *The Director* (New York: AMACOM, 1982), Chapter 7.

In general, the board of directors' time should be viewed as a scarce resource to devote to those activities in which it can uniquely and most effectively contribute to achieving organizational goals.[16] As Table 1.3 implies, board duties have historically focused on issues like financial auditing and compensation, with little or no input to the strategic management of an organization. Over the last decade, however, interest has grown in expanding the duties of the board to make it much more active in the strategic management process.[17]

Most authorities on corporate governance argue that firms should increase board involvement in the strategic management process as a way to improve the quality of strategic decisions, enabling board members to better discharge their responsibilities to represent stockholder interests.[18] One popular way to expand this involvement is by adding a strategy committee to the board's list of standing committees.[19] A strategy committee is a board committee that works with the CEO to develop corporate goals as well as strategies to reach those goals. As part of its duties, the strategy committee commonly evaluates the organization's strategic management process in order to make it more effective and efficient.

Table 1.4 shows a proposed **strategic report card** that a strategy committee might use in its evaluation of alternatives. In order to use this report card to evaluate a firm and its top management team, board members would first

TABLE 1.4

Strategic Report Card

	Key Success Attributes				Impact
	Content	Strategic Alignment	Resource Allocation	Management Process	
KEY SUCCESS ELEMENTS					
STRATEGY					
STRATEGIC IMPLEMENTATION PROGRAMS					
ORGANIZATION AND FUNCTIONS					
SYSTEMS					

SOURCE: Reprinted by permission of Donald K. Yee, "Pass or Fail? How to Grade Strategic Progress," *Journal of Business Strategy,* May/June, 1990.

define the Key Success Elements, shown in the far left column, and then they would evaluate each of these elements against the Key Success Attributes, shown across the top. For example, board members would grade a strategy on the basis of the adequacy of its content or scope, its match with the realities of the external environment including competition, the resources allocated to its accomplishment, the management process for developing and refining it, and its impact or results.

Overall, the board of directors should play a role in the strategic management of an organization. One barrier to this involvement, however, is the conviction of some managers and management scholars that the most effective and creative strategies emerge from interaction between the CEO and key subordinates.[20] For various reasons, some boards might handle strategic management issues more successfully than others. It seems reasonable, therefore, to conclude that most organizations benefit by some type of board involvement in the strategic management process.

Recent research in this area has found a positive relationship between board involvement in strategy making and a firm's financial performance.[21] The extent and type of involvement varies from firm to firm depending on factors such as the experience of board members in handling strategic management issues.

Planning Staff's Role in Strategic Management

The job of running the strategic management process can grow so large that the CEO must assign employees to a team, typically called a *planning staff,* specifically to help with the task. In a smaller organization, the CEO might simply appoint someone to act as a planning assistant. In a medium-sized to large organization, the CEO might establish a planning committee or even a planning department headed by its own director or vice president for organizational planning. A planning staff generally produces advisory reports by gathering and analyzing data and making recommendations to the CEO concerning various strategic management decisions.

In the past, the strategic management process has been heavily influenced by planning departments within organizations. Employees within these departments often designed and implemented strategic management systems while CEOs took a hands-off attitude, basically allowing the planners wide freedom in carrying out their duties. More recently, however, CEOs have begun taking more active roles in strategic management, especially in giving planning departments more guidance and direction. This activism of CEOs is generally seen to have reduced some of the influence of planning departments over the strategic management process.[22] Strategic management has returned to the domain of the line manager or general manager.

The role, influence, and involvement of each of the participants—CEO, board of directors, and planning staff—in the organization's strategic management process have changed significantly over the last several decades. This change will undoubtedly continue. Regardless of the specific role that each group will play in the future, they will have to work together as a team in order to best shape the strategic management process of their organization.

BENEFITS OF STRATEGIC MANAGEMENT

An organization can reap several benefits from effective strategic management. Perhaps the most important benefit is higher profit. Although past studies have concluded that strategic management does not always increase profitability, a significant number of recent investigations have suggested that a well-designed strategic management system can boost profits.[23]

In addition to financial benefits, organizations may gain other advantages by implementing strategic management programs. For example, strategic management can strengthen organization members' commitment to attaining long-term goals. Increased commitment normally accompanies participation in setting goals and strategies for reaching those goals. In addition, when strategic managers emphasize assessing the organization's environment, the organization reduces the chance of being surprised by movements within the marketplace or by actions of competitors that could put the organization at a sudden disadvantage. These potential benefits also explain the increased popularity of strategic management with not-for-profit and public sector organizations.

Of course, an organization cannot *guarantee* these benefits just by completing a strategic management exercise. As in most important areas of organizational life, success is never automatic and every effort risks failure. An organization's strategic management process may have inherent flaws (e.g., its environmental analysis may be incomplete). Even an organization with a refined, long-standing, highly regarded strategic management system may suffer disappointing results from decisions based on erroneous economic or market forecasts. Several large computer hardware firms such as IBM or Digital Equipment have learned this hard lesson.

HISTORICAL DEVELOPMENT OF STRATEGIC MANAGEMENT

Although managers may be eager to design and implement a strategic management system in their organization, accomplishing the task takes time. Most organizations develop their strategic management processes over periods of several years, adjusting and tailoring them to meet specific company needs.[24]

Figure 1.1 illustrates the developmental phases that lead firms toward their own strategic management systems. The development usually begins with a

FIGURE 1.1   Phases in the Development of a Strategic Management System

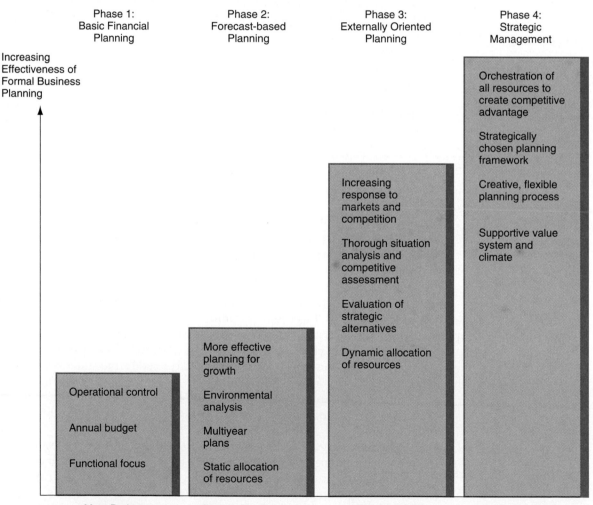

fairly simple routine of basic financial planning. During this phase, the primary concern is simply meeting budget constraints through operational control, completing the annual budgeting process, and addressing functions like operations, finance, and marketing in an isolated, nonintegrative analysis.

From these humble beginnings, the organization's perspective evolves to culminate in the process that we know as strategic management. The focus shifts over time from meeting the budget, to planning for the future, to thinking abstractly, to working to create a desired future. To create a future, decision makers orchestrate and integrate all of their organization's resources to gain a competitive advantage. Within a carefully crafted planning framework, they build flexibility into the organizational planning process, and foster a supportive, participative climate within the organization.

Managers must understand that developing an effective and efficient strategic management process in any organization can be a long and difficult task that requires sustained effort, enormous patience, and sharp political skills. In short, strategic management requires real leadership. By comparing their organizations to the system of evolutionary phases we have outlined, managers can gauge the development of strategic management in their own organizations. After realistically assessing the appropriateness of their current strategic management processes, they can begin to consider improvements and alternatives.

STRATEGIC MANAGEMENT PROCESS

We have explained strategic management as a process or series of steps. The basic steps of the strategic management process, shown in Figure 1.2, include: (1) perform an environmental analysis, (2) establish an organizational direction, (3) formulate an organizational strategy, (4) implement the organizational strategy, and (5) exert strategic control. Let's take a look at each of these steps and their places in a strategic management system.

Step 1: Perform an Environmental Analysis

The strategic management process begins with **environmental analysis,** a formal procedure to monitor the organization's environment to (a) identify present and future threats and opportunities, and (b) assess critically its own strengths and weaknesses. In this context, the organizational environment encompasses all factors both inside and outside the organization that can

FIGURE 1.2   Major Steps in the Strategic Management Process

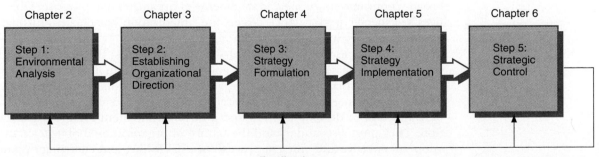

FIGURE 1.3
Sample Environmental
Factors to Monitor for
Strategic Management

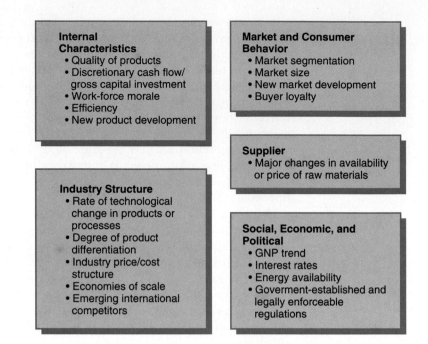

Internal Characteristics
• Quality of products
• Discretionary cash flow/ gross capital investment
• Work-force morale
• Efficiency
• New product development

Market and Consumer Behavior
• Market segmentation
• Market size
• New market development
• Buyer loyalty

Supplier
• Major changes in availability or price of raw materials

Industry Structure
• Rate of technological change in products or processes
• Degree of product differentiation
• Industry price/cost structure
• Economies of scale
• Emerging international competitors

Social, Economic, and Political
• GNP trend
• Interest rates
• Energy availability
• Goverment-established and legally enforceable regulations

influence progress toward building a sustainable competitive advantage. Figure 1.3 details some examples of environmental variables that firms commonly monitor.

The Company Example, on page 17, illustrates how one firm identified and responded to significant changes in its competitive environment. Despite a historic industry downturn, Reno Air saw an opportunity to prosper. In responding to this new environment, Reno Air defined its niche and stuck to it.

Managers must grasp the purpose of environmental analysis, recognize the multiple organizational environments in which they operate, and understand the fundamental tasks of performing an environmental analysis. These issues, along with others that arise in environmental analysis, are fully discussed in Chapter 2.

Step 2: Establish an Organizational Direction

In the second step of the strategic management process, managers establish an **organizational direction** for their firm. There are three main indicators of the direction in which an organization is moving: its vision, mission statements, and objectives. An organization's vision includes its aspirations, values, and philosophies at their most general levels. Mission statements translate broad visions into more specific statements of organizational purpose. Objectives are specific performance targets the organization has chosen, through which it hopes to succeed in its mission.

A thorough environmental analysis that pinpoints the organization's strengths, weaknesses, opportunities, and threats can often help management to establish, reaffirm, or modify its organizational direction. In order to establish an appropriate organizational direction, however, management must understand how to develop a vision and a mission statement for the organization. They must also understand the nature of organizational objectives and adopt an effective and efficient process for establishing and changing organizational direction. These issues are discussed in detail in Chapter 3.

COMPANY EXAMPLE

Smooth Landing for Reno Air

Following deregulation, the airline industry hit its nadir in the early 1990s; between 1990 and 1992, the U.S. airline industry lost $10.5 billion, wiping out all of the profits earned by the industry since the Wright brothers first took off at Kitty Hawk. This environment seemed to leave little chance for a new, entrepreneurial carrier to survive, let alone make a profit. In 1993, however, Reno Air completed its first year of operations with a profit, something that only one other scheduled carrier was able to claim.

Reno's $72 million in revenues surprised the industry; no one had given its founder, Joseph A. Lorenzo, much of a chance in mid-1992 when the airline's first plane took off.

Lorenzo (no relation to Frank Lorenzo, the former chairman of Continental Airlines) saw the industry's problems as an opportunity. As these problems seemed to grow bigger and more intractable, he saw only greater potential for Reno Air.

He began by analyzing the industry, probing its soft spots and figuring out how to turn them to his advantage. Lorenzo understood the overriding lesson of the previous decade: Don't compete against the superior resources of the big carriers; define a profitable niche and stick to it.

Lorenzo knew that Reno had to steer clear of the industry's Big Three, American, Delta, and United. Together the three carried 57 percent of domestic air traffic, but their cost structures as full-service carriers—including food, computer systems, ground equipment, and maintenance expenses—made it tough to do business profitably.

Lorenzo began with one of the most basic of all strategic decisions: choosing a home base. Locating in Reno, Nevada kept his company off the radar screens of the big carriers while giving him a foothold in the midsized city where competition was thin, and potential needs were great.

Later on, Reno closely averted head-to-head competition by abandoning a route to Minneapolis that had brought it into a price war with Northwest Airlines. Lorenzo saw his mistake and cut his losses, avoiding the kind of serious error that had grounded so many other carriers.

Next, Lorenzo recognized the limits on his expertise. He hired Jeffery Erickson, president of Midway Airlines, as Reno's CEO. When Midway filed for bankruptcy, Erickson and Lorenzo snapped up some of its best assets, including personnel and equipment that lent Reno a new cohesiveness.

The most complicated decision focused on what kind of service Reno should offer. Despite high food costs, Lorenzo decided to gain a competitive advantage over other low-cost carriers by offering some food—pretzels and cookies in coach, wine and sandwiches in first class. Reno's other costs were so low that the company could add modest services, including automated ticketing through travel agents and advance seat selection, without affecting the bottom line.

Offering those services gave Reno a key boost in its effort to win the lease of American Airlines' gates in San Jose when the big carrier decided to pull out of the market. Recognizing that frequent flier programs were the only successful way to build brand loyalty in the airline industry, Lorenzo also gained a deal to offer Reno Air passengers mileage in AAdvantage, American's frequent flier program.

SOURCE: Stephen D. Solomon, "How to Start an Airline on Your Own," *Inc.*, April 1994, pp. 52–62.

Step 3: Formulate an Organizational Strategy

The third step of the strategic management process is **strategy formulation.** Earlier, we characterized a strategy as an integrative, cohesive pattern or plan that coordinates an organization's major goals, policies, and actions. Strategy formulation, then, is the process of designing a strategy that leads to a sustainable competitive advantage.[25] Once managers have analyzed the environment and set an organizational direction, they can chart alternative competitive strategies in an informed effort to improve the organization's chances of success.

In order to formulate organizational strategy properly, managers must thoroughly understand various strategy formulation tools such as industry structure analysis, value chain analysis, the Boston Consulting Group growth–share matrix, and General Electric's multifactor portfolio matrix. Chapter 4 discusses these and other tools in great detail.

Step 4: Implementing the Organizational Strategy

The fourth step of the strategic management process is implementing strategy. This step involves acting to realize the logically developed strategies that have emerged from the previous steps of the strategic management process. Without effective implementation, an organization's strategy will fail to provide the benefits of performing an environmental analysis, establishing an organizational direction, and formulating an organizational strategy.

In order to implement organizational strategy successfully, managers must have clear positions on several, diverse issues: how to handle change within the organization as it implements the new strategy, how best to deal with organization's culture in order to ensure smooth implementation of the strategy, how strategy implementation will affect organizational structures, what different implementation approaches will realize the strategy, and what skills managers need to implement the organizational strategy successfully. Chapter 5 focuses on the implementation phase of the strategic management process and explores ways to avoid or minimize the impact of strategic implementation problems.

The progress from developing a strategic plan to achieving desired performance must, however, overcome many obstacles. Table 1.5 lists eight sources of frequent breakdowns that can hinder managers' navigation through this dangerous terrain.

Step 5: Exert Strategic Control

Strategic control is a special type of organizational control that focuses on monitoring and evaluating the strategic management process in order to im-

---

TABLE 1.5

Potential Breakdowns between Planning and Implementation

1. A customer focus does not drive the planning process.
2. Planners do not organize their information to support action by those who implement the plans.
3. The strategic planning process fails to invite input from those who will implement the plan.
4. Plans are fragmented, piecemeal, or insufficient.
5. The organization does not encourage risk-takers or champions.
6. Those responsible for implementation lack the skills they need to carry out their roles.
7. The organization lacks an adequate system for measuring the results of implementation efforts.
8. The organization does not adequately recognize or reinforce the accomplishments and victories of its implementation "heroes."

SOURCE: Based on William Sandy, "Avoid the Breakdowns between Planning and Implementation," *Journal of Business Strategy,* September/October 1991, p. 30.

prove it and ensure it functions properly. To successfully perform this strategic control task, managers must understand the process of strategic control and the role of strategic audits. In addition, managers must understand the intricacies of their management information system and how such a system can complement the strategic control process. The strategic management process within any organization is only as good as the information on which it is based.[26] These and other important issues are discussed in Chapter 6.

To simplify analysis, we have presented the strategic management process as a series of discrete steps. This facilitates learning about the components of the process and how the steps commonly relate to one another. In practice, however, managers sometimes find that an organization's strategic management effort requires that they perform several steps simultaneously, or perform them in a different order from that suggested here. Managers must be creative in designing and operating strategic management systems, and they must be flexible enough to tailor their use of those systems to the organizational circumstances that confront them.

CRITICAL CHALLENGES FOR STRATEGIC MANAGEMENT

The major steps that we have outlined are fundamental to the strategic management process. In addition, three other critical challenges for strategic decision makers have received much attention in the last decade. These challenges arise from global issues, quality issues, and social/ethical issues.

Strategic Management and Global Issues

Over the last several years, businesses' activities have tended to cross international borders more frequently. Even firms with no international operations are experiencing the impact of globalization on many markets and industries. Since this trend is expected to continue, more organizations will have to consider global issues in the future in the course of their strategic management processes.

Before managers can determine how their strategic management process can most effectively accommodate international issues, they must be fully aware of critical international variables that might significantly affect their organization. Chapter 7 elaborates on the fundamental characteristics of international management and multinational corporations. In addition, this chapter devotes sections to possible international implications for each step of the strategic management model.

Strategic Management and Quality Issues

The quality movement, spearheaded by management thinkers like the late W. Edwards Deming, has had an important impact on the way organizations perform strategic management in the 1990s. Our contemporary understanding of quality has advanced far beyond the earlier reliance on postproduction procedures (called *quality control*) to weed out manufacturing mistakes. *Quality* has come to mean an organizationwide commitment to enhance the value of a good or service to the customer at every stage of bringing it to market— from design, to production, to marketing, to postsale customer service.

Managers involved in the strategic management process at all levels need to understand the history of this movement and appreciate the important role

SKILLS MODULE

Boise Cascade's Cup Runneth Over—Finally

INTRODUCTION

Issues involving quality significantly influence the strategic management process. Review the following situation and complete the related skill-development exercise. This will give you practice in confronting the kind of dilemma that often troubles managers as they seek to improve a company's quality management strategy.

SITUATION

The Southern Operations Division of Boise Cascade Corporation favors the scaled-down, focused approach to quality improvement, but without a master plan, it took the company four years to get there. The DeRidder, Louisiana, company launched its TQM program in 1986. While the program enjoyed a success story here and there, only when it became focused in 1990 did the quality mindset begin to spread like gospel throughout the mills.

This focus started with the company's Groundwood Optimization project. The project produced annual wood-cost savings of $2.2 million and defined a whole new era in quality improvement. "We picked that project because everyone in the mill could relate to it," said Richard Greer, total quality manager. "We had been talking about the high costs of wood to the mill for some time."

Those savings—and workers' move to embrace total quality—didn't come about until the company realized that it had to do more than just announce a desire for total quality. "We weren't quite sure—after you start the people talking about the process—how you actually *use* the process," admits Dave Blencke, vice president and regional manager.

The success of the Groundwood Optimization project helped the company to realize that quality initiatives cannot take shape at the corporate management level. Said Blencke, "You have to get it going at the grass roots, which is the location level. And at that level, you know specifically what the location problems are that you want to solve. People know that inherently. All the way down to the department level, they know what they want to solve. All total quality is a tool to solve [those problems]."

SKILL DEVELOPMENT EXERCISE

You are the chief executive at Boise Cascade. You decide to expand the TQM program to the company's other divisions. What main points would you emphasize in unveiling this strategy to your division managers? Explain.

SOURCE: Tracy E. Benson, "A Business Strategy Comes of Age," *Industry Week*, May 3, 1993, pp. 43–44.

---

it plays in contemporary organizational strategy. Chapter 8 traces the evolution of the quality movement and relates the search for improved quality to the cross-functional nature of strategic management. The Skills Module previews the type of strategic and quality issues we will encounter in Chapter 8.

Strategic Management and Social/Ethical Issues

Social responsibility is the managerial obligation to act, protect, and promote both organizational interests and the welfare of society as a whole. Recognition of this obligation must affect the strategic management process.

To be socially responsible, an organization's managers need to develop thorough, thoughtful answers to such questions as:

- To which societal constituencies is the organization responsible?
- What major influences within society affect business practices?
- How can an organization conduct social audits to facilitate the strategic management process?

Issues of this nature are discussed in Chapter 9.

CRITICAL FOUNDATIONS FOR STRATEGIC MANAGEMENT

To be successful, a strategic manager must mobilize and exploit the expertise of functional specialists within the organization. The importance of the relationship between business functions and the strategic management process cannot be overestimated. Strategic management is fundamentally a cross-functional undertaking; the process should draw simultaneously on functional expertise in all areas to craft a viable strategy for the whole organization, or a major part of one. Stated conversely, a strategic management process that is either dominated by one function or passed sequentially among them (i.e., from one function to the next) is likely to produce less comprehensive and less timely results than an integrated, cross-functional process.

Traditionally, three major business functions are identified within an organization: operations or production, finance, and marketing. However, these rather general categories may obscure some debate about exactly how many major business functions organizations perform. Some management theorists argue that human resource activities constitute a major business function; others maintain that research and development constitute yet another. This text discusses all important business functions and their impacts on strategic management. Separate chapters cover operations, finance, and marketing; information on human resource management activities, research and development, and other functions is integrated throughout the text.

Operations and Strategic Management

The **operations** function is performed by those people within an organization who produce the goods or services offered to its customers. Chapter 10 discusses the essential principles of operations and explains this function's contribution to the strategic management process. This chapter addresses the appropriateness of different strategies for different types of operations, characterizes operations as a vital element of strategy, presents product design as an important operations and strategy issue, and probes the nature of strategic decision making within the operations area.

Finance and Strategic Management

Financial analysis is the process of evaluating assets, liabilities, equity, and risk, and then making decisions on the basis of these evaluations.[27] Chapter 11 relates financial concepts to strategic management. These fundamental concepts underlie any serious analysis of possible strategies; the success of the strategic management process hinges on this analysis. The chapter covers the common analytical approaches, including financial ratio analysis, break-even analysis, and net present value analysis.

Marketing and Strategic Management

Marketing has been defined as, "the process of planning and executing conception, pricing, promotion, and distribution of ideas, goods, and services to create exchanges that satisfy individual and organizational objectives."[28] Chapter 12 reveals how fundamental marketing principles relate to strategic management and how they affect situational analysis, which contributes much to the strategic management process. This chapter focuses on the strategic marketing process: analysis of consumer/product relationships, selection of

FIGURE 1.4   Framework for Strategic Management: The Model for This Text

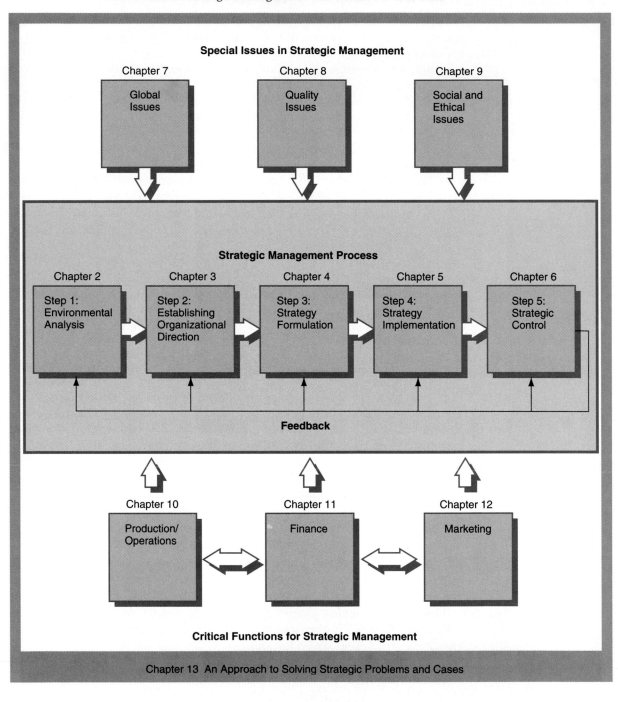

a market segmentation strategy, designing the marketing mix strategy, and implementing and controlling marketing strategy.

COMPREHENSIVE APPROACH TO ANALYZING STRATEGIC PROBLEMS AND CASES

Perhaps the most common instructional method for teaching strategic management is **case analysis.** Cases describe actual strategic management problems and invite students to analyze them critically in order to propose and defend solutions.

This text contains many cases that raise fascinating issues in strategic management. Chapter 13 details a method by which students can analyze strategic management problems and formulate recommendations. The major steps of this case analysis method are problem definition, formulation of alternative solutions to the problem, evaluation of developed alternatives, and selection and implementation of the chosen alternative. Worksheets are furnished for students to use in their analysis. The analytical method proposed in Chapter 13 is just as useful to practicing managers who face strategic management problems in real organizations.

PLAN OF THIS BOOK

Figure 1.4 outlines the overall framework for this book. It depicts all of the major topics that we have previewed in this chapter and indicates which chapter treats each one in detail. This figure will appear (with appropriate shading to highlight the relevant topic) at the beginning of each chapter to place the subject of each chapter in the context of strategic management as a whole. The figure will also serve as a review of how these diverse topics relate to one another, and it will illustrate progress in your study of strategic management.

SUMMARY

A strategy is an integrative plan or pattern of decisions that provides a road map for an organization's progress toward its goals and objectives. Strategic management is a continuous, iterative, cross-functional process aimed at keeping a strategy up to date so that the organization fits well within its environment. Typically, a firm's top management, board of directors, and planning staff contribute the most to the strategic management process. Increasingly, however, line managers, who are closer to customers and markets, and lower level employees, who must implement strategies, are playing more prominent roles.

The main steps of the process are: performing an environmental analysis establishing an organizational direction, formulating an organizational strategy, implementing that strategy, and exerting strategic control. In addition, global/international issues, social/ethical issues, and quality issues may profoundly affect an organization's strategic management process. It is critical that the strategic management process integrate input from the major business functions within the organization—operations, finance, and marketing. Each of these topics is the subject of a chapter in this text, and Chapter 13 offers guidelines for analyzing strategic management problems through case studies.

A summary checklist of questions follows the key terms. Use it to guide your analysis of problems and cases that raise fundamental strategic management issues.

KEY TERMS

strategy, p. 6
strategic management, p. 8
strategic report card, p. 11
environmental analysis, p. 15
organizational direction, p. 16
strategy formulation, p. 17

strategic control, p. 18
social responsibility, p. 20
operations, p. 21
financial analysis, p. 21
marketing, p. 21
case analysis, p. 23

CHECKLIST   Analyzing Fundamental Issues in Strategic Management

___ 1. Does the problem or case involve genuine strategic management issues?

___ 2. Are the board of directors, top management, and planning staff appropriately involved in the strategic management process?

___ 3. Are the major steps of the strategic management process appropriately ordered and integrated?

___ 4. Is organizational direction clear and well-expressed through statements of organizational mission and objectives?

___ 5. Is the strategy appropriate, given the existing organizational direction and the results of the environmental analysis?

___ 6. Has the strategy been appropriately implemented (successfully translated into action)?

___ 7. Does the focus on exerting strategic control improve the strategic management process appropriately?

___ 8. Have the impacts of global issues on the strategic management process been assessed?

___ 9. Have the impacts of quality issues on the strategic management process been considered?

___ 10. Have the impacts of social/ethical issues on the strategic management process been taken into account?

___ 11. Are the operations, finance, and marketing functions properly mobilized and utilized?

Additional Readings

Andrews, Kenneth R. *The Concept of Corporate Strategy.* Homewood, Ill.: Richard D. Irwin, 1987.

Ansoff, H. Igor, and E. McDonnell. *Implanting Strategic Management,* 2d ed. Englewood Cliffs, N.J.: Prentice-Hall, 1990.

Chakravarthy, Balaji, and Yves Doz. "Strategy Process Research: Focusing on Corporate Self-Renewal," *Strategic Management Journal,* 13 (Special Issue, Summer 1992), pp. 5–14.

Drucker, Peter. "The New Society of Organizations." *Harvard Business Review.* September/October 1992, p. 95.

Jacobson, Robert. "The 'Austrian' School of Strategy." *The Academy of Management Review,* October 1992, p. 782.

Mintzberg, Henry. "The Design School: Reconsidering the Basic Premises of Strategic Management." *Strategic Management Journal* 11, no. 3 (1990), pp. 171–195.

C A S E

STRATEGIC FACE-LIFT FOR SEARS, ROEBUCK

The February 1993 unveiling of yet another new image for Sears, Roebuck & Co. brought a collective yawn from the analysts gathered in Chicago for the announcement by the nation's third largest retailer. Over the next few months, however, the yawns turned to appreciative smiles, especially among shareholders. By the end of the year, the 800-store chain had bounced back from the previous year's record loss to a record profit, and delivered a 19 percent return on equity to its investors. Sears achieved this success, in large part, because it was able to do in one year what it had planned to do in three years: chop $328 million after taxes out of its annual costs.

Veteran observers saw one key difference between those previous, cosmetic makeovers and the most recent, substantive face-lift: its architect, Arthur C. Martinez, a Saks Fifth Avenue veteran who had joined Sears a year earlier as chairman of its merchandise group. Martinez unleashed an ambitious strategy to turn Sears into a competitive, moderately priced department store. Martinez's strategy emphasized selling apparel, which is profit-rich, while defending Sears's market share in hardware and appliances. It included a $4 billion plan to renovate stores, build more free-standing hardware stores, and move furniture into separate emporiums.

Martinez said that he began his job with three objectives: sell or close operations that were unprofitable or that diverged from Sears's new strategy, assemble a new management team, and put the new merchandising plan to work. In May 1993, step 1 closed Sears's 97-year-old catalog business, which had been losing $140 million a year.

Clearing the organizational decks was next. The 3,400 employees who accepted the company's early retirement offer included the heads of the marketing, public relations, retail, and automotive divisions. Martinez, who said that he wanted "people with a bias toward action," ended up commanding a mix of veteran Sears hands who led the home group and intimate apparel division as well as newcomers who led the advertising and women's apparel units—the two areas undergoing the most rapid changes.

Although clothing accounted for only 26 percent of Sears's annual store sales of about $28.7 billion, it brought in some 60 percent of the merchandise unit's profits. Because higher apparel sales also increased store traffic, Sears wanted to boost apparel's share to about 40 percent of store sales. Martinez's priorities included paying shoe salespeople on commission, getting more salespeople on the floor, and seeing that store racks stayed well-stocked.

To raise consumer awareness of the changes, Sears boosted its $1 billion marketing budget by 9 percent. It also began increasing the number of national brands it offered, from 40 percent to half of its merchandise mix. (The other 50 percent was private-label goods.)

Sears's new operational strategy had its costs. The big marketing push was expensive; industry analysts estimated that the company spent $60 million more on advertising in the fourth quarter of 1993 than in the year-earlier period. Shifting funds from traditional media such as newspaper inserts to newer, less-proven forms such as infomercials, and sponsoring a 30-city concert tour by singer Phil Collins also cost Sears money, and exposed the firm to risks. Yet the risks seemed to pay off. Sears's $40 million print and broadcast campaign, "Softer Side of Sears," improved the company's image among women, and apparel sales rose.

DISCUSSION QUESTIONS

1. How effectively did Martinez address the key questions in strategy development? Explain.

2. How well did Sears implement the strategy?

3. Evaluate the risks that Sears took. Do you consider them worthy ones? What are some others you would propose?

4. If you were chairman, how would a drop in profits or a surge in reorganization costs affect the various components of your overall strategic management plan at Sears?

SOURCES: Gregory A. Patterson, "'Face Lift' Gives Sears a Fresh Look and Better Results," *The Wall Street Journal,* July 20, 1993, p. B4; "Sears Earnings Signal Recovery in Retail Lines," *The Wall Street Journal,* July 21, 1993, p. A3; "Sears Funds Some New Marketing Projects," *The Wall Street Journal,* February 16, 1994, p. B3.

Notes

1. Andrew Pollack, "Sega Takes Aim at Disney's World," *New York Times,* July 4, 1993, Section 3, p. 1; Frederic M. Biddle, "The Profit Machine: NordicTrack Is the Muscle behind Top-Ranked CML," *Boston Globe,* June 8, 1993, p. 31; Bridget O'Brian, "Losing Altitude: Once-Solid Delta Air Is Burdened by Cost of European Foray," *The Wall Street Journal,* June 25, 1993, p. A1; David Hamilton, "After Initial Fuzziness, AT&T Clears Up Signal to Asia," *The Wall Street Journal,* June 30, 1993, p. B4; Joseph Pereira, "Footware Fad Makes Nike, Reebok Run for Their Money," *The Wall Street Journal,* June 24, 1993, p. B1.

2. R. A. Gordon and J. E. Howell, *Higher Education for Business* (New York: Columbia University Press, 1959).

3. M. Leontiades, "The Confusing Words of Business Policy," *Academy of Management Review,* January 1982, p. 46.

4. Mathew J. Kiernan, "The New Strategic Architecture," *The Executive,* February 1993, pp. 7–21.

5. H. Igor Ansoff, *Implanting Strategic Management* (Englewood Cliffs, N.J.: Prentice-Hall, 1984).

6. James Brian Quinn, *Strategies for Change* (Homewood, Ill.: Richard D. Irwin, 1980), p. 7.

7. Henry Mintzberg, "Patterns in Strategy Formation," *Management Science* (1978), pp. 934–948.

8. C. K. Prahalad and G. Hamel, "The Core Competence of the Corporation," *Harvard Business Review,* May/June 1990, pp. 79–91.

9. H. Mintzberg and J. Waters, "Of Strategies, Deliberate and Emergent," *Strategic Management Journal,* 1985, pp. 257–272.

10. Rich Tetzel, "Steve Jobs Leaves Hardware Behind," *Fortune,* March 8, 1993, p. 10.

11. David Nadler and Deborah Ancona, "Team-Work at the Top," in *Organizational Architecture,* ed. by D. Nadler, M. Gerstein, and R. Shaw (San Francisco: Jossey-Bass, 1992).

12. Henry Mintzberg, "Strategy-Making in Three Modes," *California Management Review,* Winter 1973, pp. 44–53.

13. Roy Forman, "Strategic Planning and the Chief Executive," *Long Range Planning* 21 (August 1988), pp. 57–64.

14. George Grune, "Strategic Planning at the Reader's Digest Association," speech given at the annual meeting of the Crummer Graduate School of Business, Corporate Council, Rollins College, 1986.

15. B. Baysinger and H. Butler, "The Composition of Boards of Directors and Strategic Control," *Academy of Management Review* (1990), pp. 72–81.

16. Ada Demb, Danielle Chouet, Tom Lossius, and Fred Neubauer, "Defining the Role of the Board," *Long Range Planning* 22 (February 1989), pp. 60–68; R. H. Rock and Marv Eisthen, "Implementing Strategic Change," in *The Management Handbook,* ed. by K. J. Albert (New York: McGraw-Hill, 1983).

17. Joseph Rosenstein, "Why Don't U.S. Boards Get More Involved in Strategy?" *Long Range Planning* 20, no. 3 (1987), pp. 30–34.

18. Kenneth R. Andrews, "Corporate Strategy as a Vital Function of the Board," *Harvard Business Review,* November/December 1981, pp. 174–184.

19. J. Richard Harrison, "The Strategic Use of Corporate Board Committees," *California Management Review* 30, no. 1 (Fall 1987), pp. 109–125.

20. Rosenstein, "Why Don't U.S. Boards."

21. W. Judge and C. Zeithaml, "Institutional and Strategic Choice Perspectives on Board Involvement in the Strategic Decision Process," *Academy of Management Journal,* October 1992, pp. 766–794.

22. "The New Breed of Strategic Planner," *Business Week,* September 17, 1984, pp. 62–66.

23. As an example of studies showing that strategic management does not always increase productivity, see R. Fulmer and L. Rue, "The Practice and Profitability of Long-Range Planning," *Managerial Planning* 22 (1974), p. 1; as an example of the opposite view, see Richard Robinson, Jr., "The Importance of Outsiders in Small Firm Strategic Planning," *Academy of Management Journal* 25, no. 1 (March 1982), p. 80.

24. Frederick W. Gluck, Stephen P. Kaufman, and A. Steven Walleck, "Strategic Management for Competitive Advantage," *Harvard Business Review,* July/August 1980, pp. 154–161.

25. Pankaj Ghemawat, *Commitment: The Dynamic of Strategy* (New York: Free Press, 1991).

26. M. D. Skipton, "Helping Managers to Develop Strategies," *Long Range Planning* 18, no. 2 (April 1985), pp. 56–68.

27. Robert Hartl, *Basics of Financial Management* (Dubuque, Ia.: William C. Brown Publishers, 1986), pp. 4–5.

28. J. Paul Peter and James H. Donnelly, Jr., *Marketing Management: Knowledge and Skills,* 4th ed. (Burr Ridge, Ill.: Richard D. Irwin, 1995), p. 7.

PART II

Strategic Management Process

Part II builds upon Part I by discussing in detail the five major steps in the strategic management process. Chapter 2 discusses the importance of environmental analysis to provide data for sound strategic management decisions. Chapter 3 concerns establishing an organization's vision, mission, and objectives to provide direction. Chapter 4 emphasizes strategy formulation, determining appropriate actions to move the organization in its chosen direction. Chapter 5 discusses strategy implementation, the process of putting formulated strategies into action. Chapter 6 focuses on strategic control to evaluate, monitor, and improve the organization's effectiveness. Careful study of this section should provide a foundation for analyzing strategic management problems and cases.

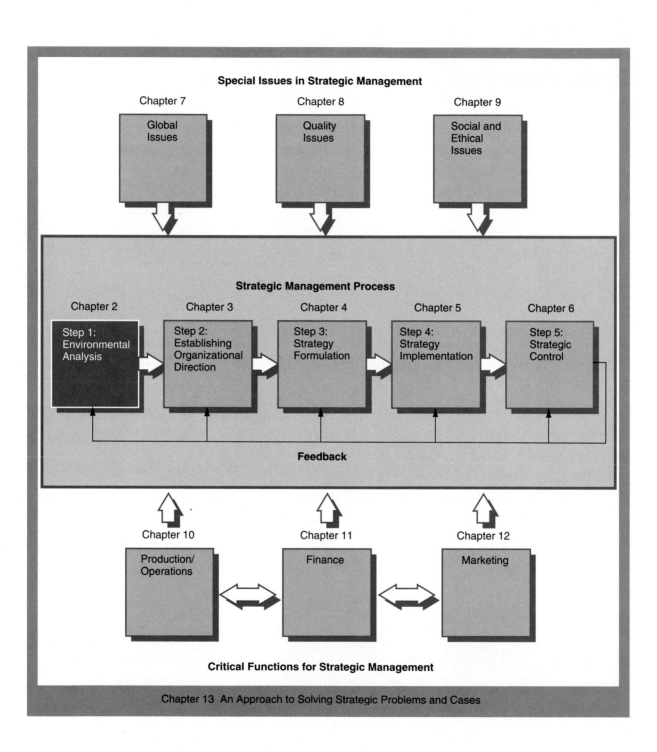

Special Issues in Strategic Management

Chapter 7

Global
Issues

Chapter 8

Quality
Issues

Chapter 9

Social and
Ethical
Issues

Strategic Management Process

Chapter 2

Step 1:
Environmental
Analysis

Chapter 3

Step 2:
Establishing
Organizational
Direction

Chapter 4

Step 3:
Strategy
Formulation

Chapter 5

Step 4:
Strategy
Implementation

Chapter 6

Step 5:
Strategic
Control

Feedback

Chapter 10

Production/
Operations

Chapter 11

Finance

Chapter 12

Marketing

Critical Functions for Strategic Management

Chapter 13 An Approach to Solving Strategic Problems and Cases

Environmental Analysis

Chapter 1 introduced the concept of strategy and described the strategic management process in very general terms. Chapter 2 focuses on the initial step of this process, environmental analysis. Companies undertake environmental analysis to ferret out information that they use in every step of the strategic management process.

We begin with the basics, describing the nature of environmental analysis and why companies devote resources to it. We then define the different levels of environments—general, operating, and internal environments—that organizations try to understand and analyze. Next, we discuss SWOT (*S*trengths, *W*eaknesses, *O*pportunities, *T*hreats) analysis and examine the general problems top managers face in their efforts to make sense of the environments in which they operate or plan to operate. We then introduce techniques for carrying out SWOT analysis and conclude the chapter by offering ideas for evaluating the overall environmental analysis effort.

ENVIRONMENTAL ANALYSIS: DEFINITION AND RATIONALE

As we noted in Chapter 1, environmental analysis is the process of monitoring an organization's environments to identify strengths, weaknesses, opportunities, and threats that may influence the firm's ability to reach its goals. We define the **organizational environment** generally as the set of forces, both outside and inside the organization, that can affect performance.

If an organization were a closed system with no input from outside, its environment would be inconsequential; as an open system, subject to a broad range of outside inputs and influences, the organization depends for its survival on effective evaluation of its environment. An organization's success or failure depends on how accurately its top management team reads the environment, and how effectively they respond to it.[1] Accordingly, managers at various levels of the organization and in various functional departments spend a great deal of time and effort gathering and analyzing data related to what they see as important environmental factors.

Large firms often rely on outside board members for advice and counsel on long-range political or macroeconomic matters. The CEO, with help from internal functional experts from marketing, research, new product development, or production, must develop a solid grasp on the strategic issues at work in the competitive environment of the firm's industry. Internal staffers, such as planners, financial analysts, and personnel specialists, must always stay abreast of new techniques and methods that define the best practices in their respective professions in order to keep their input to the process valuable.

Clearly, many people spread throughout an organization contribute to environmental analysis. This fact underscores the importance of organizing effectively for environmental analysis. To assure themselves that they will have the information they need to make strategic decisions, top managers must think carefully about who should gather what information and how to structure the flow of that information so that they can use it most effectively.[2] Because the organization must gather and act on diverse information in a timely manner, cross-functional teams of internal specialists can often perform environmental analysis most effectively.[3]

Many companies cite valuable benefits from environmental analysis. At Connecticut General Insurance Company, for example, the overriding purpose of environmental analysis is to help management to respond to *critical issues* in the environment. Sun Oil Exploration and Production Company has stated a similar purpose for its environmental analysis: to explore *future conditions* of the organizational environment and to incorporate what it learns into organizational decision making. Sears, Roebuck has stated another main purpose in undertaking environmental analysis: to identify current *emerging issues* that are significant to the company, assign priorities to these issues, and develop a plan for handling each of them.

Upon examination, these environmental analysis efforts generally focus on identifying present and future strategic issues and planning how to deal with these issues. This overall process is sometimes termed *strategic issue management*.[4]

BASIC STRUCTURES OF ENVIRONMENTS

In order to perform an environmental analysis, a manager must understand the basic structures of organizational environments. Analysts typically divide the environment of an organization into three distinct levels: the general environment, the operating environment, and the internal environment.[5] Figure 2.1 illustrates the relationship of each of these levels with the others and with the organization at large. The figure also shows the various components that make up each level. Managers must be aware of these three environmental levels, know what factors they include, and try to understand how each factor and the relationships among the factors affect organizational performance. They can then manage organizational operations in light of this understanding.

General Environment

The **general environment** is that level of an organization's external environment with components that are broad in scope and have long-term implications for managers, firms, and strategies. What are these components?

The economic component of the general environment indicates the distribution and uses of resources within an entire society. Examples of factors within the economic component are gross national product growth, the inflation rate, productivity growth, employment rates, balance of payments issues, interest rates, tax rates, and consumer income, debt, and spending patterns.[6]

FIGURE 2.1 The Organization, the Levels of Its Environment, and the Components of Those Levels

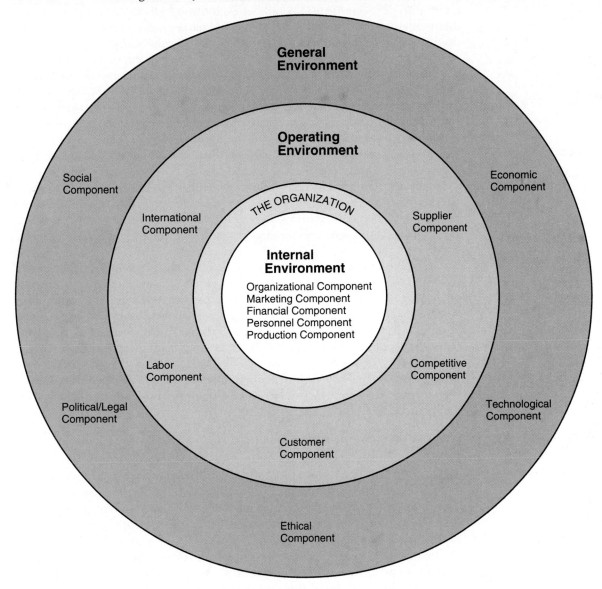

The social component of the general environment describes characteristics of the society in which the organization exists. Literacy rates, education levels, customs, beliefs, values, lifestyles, the age distribution, the geographic distribution, and the mobility of the population all contribute to the social component of the general environment. Two areas in this cluster receive special attention from corporate leaders today: the quality of public education and the aging of the Baby Boom generation of consumers. Corporate decision makers' concern with education reflects their determination to maintain the general quality of the labor force in the long term. Their attention to Baby Boomers focuses on the implications for demand for goods and services as the U.S. population ages.[7]

The political component of the general environment relates to government attitudes toward various industries, lobbying efforts by interest groups, the regulatory climate, platforms of political parties, and (sometimes) the predispositions of candidates for office. The legal component of the general environment consists of laws that members of society are expected to follow. In the United States, many legal constraints affect an organization's operations, including the Clean Air Act, the Occupational Safety and Health Act, the Consumer Product Safety Act, and the Energy Policy and Conservation Act. Naturally, over time new laws are passed and old ones rescinded.

The technological component of the general environment includes new approaches to producing goods and services: new procedures as well as new equipment. For example, the trend toward using robots to improve productivity is closely monitored by many of today's managers. The technological component of today's general environment also relates to the concepts and techniques of total quality management and continuous quality improvement. Chapter 8 examines the relationship between technology and quality in more detail.

Ethical norms of a society are elements of its culture that specify in more general ways the behavior that individuals and organizations expect of one another, but that are not prescribed by law. As the above list of laws implies, many ethical norms (e.g., consumer and worker safety and environmental protection) that are important to a society's long term future, but are seen as receiving inadequate attention, often become translated into laws. For example, in the 1950s a manager who allowed the nearby river to be polluted by run-off from a manufacturing plant was violating an ethical norm. In the 1990s, that same manager would be violating environmental protection laws. These and related issues are considered more fully in Chapter 9.

Operating Environment

The **operating environment,** sometimes termed the *competitive environment,* is that level of the organization's external environment with components that normally have relatively specific and immediate implications for managing the organization. As Figure 2.1 indicates, the major components of the operating environment are customers, competitors, labor, suppliers, and global/international issues.

The customer component of the operating environment reflects the characteristics and behavior of those who buy the organization's goods and services. Describing in detail those who buy the firm's products is a common business practice. Such profiles help management generate ideas about how to improve customer satisfaction.

The competitor component of the operating environment consists of rivals that an organization must overcome in order to reach its objectives. Understanding competitors is a key factor in developing an effective strategy, so analyzing the competition is a fundamental challenge to management. Basically, competitor analysis is intended to help management appreciate the strengths, weaknesses, and capabilities of existing and potential competitors and predict their responses to strategic initiatives.[8]

The labor component of the operating environment is made up of influences on the supply of workers available to perform needed organizational tasks. Issues such as the skill levels, union membership, wage rates, and average ages of potential workers are important to the operation of the organization. Managers often overlook another important issue: the attractiveness of working for a particular organization, as perceived by potential workers.

The supplier component of the operating environment includes the influence of providers of nonlabor resources to the organization. The firm purchases and transforms these resources during the production process into final goods and services. How many vendors offer specified resources for sale, the relative quality of materials they offer, the reliability of their deliveries, the credit terms they offer, and the potential for strategic linkages—all such issues affect managing this element in the operating environment.

The global/international component of the operating environment comprises all factors related to global issues. Though not all organizations must deal directly with international issues, the number that do is increasing dramatically. Significant aspects of the international component include the laws, political practices, cultures, and economic climates that prevail in the countries in which the firm does business.[9] Important elements in each of these categories are presented in Table 2.1. Figure 2.2 illustrates one

---

TABLE 2.1

International Component of the Operating Environment

Legal Forces	Cultural Forces
Legal traditions	Customs, norms, values, beliefs
Effectiveness of legal system	Language
Treaties with foreign nations	Attitudes
Patent/trademark laws	Motivations
Laws affecting business firms	Social institutions
	Status symbols
	Religious beliefs

Economic Forces	Political Forces
Level of economic development	Form of government
Population	Political ideology
Gross national product	Stability of government
Per-capita income	Strength of opposition parties and groups
Literacy level	Social unrest
Social infrastructure	Political strife and insurgency
Natural resources	Government attitude toward foreign firms
Climate	Foreign policy
Membership in regional economic blocks	
Monetary and fiscal policies	
Nature of competition	
Currency convertibility	
Inflation	
Taxation system	
Interest rates	
Wage and salary levels	

SOURCE: Reproduced from Arvind V. Phatak, *International Dimensions of Management*, 3d ed. (Boston: Kent Publishing, 1992), p. 6, with the permission of South-Western College Publishing. Copyright 1992 by South-Western College Publishing. All rights reserved.

FIGURE 2.2
World Changes in
the 1990s

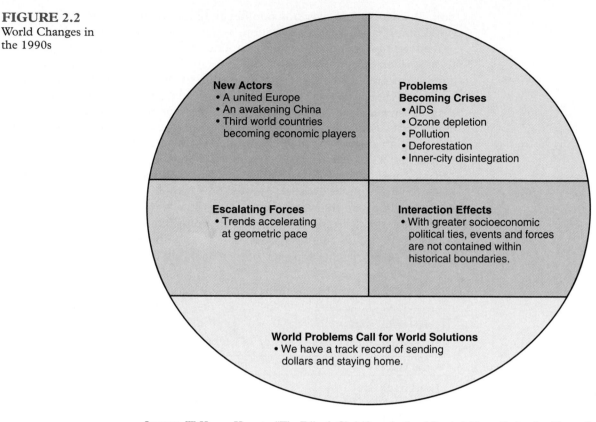

SOURCE: W. Harvey Hegarty, "The Editor's Chair/Organizational Survival Means Embracing Change," *Business Horizons,* November/December 1993, p. 2. Reprinted from *Business Horizons* (November–December 1993). Copyright 1993 by the Foundation for the School of Business at Indiana University. Used with permission.

observer's perspective on important forces that affect the international component of the operating environment of the 1990s. Note that while Table 2.1 provides a general list of potentially important issues from which firms can begin to analyze the international components of their operating environments, Figure 2.2 details underlying factors critical to understanding, and managing in, the operating environment of the 1990s. See Chapter 7 for further discussion of international issues.

Taken as a group, the five components of the operating environment define the territory or domain in which an organization resides. The structure of key relationships within this operating environment (or environments if a firm operates in multiple industries) will determine the firm's profit potential, as well as its prospects for achieving a sustainable competitive advantage.[10,11] Our definition of strategic management leads us to discuss the operating environment throughout the text. In particular, Chapter 4's discussion of strategy formulation uses environmental analysis to devise the organization's strategy.

Internal Environment

The organization's **internal environment** includes forces that operate inside the organization with specific implications for managing organizational performance. Unlike components of the general and operating environments, which act from outside the organization, components of the internal environment come from the organization itself. Table 2.2 lists a number of important components of the internal environment.

These aspects of an organization's internal environment collectively define both trouble spots that need strengthening and core competencies that the firm can nurture and build. By systematically examining its internal activities (production, marketing, etc.), a firm can better appreciate how each activity might add value or contribute significantly to shaping an effective strategy. Michael Porter has proposed a method for such an evaluation called *value chain analysis*.[12] Value chain analysis can identify internal core competencies, which, in concert with an external industry structure, are seen as the critical elements of long-term competitive advantage and profitability.[13] Chapter 4 will use the concepts of core competence and value chain analysis to enrich our discussion of the strategy formulation stage of the overall strategic management process.

The Skills Module gives you the opportunity to observe and apply environmental analysis issues in a real firm. Gerber Products has had to conduct a thorough environmental analysis in the face of a declining share of a changing market.

TABLE 2.2

Components of the Internal Environment

Organizational Component	Personnel Component
Communication network	Labor relations
Organization structure	Recruitment practices
Record of success	Training programs
Hierarchy of objectives	Performance appraisal system
Policies, procedures, rules	Incentive system
Ability of management team	Turnover and absenteeism

Marketing Component	Production Component
Market segmentation	Plant facility layout
Product strategy	Research and development
Pricing strategy	Use of technology
Promotion strategy	Purchasing of raw materials
Distribution strategy	Inventory control
	Use of subcontracting

Financial Component
Liquidity
Profitability
Activity
Investment opportunity

SKILLS MODULE
Environmental Analysis at Gerber

INTRODUCTION

We have discussed the structure of the organizational environment at some length. Review the following situation at Gerber and then complete the skill-development exercise. This will help you develop the ability to determine the impact of various environmental factors at different environmental levels on organizational success.

SITUATION

Feeding a baby isn't easy, but it's just as tough to create and sell the foods to feed a baby. The numbers are working against the big baby-food makers. Overall sales, measured in pounds, dropped 6 percent in the latest quarter, and the trend isn't likely to reverse with the Baby Boom generation graying and more women exiting their childbearing years.

Gerber Products Co., the nation's largest maker of baby food, has been losing market share to its rivals; within the most recent 12-week period, Gerber's sales declined nearly 3 percent. A 5.5 percent price increase, which rivals didn't immediately match, may have helped the competition post sales increases at Gerber's expense.

Yet the Fremont, Michigan, company maintains control of 71.2 percent of the shrinking market, selling far more peach compote and pureed beets than Beech-Nut (with 14.5 percent) and Heinz (with 11.1 percent) combined. Still, though Gerber is stocked in nearly half of the nation's supermarkets, the company has had a tough year: Its market share tumbled 1.5 percent, its new president resigned under mysterious circumstances, and it is accused, with its top rivals, of two decades of price fixing.

The changing market has led Gerber and its rivals to branch out, their growth strategies based on brand extensions. Success is mixed.

To increase overall sales, both Gerber and Beech-Nut are targeting groups with higher-than-average birth rates. For Hispanics, who buy more prepared baby food than many other ethnic groups, Gerber has unveiled a tropical line, made with fruits such as papayas and mangoes. Though successful tests in New York and Miami led to a national rollout last year, quarterly sales of the line dropped 17 percent. Beech-Nut's tropical line remains in the test marketing stage.

Angling for the toddler market, the three-year-old Gerber's Graduates line offers finger foods, snacks, and microwaved entrees. Sales of the 23-item line rose 51 percent in the most recent 12 weeks to $9.6 million, but analysts say that is short of expectations. An aggressive marketing campaign hasn't convinced people that toddler foods are anything but an unnecessary and expensive convenience item. Since a parent can easily serve macaroni and cheese, buying a six-ounce entree for $1.19 "just doesn't make sense," says Dick Landwehr, a buyer for Schultz Sav-O Stores in Milwaukee. Sales of Beech-Nut's Table Time microwaved meals rose 38 percent to $1.3 million in the same period.

Gerber has no plans to enter the hottest growth area in the marketplace—organic baby food. Although Beech-Nut discontinued its two-year effort after sales fell 44 percent, the market is healthy for Earth's Best, which saw sales climb more than 9 percent to $53.2 million for the same 12-week period.

Gerber maintains that it sets the standard for baby food, and its products show little or no traces of pesticide chemicals. Says spokesman Steve Poole, "That's as good as organic can claim to be." Analysts concur with Gerber's reluctance to enter the organic market. Says one, "It would raise the question, 'What's wrong with the other stuff?'"

SKILL DEVELOPMENT EXERCISE

Based on the situation described, list the one component from each environment—general, operating, and internal—that you think is the most critical for Gerber to deal with effectively. State your reasons for selecting this item, and make a recommendation to Gerber's top managers about what actions they should take with respect to it.

SOURCE: Carl Quintanilla, "Gerber Stumbles in a Shrinking Market," *The Wall Street Journal*, July 6, 1993, pp. B1, B5.

INTRODUCTION TO SWOT ANALYSIS

Gathering data about the general, operating, and internal environments provides the raw material from which to develop a picture of the organizational environment. **SWOT analysis** refines this body of information by applying a general framework for understanding and managing the environment in which an organization operates. (The acronym SWOT stands for Strengths, Weaknesses, Opportunities, Threats.) In many respects, the sophisticated analytical techniques discussed throughout the text are further refinements of basic SWOT analysis. In addition, students have repeatedly told us that SWOT is an excellent way to begin a case analysis. SWOT analysis attempts to assess the internal strengths and weaknesses of an organization and the opportunities and threats that its external environment presents. SWOT seeks to isolate the major issues facing an organization through careful analysis of each of these four elements. Managers can then formulate strategies to address key issues. Table 2.3 lists several key questions in each area that managers often address when performing SWOT analysis.

Although these questions may help direct a SWOT analysis, a great deal of work is required to answer them properly and to put them into perspective. For example, the analyst must assess the relative importance of each issue and the issue's potential impact on the firm and its strategy. Furthermore, the priority or relative importance of each issue may vary for strategies formulated at the corporate, business, or functional levels. We will distinguish among these levels of strategy in Chapter 4.

The case at the end of the chapter invites you to undertake a SWOT analysis for Ryka, a women's athletic shoe company. Ryka is a rapidly growing firm that generated annual revenues of $12 million in 1992. As you will see, it is also one of a handful of contemporary firms, along with Ben & Jerry's and the Body Shop, to link business strategy to social activism.

Understanding and Managing the Environment: SWOT and the Problem of Interpretation

Table 2.3 gives us some indication of the complexities of understanding and managing the environments in which managers operate. A multitude of environmental forces demand attention. Stated differently, the simplicity of SWOT analysis masks a great deal of individual and organizational complexity. For an individual manager who must complete an environmental analysis, the primary concerns are gathering and interpreting massive quantities of data about the most significant environmental forces, and then deciding what action to take in response to them. Because interpretation represents a form of judgment, interpretations, like judgments, often differ from manager to manager, even within the same firm. For example, one manager may see an environmental factor, say freer trade among nations, as an opportunity for market expansion, while another may focus on the threat of increased competition from international rivals.

This type of interpretation, often called **sensemaking,** by top managers has become the focus of a great deal of recent research by strategic management scholars.[14] This research brings the tools of psychology into the study of the strategic management process. Before it began, scholars paid little attention to sensemaking, either dismissing it as a type of mysterious black box or making some overly simple assumptions about its techniques. Mintzberg's

---

TABLE 2.3

Important Considerations for SWOT Analysis

Internal Analysis

Strengths	Weaknesses
A distinctive competence?	No clear strategic direction?
Adequate financial resources?	A deteriorating competitive position?
Good competitive skills?	Obsolete facilities?
Well thought of by buyers?	Subpar profitability because . . . ?
An acknowledged market leader?	Lack of managerial depth and talent?
Well-conceived functional	Missing any key skills or competencies?
area strategies?	Poor track record in implementing
Access to economies of scale?	strategy?
Insulated (at least somewhat)	Plagued with internal operating problems?
from strong competitive	Vulnerable to competitive pressures?
pressures?	Falling behind in R&D?
Proprietary technology?	Too narrow a product line?
Cost advantages?	Weak market image?
Competitive advantages?	Competitive disadvantages?
Product innovation abilities?	Below-average marketing skills?
Proven management?	Unable to finance needed changes
Other?	in strategy?
	Other?

External Analysis

Opportunities	Threats
Enter new markets or segments?	Likely entry of new competitors?
Add to product line?	Rising sales of substitute products?
Diversify into related products?	Slower market growth?
Add complementary products?	Adverse government policies?
Vertical integration?	Growing competitive pressures?
Ability to move to better	Vulnerability to recession and business
strategic group?	cycle?
Complacency among rival	Growing bargaining power of customers
firms?	or suppliers?
Faster market growth?	Changing buyer needs and tastes?
Other?	Adverse demographic changes?
	Other?

SOURCE: Adapted from Arthur A. Thompson, Jr., and A. J. Strickland III, *Strategic Management: Concepts and Cases* 7th ed. (Plano, Tex.: Business Publications, 1993), p. 88.

---

continuing research on how top managers really work, as opposed to the overly rational way they are often assumed to work, opened the door for renewed interest in sensemaking.[15] Herbert Simon's pioneering work on the cognitive limits inherent in managerial decision making (for which he was awarded the Nobel Prize) can be seen as the real wellspring for this research emphasis.[16]

The concept of strategic sensemaking has come to include a set of managerial activities that are basic to the task of environmental analysis—scanning, interpretation, and action-choice. In this text, we cover the first two topics in this chapter and the third in Chapter 4, in our discussion of strategy formulation.

The Aim of SWOT: Identifying and Managing Strategic Issues

SWOT analysis forces managers to better understand and respond to those factors that have the greatest importance for the firm's performance. We call these factors **strategic issues.** A strategic issue is an environmental factor, either inside or outside the organization, that is likely to have an impact on the ability of the enterprise to meet its objectives.[17]

It should be emphasized that strategic issues rarely arrive on a top manager's desk neatly labeled. Instead, data from SWOT analysis of the environment identify new technologies, market trends, new competitors, and employee morale trends. They require interpretation and translation before they are labeled *strategies*. Often, managers draw upon their experience to categorize issues as controllable or uncontrollable, as threats or opportunities. These categories then determine how an issue appears to an individual manager, how well it can be sold to other managers, and what action the firm subsequently takes.[18]

Clearly, not all issues are equally important to all organizations. Some organizations are much more sensitive to certain issues than others. Table 2.4 shows the sensitivity of a telephone equipment company and a major oil company to six different issues, or environmental factors. This example clearly supports the position that managers must carefully determine which issues have the most significant or strategic influence on organizational success. The Company Example illustrates how one top manager can look at the same situation as his predecessors, see a different set of strategic issues, and interpret them in a way that supports a different corporate strategy.

Scanning, Forecasting, and Other Data Sources for SWOT

All but the smallest organizations require cross-functional cooperation to gather data about present and future environments (sometimes termed

---

TABLE 2.4

Sensitivity of Two Companies to the Same Environmental Factors

Telephone Equipment	Manufacturer	Oil Company
GNP	Medium	High
Government capital spending	Very high	Low
Technical change	Very high	Medium/Low (except for electric car)
Sociological change	Very high (communication habits)	Very high (private car use)
Environmental pollution	Low	High
Middle East political risks	Low	High

SOURCE: Reprinted from *Long Range Planning*, March 1973, Basil W. Denning, "Strategic Environmental Appraisal," p. 25. Copyright 1973, with kind permission from Elsevier Science Ltd., The Boulevard, Langford Lane, Kidlington, OX5 1GB, UK.

COMPANY EXAMPLE

Kodak's Sharpshooter Surveys the Scene

Kodak, described as one of the most bureaucratic, wasteful, paternalistic, slow-moving—and beloved—companies in America, is ready to go down the path of restructuring—again. After five attempts in the past decade, the Rochester, New York, company has gotten serious. Frustrated board members, pressured by investors, fired the chairman and brought in one of American industry's best and brightest, Motorola Chairman George M. C. Fisher.

Although Fisher is too busy mapping out a strategic plan to disclose any further plans, he has already angered many analysts and investors with his initial promise: "Kodak has a great franchise, and my hope is to build on that to get exciting growth." Critics say that is impossible. They would prefer to see Kodak run as a mature cash cow, cutting costs, especially through massive layoffs, to generate as much cash flow as possible, buying in shares, and paying big dividends.

Fisher already faces competitive inroads on Kodak's highly profitable film and photographic-paper businesses, where gross margins can be as high as 80 percent. But Japan's Fuji Photo Film and private-label brands are undercutting Kodak's prices and eroding its market share, which in the past five years has fallen from about 80 percent to 70 percent. Lowering prices in 1994 helped stem the slide; next up is a film called Funtime aimed at the low-end market and priced 20 percent below Kodak's Standard Gold brand. It will only be sold during the spring and fall, not during peak picture times of summer and Christmas.

The trend toward lowering prices could stymie any growth plans. Kodak needs a large cash flow to finance a move it must make into electronics—a small, fast-growing arena where its products have great potential—and out of chemicals, a mature, slow-growth industry. Fisher, renowned at Motorola for forming strategic alliances with other electronics companies to gain technologies or market toeholds, will likely be searching Kodak's labs for overlooked ideas to push into the market.

Margin pressures may also lead to deeper cuts. Kodak has already spun off its Eastman Chemical division. Publicly, it says that its Sterling Drug division is not for sale; that stance may simply be timing, though, for health-care reform is battering the market values of drug companies.

Still, Fisher is optimistic about Kodak and its core product. He—and analysts—think he can stem the outward flow of market share and attain big growth overseas. After all, as Kodak executives like to point out, half of the world's citizens don't take pictures yet.

SOURCE: Peter Nulty, "Kodak Grabs for Growth Again," *Fortune,* May 16, 1994, pp. 76–78.

---

scanning and forecasting, respectively) and to try to make sense of it all. This is a direct result of the complexity and constant change in the environments in which organizations operate, environments that one executive could never fully understand and manage.

SWOT analysis becomes a team effort performed jointly by functional specialists from marketing, production, finance, etc. These experts review the environments closest to their specialities, and bring issues they see as critical to the attention of their peers from other functions, as well as general managers who have responsibilities for overall or integrated SWOT analysis. At this stage in the SWOT analysis, the team debates issues, brings conflicts between functions to the surface, prioritizes issues, and plans actions.

In another, more formal method for assessing external environmental factors as part of a SWOT analysis, managers can gather and analyze feedback from key employees. Environmental assessment specialists for the Sun Oil Exploration and Production Company developed such a system to rate the relative importance of various external environmental factors. Key employees

TABLE 2.5

Some Questions to Determine the Relevance of Environmental Factors

1. If you could have perfect information about five external factors that affect our operation, what would they be? (For example, crude oil prices, GNP deflator, etc.)
2. What five external factors do you see as the major threats to our business?
3. What five factors would you like to know about our competitors' future plans?
4. If you were asked to define a company strategic direction, what five external factors would you feel would be most critical in performing this task?
5. What five external areas would be the most likely to show changes which would be most favorable to the company's future?

SOURCE: Allen H. Mesch, "Developing an Effective Environmental Assessment Function," *Managerial Planning*, March–April 1984, p. 19. Reprinted by permission of The Planning Forum, The International Society for Strategic Management and Planning.

from various functions at Sun were asked to respond to the questions listed in Table 2.5, and their answers were analyzed. Sun's specific objective was to guide top managers in understanding the external environment in which the firm operated and to give them some perspective on possible future events that might pose threats or offer opportunities.[19]

Managers can modify this basic data gathering method to tap other sources of information, such as customers or consultants. For example, many firms routinely conduct extensive interviews with follow-up questionnaires through their marketing departments to get feedback on customer satisfaction or dissatisfaction. This research can be viewed as assessing the customer component of the firms' environments. Likewise, a firm with an active international business might survey a small group of outside consultants (such as Kissinger and Associates, headed by former Secretary of State Henry Kissinger). By analyzing the consultants' responses, the firm could develop a better understanding of the political risks involved in expanding operations in a particular country. These two data gathering efforts have very different focuses, but both can be seen as forms of environmental scanning.

Information gathered from key employees can also help managers better understand the *internal* environment of the organization. In this situation, the questions focus on the primary components of the internal environment: the organizational component, marketing component, financial component, personnel component, and production component. Table 2.6 presents several questions that might be asked in connection with such an internal analysis. Part IV of this text examines production, finance, and marketing with emphasis on how these functions might contribute to cross-functional analysis. Studies have tried to identify the specific data sources on which managers base their environmental analyses. One study found that managers seek important information from daily newspapers such as *The New York Times*, publications of industry groups such as The Conference Board, business magazines such as *Fortune*, consultants, government publications, and seminars. These same businesspeople rated literary magazines such as *The New Yorker*, universities, professional association reports from groups such as the World Future

---

TABLE 2.6

Sample Questions for an Internal Environmental Analysis

ORGANIZATIONAL COMPONENT

Is the organizational culture well-matched to the requirements of the competitive environment?

Does the company delegate authority appropriately?

Is the organization structure of the company appropriate?

Are jobs and performance goals clearly understood by workers?

MARKETING COMPONENT

Is market research used to best advantage?

Is advertising used efficiently and effectively?

Can the product distribution system be improved?

FINANCIAL COMPONENT

Does analysis of the income statement reveal potential improvements?

Does analysis of the balance sheet reveal potential improvements?

Can break-even analysis be used to better align costs in relation to profits?

PERSONNEL COMPONENT

Are training programs adequate?

Can procedures for recruitment and selection of employees be improved?

Is the performance appraisal system fair and accurate?

PRODUCTION COMPONENT

Can the organization improve its level of technology?

Can the flow of work within the plant be made more efficient?

What form does the quality improvement system take?

Society, academic journals such as the *Harvard Business Review,* and privately published newsletters such as the Kiplinger Letter as relatively unimportant sources of external information.[20]

Figure 2.3 provides a general overview of the data sources that managers can use for environmental analysis. Several additional sources of data available to managers are cited in the Appendix to Chapter 13.

Scanning Systems   Scanning systems can take many different forms. Perhaps the most widely accepted method for categorizing these systems divides them into three types.[21]

1. Irregular scanning systems: These consist largely of ad hoc studies, often in response to environmental crises (such as an energy shortage). They focus mainly on the past in an effort to identify events that have already taken place. Emphasizing intermediate or short-run reactions to crises, irregular scanning systems pay little attention to future environmental events.
2. Regular scanning systems: These systems revolve around regular reviews of the environment or selected strategic environmental components. These reviews are often made annually. Because such a scan is perceived as decision oriented, management commonly reviews the results during decision

FIGURE 2.3   General Sources of Information for Environmental Analysis

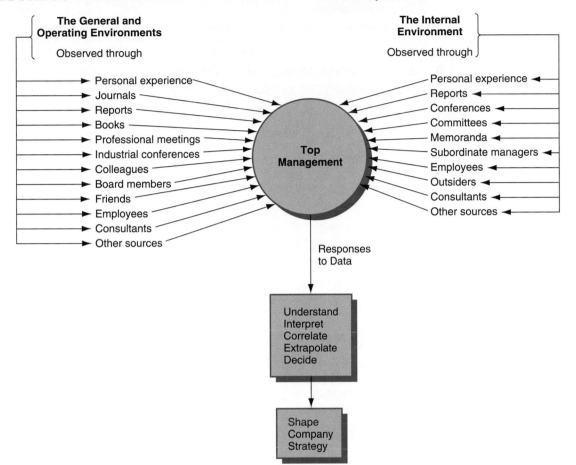

opportunities such as annual planning exercises. The focus of such a system is primarily retrospective, but some thought is given to future conditions assumed to be evolving within the environment.

3. Continuous scanning systems: These systems constantly monitor components of the organizational environment. Such scanning is an ongoing activity and is not performed by a committee set up temporarily for the sole purpose of completing a scan. Established boundary-spanning offices often coordinate this activity. Continuous scanning systems tend to be more future oriented than either irregular or regular systems.

Table 2.7 compares these three scanning systems along several dimensions. As one moves from the irregular model to the regular model to the continuous model, scanning activities generally become more sophisticated and have longer-term effects on organizational operations. A continuous scanning system generally reflects a serious, sustained commitment to environmental analysis. The first environmental analysis that many organizations conduct takes the form of some type of irregular system. Over time, this irregular scanning system can evolve into a regular and then into a continuous scanning system.

TABLE 2.7

Comparison of Scanning Models

Irregular Model	Regular Model	Continuous Model
MEDIA FOR SCANNING ACTIVITY		
Ad hoc studies	Periodically updated studies	Structured data collection and processing systems
SCOPE OF SCANNING		
Specific events	Selected events	Broad range of environmental systems
MOTIVATION FOR ACTIVITY		
Crisis initiated	Decision and issue oriented	Planning process oriented
TEMPORAL NATURE OF ACTIVITY		
Reactive	Proactive	Proactive
TIME FRAME FOR DATA		
Retrospective	Primarily current and retrospective	Prospective
TIME FRAME FOR DECISION IMPACT		
Current and near future	Near-term	Long-term
Organizational makeup		
Various staff agencies	Various staff agencies	Environmental scanning unit

SOURCE: Liam Fahey and William R. King, "Environmental Scanning for Corporate Planning," *Business Horizons,* August 1977, p. 63. Reprinted from *Business Horizons* (August 1977). Copyright 1977 by the Foundation for the School of Business at Indiana University. Used with permission.

However, regardless of the scanning approach selected, we must emphasize that the *interpretation* of the data, not the quantity or timing of the data collected, determines how the data are used in making strategic decisions.

Forecasting Systems   Environmental forecasting, a critical step in SWOT analysis, is the process of identifying strategic issues that will affect an organization's environment at some future time. Most companies find that forecasting future strategic issues is critical to organizational success.

When they perform environmental forecasts, managers try to predict the future status of strategic issues at each environmental level. An organization's environmental forecasts commonly include economic forecasts, social forecasts, political forecasts, and technological forecasts. For example, technological innovations in microelectronics and telecommunications could shift literally millions of jobs back to the home and out of the factories and offices into which the Industrial Revolution swept them.[22] Managers who judge this technological issue to be important to the future success of their organizations should already be busy planning how to cope with this trend if and when it materializes.

Naturally, the types of forecasts made by any one organization depend on the unique situation confronting that organization. Several environmental trends, however, are commonly followed by firms in very different industries. These trends are shown in Table 2.8.

TABLE 2.8

Important External and Internal Environmental Trends

EXTERNAL TRENDS

1. Trends in the global market place (protectionism versus free trade)
2. Growth of government as a customer
3. Development of the European Community
4. Business with socialist countries
5. Economic and political trends in developing countries
6. Monetary trends
7. Inflationary trends
8. Emergence of the multinational firm
9. Technology as a competitive tool
10. Bigness as a competitive tool
11. Saturation of growth
12. Emergence of new industries
13. Technological breakthroughs
14. Growth of the service sector
15. Affluent consumers
16. Changes in age distributions of customers
17. Selling to reluctant consumers
18. Social attitudes toward business
19. Government controls
20. Consumer pressures
21. Union pressures
22. Impact of society's concern with ecology
23. Impact of zero-growth advocates
24. Shrinking product life cycles
25. Intra-European nationalism
26. Conflict between multinational firms and national interests
27. Public distrust of business
28. Shrinking forecasting horizons
29. Strategic surprises
30. Competition from developing countries
31. Strategic resource shortages
32. Redistribution of power within the firm
33. Changing work attitudes
34. Pressures for employment maintenance

INTERNAL TRENDS

1. Size
2. Complexity
3. Structure
4. Systems
5. Communications
6. Power structure
7. Role definitions

Continued

TABLE 2.8

Continued

8. Centralization/decentralization
9. Values and norms
10. Management style
11. Management competence
12. Logistical competence
13. Capital intensity
14. Technological intensity
15. Product diversification
16. Market diversification
17. Technological diversification
18. Other

SOURCE: Adapted from H. Igor Ansoff, "Strategic Issues Management," *Strategic Management Journal* 1 (1980):139. Copyright 1980 by John Wiley & Sons. Reprinted by permission of John Wiley & Sons, Ltd.

TABLE 2.9

Methods of Environmental Forecasting

1. *Expert opinion.* Knowledgeable people are selected and asked to assign importance and probability ratings to various possible future developments. The most refined version, the Delphi method, puts experts through several rounds of event assessment, where they keep refining their assumptions and judgments.
2. *Trend extrapolation.* Researchers fit curves (linear, quadratic, or *S*-shaped growth curves) through past time series to serve as a basis for extrapolation. This method can be very unreliable if new developments alter the expected direction of movement.
3. *Trend correlation.* Researchers correlate various time series in the hope of identifying leading and lagging relationships that can support forecasts.
4. *Dynamic modeling.* Researchers build sets of equations to try to describe the underlying system. The coefficients in the equations are fitted through statistical means. Econometric models of more than 300 equations, for example, are used to forecast changes in the U.S. economy.
5. *Cross-impact analysis.* Researchers identify a set of key trends (those high in importance and/or probability) and ask, "If event A occurs, what will be the impact on all other trends?" The results are then used to build sets of "domino chains," with one event triggering others.
6. *Multiple scenarios.* Researchers build pictures of alternative futures, each internally consistent and with a certain probability of happening. The major purpose of the scenarios is to stimulate contingency planning.
7. *Demand/hazard forecasting.* Researchers identify major events that would greatly affect the firm. Each event is rated for its convergence with several major trends taking place in society and for its appeal to each major public group in the society. A higher convergence and appeal increases the probability that the event will occur. The highest-scoring events are then researched further.

SOURCE: Based on James R. Bright and Milton E. F. Schoeman, *A Guide to Practical Technological Forecasting* (Englewood Cliffs, N.J.: Prentice-Hall, 1973).

Many environmental forecasting techniques are available to managers. Some of these techniques (such as seeking expert opinions) can be fairly simple; others (such as trend extrapolation) can be quite complex. Some organizations may need to hire experts from outside the organization to apply these methods properly. Several forecasting techniques are presented and defined in Table 2.9.

EVALUATING THE ENVIRONMENTAL ANALYSIS PROCESS

Organizations perform environmental analysis to help them achieve their goals effectively and efficiently. Naturally, some environmental analysis efforts are better than others. Hence, it is crucial to evaluate the environmental analysis process like any other organizational activity.

Some of the important characteristics of appropriately implemented environmental analyses are discussed below. These characteristics can be used as a set of standards against which to compare a particular firm's environmental analysis activities.[23]

A Successful Environmental Analysis Is Linked Conceptually and Practically to Current Planning Operations   If the environmental analysis system is not linked to planning, the results of the analysis will contribute little toward establishing the direction the organization will take in the long run. One method commonly used to achieve this vital integration is to involve key organizational planners in some facet of environmental analysis. To ensure a strong link between planning and environmental analysis at Atlantic Richfield, for example, the manager of environmental issues is directly responsible to the director of issues and planning.[24]

A Successful Environmental Analysis Is Responsive to the Information Needs of Top Management   The client for whom environmental analysis is performed is the firm's top management team. Environmental analysts must thoroughly understand and meet the information needs of the high-level managers within their organizations. They must recognize that these information needs may change over time and adjust the environmental analysis process in accordance with such changes.

A Successful Environmental Analysis Is Continually Supported by Top Management   To be successful, any organizational effort needs the support and encouragement of top management. Environmental analysis activities are no exception. They will be perceived as important by organization members only to the extent that such support is apparent. Without this support, environmental analysis activities will be wasted.

A Successful Environmental Analysis Is Completed by Analysts Who Understand the Skills a Strategist Needs   Environmental analysts should focus on identifying existing and potential strengths, weaknesses, opportunities, and threats suggested by components of the organization's environment. Strategists must interpret the results of environmental analysis in light of their in-depth understanding of company operations. The analyst must share the strategist's skills to contribute to an effective strategy.

SUMMARY

Environmental analysis is the process of monitoring the organizational environment to identify both present and future strengths, weaknesses, opportunities, and threats that may influence the firm's ability to reach its goals. Environmental analysis is done, not by gods, but by humans; therefore we must recognize that human limitations, prior experiences, and biases will affect environmental analysis.

For purposes of analysis, a firm's environment can be divided into three main segments, or levels: the internal environment (consisting of organizational, marketing, financial, personnel, and production components), the operating environment (consisting of the supplier, competition, customer, labor, and international components), and the general environment (consisting of the economic, technological, ethical, political/legal, and social components).

Several techniques are available to help managers develop a useful environmental analysis, all of them developed from basic analysis of strengths, weaknesses, opportunities, and threats—SWOT analysis. More specifically, scanning and forecasting techniques can become parts of the SWOT analysis effort. Scanning is a technique in which the manager reviews data from various levels of the organizational environment in order to keep abreast of critical environmental issues and events. Forecasting is a technique in which the manager attempts to predict the future characteristics of the organizational environment and hence to make decisions today that will help the firm deal with the environment of tomorrow.

Having implemented an environmental analysis process, top managers should continually evaluate and improve it. The process should be linked to current planning operations, responsive to the information needs of key managers, supported by top managers, and performed by people who understand strategy.

The Checklist presents a summary of questions based on this chapter. Use it in analyzing strategic management problems and cases that focus on environmental analysis issues.

KEY TERMS

organizational environment, p. 31
general environment, p. 32
operating environment, p. 34
internal environment, p. 36
SWOT analysis, p. 39

sensemaking, p. 39
strategic issues, p. 41
scanning, p. 42
forecasting, p. 42

CHECKLIST

Analyzing Environmental Issues in Problems and Cases

___   1.   Does the strategic management problem or case raise environmental analysis issues?

___   2.   Are factors in the general environment being appropriately considered as part of the environmental analysis?

___   3.   Are factors in the operating environment being appropriately considered as part of the environmental analysis?

___ 4. Are factors in the internal environment being appropriately considered as part of the environmental analysis?

___ 5. In what way is the firm organizing its SWOT analysis?

___ 6. Does the organization have a properly functioning environmental scanning system?

___ 7. Is environmental forecasting properly employed during the environmental analysis process?

___ 8. Does the organization spend enough time evaluating and improving its environmental analysis process?

Additional Readings

Diffenbach, John, "Corporate Environmental Analysis in Large U.S. Corporations." *Long Range Planning* 16, no. 3 (1983), pp. 107–116.

Drucker, Peter F. "Managing for Tomorrow." *Industry Week,* April 14, 1980, pp. 54–64.

———. *Managing in Turbulent Times.* New York: Harper & Row, 1980.

Goss, Tracey, Richard Pascale, and Anthony Athos. "The Reinvention of the Roller Coaster: Risking the Present for a Powerful Future." *Harvard Business Review,* November/December 1993, p. 97.

Guth, William D. *Handbook of Business Strategy.* Boston: Warren, Gorham & Lamont, 1985.

Heath, Robert, and Associates. *Strategic Issue Management.* San Francisco: Jossey-Bass, 1988.

Hofstede, Geert. *Culture's Consequences: International Differences in Work Related Values.* Beverly Hills, Calif.: Sage, 1980.

Nadler, David, Marc Gerstein, and Robert Shaw. *Organizational Architecture.* San Francisco: Jossey-Bass, 1992.

Thomas, James B., Shawn M. Clark, and Dennis Gioia. "Strategic Sensemaking and Organizational Performance." *Academy of Management Journal,* April 1993, pp. 239–270.

C A S E

RYKA'S SWOT ANALYSIS HELPS IT TO TAKE ON THE BIG GUYS

Finding a product niche wasn't difficult for Sheri Poe; keeping it to herself was the hard part.

When Poe came up with the idea for a women's athletic shoe, the competition was a vast wasteland—no one else had a shoe like hers—yet overwhelmingly formidable, due to competitors' brand recognition and marketing and advertising budgets. But Poe made Ryka, her Norwood, Massachusetts, company, something different: Its shoes were designed *for* a woman's foot, *based on* a woman's foot, not on a smaller version of a man's foot. "Women have different hips and pelvises and their feet strike the ground differently," said Poe. "We developed a special last (a block of foot-shaped plastic on which shoes are made) that takes that into consideration."

Poe said that retailers recognized the need for Ryka's shoes, and industry analysts agreed that Ryka was the only athletic shoemaker designing strictly for women. (Its giant competitors have since adopted special lasts more friendly to the female foot.) Like all small companies entering crowded markets, however, Ryka needed to get attention for its innovation. Also, no upstart company can compete in a market where athletic-shoe companies spend hundreds of millions of dollars on advertising.

With a smaller budget, Ryka has ventured onto smaller avenues. Its marketers discovered that the syndicated TV fitness show hosted by Jake Steinfield, a Hollywood body trainer, had a 70 percent female audience. Ryka gave the bodybuilder an undisclosed amount of stock and a small stipend to outfit his assistants in Ryka shoes.

Quality control is another problem common to small companies. Ryka confronted difficulties perfecting its patented technology—a nitrogen molding resembling clear-rubber bouncing balls that fit into the foundation of the shoe. Quality problems, including poor stitching, prompted one athletic-shoe chain to return almost its entire fall shipment to Ryka. The company corrected the molding problems and its distributors became happier. "We think their technology is excellent," said a spokesman for Jordan Marsh. "Their styling is definitely contoured for a woman's foot."

The marketing message continued to focus on shoes made by women for women. This was no accident, since the idea for Ryka arose during Poe's latent recovery from a sexual assault 21 years earlier. She wove her story into a marketing message that helped boost Ryka's sales 53 percent in 1992, to $12 million. A hard-edged print advertising campaign inspired by Poe's intimate history juxtaposed the image of a woman working out with the photo of a teary-eyed woman, with copy that read: "Sometimes the only way to work it out is to work it out."

Though the campaign received mixed reviews, it worked. The six-year-old company expected to grow another 53 percent in 1993 to more than $18 million in sales. Through a foundation that Poe established, groups helping women who have been victims of violent crimes receive 7 percent of company profits. Such moves boost Ryka's profile and further define its niche as shoes made for women, by women.

DISCUSSION QUESTIONS

1. Based on Table 2.3, what is your assessment of Ryka's strengths, weaknesses, opportunities, and threats?

2. What would you consider the most significant factor in each of these four groupings?

3. What would you recommend that Poe do about each of these four environmental factors?

4. What three environmental trends do you see as potentially critical to Ryka's future success? Explain why.

5. How should the firm prepare itself for these trends?

SOURCES: *Business Week*, June 14, 1993, pp. 82–83; Suzanne Alexander, "Tiny Ryka Seeks a Foothold with Sneakers for Women," *The Wall Street Journal*, July 31, 1989, p. B2.

Notes

1. Samuel C. Certo, *Modern Management: Diversity, Quality, Ethics, in the Global Environment*, 5th ed. (Boston: Allyn & Bacon, 1994), pp. 41–42.

2. Lawrence Rhyne, "The Relationship of Information Usage Characteristics to Planning System Sophistication," *Strategic Management Journal* 6 (1985), pp. 319–337.

3. Jon Katzenbach and Douglas Smith, *The Wisdom of Teams* (Boston: Harvard Business School Press, 1993).

4. Jane Dutton and Edward Ottensmeyer, "Strategic Issue Management Systems: Forms, Functions, and Contexts," *Academy of Management Review* 12 (1987), pp. 355–365.

5. Philip S. Thomas, "Environmental Analysis for Corporate Planning," *Business Horizons,* October 1974, pp. 27–38.

6. For more information about several of these examples, see Abraham Katz, "Evaluating the Environment: Economic and Technological Factors," in William D. Guth, ed., *Handbook of Business Strategy* (Boston: Warren, Gorham & Lamont, 1985), pp. 2–9.

7. For an illustration of how such factors can affect strategic management, see P. D. Cooper and G. Miaoulis, "Altering Corporate Strategic Criteria to Reflect the Changing Environment: The Role of Life Satisfaction and the Growing Senior Market," *California Management Review* 31 (Fall 1988), pp. 87–97; and "Saving Our Schools," *Business Week,* September 14, 1992, pp. 70–78.

8. R. S. Wilson, "Managing in the Competitive Environment," *Long Range Planning* 17, no. 1 (1984), pp. 50–63.

9. Peter Wright, "MNC—Third World Business Unit Performance: Application of Strategic Elements," *Strategic Management Journal* 5 (1984), pp. 231–240.

10. Michael Porter, *Competitive Advantage* (New York: Free Press, 1985).

11. Pankaj Ghemawat, *Commitment: The Dynamic of Strategy* (New York: Free Press, 1991).

12. Porter, *Competitive Advantage.*

13. C. K. Prahalad and G. Hamel, "The Core Competence of the Corporation," *Harvard Business Review,* May/June 1990, pp. 79–91.

14. James Thomas, Shawn Clark, and Dennis Gioia, "Strategic Sensemaking and Organizational Performance," *Academy of Management Journal* 36, no. 2 (April 1993), pp. 239–270.

15. Henry Mintzberg, *The Nature of Managerial Work* (New York: Harper & Row, 1973).

16. Herbert Simon, *Administrative Behavior,* 2d ed. (New York: Free Press, 1957).

17. Edward Ottensmeyer and Jane Dutton, "Interpreting Environments and Taking Action: Types and Characteristics of Strategic Issue Management Systems," in Charles Snow, ed., *Strategy Organization Design and Human Resource Management* (Greenwich, Conn.: JAI Press, 1989).

18. Jane Dutton and Susan Jackson, "Categorizing Strategic Issues," *Academy of Management Review* 12 (1987), pp. 76–90.

19. Allen H. Mesch, "Developing an Effective Environmental Assessment Function," *Managerial Planning* 32, no. 5 (March/April 1984), pp. 17–22.

20. Subhash C. Jain, "Environmental Scanning in U.S. Corporations," *Long Range Planning* 17, no. 2 (1984), pp. 117–128.

21. Liam Fahey and William R. King, "Environmental Scanning for Corporate Planning," *Business Horizons,* August 1977, pp. 61–71.

22. Boas Shamir and Ilan Solomon, "Work-at-Home and the Quality of Working Life," *Academy of Management Review* 10, no. 3 (1985), pp. 455–464.

23. This section is based on Engledow and Lenz, "Whatever Happened to Environmental Analysis"; Eli Segev, "Analysis of the Business Environment," *Management Review* (1979), p. 59.

24. B. Arrington, Jr., and R. N. Sawaya, "Issues Management in an Uncertain Environment," *Long Range Planning* 17, no. 6 (1984), pp. 17–24.

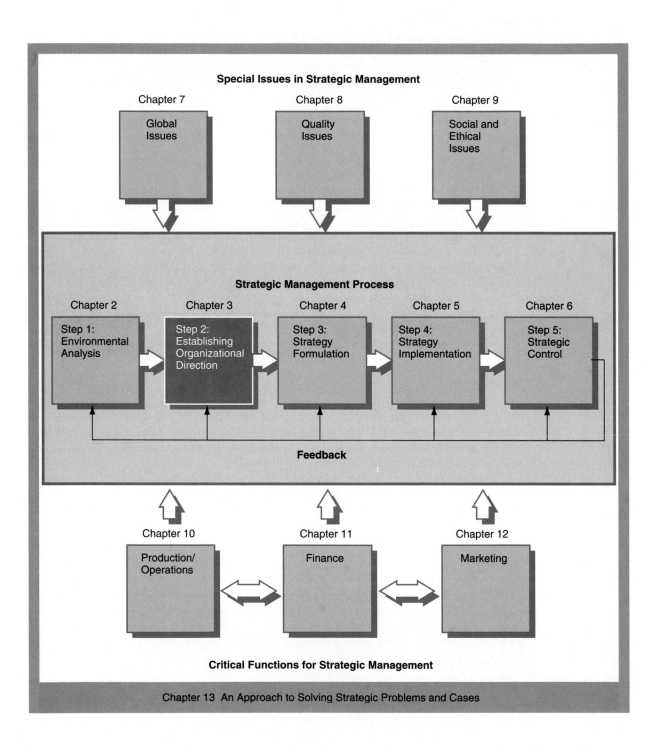

Special Issues in Strategic Management

Chapter 7

Global Issues

Chapter 8

Quality Issues

Chapter 9

Social and Ethical Issues

Strategic Management Process

Chapter 2

Step 1: Environmental Analysis

Chapter 3

Step 2: Establishing Organizational Direction

Chapter 4

Step 3: Strategy Formulation

Chapter 5

Step 4: Strategy Implementation

Chapter 6

Step 5: Strategic Control

Feedback

Chapter 10

Production/ Operations

Chapter 11

Finance

Chapter 12

Marketing

Critical Functions for Strategic Management

Chapter 13 An Approach to Solving Strategic Problems and Cases

Establishing Organizational Direction

In Chapter 2, we discussed environmental analysis, the first step of the strategic management process. That chapter covered the fundamentals of environmental analysis, structures, and interpretations. This chapter focuses on establishing organizational direction, the step of the strategic management process that immediately follows environmental analysis.

Top managers commonly use three key devices to establish and document the direction in which they wish an organization to move: vision, mission, and objectives. Essentially, organizational vision and mission establish the general direction of the firm, and organizational objectives narrow the focus to define more specific targets. Only after incorporating the results of a thorough environmental analysis can managers formulate visions, develop missions, and set consistent and compatible objectives.

FUNDAMENTALS OF ORGANIZATIONAL VISION AND MISSION

Two steps are critical in establishing and maintaining direction in any organization: (1) articulating a vision of the organization's future and (2) translating that vision into a mission that defines the organization's overarching purpose. The section below on the nature of organizational objectives explains how general visions and missions become more tangible as they are translated into focused action. Chapter 4 develops this topic further.

Many successful firms see vision and mission statements as powerful shapers of effective corporate cultures. Taken together, vision and mission statements present the values, philosophies, and aspirations that guide organizational action. These statements provide motivation, and possibly inspiration, to current and future members of the organization. In the sections below, we define and discuss the importance of these potentially powerful concepts.

What Is Organizational Vision?

As part of the strategic management process, an organizational **vision** encapsulates the organization's values and aspirations in the most general terms, without specific statements about the strategies used to attain them. A corporate vision provides a point of connection for various internal and external stakeholders. In his book, *The Fifth Discipline,* Peter Senge points out that an organizational vision is the answer to the question, "What do we want to create?"[1] Senge further explains that shared visions in organizations ". . . create a sense of commonality that permeates the organization and gives coherence to diverse activities." As a result, "[w]ork becomes part of pursuing a larger purpose embodied in the organization's products and services."[2]

Colgate executive Reuben Mark emphasized this need for a vision to transform work when he said, "You're never going to get anyone to charge the machine guns only for financial objectives. It's got to make them feel better, feel part of something."[3] John Rollwagen, former CEO of Cray Research, has reported that this sense of being part of something was brought about at Cray by people seeing themselves working to make the world's fastest computers in partnership with founder and supercomputer design genius Seymour Cray, even though few employees had actually met Cray. These examples illustrate the potential power of a corporate vision to focus the collective energy of insiders and to give outsiders a better idea of what an organization really is.

However, nothing comes without a price. In order to translate the potential power of a vision into real power, organizational leaders need to recognize certain characteristics of visions and how they work. First, developing a vision that is truly shared across an organization, one that generates excitement and commitment, can be a difficult and time-consuming process. According to Senge, this is one reason why a corporate vision often represents the ideas of one or a few people at the very top of the corporate hierarchy, and why it seems to focus more on gaining compliance than on building commitment.[4] Of course, an individual, often a founder, can have a powerful impact on a corporation's vision. However, famous stories of successful visions—James Lincoln at Lincoln Electric, Edwin Land at Polaroid, Andrew Grove at Intel—involve visions that have been widely shared across entire organizations. Often these stories neglect the work that corporate leaders devote to getting others to commit to those leaders' views.[5]

Second, the methods by which a leader tries to sell a vision to others in the organization seem critical. William O'Brien of Hanover Insurance has stated that, "Being a visionary leader is not about giving speeches and inspiring the troops. How I spend my day is pretty much the same as how any executive spends [the] day. Being a visionary leader is about solving day-to-day problems with my vision in mind."[6]

Third, leaders must recognize the complexity of changing an outmoded vision to reflect new realities, possibly those uncovered during environmental analysis. News reports in the mid-1990s recount the Herculean efforts of U.S. corporations to re-create or redefine themselves in order to adapt to new competitive forces. Sears, General Motors, AT&T, and Motorola are examples of firms working to redefine themselves through updated visions of the future, and through new objectives and strategies that might flow from new visions.

The breakup of AT&T spawned seven "Baby Bell" firms (e.g., Bell Atlantic, NYNEX, US West, etc.) spread geographically around the United States. Leaders in these seven new firms have reported enormous difficulties in moving their shared visions away from taking orders from a far-off central office (i.e., AT&T) toward independent action, away from a singular focus on providing local telephone service toward greater diversification.[7] Table 3.1 shows how one firm stated its vision.

TABLE 3.1

Delta's Vision

Getting 74,000 people to agree on anything is no small task. Having spoken with people throughout the Delta system, I can assure you we not only have a shared vision, but also the shared determination to see it reflected in the service we provide.

Much has changed since Delta flew our first passengers in 1929. One thing has not: our commitment to excellence and superior customer service. That commitment is at the core of our vision for the future—one that will see Delta build on its traditional strengths to prosper in a highly competitive global marketplace.

In short, we want Delta to be the **Worldwide Airline of Choice.**

> **Worldwide,** because we are and intend to remain an innovative, aggressive, ethical, and successful competitor that offers access to the world at the highest standards of customer service. We will continue to look for opportunities to extend our reach through new routes and creative global alliances.

> **Airline,** because we intend to stay in the business we know best—air transportation and related services. We won't stray from our roots. We believe in the long-term prospects for profitable growth in the airline industry, and we will continue to focus time, attention, and investment on enhancing our place in that business environment.

> **Of Choice,** because we value the loyalty of our customers, employees, and investors. For passengers and shippers, we will continue to provide the best service and value. For our personnel, we will continue to offer an ever more challenging, rewarding, and result-oriented workplace that recognizes and appreciates their contributions. For our shareholders, we will earn a consistent, superior financial return.

That is the Delta vision. Our challenge, at one of the most critical times in our history, is to realize that vision and to build on our position as a world leader in aviation.

How? By continuing to control costs while providing excellent, high-value service. By taking steps to keep up with innovative competitors and alliances. By knowing how to operate in diverse markets and attract new customers. By recognizing that established ways of doing business that may have served us well in the past will not sustain us in the future. And by remembering at all times that people—customers, our personnel, and shareholders—are our competitive edge.

As we adapt to the new realities of a dynamic international marketplace and changing world, some of the old ways of doing business will no longer apply. But one principle remains paramount: putting people first. This airline is a "people business." Service is the cornerstone of our operation. We will work as a team to meet the needs of our customers with the quality dependable service they have come to expect. With a strong route system; a safe, dependable fleet; and uncompromising integrity, Delta will make its vision a reality and live up to a hard-earned, well-deserved reputation as the **Worldwide Airline of Choice.**

SOURCE: *SKY,* December 1993, p. 10. Delta's Vision For The Future is provided courtesy of Delta Air Lines, Inc.

Vision and Performance

Some evidence suggests that vision-driven companies outperform their competitors in the marketplace. Collins and Porras studied firms identified as visionary by other executives. They found that visionary firms, as a group, performed 55 times better than the overall stock market, and, taken individually, performed 8 times better than their nonvisionary competitors.[8]

Despite this observed link between vision-driven action and performance, some high-profile executives reject the notion that a corporate vision is important. Shortly after taking over as CEO of IBM, Louis Gerstner, Jr. stated, "There's been a lot of speculation as to when I'm going to deliver a vision of IBM. The last thing IBM needs right now is a vision."[9] Gerstner believed that what IBM needed most was a return to basic "blocking and tackling" skills, such as reducing costs and improving market focus. Chrysler's CEO, Robert Eaton, has voiced agreement: "Internally, we don't use the word *vision*. I believe in quantifiable short-term results—things we can all relate to—as opposed to some esoteric thing no one can quantify."[10]

What could account for such variation in views on the topic of vision? Noel Tichy, author and consultant, offers two answers. First, the need for and importance of a vision may differ by industry; a firm operating in a mature industry, such as an automobile component manufacturer, may need a vision less than a firm in an industry, such as biotechnology, that demands a "radically new idea to win in the marketplace."[11] Second, firms experiencing severe financial problems, as IBM was in the mid-1990s, need to focus on short-term survival before they can spare attention for longer-term matters related to vision; one source explains that, "the patient has to survive before you can [set] a workout schedule."[12]

Apart from their direct operating results, some vision-driven firms clearly behave very differently from their more traditional cousins. Consider this statement that appeared in Ben & Jerry's 1990 annual report: "Ben & Jerry's has yet to print nutritional information on packaging of its original super-premium ice cream; it has no paid parental leave policy, and it has only one minority in a senior management position. In the case of energy, due to inadequate record-keeping the company is unable to report on energy conservation actions. Relations with franchises have improved; even so, the company's communication with franchises . . . has been uneven."[13]

The type of corporate behavior reflected in this self-critical passage or in the Body Shop's decision not to advertise in an advertising-driven industry—cosmetics—has caused one observer to note a growing distinction between traditional firms, which try to position an image, and nontraditional firms that seek rather to express their true characters to realize their visions.[14] Table 3.2 shows the differences in these two approaches.

What Is Organizational Mission?

Organizational **mission** is the overarching purpose for which an organization exists. It provides an answer to the question, "Why do we exist?" Senge points out that successful organizations "have a larger sense of purpose that transcends providing for the needs of shareholders and employees. They seek to contribute to the world in some unique way, to add a distinctive source of value."[15] In general, a firm's organizational mission statement contains such

TABLE 3.2

Differences between Image Positioning and Character Expression

Image Positioning	Character Expression
To make company or product appealing	To build trust in business relationship
Image leads, reality may follow	Reality leads
Exaggerate trivial differences	Dramatize significant differences
Make claims, support with artificial evidence	Don't make claims, find ways to believably behave differently
Image positioning works even if it's at odds with reality	Consumers hunger for companies they trust. Images at odds with reality risk mistrust.
Communications are seen as messages to convey image	Communications are seen as behavior to express character
Depends on company-sponsored communications	Depends on news media and customer word-of-mouth
Marketing seen as separate from delivery of goods and services	Marketing seen as integral to development and delivery of goods and services

SOURCE: Peter Laundy, "Learning from the Laramie Lawyer's Letter," *Design Statements,* a journal of The American Center for Design, Fall 1992.

information as what types of products or services the organization produces, who its customers tend to be, and what core values it holds. **Core values** provide an answer to the question, "How do we want to act, consistent with our mission, along the path toward achieving our vision?"[16]

Many firms summarize and document their organizational missions in **mission statements.** Table 3.3 presents sample mission statements for several organizations, including: Great Scot Supermarkets, a small midwestern grocery store chain in Indiana; Federal Express, an international shipping company; and The Crummer School, a small graduate school of business at Rollins College in Winter Park, Florida.

Contents of Mission Statements

The kind of information contained in a mission statement varies from organization to organization, but most mission statements address some common themes.[17] These themes include:

- *Company product or service:* This information identifies the goods and/or services produced by the organization—what the company offers to its customers.
- *Markets:* This information describes the markets and customers that the organization intends to serve. Who these customers are and where they are located are common themes.

TABLE 3.3

Organizational Mission Statements

GREAT SCOT SUPERMARKETS

Great Scot Supermarkets is a progressive, growth-oriented company recognized as a regional leader in retail foods. We will continue to strive to improve our responsiveness to the needs and concerns of our customers, employees, suppliers, and the communities in which we serve. This will be accomplished through the development of our employees, an emphasis on volume, and profitability. We intend to expand within our existing marketing areas to both protect and improve our positions. As personnel and finances are adequate and opportunities arise, our growth will continue in other areas.

FEDERAL EXPRESS

Federal Express is committed to our People-Service-Profit philosophy. We will produce outstanding financial returns by providing totally reliable, competitively superior, global air–ground transportation of high-priority goods and documents that require rapid, time-certain delivery. Equally important, positive control of each package will be maintained utilizing real-time electronic tracking and tracing systems. A complete record of each shipment and delivery will be presented with our request for payment. We will be helpful, courteous, and professional to each other and the public. We will strive to have a completely satisfied customer at the end of each transaction.

THE CRUMMER SCHOOL

The mission of The Crummer School is to improve management through formal education programs stressing an administrative point of view, research and publication involving new knowledge and teaching materials, and relationships with businesses and the community. In fulfilling this mission the School is committed to programs that emphasize high quality, innovation, problem solving, and the application of management theory. The emphasis of The Crummer School is on the full-time MBA program. The primary target market for this core business is the national pool of applicants, with or without academic backgrounds in business, but including those who have business experience.

- *Technology:* This information generally includes such topics as the techniques and processes by which the organization produces goods and services. This discussion may consist largely of a broad description of organizational production techniques and quality-enhancing methods.
- *Company objectives:* Most mission statements refer to company objectives. For many firms, these include the general ways they propose for dealing with key stakeholders, such as shareholders, customers, or employees.
- *Company philosophy or core values:* A statement of company philosophy (sometimes called a *company creed*) commonly appears as part of the mission statement. A *company philosophy* statement reflects the basic beliefs and values that should guide organization members in conducting organizational business. Table 3.4 describes the Baxter Travenol Company and summarizes its philosophy or core values.
- *Company self-concept:* Mission statements inevitably contain or are accompanied by information on the self-concept of the company. Company self-

---

TABLE 3.4

Baxter Travenol: Description and Philosophy

Baxter Travenol is engaged in the worldwide development, manufacture, and sale of a diversified line of medical-care products and related services. These products and services are used principally by hospitals, blood centers, clinical laboratories, and dialysis centers, and by patients at home under physician supervision. Baxter Travenol products are manufactured in 17 countries and bring quality therapy to millions of patients in more than 100 countries.

FUNDAMENTAL PRINCIPLES

At Baxter Travenol, we are committed to:
Improving health care for people around the world
Meeting the highest standards in responsible corporate citizenship
Attaining a position of leadership in each of the health care markets we serve
Providing our customers with products and services of consistently high quality and value
Sustaining a strong spirit of teamwork through mutual commitment, dedication, and loyalty within our employee family
Achieving consistent, long-term financial growth and the best possible return to our stockholders

SOURCE: 1984 Baxter Travenol Annual Report. Baxter Travenol Laboratories, Inc. See also Baxter Travenol Annual Report, 1993.

---

concept is the company's own view or impression of itself. In essence, the company arrives at this self-concept by assessing its strengths, weaknesses, competition, and ability to survive in the marketplace.

- *Public image:* Mission statements generally contain some reference, either direct or indirect, to the type of impression that the organization wants to leave with its public. In the end, of course, it is not the image that top managers want to project that is important; but the image that the public actually forms. Table 3.2 provides insight into this process.

Such themes, then, as company product or service, market, technology, company goals, philosophy, self-concept, and public image are commonly addressed in a statement of organizational mission and companion statements. Table 3.5 presents a mission statement and related information prepared by Levi Strauss & Company. The Skills Module presents an opportunity for students to develop a mission statement.

TABLE 3.5

Levi Strauss & Company: Mission Statement and Related Information

---

MISSION STATEMENT

The mission of Levi Strauss & Co. is to sustain profitable and responsible commercial success by marketing jeans and selected casual apparel under the Levi's brand.

Continued

TABLE 3.5

Continued

We must balance goals of superior profitability and return on investment, leadership market positions, and superior products and service. We will conduct our business ethically and demonstrate leadership in satisfying our responsibilities to our communities and to society. Our work environment will be safe and productive and characterized by fair treatment, teamwork, open communications, personal accountability and opportunities for growth and development.

ASPIRATION STATEMENT

We all want a company that our people are proud of and committed to, where all employees have an opportunity to contribute, learn, grow and advance based on merit, not politics or background. We want our people to feel respected, treated fairly, listened to and involved. Above all, we want satisfaction from accomplishments and friendships, balanced personal and professional lives, and to have fun in our endeavors.

When we describe the kind of Levi Strauss & Co. we want in the future what we are talking about is building on the foundation we have inherited: affirming the best of our company's traditions, closing gaps that may exist between principles and practices and updating some of our values to reflect contemporary circumstances.

WHAT TYPE OF LEADERSHIP IS NECESSARY TO MAKE OUR ASPIRATIONS A REALITY?

New Behaviors: Leadership that exemplifies directness, openness to influence, commitment to the success of others, willingness to acknowledge our own contributions to problems, personal accountability, teamwork and trust. Not only must we model these behaviors but we must coach others to adopt them.

Diversity: Leadership that values a diverse work force (age, sex, ethnic group, etc.) at all levels of the organization, diversity in experience, and a diversity in perspectives. We have committed to taking full advantage of the rich backgrounds and abilities of all our people and to promote a greater diversity in positions of influence. Differing points of view will be sought; diversity will be valued and honesty rewarded, not suppressed.

Recognition: Leadership that provides greater recognition—both financial and psychic—for individuals and teams that contribute to our success. Recognition must be given to all who contribute: those who create and innovate and also those who continually support the day-to-day business requirements.

Ethical Management Practices: Leadership that epitomizes the stated standards of ethical behavior. We must provide clarity about our expectations and must enforce these standards through the corporation.

Communications: Leadership that is clear about company, unit, and individual goals and performance. People must know what is expected of them and receive timely, honest feedback on their performance and career aspirations.

Empowerment: Leadership that increases the authority and responsibility of those closest to our products and customers. By actively pushing responsibility, trust and recognition into the organization we can harness and release the capabilities of all our people.

SOURCE: Reprinted with permission from the Feb. 1993 issue of *Training* Magazine. Copyright 1993. Lakewood Publications, Minneapolis, MN. All rights reserved. Not for resale.

SKILLS MODULE
Wal-Mart's Growth Clouds Its Organizational Direction

INTRODUCTION

Establishing an organizational mission and direction is a critical step in the strategic management process. Review the following situation at Wal-Mart and then complete the related skill-development exercise. The exercise affords you the opportunity to review and revise Wal-Mart's organizational vision and strategy.

SITUATION

In the eyes of its detractors, Wal-Mart is the evil behemoth of retailing. The Arkansas-based chain is bigger than K mart and Sears combined, and nearly as big as the entire U.S. department store industry. It is also responsible for putting countless small-town retailers out of business and turning rural downtown areas into ghost towns. Wal-Mart's newest venture, supercenters that combine supermarkets and discount stores, are going up at the rate of more than one a week, and its buyout of a failing Canadian chain's 122 stores provides it with the means for a major thrust across the northern border.

After hearing the chorus of criticism, it would surprise many that, despite its seeming vastness, Wal-Mart controls less than 15 percent of the general merchandise business in the United States, and probably less than 3 percent of the grocery business.

The dichotomy of trying to remain a small-town, aw-shucks shopkeeper while becoming a card-carrying member of the Fortune 500 has presented mixed, albeit still rosy fortunes. In 1993, for example, Wal-Mart's routinely double-digit sales increases fell below budget and declined toward the industry's typical 5 percent. By year's end, however, sales rose 21 percent, to $67.3 billion, while profits increased 17 percent to $2.3 billion.

It was a watershed year for Wal-Mart and all of its retail operations—Sam's Club buyer's-club stores, domestic and international Wal-Mart stores and supercenters, and McLane Co., the country's leading supplier to convenience stores. The company is now so big that it risks creating diseconomies of scale. Its very size, for example, threatens its ability to restock shelves in time to catch trends. Bill Fields, president of the Wal-Mart Stores division, was taken aback recently when he asked one vendor how long it would take to stock one circle rack in each of the chain's 2,500 stores. "Eight months," he was told.

Wal-Mart's corporate culture is also threatened. The chain's late founder, Sam Walton, led from the top, but ran the company from the bottom. Growth has forced Wal-Mart to add more management layers, however, and to restructure into four divisions, themselves further divided by geographic region.

CEO David Glass, for example, now has five levels of management between him and the store manager. "Wal-Mart has achieved the size where you can't run the company," he freely admits. "Nobody can run an $80 billion retail company." His view is to simplify—run it one store at a time. The 25 to 35 Wal-Marts the company plans to build in the Northeast in 1994 will be a good test. Wal-Mart will make its first foray onto Long Island, home to 7 million people—about three times the population of Arkansas, where Wal-Mart has 77 stores—and just as far removed in regional style and taste.

The company will depend on its information infrastructure, a point-of-sale replenishment system, to customize merchandise selections for individual outlets. Already, some 40 regional buyers make sure that Portland, Oregon gets a different color palette than Portland, Maine. But there are glitches. In February, when lawns were covered with snow, stores in Maine were receiving bags of grass and fertilizer. Wal-Mart plans to customize each linear foot of space within its stores using data on purchasing variables. Figuring out the technology will help the chain market down to the household level, increasing sales per square foot and driving down operating costs.

SKILL DEVELOPMENT EXERCISE

Based on the information you have just read, write a mission statement for Wal-Mart. Keep in mind the process of establishing organizational direction.

SOURCE: Bill Saporito, "And the Winner Is Still . . . Wal-Mart," *Fortune*, May 2, 1994, pp. 62–70.

THE NATURE OF ORGANIZATIONAL OBJECTIVES

The first part of this chapter has outlined the role of vision and mission in establishing the character and general direction of the firm. This part focuses on establishing progressively more specific direction through the use of organizational objectives. We will define the term *organizational objectives,* explain their importance, describe two major types of objectives in organizations, and discuss different areas in which organizations should formulate objectives.

What Are Organizational Objectives?

An **organizational objective** is a target toward which an organization directs its efforts. The importance of establishing appropriate objectives for an organization cannot be overemphasized. Clear objectives provide the basic foundation for strategy formulation, strategy implementation, and action planning. Organizational objectives can be used much as navigators use the North Star: you "sight it on your compass and then use it as a means of getting back on track when you stray."[18]

Types of Objectives in Organizations

Organizations typically have two different sets of objectives. **Short-run objectives** identify targets that the organization wants to reach within one or two years. **Long-run objectives** are targets that the organization wants to reach within three to five years.

These two types of organizational objectives differ in significant ways. The most apparent difference, of course, is the period of time within which the organization is attempting to reach the objective. Another important difference between these objectives is how specifically they are written. In general, short-run objectives tend to give more detail about such issues as who will accomplish exactly what tasks, when they will accomplish those tasks, and in what organizational areas they fall.

Areas for Organizational Objectives

Since the early history of business and industry, most organizations have focused on one primary objective: making a profit.[19] Peter Drucker, perhaps the most influential business writer of modern times, has pointed out errors in managing an organization by focusing primarily on only one objective.[20] According to Drucker, organizations should aim at achieving several objectives. Objectives should cover all areas important to the operation of the firm. Drucker has noted eight key areas in which long-run and short-run organizational objectives should be set. Note how well these areas match up to the general themes of mission statements:

1. *Market standing:* The position of an organization—where it stands—relative to its competitors. One of the organization's objectives should indicate the position it wants to achieve relative to its competitors.
2. *Innovation:* Any change made to improve methods of conducting organizational business. Organizational objectives should indicate innovations the organization wants to implement.
3. *Productivity:* The level of goods or services produced by an organization relative to the resources used in the production process. Organizations that use fewer resources to produce specified levels of products are said to be

more productive than organizations that require more resources to produce at the same level. Objectives should set targets.

4. *Resource levels:* The relative amounts of various resources held by an organization, such as inventory, equipment, and cash. Most organizations should set objectives to indicate the relative amounts of each of these assets that they want to hold.

5. *Profitability:* The ability of an organization to earn revenue dollars beyond the expenses necessary to generate the revenue. Organizational objectives commonly indicate the levels of profitability that firms seek.

6. *Manager performance and development:* The quality of managerial performance and the rate at which managers are developing personally. Because both of these areas are critical to the long-term success of an organization, emphasizing them by establishing and striving to reach related organizational objectives is very important.

7. *Worker performance and attitude:* The quality of nonmanagement performance and such employees' feelings about their work. These areas are also crucial to long-term organizational success. The importance of these considerations should be stressed through the establishment of organizational objectives.

8. *Social responsibility:* The obligation of business to help improve the welfare of society while it strives to reach other organizational objectives. Only a few short years ago, setting organizational objectives in this area would have been somewhat controversial. Today, however, such objectives have become commonplace and are considered very important. Note the emphasis placed on this factor in the mission statements of Great Scot and Levi Strauss, shown earlier.

Note in Figure 3.1 that Rockwater, a global engineering and construction firm, has developed four clusters, or groupings, of objectives toward which it works—financial, customer, internal, and growth objectives. Note also that these four sets of objectives are united via the firm's strategy, a topic we will examine in depth in Chapter 4.

Characteristics of High-Quality Organizational Objectives

Objectives exist in some form in virtually all organizations. The quality of objectives, of course, largely determines how useful they actually are. Several guidelines have been developed over time to help managers develop high-quality organizational objectives.

Specific Objectives   Specific objectives indicate exactly what should be accomplished, who should accomplish it, and within what time frame they should accomplish it. Specific details eliminate confusion about objectives and ensure that all organization members know and understand what is expected of them. Furthermore, the step in the strategic management process that follows setting an organizational direction deals with formulating organizational strategy. In general, more specific objectives make it easier for management to develop strategies to reach them. Specific, high-quality organizational objectives provide a foundation on which managers can construct appropriate organizational strategies.

Levels of Effort   Objectives should be set high enough that employees must extend themselves somewhat to achieve them. On the other hand,

FIGURE 3.1   Rockwater's Organizational Objectives

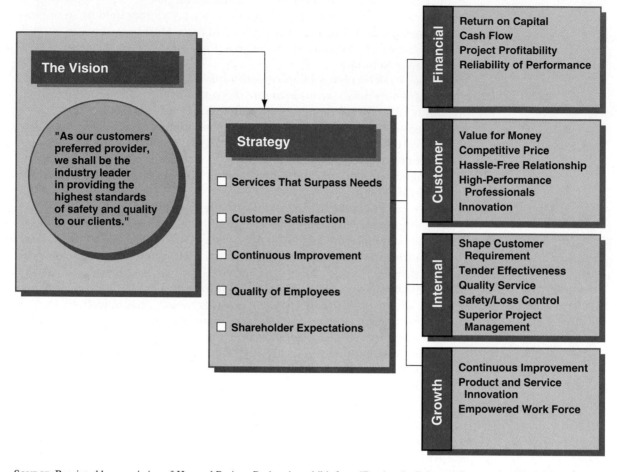

objectives should not be set so high that employees become frustrated and stop trying! Happily, objectives that challenge employees' abilities are generally more interesting and more motivating than easily attained objectives.[21] Managers should establish reachable organizational objectives, and all organization members should share this view. Workers who view objectives as impossible to reach may utterly ignore the objectives as an indicator of how they should apply their time and effort.

Changing Objectives   Managers must continually assess the organizational environment to recognize when organizational objectives need changes, and they must encourage all organization members to identify changes they think the firm should make.

Measurable Objectives   A measurable objective, sometimes called an **operational objective,** is an objective stated in such a way that an attempt to attain it can be compared to the objective itself to determine whether it actually has been attained. Confusion about whether an objective has been attained can result in conflict and poor relations between managers working at different levels of a firm.

Consistent Long-Run and Short-Run Objectives   Managers should establish organizational objectives that reflect a desirable mix of time frames and that support one another. Long-term objectives must be consistent with the organizational vision and mission, setting targets to be hit within a three-year to five-year period. Short-run objectives must be consistent with long-run objectives, setting targets to be reached within one or two years. As a general rule, shorter-run objectives should be derived from, and lead to the attainment of, longer-run objectives.

Figure 3.2 continues the example of Great Scot Supermarkets, which we introduced earlier. It illustrates objectives for that firm consistent with its organizational mission.

THE PROCESS OF ESTABLISHING ORGANIZATIONAL DIRECTION

The first two parts of this chapter have discussed the fundamentals of organizational visions, missions, and objectives. This section focuses on the *process* of establishing an organizational direction. This process consists of three major steps: (1) reflecting on the results of environmental analysis, (2) developing an appropriate vision and mission, and (3) establishing appropriate organizational objectives. The Company Example discusses a facet of organizational direction at Pillsbury.

Step 1: Reflecting on the Results of Environmental Analysis

Environmental analysis should provide managers with adequate information for *reflection*. It should draw data from all levels of the organizational environment—the general, operating, and internal environments. Analysis of this information, often performed by a cross-functional team, should establish the relevance of these data, and of various other issues, to the organization's performance.

Step 2: Developing an Appropriate Vision and Mission

Information derived from environmental analysis serves as a solid foundation on which to build an organizational vision and mission. Once managers understand both the internal and external organizational environments, they are better equipped to develop an appropriate vision and mission for the organization. These vision and mission statements reflect the organization's relationship to its environment and thereby increase the probability of its long-term survival. In addition, a mission statement identifies the organization's core values, which specify how it will act as it moves to fulfill its vision.

Step 3: Developing Appropriate Organizational Objectives

After developing vision and mission statements the organization needs to set organizational objectives that are consistent with its vision and mission. Because of the fundamental importance of profit in the business context, we focus our discussion on setting profit objectives. Remember that firms set objectives in many areas, as discussed earlier (market share, innovation, productivity, resource levels, manager and worker performance and development, and social responsibility) in addition to profitability. However, since

FIGURE 3.2 Consistency of Possible Mission and Objectives for Great Scot Supermarkets

Mission

Great Scot Supermarkets is a progressive growth-oriented company recognized as a regional leader in retail foods. We will continue to strive to improve our responsiveness to the needs and concerns of our customers, employees, suppliers, and the communities in which we serve. This will be accomplished through the development of our employees, and emphasis on volume, and profitability. We intend to expand within our existing marketing areas to both protect and improve our positions. As personnel and finances are adequate and opportunities arise our growth will continue in other areas.

Serves as foundation for . . .

When accomplished, results in the accomplishment of . . .

Long-Run Objectives

• Make Great Scot above the grocery store industry average for profitability.

• Improve competitive position within market areas.

• Develop and hire employees for present as well as future needs.

Serves as foundation for . . .

When accomplished, results in the accomplishment of . . .

Short-Run Objectives

• Achieve major reductions in wage expenses.
• Reduce warehouse expenses.
• Buy quality products at lower costs.

• Review and evaluate sales run by competition.
• Match prices offered by competition on high-volume items.
• Encourage store tours by community groups.

• Conduct training programs for cashiers.
• Maintain competitive wage rates.
• Advertise job openings in trade publications.

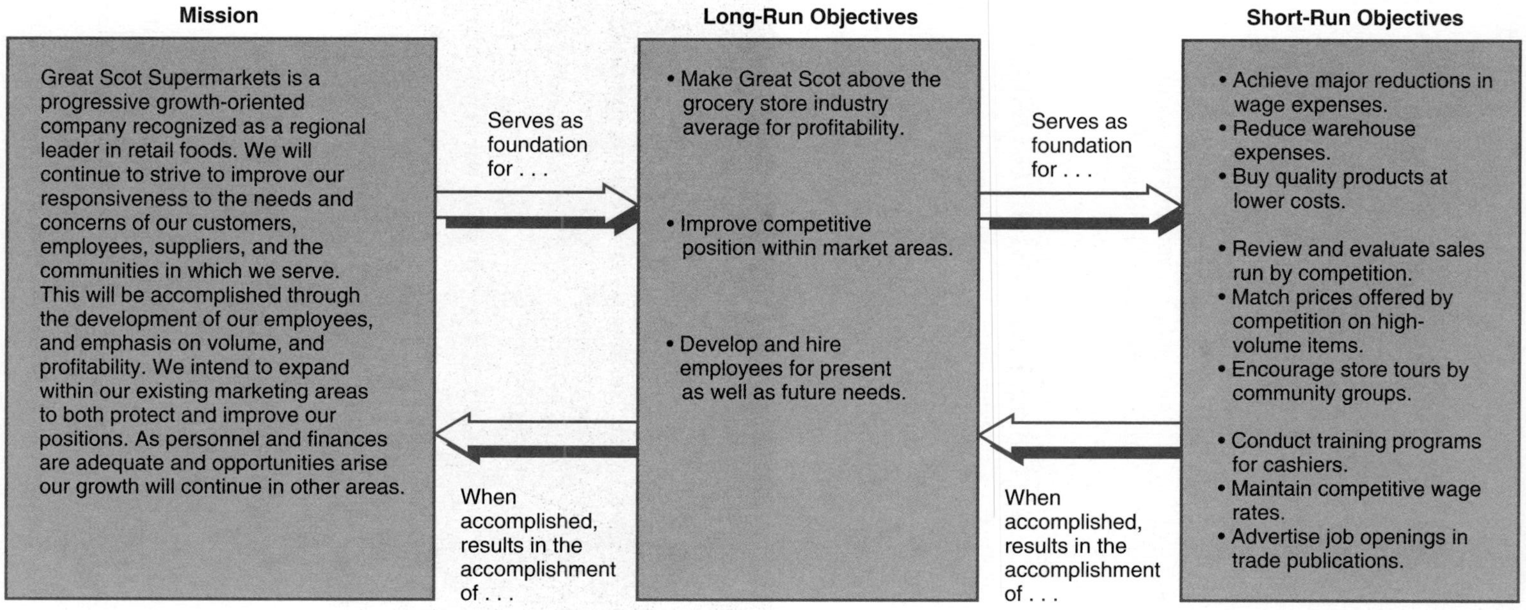

COMPANY EXAMPLE

Communal Kitchen Charts Pillsbury's Consumer Strategy

Every weekday, more than 2,000 consumers call Pillsbury's toll-free hotline with complaints, questions, and compliments about the company's products. The phone number, printed on Pillsbury packages, promotes a service the Minneapolis manufacturer is more than happy to provide.

As the mix of packaged-foods manufacturers becomes broader and more competitive, sellers of branded goods like Pillsbury are using their toll-free consumer hotline operations to outgun the growing number of private-label products. Although the phone service costs Pillsbury, a unit of Grand Metropolitan PLC, several million dollars a year, the benefits are part of the company's mission of being responsive to its products' users and attuned to trends and changes.

Pillsbury's consumer-service center employees—mostly women, all with college degrees and backgrounds in home economics or nutrition—placate unhappy consumers and make satisfied ones even happier. The Pillsbury phone respondents are themselves satisfied; turnover is low—the last replacement was hired four years ago, pay is around $25,000 a year, and Pillsbury makes sure that these experienced workers are supplied with the best materials available. An extensive computerized database and fat technical manuals, as well as plenty of cookbooks, are close at hand.

The calls function as "a wonderful research tool" and act as a safety net, says Paul Walsh, Pillsbury's chief executive. "If we have a problem with a product, we want to be the first to hear about it."

The calls also provide Pillsbury with important information for its many operations, from product development and marketing to quality assurance and manufacturing. Susan Shlosberg, the company's vice president of consumer relations and technical services, leads an eight-person support staff to analyze data from the calls and expand on it; asking callers about product concepts was a recent idea.

Calls are taped, but each caller's privacy is protected. Shlosberg often plays recordings for product managers and plant employees, letting them hear from the source what consumers think about Pillsbury and its products.

SOURCE: Richard Gibson, "Pillsbury's Telephones Ring with Peeves, Praise," *The Wall Street Journal,* April 20, 1994, pp. B1–B4.

objectives in each of these other areas are ultimately focused on improving the firm's long-term profitability, we believe that profit objectives merit detailed discussion.

Nature of Profitability Objectives   **Profitability objectives** set targets for revenue an organization should earn beyond the expenses necessary to generate the revenue. Profitability objectives commonly state target returns on assets (ROAs), net profit margins, and returns on stockholders' equity. Table 3.6 lists these measures of profitability, defines them, and explains how to calculate them. Although the basic concept of referring to such objectives to manage organizations is not new, their role in strategic management has renewed interest in them.[22]

Guidelines for Establishing Profitability Objectives   Managers generally establish profitability objectives by collecting and analyzing information that compares specific organizational data to similar data for other organizations or groups of organizations. Gathering and analyzing this information enables managers not only to evaluate an organization's current profit performance, but also to determine how high to set profitability objectives.

TABLE 3.6

Profitability Objectives

Profitability Objectives	Description	Calculation Method[a]
Net profit margin	Organizational objective that focuses on the amount of net profit an organization earns in relation to the level of sales it attains	$\dfrac{\text{Net profit}}{\text{Sales}}$
Return on assets (ROA)	Organizational objective that focuses on the amount of net profit an organization earns in relation to its total assets	$\dfrac{\text{Net profit}}{\text{Total assets}}$
Return on stockholders' equity ROE	Organizational objective that focuses on the amount of net profit an organization earns in relation to its equity	$\dfrac{\text{Net profit}}{\text{Stockholders' equity}}$

[a] These ratios are expressed as percentages.

To illustrate how this process works, consider the task of setting objectives for net profit margin, return on assets, and return on stockholders' equity at McDonald's Corporation. Managers would normally begin by gathering past information to get a very broad view of comparable figures for business organizations in general. One source of such information is the industrial composite that appears periodically in Value Line's *Selection and Opinion*. This industrial composite averages profitability data for over 900 industrial, retail, and transportation companies that account for about 80 percent of the income earned by all U.S., nonfinancial corporations.

In addition to this industrial composite information, McDonald's Corporation managers would probably seek to evaluate the performance of companies more closely related to the fast-food business. Information about profitability performance for the restaurant industry, in general, as well as for specific competitors such as Wendy's International, would be very valuable. Information of this sort is also available periodically in Value Line's *Selection and Opinion*.

After gathering all of this information, McDonald's managers would compare it to data compiled on their own company (see Figure 3.3). Analysis of this information would probably lead McDonald's managers to conclude that their firm was performing competitively in the areas of net profit margin, return on investment, and return on stockholders' equity. Significantly unfavorable comparisons in any of these areas would have alerted McDonald's managers that improvement was possible and that profitability objectives should be revised upward. The current data indicate that perhaps the same or slightly higher profitability objectives would be appropriate for McDonald's in the next operating period.

McDonald's managers must also consider, however, that the information they gathered reflects one year only. Gathering the same information and

FIGURE 3.3   McDonald's Profitability Performance

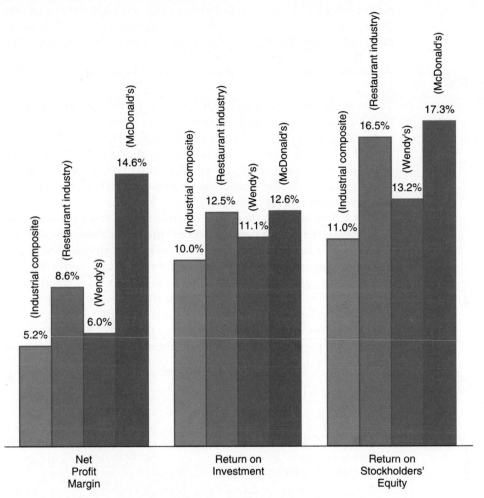

SOURCE: Data from *The Value Line Investment Survey,* June 24, 1994, pp. 294, 302, 312. Note that industrial composite figures are author estimates based on Value Line composites for individual industries.

making the same comparisons for a five-year period might reveal desirable or undesirable trends that organizational objectives should address.

The case at the end of the chapter is designed to give you some experience in spotting issues that may affect the objectives that a company establishes for itself.

DEVELOPING INDIVIDUAL OBJECTIVES

After setting overall organizational objectives, managers must continue to develop an effective and efficient pattern of objectives within an organization culminating in establishment of objectives for each individual working in significant organizational segments. **Individual objectives** are targets that specific people within an organization attempt to reach. Individual objectives are designed so that accomplishing each one contributes to the accomplishment of the broader objectives of the department. In turn, the accomplishment of departmental objectives contributes to the accomplishment of objectives for the organization as a whole. Individual objectives help individual workers understand exactly what they are expected to contribute to their departments.

SUMMARY

Three main organizational ingredients are commonly used to establish organizational direction: vision, mission, and objectives. An organization's vision states its goals and directions in the most general terms. It answers the question, What do we want to create? Organizational mission is the purpose for which an organization exists. Mission statements commonly address the topics of company core values, products or services, markets, technologies, philosophies, self-concepts, and images.

Organizational objectives are specific targets toward which the organization directs its efforts. Objectives reflect the organization's vision and mission. They provide important guidance for managers' decisions and for initiatives to increase organizational efficiency and to evaluate performance. Short-run and long-run objectives focus on such areas as market standing, innovation, resource levels, profitability, manager performance and development, worker performance and attitude, and social responsibility.

To establish organizational direction effectively, managers should develop a consistent pattern of organizational vision, mission, and objectives.

KEY TERMS

vision, p. 55
mission, p. 58
core values, p. 59
mission statements, p. 59
organizational objective, p. 64

short-run objective, p. 64
long-run objective, p. 64
operational objective, p. 66
profitability objective, p. 69

CHECKLIST

Analyzing Organizational Direction in Problems and Cases

____ 1. Does the strategic problem or case involve issues related to organizational direction?

____ 2. Does the case show evidence of a clear organizational vision and mission?

____ 3. Does the organizational mission appropriately reflect the organizational environment?

____ 4. Does the situation involve organizational objectives that appropriately reflect the organizational mission?

____ 5. Are suitable types of objectives employed?

____ 6. Have objectives been established in all areas critical to organizational success?

____ 7. Are the objectives that are apparent in the case or situation high-quality objectives?

____ 8. Are individual objectives sufficiently emphasized?

____ 9. Is an acceptable process for establishing organizational direction apparent in the situation or case?

Additional Readings

Chajet, Clive. "The Making of a New Corporate Image," *Journal of Business Strategy*, May/June 1989, p. 18.

Kolesar, Peter J. "Vision, Values, and Milestones: TQM at Alcoa." *California Management Review*, Spring 1993, p. 133.

Langeler, Gerard H. "The Vision Trap." *Harvard Business Review*, March/April 1992, p. 46.

Mitroff, Ian I. *Stakeholders of the Organizational Mind*. San Francisco: Jossey-Bass, 1983.

Ruch, Richard S., and Ronald Goodman. *Image at the Top*. New York: Free Press, 1983.

Schoemaker, Paul J. H. "How to Link Strategic Vision to Core Capabilities." *Sloan Management Review*, Fall 1992, p. 67.

Smith, Patrick. "How to Present Your Firm to the World," *Journal of Business Strategy*, January/February, 1990, p. 32.

CASE

INTEL STRATEGY TAKES A CHANCE

Andy Grove is taking a big risk. The CEO of Intel, maker of microprocessor chips, is basing his business strategy on an assumption. Grove guesses that AT&T, IBM, Matsushita, Motorola, Philips, Sega, and Sony can't keep up with his firm. He's sure enough that he's gambling nearly a third of Intel's revenues, $3.5 billion in 1994, that the company will dominate a slew of businesses in which it has no experience.

Such aggressiveness has worked in the past. The so-called "Mad Hungarian" poured money into product development and factories to establish the Santa Clara, California, company as the hardware companion of Bill Gates's software champ, Microsoft. Today, Intel supplies the microprocessors in about three-quarters of all PCs sold. Its gross profit margin is 58 percent; net earnings last year were $2.3 billion on sales of $8.8 billion, making Intel the most profitable company of its size in the world. Its size is fluid, however; Intel is growing so fast, it doubles in size roughly every two years.

So, Grove might ask, what is the risk in his gamble? The firm faces growing competition from other chip makers, notably the RISC chip, an inexpensive, ultrafast microprocessor developed by IBM, Motorola, and Apple Computer and featured in Apple's PowerPC series. Also clonemakers have scored a crucial victory in a lawsuit affirming their right to copy Intel codes governing the behavior of microprocessors.

Grove thinks that his company can stay on top by flooding the market with ever faster, yet still inexpensive, chips. Its newest chip, the Pentium, is proof of how fast Intel can move. The chip crunches data at almost twice the rate of the best-selling chip today (also Intel's). The goal is simple: create chips to enable PC producers to double the performance of their machines at every price point every year. New, more powerful chips should appear every year or two.

Pushing down prices is part of the objective. Grove argues that what Intel loses in profit margins it can more than make up in volume. He says he doesn't care about margin percentages. "I want to increase dollar profits, and they are a product of margin times unit volume."

Grove anticipates that volume will grow not from corporate customers, but from the demands of consumers and home-office users for convenience and novelty. The ultimate aim: to transform the PC powered by Intel chips into an all-purpose consumer device for heading down the information superhighway, controlling the TV, VCR, telephone, answering machine, and so on.

Two lines, printed on fortune cookie slips, conveyed Grove's strategy to Intel's 29,500 employees:

1. Job 1

2. Make the PC "IT"

Grove says the first line is a reminder to strengthen Intel's No. 1 position in the microprocessor market and establish Pentium as the best-selling microprocessor faster than any before it. Line 2 refers to Grove's desire to turn the PC into the cornerstone of 21st-century information technology.

Getting there, says Grove, is easier because there is competition. If it wasn't for the threat of PowerPC, and what he calls the "megabattle," Intel would not be moving so quickly. "We are making gutsier moves investment-wise, pricing-wise, every way, because we've got a competitive threat," he says. "The net result is we'll get to advance to the next level of competition."

DISCUSSION QUESTIONS

1. What is Grove's vision for Intel? What is Intel's mission?

2. How effectively do Intel's organizational objectives define and fulfill its mission?

3. What is the purpose of the fortune cookie slips?

4. How well do Grove's objectives for Intel contribute to the objective of profitability?

SOURCE: David Kirkpatrick, "Intel Goes for Broke," *Fortune*, May 16, 1994, pp. 62–68.

Notes

1. Peter Senge, *The Fifth Discipline: The Art and Practice of the Learning Organization* (New York: Doubleday, 1990), p. 206.

2. Ibid., p. 207–208.

3. B. Dumaine, "What the Leaders of Tomorrow See," *Fortune*, July 3, 1989, pp. 49–62.

4. Senge, *Fifth Discipline*, p. 206.

5. Thomas Stewart, "GE Keeps Those Ideas Coming," *Fortune*, August 12, 1991, pp. 41–49.

6. Senge, *Fifth Discipline*, p. 217.

7. Edward Ottensmeyer and Robert McGowan, "US West: The Architecture of Corporate Transformation," *Business Horizons*, January/February 1991.

8. Reported in Chris Lee, "The Vision Thing," *Training*, February 1993, pp. 25–32.

9. Michael Miller and Laurie Hays, "Gerstner's Nonvision for IBM Raises a Management Issue," *The Wall Street Journal*, July 29, 1993, pp. B1, B6.

10. Douglas Lavin, "Robert Eaton Thinks 'Vision' Is Overrated and He's Not Alone," *The Wall Street Journal*, October 4, 1993, pp. A1, A8.

11. Ibid., p. A1.

12. Miller and Hays, "Gerstner's Nonvision," p. B6.

13. Reported in Peter Laundy, "Learning from the Laramie Lawyer's Letter," *Design Statements*, Fall 1992, pp. 3–11.

14. Ibid., p. 5.

15. Senge, *Fifth Discipline*, pp. 223–224.

16. Ibid., p. 224.

17. This discussion is based largely on John A. Pearce II, "The Company Mission as a Strategic Tool," *Sloan Management Review,* Spring 1982, pp. 15–24.

18. Marshall E. Dimock, *The Executive in Action* (New York: Harper and Brothers, 1945), p. 54. For a more recent discussion of this issue, see Samuel C. Certo, *Principles of Modern Management: Functions and Systems,* 4th ed. (Boston: Allyn & Bacon, 1989), pp. 59–60.

19. Gordon Donaldson, "Financial Goals and Strategic Consequences," *Harvard Business Review,* May/June 1985, pp. 57–66.

20. Peter F. Drucker, *The Practice of Management* (New York: Harper & Row, 1954), pp. 62–65, 126–129.

21. For more information about the effect of challenge on motivation of workers, see Frederick Herzberg, "One More Time: How Do You Motivate Employees?" *Harvard Business Review,* January/February 1968, pp. 53–62. Due to its continuing relevance for modern managers, this article has been reprinted: *Harvard Business Review,* September/October 1987, pp. 109–120.

22. John H. Quandt, "Setting Strategy Using Variable ROI Analysis," *The Journal of Business Strategy* 5, no. 1 (Summer 1984), pp. 77–79.

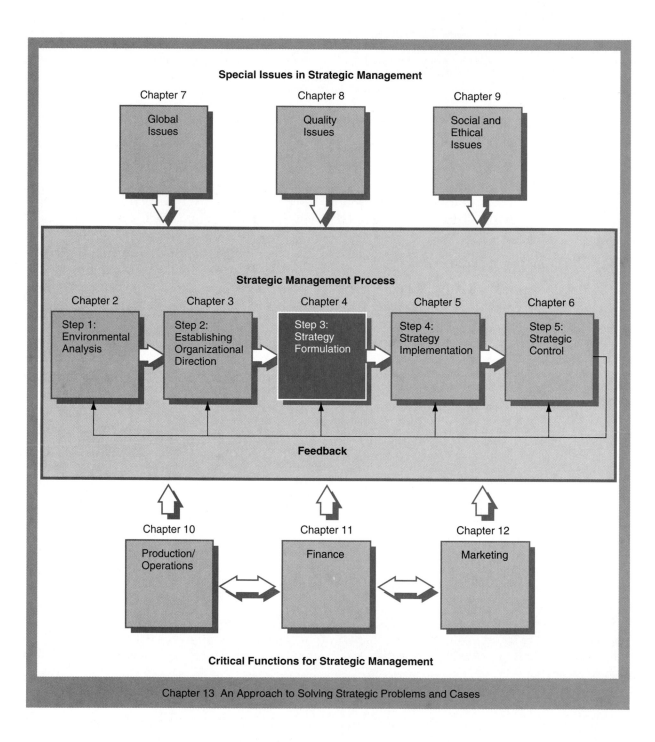

Special Issues in Strategic Management

Chapter 7

Global Issues

Chapter 8

Quality Issues

Chapter 9

Social and Ethical Issues

Strategic Management Process

Chapter 2

Step 1: Environmental Analysis

Chapter 3

Step 2: Establishing Organizational Direction

Chapter 4

Step 3: Strategy Formulation

Chapter 5

Step 4: Strategy Implementation

Chapter 6

Step 5: Strategic Control

Feedback

Chapter 10

Production/ Operations

Chapter 11

Finance

Chapter 12

Marketing

Critical Functions for Strategic Management

Chapter 13 An Approach to Solving Strategic Problems and Cases

CHAPTER 4

Strategy Formulation

Formulating a strategy for an organization involves developing a cohesive plan for achieving objectives by adapting the organization in an appropriate way to its environment. A strategy represents the embodiment of the organization's best efforts to think smart about its future—how to position its goods or services against those of competitors, how to forge tight linkages with its customers, how to build upon or develop its internal competencies, how to prepare for environmental shifts, how to diversify its portfolio of goods or services in ways that build synergy for future competitive strength.

Strategy formulation is primarily an analytical effort that relies heavily on executive judgment and creativity. It draws critical input from the environmental analysis techniques introduced in Chapter 2 in its focus on achieving an adaptive fit for the firm in its environments. Strategy, as we defined it in Chapter 1, is seen as an integrative plan that provides more specific details than the vision or mission statement discussed in Chapter 3. It further refines the general notions of what the organization wishes to create or what its overarching purposes are.

In this chapter, our discussion of strategy formulation is built around the three levels at which organizations formulate strategies. We first discuss business-level strategies, through which firms search for sustainable competitive advantage in their specific industries. We center our presentation around Michael Porter's well-known framework for analyzing the structure of an industry and its profit potential, identifying alternative business-level strategies built on foundations of either differentiation or cost leadership. In this section, we also discuss the enormous difficulties that complicate competitor analysis, and efforts to build sustainable competitive advantage in any industry.

Second, we turn our attention to functional-level strategies which govern management of internal organizational functions (e.g., finance, marketing, R&D) in order to add value to goods and services by mobilizing core competencies. Here, we draw upon Porter's work on the power of value chain analysis to ". . . disaggregate a firm into its strategically relevant activities in order to understand the behavior of costs and the existing and potential sources of differentiation."[1] We consider the ways in which internal activities both support and shape business-level strategies.

Third, we consider corporate or multibusiness strategies, defined here as strategies that seek synergy for an organization through the skillful assembly of a portfolio of businesses or business units, often stretching across several diverse industries. This section explores one fundamental question: How can diversification be managed for long-run effectiveness?

FORMULATING BUSINESS-LEVEL STRATEGIES

Shaping a **business-level strategy** involves making decisions for an entire organization that operates in a single industry. Cray Research, for example, operates only in the supercomputer industry, so its only strategy focuses on that one industry and Cray's position in it. Larger or more diversified firms formulate business-level strategy for strategic business units (SBUs) or product divisions. For example, MTV and Nickelodeon are separate units of Viacom, a diversified entertainment company. Their strategies are developed at the operating unit level, to reflect product and environmental differences. The results are then incorporated into Viacom's corporate strategy, which encompasses business-level strategies for television and radio stations, as well as cable systems.

Business-level strategy making, thus, focuses on a single industry and a few closely related industries that may affect it. Shaping a business-level strategy is a firm's answer to the question, How will we compete in this industry in a way that builds sustainable competitive advantage and, therefore, above-average profitability? As we indicated in Chapter 2, answering this basic question begins with some variation of SWOT analysis.

We begin our discussion in this section by focusing on the opportunities and threats that emerge from analysis of an industry's structure and the critical forces that shape competition and profitability within it. We then turn to the general consideration of strengths (or core competencies) and weaknesses and their effects on business-level strategy. We then use this as a jumping off point for our discussion of functional-level strategies.

Industry Structure Analysis and Competitive Positioning

Michael Porter's framework for industry analysis provides a powerful analytical device for the business strategist.[2] By assessing separately and collectively the strengths of five competitive forces, which shape all industry environments, business-level strategists are better able to position their businesses within their industries. These five forces are (1) the threat of new entrants, (2) the bargaining power of suppliers, (3) the bargaining power of buyers, (4) the threat of substitute products, and (5) the rivalry among existing competitors. Figure 4.1 shows these five forces, plus a number of factors that shape each of them. We discuss each of these critical forces in the sections below.

Threat of New Entrants   Any firm that considers entering an industry brings new capacity and a desire to gain market share and profits, but whether it actually enters the industry depends on several **barriers to entry.** (A number of these are shown in Figure 4.1.) Established firms in an industry may create barriers to entry through experience curve effects, since their cumulative experience in producing and marketing a product often reduces their per-unit costs below those of inexperienced firms. In general, higher entry barriers reduce the likelihood that outside firms will enter the industry.

Thus, a picture emerges of firms that already compete in an industry attempting to create and defend barriers that other firms must overcome to compete themselves. In effect, industry pioneers work hard to set a high price of admission for those who come later. Examples abound of industries where admission is costly (or unaffordable). The soft drink industry is dominated by a few strong competitors, notably Coca-Cola and Pepsi-Co, whose dominance

FIGURE 4.1   Elements of Industry Structure

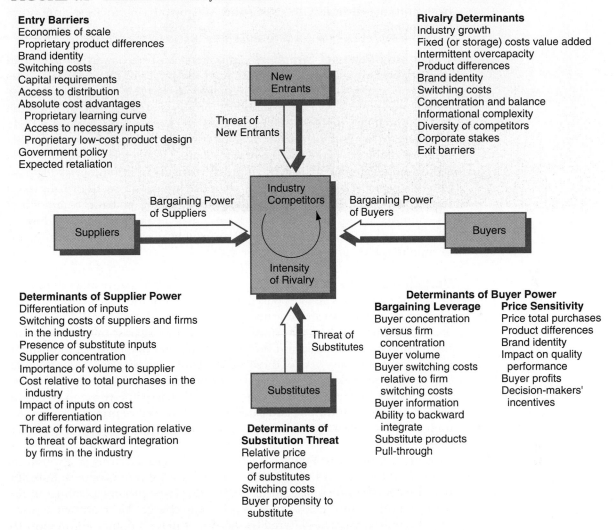

Entry Barriers
Economies of scale
Proprietary product differences
Brand identity
Switching costs
Capital requirements
Access to distribution
Absolute cost advantages
  Proprietary learning curve
  Access to necessary inputs
  Proprietary low-cost product design
Government policy
Expected retaliation

Rivalry Determinants
Industry growth
Fixed (or storage) costs value added
Intermittent overcapacity
Product differences
Brand identity
Switching costs
Concentration and balance
Informational complexity
Diversity of competitors
Corporate stakes
Exit barriers

New Entrants

Threat of New Entrants

Industry Competitors

Intensity of Rivalry

Bargaining Power of Suppliers

Suppliers

Bargaining Power of Buyers

Buyers

Determinants of Supplier Power
Differentiation of inputs
Switching costs of suppliers and firms
  in the industry
Presence of substitute inputs
Supplier concentration
Importance of volume to supplier
Cost relative to total purchases in the
  industry
Impact of inputs on cost
  or differentiation
Threat of forward integration relative
  to threat of backward integration
  by firms in the industry

Threat of Substitutes

Substitutes

Determinants of Substitution Threat
Relative price
  performance
  of substitutes
Switching costs
Buyer propensity to
  substitute

Determinants of Buyer Power

Bargaining Leverage	**Price Sensitivity**
Buyer concentration	Price total purchases
versus firm	Product differences
concentration	Brand identity
Buyer volume	Impact on quality
Buyer switching costs	performance
relative to firm	Buyer profits
switching costs	Decision-makers'
Buyer information	incentives
Ability to backward	
integrate	
Substitute products	
Pull-through	

SOURCE: Adapted and reprinted with the permission of The Free Press, an imprint of Simon & Schuster from COMPETITIVE AD-VANTAGE: Creating and Sustaining Superior Performance by Michael E. Porter. Copyright © 1985 by Michael E. Porter.

of distribution channels represents an especially effective barrier to entry. By one industry estimate, over 1,000 new soft drink products are developed each year; but only a few ever make it into the supermarket due to the barriers created by Coke and Pepsi. There is an important lesson here—entry barriers do not always emerge simply from the nature of an industry; they are created by competitors striving to develop their own sustainable competitive advantages.

Sometimes, of course, barriers can be overcome. A proprietary product innovation developed by a new competitor or a new product for a neglected market niche can leapfrog established competitors, and thus overcome entry barriers. Canon's small copiers gained market share in an industry previously dominated by Xerox. Reebok gained a substantial share of the athletic shoe market by catering initially to a rapidly growing niche—aerobics classes—that had been overlooked by industry leaders such as Nike. Fox Broadcasting lured a significant share of the young television viewing audience away from entrenched rivals CBS, NBC, and ABC by offering focused, innovative programming.

Bargaining Power of Suppliers   Suppliers can be a powerful force in an industry because they may be able to raise the prices of raw materials or reduce their quality. In general, when suppliers are few (i.e., the supplier industry is concentrated), when the suppliers' products are essential, or when the cost of switching suppliers is high, the bargaining **power of suppliers** is high. Suppliers, through their pricing decisions and the competitive strength that supports them, can capture some profit potential in the industry or industries they supply. Thus, in an attractive industry structure, a firm has a strong position relative to its key suppliers. Industries like breakfast cereals or baby foods feature suppliers that are highly competitive sellers of basic commodities (economists would call them *price takers*), such as farmers. Such industries offer buyers significant advantages in bargaining power. Other determinants of supplier power are listed in Figure 4.1.

Bargaining Power of Buyers   Buyers in industry structure analysis include both final consumers and key purchasers throughout the distribution process. The **power of buyers** can force an industry's prices down, bargain for higher quality or more services, play industry competitors against one another, and threaten to integrate backward (i.e., make what they need instead of buying it from another industry). All of these tactics reduce supplier industry profitability. For example, relatively small consumer-products manufacturers may sell to large retailers, such as Sears or Wal-Mart. They have little room to negotiate with such dominant buyers, and cannot expect to receive premium prices for their products. Several determinants of buyer power are shown in Figure 4.1.

Threat of Substitute Products   In a broad sense, all firms in an industry compete with firms in industries that produce substitute products. **Substitution threats** limit potential returns in an industry by placing a ceiling on the prices that firms in the industry can profitably charge. More attractive price-performance alternatives offered by substitutes place a tighter lid on industry profits. For example, the prices charged by a movie theater are affected by the prices of entertainment alternatives, such as cable television. Similarly, the prices vacation travelers pay to airlines for relatively short flights are influenced by the prices of auto or train travel. Some determinants of the degree of substitution threat are shown in Figure 4.1.

Rivalry among Existing Competitors   Porter's concept of **rivalry among competitors** comes closest to what we normally think of as competition in a business setting. Rivalry is the arena of competitive game playing, i.e., taking steps in direct or indirect opposition to those of competitors to build a more defensible position.[3] Rivalry creates exciting headlines for the business press—Coke versus Pepsi in the cola wars, AT&T versus MCI, Reebok versus Nike—the list could go on indefinitely. We are less interested in the specific actions of individual competitors to outfox one another, however, and more interested in the nature of rivalry in the industry as a whole, and the factors that cause rivalry to take a certain shape. Industry rivalry can be described with terms like *price competitive, advertising intensive, technology based,* or *service focused.* For example, technology-based rivalry would describe an industry like biotechnology, where the rivalry is based on applied research and the development of breakthrough drugs. Rivalry of this sort spurs firms to compete to attract the best scientific talent to their side, and winning these bidding wars for the best people may be the key factor in determining future competitive advantage.

Of the factors that shape rivalry in an industry, the most powerful may be industry growth or life cycle stage. Slow demand growth, due to either economic fluctuations or life cycle factors, can transform industry rivalry, for example, in the direction of brutal price competition and away from advertising wars that emphasize product differences. This is especially true when exit barriers are high for industry rivals. This scenario describes the personal computer industry in the early 1990s. As the technology became standardized, rivals could no longer sell unique products for premium prices, they had to slash prices and search for profits through low-cost manufacturing and distribution systems.

Strategy Alternatives

In Porter's framework, analysis of these five forces should guide the development of business strategy. For example, a firm has the best chance of high profitability in an industry characterized by high barriers to entry and weak competitors, weak substitutes, weak buyers, and weak suppliers. Although few industries offer all of these characteristics, the key to strategy formulation is to focus on the particular opportunities and threats in the industry. For example, in an industry with high entry barriers, competition from new entrants may be a minor concern in strategy formulation. Efforts may focus instead on changing the structure of the industry via backward integration (buying out suppliers), forward integration (buying out distribution channels), or horizontal integration (buying out existing competitors).

Typically, however, competitive analysis focuses on rivalry among existing competitors and on the formulation of strategies to outperform other firms in the industry. Porter suggests that firms can choose among three generic strategies: overall cost leadership, differentiation, and focus. The skills and resources needed and the organizational requirements of these strategies are shown in Table 4.1.

By pursuing an **overall cost leadership strategy,** a firm tries to earn above-average returns in its industry despite the presence of strong competitive forces. Cost leadership is accomplished through a consistent emphasis on efficient production of a good or service. Firms that follow cost leadership strategies are often referred to as *low-cost producers* in their industries. This strategic option is popular among firms that have high-volume production facilities and relatively high market shares in their industries. Cost leadership strategies often depend on favorable access to raw materials and the need for considerable financial resources to stay ahead of competitors in acquiring the most efficient manufacturing equipment. However, cost leaders are not always the largest producers in an industry. Southwest Airlines, a growing regional air carrier, has committed itself to a cost leadership strategy. It consistently turns a profit in the problem-plagued U.S. airline industry because its cost per available seat mile is roughly 80 percent of those of its larger rivals. The Company

TABLE 4.1

Porter's Three Generic Strategies and Their Requirements

Generic Strategy	Commonly Required Skills and Resources	Common Organizational Requirements
Overall cost leadership	Sustained capital investment and access to capital Process engineering skills Intense supervision of labor Products designed for ease in manufacture Low-cost distribution system	Tight cost control Frequent, detailed control reports Structured organization and responsibilities Incentives based on meeting strict quantitative targets
Differentiation	Strong marketing abilities Product engineering Creative flair Strong capability in basic research Corporate reputation for quality or technological leadership Long tradition in the industry or unique combination of skills drawn from other businesses Strong cooperation from channels	Strong coordination among functions in R&D, product development, and marketing Subjective measurement and incentives instead of quantitative measures Amenities to attract highly skilled labor, scientists, or creative people
Focus	Combination of the above policies directed at the particular strategic target	Combination of the above policies directed at the particular strategic target

SOURCE: Adapted and reprinted with the permission of The Free Press, an imprint of Simon & Schuster from COMPETITIVE STRATEGY: Techniques for Analyzing Industries and Competitors by Michael E. Porter. Copyright © 1980 by The Free Press.

Example illustrates a cost-leadership strategy. Kohl's Corporation, a rapidly growing department store chain, relies on a low-cost strategy to support it in the highly competitive world of retailing.

A **differentiation strategy** involves creating and marketing unique products for a mass market that command premium prices. Differentiators lead firms to work to develop unique brand images (Levi's jeans), unique technology (Intel's computer chips), unique features (Jenn-Air electric ranges), unique distribution channels (Tupperware), unique customer service (Four Seasons Hotels), or the like. Differentiation is a viable strategy for earning above-average returns in industries where customers perceive that premium prices

COMPANY EXAMPLE

Kohl's Pioneers New Retail Niche

Parquet floors and carpeting instead of linoleum; soft lighting rather than fluorescent strips; name-brand merchandise stacked on oak tables, not piled in mesh or melamine bins. The atmosphere in Kohl's Corp.'s 92 stores is markedly different from those in its competitors' outlets: discount stores and upscale department stores.

For Kohl's, it's all part of an overall strategy that industry analysts say has put the pioneering chain into a league of its own—appealing to Middle America's desire to shop in attractive stores that offer brand-name clothing at discount prices.

It's a simple concept—pleasant stores offering cutthroat prices—that has translated well to the eight states where the Wisconsin-based retailer operates. Kohl's plans to open 18 or more new stores annually for the next five years, focusing first on cities on the East and West coasts. At first glance, it may seem a tough sell; the Northeast is especially crowded with both discounters and upscale retailers. But analysts say shoppers will soon discover the difference. According to New York retail consultant Kurt Barnard, Kohl's has built a reputation for being a skillful merchandiser that frequently outflanks competitors. "They're very savvy."

Kohl's has to be savvy to afford the ambience of a department store while selling at such reduced prices. Gross margins are about 8 percent below those of other department stores, yet it generates a high return on sales—almost 11 percent in 1993.

Having better access than its competitors to popular brand names has helped Kohl's make competitive inroads, but the real key is keeping a tight rein on costs. Much of the company's initial cost savings comes from land purchases; whether for a free-standing or mall unit, it locates stores where real estate is cheap. Further, Kohl's uses only 15 percent of a store's square-footage for storage; competitors use up to 40 percent. To save labor costs, merchandise displays encourage self-selection, while checkout counters are found not in individual departments, but by store exits in discount-store-style clusters. Savings will continue with the company's expansion; Kohl's plans to keep its new locations within 400 miles of its distribution centers to speed up restocking.

Retail experts expect strong profits, due in large part to Kohl's aggressive, but down-to-earth, management style, which befits an era where level-headedness rather than glitz is paramount. The numbers are impressive: Sales at stores opened at least a year have risen at least 8 percent annually, and total sales rose 16 percent in 1993 to $1.3 billion.

SOURCE: Christina Duff, "Kohl's of the Midwest Maps an Invasion of Both Coasts," *The Wall Street Journal*, May 12, 1994, p. B4.

can bring them goods or services that are distinctly better than the lower cost versions. Differentiators (or premium product producers) define the high end of a given industry, to the extent that the industry structure and associated life cycle permit enough difference among products to allow a high end. In perishable consumer goods, for example, differentiators sell highly advertised, branded products—Perdue chickens, Heinz ketchup—rather than store labels.

A **focus strategy** seeks to segment markets and appeal to only one or a few groups of consumers or organizational buyers. A firm that limits its attention to one or a few market niches hopes to serve those niches better than firms that seek to influence the entire market. For example, products such as Rolls-Royce automobiles, Cross pens, and Hartmann luggage are designed to appeal to the upscale market and serve it well rather than trying to compete in the mass market. Not all niche players focus on upscale markets where they can command premium prices. Many combine narrow focuses with low-cost strategies to provide products to targeted customer niches. This group might include a small, regional packaging manufacturer that focuses on a small set

TABLE 4.2

Risks Associated with Porter's Three Generic Strategies

Risks of Cost Leadership Strategy	Risks of Differentiation Strategy	Risks of Focus Strategy
Cost leadership is not sustained • competitors imitate • technology changes • other bases for cost leadership erode	Differentiation is not sustained • competitors imitate • bases for differentiation become less important to buyers	The focus strategy is imitated The target segment becomes structurally unattractive • structure erodes • demand disappears
Proximity in differentiation is lost	Cost proximity is lost	Broadly targeted competitors overwhelm the segment • the segment's differences from other segments narrow • the advantages of a broad line increase
Cost focusers achieve even lower cost in segments	Differentiation focusers achieve even greater differentiation in segments	New focusers subsegment the industry

SOURCE: Adapted and reprinted with the permission of The Free Press, an imprint of Simon & Schuster from COMPETITIVE ADVANTAGE: Creating and Sustaining Superior Performance by Michael E. Porter. Copyright © 1985 by Michael E. Porter.

of customers. Manufacturing economics (which determine the smallest efficient plant size) and low overhead allow these niche players to compete effectively on the basis of low delivered cost.

By implementing one of these generic strategies a firm tries to build a competitive advantage in an industry. However, each exposes the firm to risks that threaten its sustainability over time. These risks are shown in Table 4.2. For example, a well-designed and implemented focus or niche strategy may do so well that it grows a niche market until major competitors begin to find it attractive. Pepsi's recent move into clear or colorless soft drinks follows the work of smaller firms, such as Clearly Canadian, to develop this niche market.

The Skills Module gives you an opportunity to analyze and discuss the strength and weakness of the focus strategy of one small business in the service sector.

Industry Structures and Competitive Strategies—Additional Challenges

A few additional comments can help put the Porter framework in perspective. First, there is nothing deterministic or mechanical about industry analysis. Answering the critical questions to size up the structure of an industry involves few equations and much executive judgment. The same biases and human limitations that influence efforts to interpret the environment are at work

SKILLS MODULE

KangaKab Venture Rides Twisting Road

INTRODUCTION

We have introduced three generic strategies and noted the general requirements and risks associated with each one. Translating these ideas into specific actions in specific firms is the basic challenge, however, not only to students in a strategic management course but to practicing managers in every industry. Read the short description of KangaKab and its industry and complete the skill development exercise. This should help you to understand and appreciate the challenges of developing a strategy that yields a sustainable competitive advantage.

SITUATION

It was an idea borne of exasperation. Ad executive Judith London had to leave a business meeting early to drive her kids from school to the babysitter's house. When her complaint was echoed by colleague David Parkin, the two realized that there must be thousands of working parents in the same situation. There were, and their numbers were growing: in 1993, the U.S. Census Bureau counted 8.7 million dual-income households with children under 18 and annual incomes above $50,000—24 percent more than in 1989.

Thus was born the idea for KangaKab Inc., a children's ride service that London and Parkin started in 1992. During the next six months, the partners refined their business idea by meeting with a focus group, composed mainly of employed mothers; they also raised $34,000 from family and friends to buy three vans, ran newspaper ads to recruit drivers, and solicited initially wary customers.

The Marlton, New Jersey, company's five-van fleet transports about 150 children a week at a usual per-trip rate of $6 a child. One van's midday ferrying job might generate $30 for KangaKab; Parkin's 75-minute afternoon run carrying 12 youngsters brings in practically a dollar a minute. The partners expect to turn their first profit in 1994 on projected revenue of $250,000. In an effort to accelerate growth, they began franchising the concept in several states in 1993; so far, they have sold three franchises.

KangaKab is not the only entrepreneur throwing a lifeline to working parents whose most valuable commodity has become time; recent startups include nanny referral networks and children's fitness centers. KangaKab is not alone, or even the first, to enter the business of juvenile transportation. Kid's Kab International Franchise Corp., formed in Troy, Michigan, in 1991, claims to be the nation's biggest, deriving about $500,000 in annual revenue from 32 franchisees in 14 states. Pamela Henderson, founder, president, and mother of three, says her company plans to open 28 more franchises this year and license operations in Canada and the United Kingdom.

Henderson cautions that the business is much more than buying a van and making appointments with parents. Annual liability and collision insurance coverage in suburban areas typically costs $2,500 a vehicle; various regulatory approvals and friendly, reliable drivers also are required. (KangaKab's roster includes a retired bank vice president.) Even then, making money is not easy; routes must be carefully structured to maximize the number of paying passengers per trip.

Parkin might add that the business requires one more thing: patience. He goes through two bags of sunflower seeds a day while calming himself in heavy traffic amid the din of voices chanting, "Dave has a bald spot!"

SKILL DEVELOPMENT EXERCISE

Using Porter's framework and the ideas presented in Tables 4.1 and 4.2, assess the situation at KangaKab. What type of focus strategy have they selected? Describe their strategy in as much detail as possible. Why have the owners chosen to compete this way? Could other firms develop other ways to compete in this industry? How should KangaKab attempt to protect its niche from competitors? What actions would you recommend that KangaKab take if other competitors, e.g., Kid's Kab, were to move into their market area? Why?

SOURCE: Michael Selz, "From School to the Doctor's Office to Home: Ride Service Does the Driving for Parents," *The Wall Street Journal,* May 6, 1994, pp. B1–B2.

here, and they may result in ineffective strategy formulation. To see these interpretive problems and the wrongheaded strategies they spawn at work in real companies, we need only to remember the tenacious hold of U.S. auto makers on their outmoded big-car strategies while consumers rushed toward Honda and Toyota for small cars.

Also, industry analysis quickly becomes *industries* analysis; one must understand the structures of adjacent industries in which suppliers, buyers, and potential entrants operate. In addition, industry structure is not static. It changes as the result of changes in the industry life cycle, and perhaps more importantly, as the result of the decisions and actions of key competitors. For example, if either Nike or Reebok were to adopt a cost leadership strategy in the athletic shoe industry, the structure of that industry would change dramatically from what it has been to date.

Some readers will no doubt wonder why firms cannot adopt differentiation and cost leadership strategies at the same time. Managers discover an inherent tension between what the two strategies demand of a firm. This is not to say that successful differentiators, for example, cannot also pay attention to costs or efficient production. Of course, they can. To compete effectively as differentiators, however, they must be driven by *that* imperative rather than the cost leadership imperative. A careful reading of Table 4.1, with its lists of the skills and organizational requirements associated with these two strategies, will reveal fundamental tensions between them. (The organizational requirements section also previews several issues we will review in the next chapter on strategy implementation.)

Many of today's most effective firms in advanced technology industries, for example, Intel in microprocessors, might be said to employ the two basic strategies in rapid succession or sequence. In developing and designing new products, they behave as differentiators. As soon as new products are developed firms know that many of them will be imitated in short order by competitors, i.e., their competitive advantage is not sustainable over time. Therefore, the firm shifts its strategic gears for the new product, focusing rapidly on low cost production and manufacturing efficiencies to enhance the profitability of a premium-priced product for the short period when it can still command a premium price. These enhanced profits, in turn, finance the costly development of the next differentiated product.

Finally, having identified three generic business-level strategies does not tell us how different firms with established positions in an industry will behave over time. Other typologies have been developed to explain how firms play out their chosen business strategies. One such typology, based on military strategy, is shown in Table 4.3.

The Challenge of Competitor Analysis: Sensemaking and Industry Structure

We pointed out in Chapter 2 that strategic issues do not arrive neatly packaged on the executive's desktop. Executives must interpret data from the competitive environment. Interpretation introduces biases and cognitive limitations of managers into the strategy-making equation, which may lead to flawed industry structure analyses. Making sense of competitor's actions and capabilities and judging their strategic impacts on a firm are key elements of industry structure analysis.

TABLE 4.3

Military Strategies for Industrial Warfare

Al Ries and Jack Trout argue that military strategy provides a useful perspective on competing in an industry. They identify four kinds of warfare, each appropriate for particular competitors in an industry.

DEFENSIVE WARFARE

Defensive strategies should be used only by market leaders such as General Motors and IBM. Defensive warfare involves protecting market share against competitors by introducing new products and services that render existing ones obsolete. Market leaders should block competitors' attempts at innovation by quickly copying any promising new products that they introduce.

OFFENSIVE WARFARE

Offensive strategies should be used by the second and third leading firms in the industry, firms that are large enough to mount sustained attacks on the market leader. Offensive warfare focuses on dissecting a leader's strength and finding a weakness where the leader is vulnerable to attack. The attack should be mounted on as narrow a front as possible, usually with a single product. For example, Federal Express became the market leader over Emory and Airborne by emphasizing its Priority One service and high reliability.

FLANKING WARFARE

Flanking strategies involve moving into uncontested areas where no markets exist, surprising competitors, and following up innovations relentlessly. This strategy also suits market followers rather than market leaders. For example, Miller flanked the industry with Lite beer and now dominates the light-beer market. Flanking is often a high-risk strategy, but successful flanking can be highly profitable.

GUERRILLA WARFARE

Guerilla strategies entail finding a niche in the market small enough to defend, while maintaining readiness to withdraw nimbly, if necessary. This strategy suits companies with small market shares.

SOURCE: Based on Al Ries and Jack Trout, *Marketing Warfare* (New York: McGraw-Hill, 1986).

A recent study of competitor analysis notes that "[i]t embodies both competitive intelligence to collect data on rivals and the analysis and interpretation of the data for managerial decision making."[4] This study also identified six serious blind spots often observed in competitor analysis methods. Table 4.4 lists these flaws and matches them with the actions that executives might take to remedy them.

Misjudging the boundaries of an industry, for example, is most readily observed in the business world when firms in one industry are blindsided by moves of firms from another industry that had not been identified as competitors. Classic examples include the watch industry's surprise at competition from semiconductor producers like Texas Instruments and its digital watches. More recently, IBM has entered the management consulting industry, with an as-yet-unknown impact on traditional consulting firms. In Porter's model, the

TABLE 4.4

Competitive Analysis Flaws and Managerial Actions

Flaws	Executive Actions
1. Misjudging industry boundaries	Change the view of the competition by focusing on competitors' intentions, seeing the industry from the entrant's eye, examining the reason for an entrant's failure, and performing an autopsy on failing competitors
2. Poor identification of the competition	Study competitors' response patterns and blind spots; survey customers and suppliers; focus on competitor's capabilities, not only on their forms
3. Overemphasis on competitors' visible competence	Study competitors' response patterns; analyze rivals' invisible functions
4. Overemphasis on where, not how rivals will compete	Study competitors' strategic intentions; study the industry from competitors' eyes
5. Faulty assumptions about the competition	Transform the cliché that competition is good into a living reality; study competitors' actions and response patterns; ensure representation of diverse groups in the competitive analysis process; teach employees about competitors; validate assumptions by discussing them with suppliers and customers
6. Paralysis by analysis	Pay attention to the staffing, organization, and mission of the competitive analysis unit; integrate competitive analysis with the managerial decision-making process; use nontraditional approaches to competitor analysis

SOURCE: Adapted from Shaker Zahra and Sherry Chaples, "Blind Spots in Competitive Analysis," *Academy of Management Executive*, May 1993, p. 7.

watch industry's flaw would be poor analysis of the threat of substitutes, and management consultants' failure to analyze potential entrants effectively.

Table 4.4 also suggests that managers can overcome faulty assumptions about competitors by involving diverse groups in the competitive analysis process. This observation reinforces our emphasis on a cross-functional perspective on strategic management, in this case the competitor analysis component, for firms operating in the complex environments of the 1990s.

The Challenge of Sustainability—Competitive Advantage over Time

In a competitive world, advantages are difficult to sustain. Table 4.2 confirms that the risks associated with Porter's three generic strategies mainly revolve around the sustainability issue. A strategy may yield a temporary advantage, but not one that can be sustained in the face of competitive moves by rivals.

Pankaj Ghemawat puts it this way: "For outstanding performance, a company has to beat the competition. The trouble is the competition has heard the same message."[5]

Ghemawat bolsters this assertion by pointing out the relative ease with which rivals can imitate new products, innovative production methods, and marketing approaches. Ghemawat proposes three ways to overcome the sustainability barrier—commitment to achieving size advantages in a targeted market, getting access to key resources or customers, and taking advantage of restrictions on the options of competitors. Thus, relatively large firms can hope to achieve sustainable advantage by retaining key inputs and locking in key customers (e.g., through high switching costs), when competitors find it structurally difficult to change directions.

One type of organizational skill—quick response—has received much attention lately as a possible source of sustainable competitive advantage.[6] Bower and Hout argue that quick response, if properly nurtured, can become both a critical organizational capability and a management philosophy, a new way of thinking about "how to organize and lead a company and how to gain a real advantage over competitors."[7] Fast organizations are thus better able to support their differentiation, cost leadership, of focus strategies than slower rivals.

A problem arises when a firm's commitments and key skills suit conditions less well as time passes. What a firm does to achieve sustainable advantage at Time 1 may put it into a weak position at Time 2. For example, Digital Equipment Corporation was a pioneer and a dominant player in the minicomputer industry. In Ghemawat's terms, the firm made a commitment to size, assembled the necessary talent, built strong relationships with its customers, and outflanked the larger IBM, which chose to defend its mainframe computer line instead of aggressively moving into the minicomputer market. However, Digital's very commitment to this market became one source of the troubles it experienced in later time periods, when that prior commitment cast it in the role of turf defender, and thus kept it from aggressively pursuing the personal computer or workstation markets as early as it might have. Bower and Hout might argue that Digital could have developed a quick response capability, developing new products faster and avoiding later stage problems.

One of the points underscored by the analyses of Ghemawat and others is the importance of a firm's collective know-how, or core competencies, in the search for sustainable competitive advantage.[8] In the following section, we turn our attention specifically to the analysis of a firm's internal strengths and weaknesses, and the core competencies on which it can build business-level strategies.

Core Competencies and Business-Level Strategy

In Chapter 1, we defined strategic management as a continuous process aimed at keeping an organization appropriately matched to its environment. We now consider the strengths and weaknesses of organizations, and their attempts to match core competencies to their competitive environments.

Core competency can be defined generally as "the collective learning in the organization."[9] This usually focuses on production and technology-related skills in diversified corporations. This definition challenges a corporation's managers to design an architecture in which these competencies can move flexibly and effectively across the diverse units of the firm.

Competencies can also influence the shape of business-level strategy. Once again, Michael Porter provides a conceptual framework for the systematic evaluation of a firm's internal activities to identify and refine those that are strategically important to a firm's search for competitive success through cost leadership or differentiation. Figure 4.2 shows the generic value chain of organizations, divided into primary activities and support activities. Through a detailed examination of these activities, separately and collectively, a firm can not only develop a better sense of its strengths and weaknesses, but it can also more powerfully understand the impact of, or value added by, each activity in relation to its chosen strategy.

Value chain analysis begins with the recognition that each firm or business unit is, in Porter's words, "a collection of activities that are performed to design, produce, market, deliver, and support its product."[10] By analyzing each value activity separately, and by determining each activity's cost and contributions, managers can judge the value of each activity to the firm's search for sustainable competitive advantage. By identifying and analyzing a firm's value activities, managers work with the core elements of its competitive advantage since the efficiency and effectiveness of each activity affects the firm's success in its low cost, differentiation, or focus strategy.

Porter divides value activities into two broad categories—primary and support activities. **Primary activities,** shown across the bottom of Figure 4.2, include inbound logistics, operations, outbound logistics, marketing/sales, and service. It is helpful to think of primary activities as a stream of related activities, beginning with the arrival and storage of raw materials or inputs to the firm's production processes; their transformation into final products; handling, storage, and distribution of outgoing finished products; marketing and sales activities to identify, reach, and motivate buyer groups; and service activities to provide customer and product support.

Support activities, as the name suggests, provide specialized and general support to primary activities. Support activities like procurement, technology development, human resource management, and infrastructure are shown at the top of Figure 4.2. It is useful to think of support activities as general business functions. For example, the procurement activity includes more functions than might be included in a purchasing department's activities, which normally focus narrowly on buying raw materials for use in manufacturing. Procurement includes the full range of processes or technologies that a firm might use to acquire anything from office supplies to critical raw materials, advertising services, temporary workers, or top managers.

Similarly, technology development and human resource management (HRM) can affect primary value activities in strategically important ways. For example, careful training and assignment of medical staff is critical to the profitability and service goals of a health maintenance organization. Technology development can affect new product design, selection of new materials, production processes, logistics, marketing, and services. This broad definition of *technology development* extends beyond the traditional research and develop-

FIGURE 4.2   The Generic Value Chain

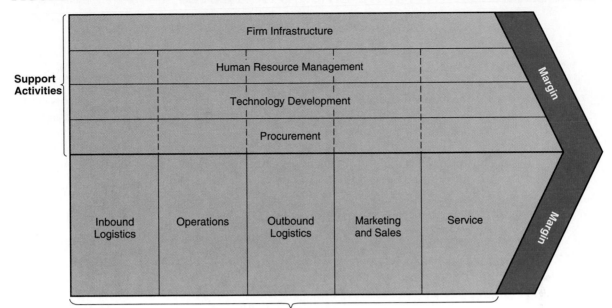

ment function to include, for example, the design of a new inventory control system and product refinements suggested by a major customer.

Firm infrastructure encompasses activities such as general management, accounting and finance, information systems, government relations, and legal affairs. Infrastructure supports primary value activities by providing both internal coordination (through systematic measurement, information flows, and strategic planning) and management of key external relationships.

As a tool for strategy formulation, value chain analysis demands not only that managers analyze each separate value activity in great detail but also that they examine the critical linkages between and among internal activities. In this way, the value chain enhances the importance of cross-functional efforts in strategy formulation. Value chain analysis calls upon managers to think creatively and broadly about how the firm goes about its activities, and about how those activities affect each other. Inevitably, such an approach draws attention to a basic reality: formulating a strategy, putting it into play, and refining it over time require the talents and energies of people from every corner of the firm. Functional strategies, then, must be analyzed and coordinated to maximize their cross-functional effects if they are to contribute optimally to a firm's overall competitive strategy.

Value chain analysis can also help firms to better understand the linkages between their value chains and those of current or potential suppliers and customers, in the interest of building a stronger competitive strategy. In the following section on functional strategies, we will look in more detail at ways to put internal activities (and the core competencies that they exploit) squarely in the middle of the strategy equation.

FORMULATING FUNCTIONAL-LEVEL STRATEGIES

Traditionally, **functional-level strategies** have been viewed as flowing harmoniously from business-level strategies. Once a business-level strategy is decided, the story goes, functional managers put together strategies that are consistent with and fully supportive of it. This may have represented wishful thinking that internal activities are always compliant, problem-free support mechanisms for the larger strategy of a business. In reality, however, this view of things as they should be may have differed significantly from things as they were.

The recent emergence of the quality movement has called attention to suboptimal operations of functions, considered separately or in combination. A growing number of firms now use benchmarking to compare their functions to those of world-class competitors. Many also aggressively employ outsourcing, deciding that an internal function can be performed more efficiently by an external supplier. These trends attest to the new ways in which firms are thinking about their functions and their functional-level strategies. Outsourcing seems to be causing a revolution in the ways organizations are structured, and the way we think about transferring functions outside the organization's traditional boundaries. *Fortune* magazine has pointed out the emerging significance of what it called the "modular organization"; *Business Week* earlier referred to the same phenomenon as creating a "hollow corporation."[11]

In the sections below, we consider several functions and appropriate functional-level strategies. For each, we focus on its ability to add value to a firm's goods or services.

Technology/Research and Development Strategies

In many industries, an organization cannot grow or even survive without generating a steady stream of new products. Research and development (R&D) specialists work to devise new products to support the business-level strategy. R&D conceives new product ideas and develops them until the products reach full production and enter the market. This process involves concept generation and screening, product planning and development, and perhaps even test marketing.

Some industry structures make R&D critical since new products can be highly profitable; still, R&D can be time consuming, expensive, and risky. For example, it is estimated that only one out of seven new product ideas ever makes it to the market. Clearly, the time and money allocated to researching and developing the other six ideas greatly increase overall R&D costs. Furthermore, an average of 30 to 35 percent of new products fail after entering the market, so *innovation strategies*—those that focus heavily on developing new products—can be very risky.[12] For this reason many organizations use *imitation* or *fast follower strategies,* rapidly copying new competitive products that do well. A number of Japanese electronics companies were quite successful in the 1970s and 1980s in copying American technology. By avoiding many R&D costs, they improved their competitive positions significantly.

In recent years, the emphasis has increased on the role of R&D in adding value through its internal linkages to manufacturing and marketing functions. We read with increasing frequency about corporate efforts to "design for manufacture" or to do "concurrent engineering"; both techniques focus on improving coordination among several functions to reduce the time a product takes to reach the market. Cross-functional communication can improve coordination and enhance the important role of the R&D function in providing the ideas and concepts needed to generate successful new product introductions or to increase the efficiency of production methods.

Operations Strategies

Specialists in this area make decisions about required plant capacity, plant layout, manufacturing and production processes, and inventory requirements. Two important aspects of operations strategy are controlling costs and improving the efficiency of plant operations. As for the technology/R&D function, manufacturing has been in the spotlight in recent years because of the total quality movement, and the tools and techniques that support this movement.

Functional-level strategies for operations in the 1990s use statistical process control, just-in-time inventory methods, continuous improvement systems, flexible manufacturing systems, and the human resource management approaches that support these quality-enhancing techniques. The work of W. Edwards Deming on quality improvement has had an increasing influence on operations strategies. Chapter 8 of this text explores the increasingly important issue of quality, and its close links to competitive strategy, while Chapter 10 offers further discussion of the operations function.

Financial Strategies

Financial specialists are responsible for forecasting and financial planning, evaluating investment proposals, securing financing for various investments, and controlling financial resources. Financial specialists contribute to strategy formulation by assessing the potential profit impacts of various strategic alternatives, using techniques such as net present value analysis, and evaluating the financial condition of the business. While much of the earlier discussion of business-level strategy emphasized product–market fit and positioning, the role of finance in strategy formulation should not be underestimated. Financial analysis answers some of the fundamental questions that drive strategy making in a firm. What will a new strategic initiative cost? What financial risk does a new strategy present versus the risk of an existing strategy? What is the lowest-cost method of financing a new initiative? Chapter 11 of this text discusses financial issues in greater detail.

Marketing Strategies

Marketing specialists determine the appropriate markets in which to offer products and they develop effective marketing mixes. (The marketing mix includes four strategic elements: price, product, promotion, and channels of distribution.) Chapter 12 of this text covers marketing strategy in greater detail, and provides insight into how the marketing function takes a product into the marketplace, and how it carries critical feedback from that marketplace back to a firm's leaders to help them fine-tune or revise a strategy.

TABLE 4.5

Effective and Ineffective Human Resource Management

Characteristics of Effective Companies	Characteristics of Ineffective Companies
Genuine concern for people; a positive view of employees as assets	Do not view employees as important assets; show little concern for work force
Good training, development, and advancement opportunities	Managed autocratically or bureaucratically; rigid and inflexible
Pay well; good compensation programs	Little or no employee development; an ineffective internal advancement process
Able to retain employees; low turnover	Poor internal communication
Good internal communication; open communication	Unclear or outdated policies; inconsistently administered and altered in difficult times
Top management committed to and supportive of HR [human resources]	High turnover
Encourage employee participation.	

SOURCE: Adapted from S. W. Alper and R. E. Mandel, "What Policies and Practices Characterize the Most Effective HR Departments, *Personnel Administrator,* vol. 29, no. 11, 1984. Copyright 1984 The American Society for Personnel Administration, 606 North Washington Street, Alexandria, Virginia 22314. Reprinted with the permission of *HRMagazine* published by the Society for Human Resource Management, Alexandria, Va.

Human Resource Strategies

In general, the human resource function is concerned with attracting, assessing, motivating, and retaining the employees the firm needs to run effectively. This function is also responsible for affirmative action planning and evaluating the safety of the work environment. Collectively, the set of decisions concerning these issues define the human resource strategy for the business.[13]

Like other strategies, human resource strategies are based on both external and internal analysis. External analysis includes tracking developments in laws and regulations that affect employment (such as equal employment opportunity laws), studying changes in labor unions and labor negotiations, and analyzing changes in the labor market. Internal analysis includes investigating specific problem areas such as low productivity, excessive turnover, or high accident rates. In addition, human resource strategies may involve analyzing and proposing changes in organizational structure and climate.

Table 4.5 lists several characteristics of effective and ineffective human resource management. Table 4.6 presents a portion of the human resource strategy for Merck and Company. As is appropriate for all functional-level strategies, it identifies goals specific to the operational level and specifies tasks that must be performed to reach these goals.

TABLE 4.6

Excerpts from Merck and Company's Human Resource Strategy

Develop new and more effective ways to accommodate employee participation in joint problem-solving areas and in appropriate policy/practice development.

Opinion surveys, face-to-face meetings, focus groups, quality circle groups, and labor–management committees have added channels for employees to express their concerns and suggestions. These are just the start of many avenues which will be explored to improve participation and two-way communications between employees and supervisors.

There continues to be room for and need for expanding and improving employee participation. This will be achieved through improved two-way communication between employees and supervisors. Managers and supervisors need to fully understand and to put into practice the belief that the commitment of people is better assured when they are involved in the decision-making process.

SUMMARY OF ACTION PLANS

- Application of focus group techniques to develop or revise policies and procedures (successfully tested in 1980 with the Performance Appraisal Program and the Salary Administration Program).
- Continue to measure the effectiveness of management policies, practices, and programs.

PRIORITY 10

Develop innovative approaches to organization design, job design and scheduling, and advanced office systems to improve productivity.

Strengthen our capabilities for more effective organization planning to ensure capability of supporting business plans and objectives. It is critical that skills be broadened in long-term organization planning and in the redesign of jobs and work.

Attract talented professionals who want more flexibility in the workplace.

We will continue our investigation into advanced office systems and the expansion of office automation, which have significant human implications. There is a need to coordinate a stronger planning effort—on a corporatewide basis—between the three elements that are essential to make advanced office systems work effectively. These three elements include the technical (MIS), the physical office design (Engineering), and the behavioral (Human Resources). Given that Merck is office-worker intensive and will become more so in the future, this planning effort has significant implications for the Company's productivity efforts.

SUMMARY OF ACTION PLANS

- Continue to develop skills for effective organization planning and implementation of Advanced Office Systems.
- Expand flexible working hours and test new scheduling and work pattern approaches.
- Continue to improve consulting skills of H.R. professionals.

SOURCE: G. T. Milkovich and J. D. Phillips, "Human Resource Planning at Merck & Co.," in L. Dyer, ed., *Human Resource Planning: A Case Study Reference Guide to the Tested Practices of Five Major U.S. and Canadian Companies* (New York: Random House, 1985).

FORMULATING CORPORATE-LEVEL STRATEGIES

Top managers formulate corporate-level strategies, or multibusiness strategies, to achieve sustainable synergy for an organization by assembling a portfolio of businesses or business units, which may stretch across a diverse set of industries. For example, General Electric's portfolio of businesses ranges from jet engines to financial services to a television network (NBC) to appliances to medical instruments to light bulbs. The firm's overarching plan seeks to hold together these diverse businesses to form a synergistic whole that combines individual industry structures and business-level strategies. This plan is the firm's **corporate-level strategy.**

A well-conceived corporate-level strategy guides corporate managers' efforts to manage their portfolios of businesses in much the same way that the stated objectives of a mutual fund guide the fund manager's decisions about what securities to buy, what to hold, and what to sell. Corporate strategy focuses on a portfolio of businesses, however, instead of a portfolio of stocks or bonds. A corporate strategy also guides the top managers' decision about the roles that various businesses will play in the portfolio, and thus on how resources should move from one business to another.

In this section, we first review the factors that explain most organizations' transformations from single-business firms to multibusiness firms that need corporate-level strategies. We then discuss approaches to managing for synergy across a diverse set of businesses or business units.

Diversification—Approaches to Assembling a Portfolio

What explains the emergence of multibusiness strategies? Why and how do single businesses decide to form portfolios of businesses? Answers to these basic questions may cite several motives, but we believe they center on four—growth goals, risk management, special expertise, and industry structure.

Growth Goals

An organization that operates in a single industry has chosen to concentrate its efforts and hitch its wagon to the future of that one industry. What happens if industry growth slows? The organization's leaders have a strategic choice to make. They can stay focused on that one industry and seek to strengthen their competition position within it; they may have to resign themselves to a future of slower growth, but continuing profitability. If they are not satisfied with their industry's growth picture and want better results for their shareholders (and possibly more interesting work for themselves), they may explore alternative ways to move away from a single-business strategy.

Once they decide to build a multibusiness corporate portfolio to improve their firm's growth, managers can accomplish this goal in many ways. Often, as shown below, they may seek to acquire other, existing firms in horizontal integration, vertical integration, or diversification strategies.

Horizontal Integration   In this strategy, the firm seeks to grow by acquiring competing firms in the same line of business. Such a move can quickly increase the size, sales, profits, and potential market share of an organization. Horizontal integration represents the strategic alternative that is closest to a firm's former single-business strategy. This form of integration via acquisition seeks the same result as market penetration efforts taken by a firm—that is, it results in a firm increasing its share of, and thus growth in, an industry that may be growing slowly overall.

Vertical Integration   In this strategy, the firm seeks to grow by acquiring other organizations in its channel of distribution. When an organization purchases its suppliers, it engages in *backward* vertical integration. An organization that purchases other firms that are closer to the end users of the product such as wholesalers and retailers engages in *forward* vertical integration. Vertical integration gives greater control over a line of business and increases profits through greater efficiency or better selling efforts.[14] Some vertical integration moves are carried out, not through acquisition, but by launching new manufacturing efforts. Instead of acquiring one of its key suppliers, the firm simply begins producing that supply. A soup company may acquire a metal-can maker to pursue vertical integration by acquisition. A personal computer maker may begin making its own semiconductors to pursue vertical integration by launching a new venture.

Diversification   In this strategy, a firm seeks to grow by acquiring firms in industries or lines of business that are new to it. When the acquired firm has production technology, products, channels of distribution, and/or markets similar to those of the purchasing firm, the strategy is called *related* or *concentric diversification*. This strategy is useful when shared resources can improve the organization's efficiency or market impact. H. J. Heinz, with its packaged-food related diversification, is an example of this form of diversification.

When the acquired firm is in a completely different line of business, the strategy is called *unrelated* or *conglomerate diversification*. The General Electric portfolio mentioned earlier provides an example of this form of diversification. Both related and unrelated diversification efforts often begin with the goal of achieving higher growth rates than a single industry can offer.

Risk Management

The push to expand beyond a single business, and thus the need for a multi-business strategy, often results from a firm's desire to spread its risk across more than one industry. In much the same way that a mutual fund manager might choose a wide variety of stocks from different sectors of the economy to balance the risk of an entire portfolio, an organizational strategist might steer a firm away from the risks inherent in operating in only one industry. The risk of pinning all of their hopes on the metal container industry motivated the top managers of American Can Co. to diversify into insurance and financial services; eventually, the firm changed its name to Primerica after selling off its container operation altogether.

Special Expertise

Organizations often seek to build multibusiness portfolios to exploit some special expertise that they believe they possess that will add value to an acquired organization in a new industry. They believe they possess a core competence that is transferable into a new industry or industry segment. H. J. Heinz acquired Weight Watchers and Ore-Ida Potatoes, for example, to provide their operations with distribution clout.

Industry Structure

Before building a multibusiness portfolio, an organization needs to carefully consider the structure of the industry into which it plans to move with special emphasis on the question of how it can develop a sustainable competitive advantage there. Just because a high-growth industry is featured regularly in the business press is no justification for trying to move into it! The high entry costs of moving into a high-growth industry often consume much of the potential profit that it might generate. One of the classic stories of diversification failure is Exxon's attempted move into the office equipment business in the early 1980s, when that industry was growing rapidly. Exxon spent a great deal of money acquiring an assortment of small manufacturers and building a sales force, only to recognize that the highly visible Exxon name and vast resource base was not powerful enough to overcome the industry dominance of well-entrenched rivals like IBM, Xerox, etc.

Business Portfolio Models—Approaches to Managing a Portfolio for Sustainable Synergy

Business portfolio models are tools for analyzing (1) the relative position of each of an organization's businesses in its industry, and (2) the relationships among all of the organization's businesses. Two approaches to developing business portfolio models are the Boston Consulting Group's growth–share matrix and General Electric's multifactor portfolio matrix.

BCG Growth–Share Matrix

The Boston Consulting Group, a management consulting firm, developed and popularized an approach to multibusiness strategy making called the **growth–share matrix,** shown in Figure 4.3. The basic idea is that a firm should have a balanced portfolio of businesses in which some generate more cash than they use to help support others that need cash to develop and become profitable. The role of each business is determined on the basis of two factors: the growth rate of its market and its share of that market.

The vertical axis indicates the market growth rate, measured as the annual percentage growth of the market (current or forecasted) in which the business operates. Anything under 10 percent is typically considered a low growth rate and anything above 10 percent a high growth rate. However, depending on the industries being evaluated, other percentages are used.

The horizontal axis indicates market share dominance, or relative market share, computed by dividing the firm's market share (in units) by the market share of its largest competitor. For example, a relative market share of 0.2 means that the sales volume of the business is only 20 percent of the market leader's sales volume; a relative market share of 2.0 means that the business produces a sales volume twice that of the next largest competitor. A relative market share of 1.0 is set as the dividing line between high and low share. Each of the circles in Figure 4.3 represents the relative revenue of a single business; a larger circle represents more sales than a smaller circle.

The growth–share matrix places businesses in four cells, which reflect the four possible combinations of high and low growth with high and low market share. These cells represent particular types of businesses, each of which has a particular role to play in the overall business portfolio. The cells are labeled:

1. *Question marks* (sometimes called *problem children*): Businesses that operate in high-growth markets, but have low relative market shares. Most busi-

FIGURE 4.3
BCG's Growth–Share
Matrix

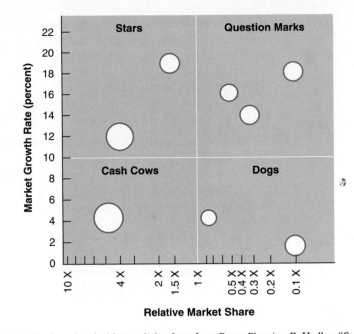

SOURCE: Adapted and reprinted with permission from *Long Range Planning*, B. Hedley, "Strategy and The Business Portfolio," February 1977, Elsevier Science Ltd., Pergamon Imprint, Oxford, England.

nesses start off as question marks either entering high-growth markets that already have market leaders, or operating as one of many small competitors in emerging industries. A question mark generally needs a lot of funds; it must keep adding plant, equipment, and personnel to keep up with a fast-growing industry that it wants to overtake or become the leader. The term *question mark* is well-chosen, because the organization has to think hard about whether to keep investing funds in the business or to get out.

2. *Stars:* Question-mark businesses that have become successful. A star is a market leader in a high-growth market, but it does not necessarily provide much cash. The organization has to spend a great deal of money keeping up with the market's rate of growth and fighting off competitors' attacks. Stars often consume cash rather than generating it. Even so, they are usually profitable in time.

3. *Cash cows:* Businesses in markets with low annual growth that have large market shares. A cash cow produces a lot of cash for the organization. The organization does not have to finance a great deal of expansion because the market's growth rate is low. Since the business is a market leader, it enjoys economies of scale and higher profit margins. The organization milks its cash-cow businesses to pay its bills and support other growing businesses.

4. *Dogs:* Businesses with weak market shares in low-growth markets. They typically generate low profits or losses, although they may bring in some cash. Such businesses frequently consume more management time than they are worth and merit elimination. However, an organization may have good reasons to hold onto a dog, such as an expected turnaround in the market growth rate or a new chance at market leadership.[15]

Strategic Alternatives   After plotting each of its businesses on the growth–share matrix, an organization's next step is to evaluate whether the portfolio is healthy and well-balanced. A balanced portfolio has a number of stars and cash cows, and not too many question marks or dogs. This balance is important because the organization needs cash, not only to maintain existing businesses, but also to develop new businesses. Depending on the position of each business, the firm can formulate one of four basic strategic goals for it:

1. *Build market share:* This goal is appropriate for question marks that must increase their shares in order to become stars. Some businesses may have to forgo short-term profits to gain market share and future, long-term profits.
2. *Hold market share:* This goal is appropriate for cash cows with strong share positions. The cash generated by mature cash cows provides critical support for other businesses and financing innovations. However, the cost of building share for cash cows is likely to be too high to be profitable.
3. *Harvest:* Harvesting involves milking as much short-term cash from a business as possible, even allowing market share to decline if necessary. Weak cash cows that do not appear to have promising futures are candidates for harvesting, as are some question marks and dogs.
4. *Divest:* Divesting involves selling or liquidating a business to invest the resources devoted to it more profitably in other businesses. Divesting is appropriate for those dogs and question marks that are not worth investments to improve their positions.

Evaluation of the Growth–Share Matrix   As an innovative approach to investigating relationships among an organization's businesses, the growth–share matrix helped stimulate interest in managing a diversified portfolio. Perhaps its main contribution came from encouraging managers to view the formulation of corporate strategy in terms of joint relationships among businesses and to take long-range views. The growth–share matrix acknowledges that businesses in different stages have different cash requirements and make different contributions to achieving organizational objectives. The growth–share matrix also provides a simple and appealing visual overview of an organization's business portfolio.

However, a variety of problems that arise with this approach suggest that it must be used cautiously in strategy formulation. Among these problems:

- The growth–share matrix focuses on balancing cash flows, whereas organizations are more likely to be interested in the returns on investment that various businesses yield.
- It is not always clear what share of what market is relevant in the analysis. For example, the analysis of Cadillac's market share would give much different results if it were determined on the basis of the overall car market rather than just the market for luxury cars.
- The growth–share matrix assumes a strong relationship between market share and return on investment. In fact, it is commonly believed that a 10 percent difference in market share is accompanied by a 5 percent difference in return on investment. However, other research has found a much weaker relationship; a 10 percent change in market share is associated with only a 1 percent change in return on investment.[16]
- Many other factors besides market share and growth rate have critical effects on strategy formulation. For example, industry structure and the core

FIGURE 4.4
GE's Multifactor
Portfolio Matrix

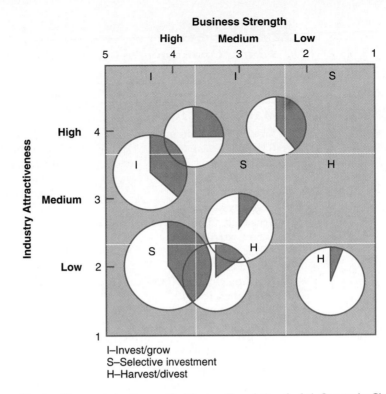

I–Invest/grow
S–Selective investment
H–Harvest/divest

competencies of the firm and its competitors are important influences that this method does not adequately consider.

- The growth–share matrix does not directly compare investment opportunities in different businesses. For example, it is not clear how to compare two question marks to decide which should be developed into a star and which should be allowed to decline.

- The approach offers only general strategy guidance without specifying how to implement such strategies.

Thus, although the growth–share matrix may provide a useful overview of a business portfolio, and it may point out some important relationships among an organization's businesses, it does not provide a complete framework for corporate strategy formulation. Several other portfolio models have been developed that overcome some of the problems inherent in the growth–share matrix. We will discuss one of them: General Electric's **multifactor portfolio matrix.**

GE's Multifactor Portfolio Matrix

This approach has a variety of names, including the *nine-cell GE matrix, GE's nine-cell business portfolio matrix,* and the *industry attractiveness–business position matrix.* It was developed at General Electric with the help of McKinsey and Company, a consulting firm. The basic matrix is shown in Figure 4.4.[17] Each circle represents an industry, and the shaded portion represents the organization's market share in that industry.

TABLE 4.7

Factors Contributing to Industry Attractiveness and Business Strength

Industry Attractiveness	Business Strength
MARKET FACTORS	
Size (dollars, units or both)	Your share (in equivalent terms)
Size of key segments	Your share of key segments
Growth rate per year:	Your annual growth rate:
Total	Total
Segments	Segments
Diversity of market	Diversity of your participation
Sensitivity to price, service features, and external factors	Your influence on the market
Cyclicality	Lags or leads in your sales
Seasonality	
Bargaining power of upstream suppliers	Bargaining power of your suppliers
Bargaining power of downstream suppliers	Bargaining power of your customers
COMPETITION	
Types of competitors	Where you fit, how you compare
Degree of concentration	in terms of products, marketing
Changes in type and mix	capability, service, production
	strength, financial strength,
	management
Entries and exits	Segments you have entered or left

SOURCE: Derek F. Abell and John S. Hammond, STRATEGIC MARKET PLANNING: Problems & Analytical Approaches, © 1979, p. 214. Reprinted by permission of Prentice-Hall, Englewood Cliffs, New Jersey.

Each of an organization's businesses is plotted in the matrix on two dimensions, industry attractiveness and business strength. Each of these two major dimensions represents a composite of a variety of factors. The two dimensions make good sense for strategy formulation, because a successful business typically operates in an attractive industry where it has the particular business strengths required to succeed. Both strengths are needed to produce outstanding performance through sustainable advantage.

To use this matrix, an organization must identify the factors that are most critical to industry attractiveness and business strength. Table 4.7 lists some of the factors that analysts commonly use to locate businesses on these dimensions.

The next step in developing this matrix is to weight each variable on the basis of its perceived importance relative to the other factors. (The weights must total 1.0.) Managers must then indicate, on a scale of 1 to 5, how low or high their business scores on that factor. Table 4.8 presents this analysis for one business. These calculations rate the business at 3.45 in industry attractiveness

---

TABLE 4.7

Continued

Changes in share	Your relative share change
Substitution by new technology	Your vulnerability to new technology
Degrees and types of integration	Your own level of integration

FINANCIAL AND ECONOMIC FACTORS

Contribution margins	Your margins
Leveraging factors, such as economies of scale and experience	Your scale and experience
Barriers to your entry or exit (both financial and nonfinancial)	Barriers to your entry or exit (both financial and nonfinancial)
Capacity utilization	Your capacity utilization

TECHNOLOGICAL FACTORS

Maturity and volatility	Your ability to cope with change
Complexity	Depths of your skills
Differentiation	Types of your technological skills
Patents and copyrights	Your patent protection
Manufacturing process technology required	Your manufacturing technology

SOCIOPOLITICAL FACTORS IN YOUR ENVIRONMENT

Social attitudes and trends	Your company's responsiveness and flexibility
Laws and government agency regulations	Your company's ability to cope
Influence with pressure groups and government representatives	Your company's aggressiveness
Human factors, such as unionization and community acceptance	Your company's relationships

---

and 4.30 in business strength. This places the business close to the high–high cell of the matrix.

Strategic Alternatives   Depending on where a business plots on the matrix, the organization can formulate three basic strategies: invest/grow, invest selectively, and harvest/divest. Businesses that fall in the cells that form a diagonal from lower left to upper right are medium-strength businesses that merit only selective investment. Businesses in the cells above and to the left of this diagonal are the strongest; they deserve invest/grow strategies. Businesses in the cells below and to the right of the diagonal are weak overall; these are serious candidates for harvest/divest strategies.

Evaluation of the Multifactor Portfolio Matrix   This approach has advantages over the growth–share matrix. First, it provides an explicit mechanism for matching internal strengths and weaknesses with external opportunities and threats, the fundamental task of strategic management. Second, as

TABLE 4.8

Illustration of Industry Attractiveness and Business Strength Computations

INDUSTRY ATTRACTIVENESS	Weight	Rating (1–5)	Value
Overall market size	0.20	4.00	0.80
Annual market growth rate	0.20	5.00	1.00
Historical profit margin	0.15	4.00	0.60
Competitive intensity	0.15	2.00	0.30
Technological requirements	0.15	3.00	0.45
Inflationary vulnerability	0.05	3.00	0.15
Energy requirements	0.05	2.00	0.10
Environmental impact	0.05	1.00	0.05
Social/political/legal	Must be acceptable		
	1.00		3.45

BUSINESS STRENGTH			
Market share	0.10	4.00	0.40
Share growth	0.15	4.00	0.60
Product quality	0.10	4.00	0.40
Brand reputation	0.10	5.00	0.50
Distribution network	0.05	4.00	0.20
Promotional effectiveness	0.05	5.00	0.25
Productive capacity	0.05	3.00	0.15
Productive efficiency	0.05	2.00	0.10
Unit costs	0.15	3.00	0.45
Material supplies	0.05	5.00	0.25
R&D performance	0.10	4.00	0.80
Managerial personnel	0.05	4.00	0.20
	1.00		4.30

SOURCE: Philip Kotler, MARKETING MANAGEMENT: Analysis, Planning, Implementation, and Control, 7e, © 1991, p. 45. Reprinted by permission of Prentice-Hall, Englewood Cliffs, New Jersey. Slightly modified from La Rue T. Hormer, *Strategic Management* (Englewood Cliffs, N.J.: Prentice-Hall, Inc., 1982), p. 310.

we have noted, the two dimensions of industry attractiveness and business strength are excellent criteria for rating potential business success.

However, the multifactor portfolio matrix also suffers from some of the same limitations as the growth–share matrix. For example, it does not solve the problem of determining the appropriate market, and it does not offer anything more than general strategy recommendations. In addition, the measures are subjective and can be very ambiguous, particularly when one is considering different businesses.[18]

In general, portfolio models provide graphical frameworks for analyzing relationships among the businesses of large, diversified organizations, and they can yield useful strategy recommendations. However, no model yet devised provides a universally accepted approach to dealing with these issues. Portfolio models should never be applied mechanically, and any conclusions they suggest must be carefully considered in light of sound managerial judgment and the firm's vision and goals, which no model can replace.

SUMMARY

Strategy formulation cannot begin at any level until the managers responsible for shaping strategy understand the context in which their strategies will unfold. Thus, they rely on some form of SWOT analysis to supply the information they need from the internal and external environments, filtered through the goals and values of vision and mission statements.

Strategy is formulated at three distinct levels: the business, functional, and corporate levels. Devised by top management, strategies are plans designed to ensure that the firm achieves its overall objectives.

We approached the formulation of strategy at the business, business-unit, or divisional level from the perspective of Michael Porter's analysis of five competitive forces: the threat of new entrants, the bargaining power of suppliers, the bargaining power of buyers, the threat of substitute products, and rivalry among competitors. We discussed the conditions under which the strategies of overall cost leadership, differentiation, and focus are appropriate and the risks associated with each. In addition we used Porter's value chain analysis to consider internal core competencies and their importance in achieving competitive advantage. Strategies that functional units adopt and strategies that link units in cross-functional ways ideally must support overall firm strategy. We touched on such issues as innovation versus imitation in the research and development function, controlling costs and boosting efficiency in the operations function, the planning and controlling tasks of financial specialists, the marketing function's responsibility for selecting markets and developing effective marketing mixes, and the need for the human resource function to develop and manage employees effectively.

We explored the roots of expansion from single-business to multibusiness organizations, and we examined two business portfolio models created to help top managers achieve sustainable synergy. The growth–share matrix enables managers to classify every business as a question mark, a star, a cash cow, or a dog; to ascertain whether the firm's roster of businesses is well-balanced among the four; and to determine what strategy is appropriate for each. The multifactor portfolio matrix attempts to quantify the strength of a business and the attractiveness of its industry. The placement of businesses in the matrix based on these two numbers is taken as an indication of the best strategy choice: investing aggressively, investing selectively, or refraining from further investment. Both models offer useful information in an interesting graphical format, but it is important to remember that they cannot generate goals or specific actions, and that they are not substitutes for sound managerial judgment and experience.

KEY TERMS

business-level strategy, p. 78
barriers to entry, p. 78
power of suppliers, p. 80
power of buyers, p. 80
substitution threats, p. 80
rivalry among competitors, p. 80
overall cost leadership strategy, p. 81
differentiation strategy, p. 82
focus strategy, p. 83

core competency, p. 90
value chain analysis, p. 90
primary activity, p. 90
support activity, p. 90
functional-level strategy, p. 92
corporate-level strategy, p. 96
growth–share matrix, p. 98
multifactor portfolio matrix, p. 101

CHECK✓LIST ## Analyzing Strategy Formulation in Situations and Cases

__ 1. Is strategy formulation the major focus of this situation or case?

__ 2. What general strategy is the organization following, and would other strategies be more likely to achieve organizational objectives?

__ 3. What business strategies does the situation or case involve?

__ 4. Would an analysis of the five competitive forces or value chain help managers formulate a more effective business strategy?

__ 5. What functional strategies are at issue in the situation or case?

__ 6. Is this a diversified corporation for which a business portfolio analysis would be useful?

__ 7. Is enough information available for management to develop and analyze a growth–share matrix or a multifactor portfolio matrix?

Additional Readings

Adler, Paul S., D. William McDonald, and Fred MacDonald. "Strategic Management of Technical Functions." *Sloan Management Review,* Winter 1992, p. 19.

Dixit, Avinash, and Barry Nalebuff. *Thinking Strategically: The Competitive Edge in Business, Politics, and Everyday Life.* New York: W. W. Norton, 1991.

Hamel, Gary, and C. K. Prahalad. "Strategy as Stretch and Leverage." *Harvard Business Review,* March/April 1993, p. 75.

Hart, Stuart. "An Integrative Framework for Strategy-Making Processes." *The Academy of Management Review,* April 1992, p. 327.

MacMillan, Ian C., and Patricia E. Jones. *Strategy Formulation: Power and Politics.* St. Paul, Minn.: West Publishing, 1986.

Normann, Richard, and Rafael Ramirez. "From Value Chain to Value Constellation: Designing Interactive Strategy." *Harvard Business Review,* July/August 1993, p. 65.

Peteraf, Margaret. "The Cornerstones of Competitive Advantage: A Resource-Based View," *Strategic Management Journal* 14 (1993), pp. 179–191.

Schofield, Malcom, and David Arnold. "Strategies for Mature Businesses." *Long Range Planning* 21/5, no. 3 (October 1988), pp. 69–76.

Stalk, George, Philip Evans, and Lawrence Shulman. "Competing on Capabilities: The New Rules of Corporate Strategy." *Harvard Business Review,* March/April 1992, p. 57.

Williams, Jeffrey. "How Sustainable Is Your Competitive Advantage?" *California Management Review,* Spring 1992, pp. 29–51.

C A S E

FORMULATING STRATEGY FOR THE SWATCH-MOBILE

Nicolas Hayek says that a chief executive has to believe in Santa Claus. The chairman of Swatch manufacturer SMH Swiss Corp. has persuaded others, most notably automobile executives, to believe along with him. He, after all, heads a company whose product—the low-cost, Swatch timepiece with the plastic band—has sold more than 100 million units since its 1983 debut, in the process becoming a collector's item. Now, although sales of Swatch's other, larger-scale products—clothing, telephones, and sunglasses—haven't taken off, Hayek and a partner, Daimler-Benz AG's Mercedes-Benz unit, are readying the prototype of the Swatchmobile.

Observers won't be able to test-drive the car until the 1996 Olympics; it won't be available for months afterward. But the interval between the announcement and the introduction of the Swatchmobile is part of Hayek's plan to make the car known to the world. To Hayek, a car is an "emotional consumer item, like a watch. I was born to sell emotional consumer products."

The Swatchmobile, a two-seater expected to come in snappy colors, will combine what Hayek calls the three most important features of the watch: affordability, durability, and stylishness. He says the car will cost well under $10,000 and measure less than 10 feet long. Not only will it perform well, says Hayek, the Swatchmobile "will have the crash security of a Mercedes."

Some question whether the marriage of Swatch and Mercedes can work. A Swatch partnership with Volkswagen AG fell apart early last year; VW officials determined that the project wouldn't turn a sufficient profit. Hayek, however, says other top auto-industry executives came begging. Confident as he is with his product, Hayek needs Mercedes for its distribution system, if not its manufacturing facilities. (Britain's Board of Trade has already asked Hayek to consider basing production there.)

Mercedes, already planning to introduce a series of small "A-class" luxury cars in 1997, thought the collaboration with Swatch a daring bid to broaden its presence in the mass market. It hasn't disclosed many details of the partnership, including how many Swatchmobiles it would aim to produce, what price it would charge, what quality standards it would set, how much it would invest, or how closely it would tie the new car to its prestigious Mercedes name.

Hayek is not reluctant to boast that the project will aim to sell 100,000 cars in the first year, possibly 1996 or 1997, and up to 1 million annually in the fifth year. The car will succeed on low price and a with-it image, he asserts.

Others take issue with Hayek's assessment. Even one of the company's own engineers says those features alone won't do it. "There are too many small cars on the market already," says Daniel Ryhiner. He maintains that the Swatchmobile's only unique selling point will be its environmental friendliness. When operating on electricity, it will emit virtually no pollutants, and when operating on gas, it will go great distances on one gallon, thanks to an engine that weighs one-tenth as much as any existing engine with equal power. Yet he concedes that even that selling point may falter. Solar products and other "green" ideas are slow starters in the marketplace, giving Hayek "a masterful public relations and marketing challenge."

DISCUSSION QUESTIONS

1. Analyze the Swatchmobile's industry using Porter's five forces model.
2. Based on your analysis, what strategy would you recommend to Mercedes and Swatch for their new product? How would you (a) produce, (b) position, and (c) price the product?
3. Based on your analysis, what do you see as the biggest threats to the strategy you proposed above? From which competitors would you expect serious retaliation in the market?

4. From the perspectives of each of the partners in the venture, what sort of diversification move does this represent? What are the risks to Mercedes and to Swatch? Explain.

SOURCE: Audrey Choi and Margaret Studer, "Daimler-Benz's Mercedes Unit to Build a Car with Maker of Swatch Watches," *The Wall Street Journal,* February 23, 1994, p. A14; and Kevin Helliker, "Can Wristwatch Whiz Switch Swatch Cachet to an Automobile?," *The Wall Street Journal,* March 4, 1994, pp. A1–A5.

Notes

1. Michael Porter, *Competitive Advantage* (New York: Free Press, 1985), p. 33.
2. Ibid.
3. Avinash Dixit and Barry Nalebuff, *Thinking Strategically* (New York: W. W. Norton, 1991).
4. Shaker Zahra and Sherry Chaples, "Blind Spots in Competitive Analysis," *Academy of Management Executive,* May 1993, p. 7; see also, E. Zajac and M. Bazerman, "Blind Spots in Industry and Competitor Analysis," *Academy of Management Review* 16, no. 1 (1991), p. 37.
5. Pankaj Ghemawat, "Sustainable Advantage," *Harvard Business Review,* September/October 1986, p. 53.
6. Amar Bhide, "Hustle as Strategy," *Harvard Business Review,* September/October 1986, p. 59; see also Joseph Bower and Thomas Hout, "Fast-Cycle Capability for Competitive Power," *Harvard Business Review,* November/December 1988, p. 110.
7. Bower and Hout, "Fast-Cycle Capability," p. 111.
8. Jeffrey Williams, "How Sustainable Is Your Competitive Advantage?" *California Management Review,* Spring 1992, p. 29.
9. C. K. Prahalad and Gary Hamel, "The Core Competence of the Corporation," *Harvard Business Review,* May/June 1990, p. 82.
10. Porter, *Competitive Advantage,* p. 36.
11. *Fortune,* February 8, 1993; *Business Week,* March 3, 1986.
12. C. Merle Crawford, *New Product Management,* 2d ed. (Homewood, Ill.: Richard D. Irwin, 1987), p. 21.
13. For a complete discussion of human resource management and strategy, see Herbert G. Henneman III, Donald P. Schwab, Hohn A. Fossum, and Lee Dyer, *Personnel/Human Resource Management,* 4th ed. (Homewood, Ill.: Richard D. Irwin, 1989). See also Cynthia A. Lengnick-Hall and Mark L. Lengnick-Hall, "Strategic Human Resources Management: A Review of the Literature and Proposed Typology," *Academy of Management Review* 13, no. 3 (1988), pp. 454–470.
14. See Ted Kumpe and Piet T. Bolwijn, "Manufacturing: The New Case for Vertical Integration," *Harvard Business Review,* March/April 1988, pp. 75–81.
15. These descriptions are based on a discussion in Philip Kotler, *Marketing Management: Analysis, Planning, and Control,* 6th ed. (Englewood Cliffs, N.J.: Prentice-Hall, 1988), pp. 41–42.
16. See Robert Jacobson and David A. Aaker, "Is Market Share All That It's Cracked Up to Be?" *Journal of Marketing,* Fall 1985, pp. 11–22.
17. This discussion is based on Kotler, *Marketing Management,* pp. 43–46.
18. David A. Aaker, *Developing Business Strategies* (New York: John Wiley & Sons, 1984), p. 237.

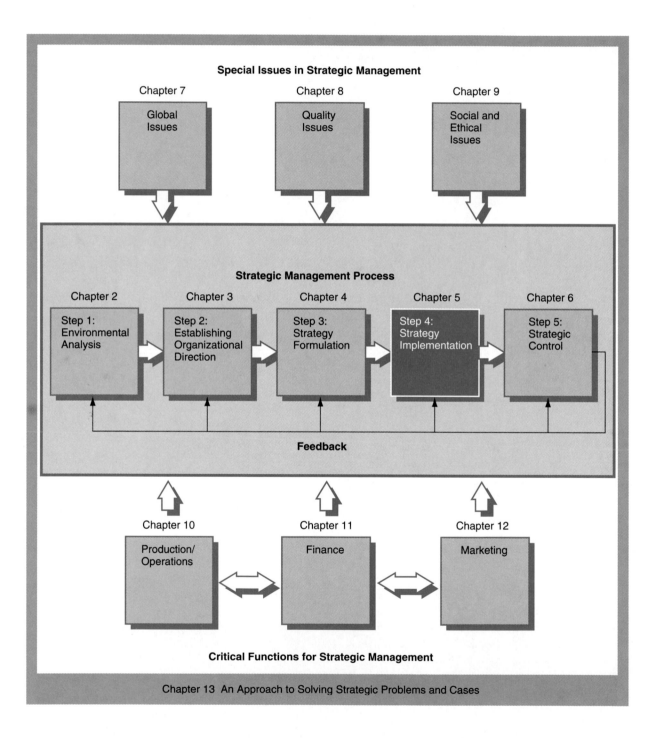

Special Issues in Strategic Management

Chapter 7

Global Issues

Chapter 8

Quality Issues

Chapter 9

Social and Ethical Issues

Strategic Management Process

Chapter 2

Step 1: Environmental Analysis

Chapter 3

Step 2: Establishing Organizational Direction

Chapter 4

Step 3: Strategy Formulation

Chapter 5

Step 4: Strategy Implementation

Chapter 6

Step 5: Strategic Control

Feedback

Chapter 10

Production/ Operations

Chapter 11

Finance

Chapter 12

Marketing

Critical Functions for Strategic Management

Chapter 13 An Approach to Solving Strategic Problems and Cases

CHAPTER

5

Strategy Implementation

In the previous chapter, we discussed a number of important issues that arise as managers formulate strategies. In this chapter, we focus on implementing those strategies—putting them into action. The success of an organization depends on how effectively it implements strategies. In fact, the first attribute listed by Thomas Peters and Robert Waterman as distinctive of excellent, innovative companies is related to the corporate view of implementation. They suggest that excellent companies have a bias for action, for getting on with the job:

> Even though these companies may be analytical in their approach to decision making, they are not paralyzed by that fact (as so many others seem to be). In many of these companies the standard operating procedure is "Do it, fix it, try it." . . . Moreover, the companies are experimenters supreme. Instead of allowing 250 engineers and marketers to work on a new product in isolation for 15 months, they form bands of 5 to 25 and test ideas out on a customer, often with inexpensive prototypes, within a matter of weeks. What is striking is the host of practical devices the excellent companies employ to maintain corporate fleetness of foot and counter the stultification that almost inevitably comes with size.[1]

As this quote suggests, effective managers often work back and forth between strategy formulation and strategy implementation. Many successful organizations do not plan every aspect of a strategy in detail and then proceed to implement it according to the predefined schedule. Rather, strategies are often partially formulated, implemented, reformulated, and extended to rapidly capitalize on strategic opportunities. Henry Mintzberg refers to this process as *crafting* a strategy: "Formulation and implementation merge into a fluid process of learning through which creative strategies evolve."[2] Thus, although this chapter focuses on implementation, remember that formulation and implementation influence each other and often evolve together.

Also, keep in mind that the managerial skills required to formulate a strategy differ significantly from those needed to implement that strategy. Formulation calls on the best analytical and technical skills that an executive or executive team can muster, while implementation draws more heavily on leadership and administrative skills of a person or team.

What forces can a top manager deploy to assist in strategy implementation? In our view, three key building blocks will, if well managed, yield effective strategy implementation—managing change, managing structure, and managing culture.

This stage of the strategic management process offers the greatest potential for wide-ranging, integrative, cross-functional methods, since strategy implementation, or acting on a strategy, involves every function and person in the organization. The top management team clearly is involved since it must assess and manage the three interrelated core elements—change, structure, and culture. Top managers depend on other managers as well as the employees of the firm, however, to translate a strategy—a plan—into a living reality. Today's business context places these managers and employees more frequently in cross-functional teams to more effectively implement strategies. Rubbermaid, Black & Decker, Ford, 3M, Microsoft, Lotus Development, General Mills, and many other U.S. firms use cross-functional teams, sometimes with self-management responsibility, to carry out implementation activities ranging from product design and development to production to sales to customer service. Firms whose strategies depend heavily on getting new products designed and manufactured efficiently and marketed quickly have achieved excellent results from cross-functional teams made up of experts from R&D, production, marketing, and finance.

We propose a five-stage model of the strategy implementation process in Figure 5.1, which is built around the three building blocks identified above. It is useful, we find, to dissect this crucial process into discrete steps of (1) determining how much the organization will have to change in order to implement the strategy under consideration and managing the change process, (2) managing the formal and informal structures of the organization, (3) managing the culture of the organization, (4) selecting an appropriate scheme to implement the strategy, and (5) evaluating implementation skills.

FIGURE 5.1
Strategic Implementation Tasks

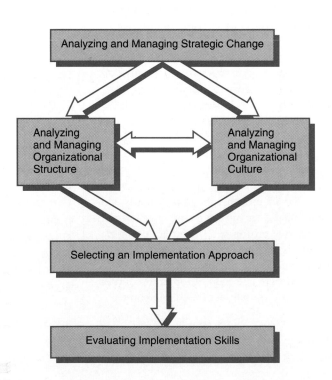

ANALYZING STRATEGIC CHANGE

A useful first step in implementing a strategy is to determine clearly how much the organization will have to change in order to succeed in the implementation. Some strategies require only minimal changes in the way a firm currently conducts its business; others require sweeping changes in its operations. For example, implementing a new pricing strategy may affect only a few people within the organization and cause very little change in day-to-day operations. However, it may require a radical change to replace a traditional organization structure based on functional boundaries with a more flexible, nontraditional structure of cross-functional teams intended to improve the firm's design-for-manufacture capabilities and its time to market.

Strategic change can be viewed as a continuum running from no variation in strategy to a complete change in an organization's mission. For analysis, it is useful to divide strategic change into the five discrete stages shown in Table 5.1. By determining the level of strategic change, managers can more accurately anticipate problems likely to arise in implementing the strategy. Typically, implementation becomes more complex with the move from a stable strategy to organizational redirection, because the number of organizational units, people, and tasks involved increases greatly. In addition, the problems involved in organizational redirection are more likely to be unique or unfamiliar. The five levels of strategic change and the implications of each for strategy implementation are discussed in the sections that follow.

Stable Strategy

A **stable strategy** essentially repeats the strategy from the previous planning period. Because this choice involves no new skills or unfamiliar tasks, successful implementation is largely a matter of monitoring activities to ensure that they are performed on schedule. At this level, experience curve effects (i.e., learning from previous experience) can help to make implementation more cost-effective and efficient.

Routine Strategy Change

A **routine strategy change** makes normal, predicted adjustments in the methods by which the firm seeks to attract customers. Firms may alter their advertising appeals, update packaging, use different pricing tactics, and change

TABLE 5.1

Levels of Strategic Change

	Industry	Organization	Products	Market Appeal
Stable strategy	same	same	same	same
Routine strategy change	same	same	same	new
Limited strategy change	same	same	new	new
Radical strategy change	same	new	new	new
Organizational redirection	new	new	new	new

distributors or distribution methods in the normal course of operations. Campbell Soup, for example, changes its radio ads with the weather. When a storm is forecasted, the commercials encourage consumers to stock up on soup before the weather worsens; after the storm has hit, the message encourages consumers to stay home and enjoy good, hot soup. Implementing such strategies requires managers to schedule and coordinate activities with ad agencies and intermediaries. In some cases, such as when the firm offers a significant price deal to intermediaries or consumers, managers must also coordinate production to ensure that enough inventory is available to handle increased demand.

An important type of routine strategy change involves positioning or repositioning a product in the minds of consumers. A classic example of this involved 7 Up, which for many years had difficulty convincing consumers that it was a soft drink and not just a mixer. By promoting 7 Up as the Uncola, the company positioned it as both a soft drink that could be consumed in the same situations as colas and an alternative to colas. This strategy proved successful, but it did not require a major change for effective implementation.

Limited Strategy Change

A **limited strategy change** involves offering new products to new markets within the same general product class. Managers must handle many variations at this level of strategic change, because products can be new in a variety of ways. For example, Extra-Strength Tylenol was a new product formulation that did not require radically different methods of production or marketing, so implementing a strategy to sell this product required no major change in Johnson & Johnson's operations. On the other hand, the creation, production, and marketing of products such as stereos, televisions, home computers, videocassette recorders, and video cameras for new or evolving markets often involve more complex implementation problems.

Radical Strategy Change

A **radical strategy change** involves a major shift for the firm. This type of change is commonly necessary to complete mergers and acquisitions between firms in the same basic industry. For example, Nestlé acquired Carnation (both of which were in the food industry), and Procter & Gamble acquired Richardson-Vicks (both in consumer products). Such acquisitions can create particularly complex problems in integrating the firms. The acquiring firm not only obtains new products and markets, but also confronts legal problems, the complexities of developing a new organizational structure, and (quite often) the need to reconcile conflicts between organizational cultures.

Radical corporate strategy change can be driven by new approaches to acquisitions and sales of businesses or business units. For example, when John F. Welch, Jr., became chairman of General Electric, the company was regarded as a "GNP company" whose growth and prosperity could never outpace those of the overall economy. Welch set out to create a company that could outpace the economy and prosper even in difficult economic times. He stripped entire levels from the corporate hierarchy and shifted resources from manufacturing businesses to fast-growing service and high-technology units. He bought NBC and automated production facilities, eliminating 100,000 employees, more than one-fourth of the work force. In his first five years as chairman, he sold 190 subsidiaries worth nearly $6 billion and spent $10 billion on 70 acquisitions. Clearly, this is a strategy of radical change, which may eventually develop into a total organizational redirection.[3]

Organizational Redirection

One form of **organizational redirection** involves mergers and acquisitions of firms in different industries. The degree of strategic change depends on how much the industries differ and on how centralized management of the new firm will be. For example, when Philip Morris, a manufacturer of cigarettes and beverages, acquired General Foods, a food products manufacturer, the redirection essentially created a single, more diversified organization operating in two similar industries. When General Motors acquired Electronic Data Systems (EDS), however, the implementation was complicated by considerable differences between the industries and between the two companies' views of appropriate business conduct. EDS personnel codes forbade employees from drinking alcohol at lunchtime or wearing tasseled shoes. GM employees who transferred to EDS were deeply dissatisfied with such rules, and over 600 of them resigned. Then Chairman Roger B. Smith had a near revolt on his hands as he attempted to reconcile the two different corporate cultures.[4]

Another form of organizational redirection occurs when a firm leaves one industry and enters a new one. For example, when one small brewery could no longer compete in the beer industry, it redirected its efforts to the trucking and packaging industries. Similarly, American Can Company redirected its business from packaging to financial services during the mid-1980s, as noted in Chapter 4.[5] This type of organizational redirection is the most complex strategy to implement. It involves changes in the firm's mission and may require development of an entirely new set of skills and technologies.

Managing Strategic Change

These broad categories can give a manager a sense of the magnitude of a newly implemented change, but they do not shed much light on how to actually manage a strategic change effort. While a fully developed discussion of managing change is outside the boundaries of this text, we do wish to present one general framework and to point the interested reader toward additional resources.

James Brian Quinn provides an outline of the steps that effective leaders often use to manage strategic change.[6] Table 5.2 shows three major sequential steps, along with the specific activities in each. Quinn's approach emphasizes the essential analytical and political roles of the executive in managing the strategic change effort and returns us to the issue of sensemaking and interpretation introduced in Chapter 2. Besides the analytical and technical skills to make sense of their environments, effective top managers also need political and leadership skills to sell those interpretations to others and to orchestrate changes that they imply.[7]

ANALYZING AND MANAGING ORGANIZATIONAL STRUCTURE

Managers must contend with two basic kinds of organizational structures. The **formal organizational structure** represents the relationships between people and functions as designed by management and conveyed in the organization

TABLE 5.2

Managing Strategic Change

INITIATING STRATEGIC CHANGE

- Build networks to sense needs
- Improve and lead the formal information system
- Amplify understanding
- Build awareness
- Change symbols
- Legitimize new viewpoints
- Develop partial solutions
- Broaden support

MOVE FROM CONCEPT TO STRATEGY

- Overcome opposition to change by finding zones of indifference and no-lose situations
- Building comfort levels; change perceived risks
- Structure flexibility
- Test trial concepts

SOLIDIFY COMMITMENT

- Create key pockets of commitment
- Keep political exposure low
- Eliminate options
- Crystallize focus and consensus; manage coalitions
- Formalize commitment; empower champions
- Design continuous strategic change process

chart. The **informal organizational structure** represents the web of social relationships based on friendships or interests shared among various members of an organization. The informal organizational structure reveals itself in the patterns of communication commonly called the *grapevine*.

When implementing a strategy, managers must consider both the formal and the informal organizational structures for three reasons. First, the existing organizational structure may or may not adequately support, or even impede, successful implementation. If the organization has so many levels of management that a strategy cannot be implemented effectively or changed rapidly to accommodate changing conditions, then successful implementation may become difficult. In some cases, effective implementation may require changes to the formal organizational structure. For example, GE shed several echelons of organizational structure under Welch and it regrouped its 15 businesses into three areas to make the company more cost-effective and responsive to change.

Second, implementation requires assigning tasks to specific management levels and personnel within the organization. A radical strategy change or organizational redirection is typically spearheaded by the chief executive officer, whereas routine strategy changes may be directed by middle management. Third, the informal organization can become a valuable tool to facilitate successful implementation. For example, if several regional managers commonly consult with each other about implementation issues, this informal network can be used to encourage rapid execution of strategic actions.

The formal organizational structure commonly displays characteristics of one of six types: the simple, functional, divisional, strategic business unit (SBU), matrix, and network structures. Schematic diagrams of these structures appear in Figure 5.2.

Simple Organizational Structure

A **simple organizational structure** has only two levels, the owner-manager and the employees. Small firms that produce only one good or service, or only a few related ones, usually exhibit this structure. A major advantage of this structure is that it allows rapid, flexible implementation of strategies and strategic changes. This advantage is a primary source of competitive advantage that can sometimes allow small firms to compete effectively with industry giants. Those independently owned and operated specialty firms we see in our communities—frozen yogurt shops, sporting goods stores—are typically structured this way, with owner and employees performing a wide range

FIGURE 5.2   Six Types of Organizational Structures

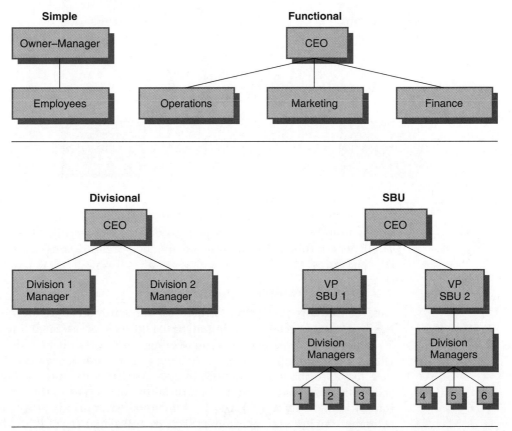

Continued

FIGURE 5.2   Continued

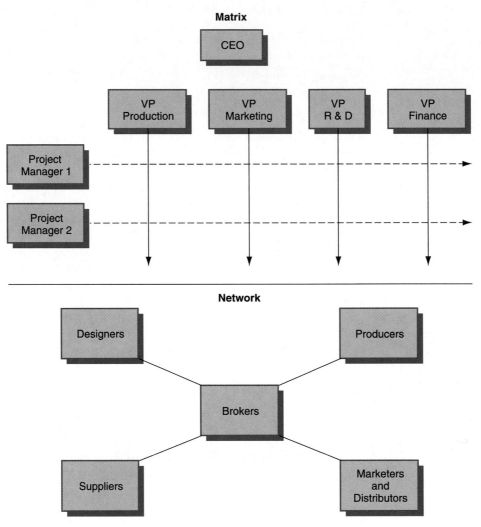

of functions. However, because success depends so heavily on the skills of a single person (the owner-manager) many such organizations do not survive in the long run.

Functional Organizational Structure

As organizations grow, their structures frequently need to be changed to reflect greater specialization in functional business areas. Such line functions as production and operations, marketing, and research and development (R&D) may be organized into departments. A **functional organizational structure** may also include a number of staff departments, such as finance and accounting or personnel and administration, that report to the CEO. Specialization is the chief advantage of a functional structure; it promotes the development of greater expertise in each area. Wal-Mart is a highly visible contemporary example of the enduring power of the functional organizational

COMPANY EXAMPLE

IBM Reorganizes Its Sales Force

Attempting to sharpen its customer focus and remain competitive, International Business Machines Corp. has undertaken the biggest reorganization of its worldwide sales and marketing force in decades. IBM intends to eliminate one or more layers of management to help transform its account executives from order-takers to business advisers.

The change reorganizes IBM's primary sales staff by industry rather than geography. Chairman Louis Gerstner had hoped to see full implementation of a less sweeping plan established by his predecessor, but he apparently decided to accelerate the effort and impose major change. The reorganization is a step that industry experts and some customers have been urging for years.

The shift to focus on industries rather than geography brings fundamental change to a company with a historic policy of promoting only from within—especially in the sales force. In setting up 14 industry areas, including banking, retail, travel, and insurance, and granting broad powers to their chiefs, IBM will fill half of the top U.S. posts with recent hires from the consulting industry.

Today, most IBM account executives report up through an intricate network of sales branches, overseen by trading area managers, who in turn report to top managers in charge of broad regions, such as New England. The new structure has account teams that bypass branch managers and report directly to the industry group heads. The move could erode the power of IBM's geographically based sales chiefs, who previously held sway over thousands of careers, and could lead to turf wars.

The biggest impact could occur overseas, where Gerstner's team has had trouble controlling some of IBM's long-autonomous executives. These country heads could see their power diminished as the loyalties of sales executives shift to industry groups within the region.

SOURCE: Bart Ziegler, "IBM Plans to Revamp Sales Structure to Focus on Industries, Not Geography," *The Wall Street Journal*, May 6, 1994, p. A3.

structure.[8] Wal-Mart's effective profit and growth performance is supported by functional excellence in its logistics, inventory control, and distribution systems. However, functional structures may suffer from coordination problems among departments that may impede effective operations, especially when a firm's goods or services become more diverse.

Divisional Organizational Structure

As a firm acquires or develops new products in different industries and markets, it may have to adopt a **divisional organizational structure.** Each division may operate autonomously under the direction of a division manager, who reports directly to the CEO. Divisions may be based on product lines (automotive components, aircraft), markets (consumers, organizational buyers), geographic areas (north, south, international), or channels of distribution (retail stores, catalog sales). Managers in each division must handle not only their own line and staff functions, but they must also formulate and implement strategies on their own with the approval of the CEO. The overall organization has staff positions (such as vice presidents of administration and operations) to assist in coordinating activities and allocating resources. The divisional organizational structure helps large companies to remain close to their markets and responsive in their strategies, but conflict can result as the divisions compete for resources. The Company Example tells of IBM's effort to organize its sales operations along industry or customer lines rather than geographic lines. This example explores the internal political problems that corporate reorganizations often face.

Strategic Business Unit Organizational Structure

When a divisional structure becomes unwieldy, giving the CEO too many divisions to manage effectively, the organization may reorganize in the form of strategic business units (SBUs) or strategic groups. The **strategic business unit organizational structure** groups a number of divisions together on the basis of similarities in such things as product lines or markets. Vice presidents are appointed to oversee the operations of the newly formed strategic business units, and these executives report directly to the CEO. The SBU structure may be useful for coordinating divisions with similar strategic problems and opportunities. However, because it imposes another layer of management, it can also slow decision making and retard the implementation process unless authority is decentralized.

Matrix Organizational Structure

A **matrix organizational structure** facilitates the development and execution of various large programs or projects. As shown in Figure 5.2, each departmental vice president listed at the top has *functional* responsibility for all projects within the function; the project managers listed down the side have responsibility for completing and implementing strategic projects. This approach allows project managers to cut across departmental lines, and it can promote efficient implementation of strategies. In effect, project groups are cross-functional teams, that exist for the duration of a project. The matrix structure does have an important disadvantage: employees often become confused about their work responsibilities and about whether they are accountable to project managers or to their functional group managers. In their study of excellent corporations, Peters and Waterman made the following observation about matrix organization structures:

> Virtually none of the excellent companies spoke of itself as having formal matrix structures, except for project management companies like Boeing. But in a company like Boeing, where many of the matrix ideas originated, something very different is meant by matrix management. People operate in a binary way: they are either a part of a project team and responsible to that team for getting some task accomplished (most of the time), or they are part of a technical discipline, in which they spend some time making sure their technical department is keeping up with the state of the art. When they are on a project, there is no day-in, day-out confusion about whether they are really responsible to the project or not. They are.[9]

Network Organizational Structure

The sixth and most recent addition to the roster of structural types is the **network organizational structure.** Since structures do not develop independently, but as ways to more effectively implement new strategies, what factors have caused this new form to develop? In a series of seminal articles, Raymond Miles, Charles Snow, and a few co-authors have documented the emergence of a variety of network structures.[10] They argue that increased global competition and rapid technological change have caused many firms to shed traditionally internal activities, to downsize to leave only what they do best. Such a firm seeks to keep responsibility only for its core competencies, its world-class or superior skills and activities. This movement has led many firms to reduce the number of layers in their management hierarchies, and to search constantly for opportunities for out-sourcing, that is, contracting with outsiders to provide services instead of performing those functions internally. For example, instead of producing the shoes it designs, Nike contracts with a set of Asian manufacturers to produce them.

A new strategic perspective drives this movement to networks. Managers have a growing sense that value chains can be rethought and reconfigured so that a firm can achieve competitive success by building for itself, not a set of tightly controlled, internally managed activities, but a set of negotiated and cooperative relationships involving several other partner firms, *all doing what they do best*. In this way, networks can come to resemble the Japanese *keiretsu*—"organizational collectives based on cooperation and mutual shareholding among groups of manufacturers, suppliers, and trading and finance companies."[11]

Unfortunately, no hard and fast rules determine when an organization needs to change its structure to reflect new environmental and strategic realities. For example, moving from a functional to a divisional structure may help a firm to meet customer needs in the markets served by the new divisions. However, the costs of setting up each new division, with its own accounting, marketing, and R&D department, new manufacturing facilities, etc., may offset the benefits gained from increased sales. Similarly, moving from a traditional, functional structure to a network involves new ways of thinking about interfirm cooperation and trust. Miles and Snow point out, for example, that network structures may fail, because, after having shed many noncore activities, a firm might find that its expertise has become too narrow and that its role in the value chain has become more vulnerable.[12]

The 1990s have brought a great deal of experimentation in defining the core tasks and processes to include in the modern organization (e.g., network structures). In addition, innovative ways of organizing to complete tasks and processes (e.g., teams), are sometimes revolutionary. Pictures of organization structures have traditionally looked like the organization charts in Figure 5.2. However, as the tradition of vertical authority and control has faced challenges from new modes of doing work, such as cross-functional teams, new ways of picturing organization structures have emerged.[13] Figure 5.3 illustrates four examples of this new generation of organization chart.

In sum, analyzing and managing organizational structure is a necessary step in strategy implementation; it forces managers to consider a strategy in relation to the tasks that must be performed to effectively implement it. The firm's current structure and personnel are often adequate for successful implementation. In some cases, a temporary change in structure may facilitate implementation without creating undue problems. In a few cases, when a particular organizational structure is so cumbersome and inefficient that it prevents the firm from implementing a good strategy effectively, the structure may need to be completely overhauled. However, other factors must be considered before management concludes that an organization's structure must be revamped. One of the most important of these factors is the organization's culture.

FIGURE 5.3
New Models for the
Modern Organization

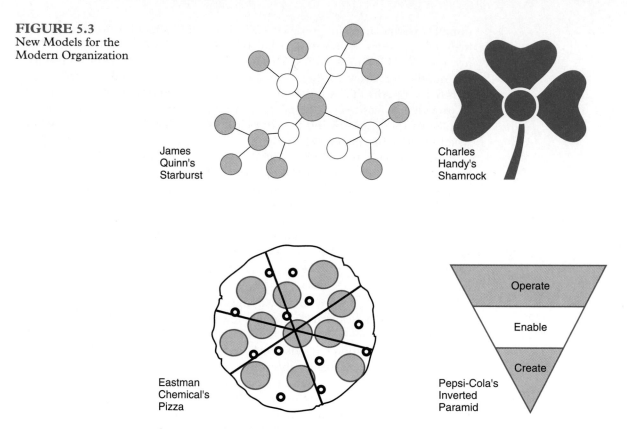

SOURCE: John Byrne, "Congratulations. You're Moving to a New Pepperoni." Reprinted from December 20, 1993 issue of *Business Week* by special permission, copyright © 1993 by McGraw-Hill, Inc.

ANALYZING AND MANAGING ORGANIZATIONAL CULTURE

Scholars have proposed many definitions of organizational or corporate culture. For the purposes of this text, we will take **organizational culture** to mean a set of shared values and beliefs that develop in an organization over time. Organizational culture affects strategy implementation by influencing the behavior of employees and, it is hoped, motivating them to achieve or surpass organizational objectives. Typically, the CEO and other present or past organization leaders exert key influence on culture. In addition, organizations often exhibit various subcultures in particular divisions or departments, which are influenced by leaders at these levels.

Organizations develop and reinforce cultures in a variety of ways. One authority identifies five primary and five secondary cultural development mechanisms.[14] The five primary mechanisms are:

1. *What leaders pay attention to, measure, and control:* Leaders can communicate their vision of the organization and what they want done very effectively by consistently emphasizing the same issues in meetings, in casual remarks and questions, and in strategy discussions. For example, if product quality is the dominant value they want to inculcate in employees, leaders may consistently inquire about the effects of any proposed changes on product quality.

2. *Leaders' reactions to critical incidents and organizational crises:* Leaders' methods for dealing with crises can create new beliefs and values and reveal underlying organizational assumptions. For example, when a firm faces a financial crisis without laying off any employees, it may broadcast the message that the organization sees itself as a family that looks out for its members.

3. *Deliberate role modeling, teaching, and coaching:* Leaders' behaviors in both formal and informal settings have important effects on employee beliefs, values, and behaviors. For example, if the CEO regularly works very long hours and on weekends, other managers may respond by spending more of their time at work, too.

4. *Criteria for allocation of rewards and status:* Leaders can quickly communicate their priorities and values by consistently linking rewards and punishments to desirable behaviors. For example, a weekly bonus for exceeding production or sales quotas may help employees to recognize the value placed on these activities and to focus their efforts appropriately.

5. *Criteria for recruitment, selection, promotion, and retirement of employees:* The types of people who are hired and who succeed in an organization are those who accept the organization's values and behave accordingly. For example, if managers who are risk takers consistently move up the organizational ladder, the organization's priorities should come through loud and clear to other managers.

The Skills Module invites you to apply these mechanisms to analyze the culture of UPS. In addition to the five primary mechanisms we've just mentioned, five secondary mechanisms contribute to the development of organizational culture:

1. *The organization's design and structure:* Designing an organization's structure offers leaders a chance to express their deeply held assumptions about the tasks and processes of the firm, the best means of accomplishing them, human nature, and the right kinds of relationships among people. For example, a highly decentralized organization suggests that leaders have confidence in the abilities of subordinate managers.

2. *Organizational systems and procedures:* Some very visible parts of organizational life influence culture, including the daily, weekly, monthly, quarterly, and annual routines, procedures, reports to file, forms to fill out, and other recurring tasks. For example, if the CEO asks for quarterly reports on all assistant managers, this requirement communicates the message that the organization values this group.

3. *Design of physical space, facades, and buildings:* Leaders who embrace a clear philosophy and management style often make that style manifest in their choices of architectural style, interior design, and decor. For example, leaders who believe in open communication may lay out office space to leave few private areas or barriers to the flow of traffic. In recent years, interior design experts have designed special work spaces for cross-functional teams.

4. *Stories, legends, myths, and parables about important events and people:* As a group develops and accumulates a history, some of this history becomes embodied in stories about events and leadership behavior.

SKILLS MODULE
UPS Reorients Its Corporate Culture

INTRODUCTION

The text outlines five primary cultural development mechanisms. Review the following situation, and then complete the related skill development exercise. This will give you an opportunity to consider some of the issues involved in creating an effective organizational culture.

SITUATION

In 1990, executives at Eastman Kodak Co. were intent on concentrating their shipping business among fewer package carriers, and United Parcel Service Inc., the nation's biggest carrier, was on the endangered list. "Every time we'd ask them about special services or discounts, I'd hear back the same thing: 'It's not in our best interest,'" said a Kodak spokesman. "Well, that's not what I was hearing from their competitors."

UPS responded to the complaints; renewed attention and volume discounts repaired the business relationship. Within three years, Kodak had increased its business with UPS by 15 percent, to 50,000 packages a week.

Kodak is only one of the many customers UPS has won over as result of what UPS insiders call the "velvet revolution." Under Chief Executive Kent Nelson, the Atlanta-based firm has discarded its we-know-what's-best-for-you imperiousness; instead, the package carrier is stressing customer satisfaction via flexible pickup and delivery times, customized shipment plans, and a $2 billion investment in technology to keep up-to-the-minute tabs on shipments. UPS has also done what many had considered unthinkable, moving away from the residential deliveries that had been its bread and butter.

Nelson says he had little choice but to change what customers saw as an aloof and rigid style: The competition had been cherry-picking many of UPS's best customers. He began the revolution in-house. In 1990, as profit margins slid toward 4 percent from nearly 7 percent two years prior, Nelson appointed four top executives to conduct an intensive review of UPS's business methods.

Key to improving customer service was beefing up the marketing staff. For years, UPS had relied on a seven-person team, too few to handle questions from both existing and potential customers. By 1992, the staff had grown to 175 and was handling 6,000 corporate inquiries annually.

The headquarters-driven overhaul of corporate culture has met little resistance from managers and supervisors in the field. Retraining helped, but executive compliance is more easily explained by UPS's compensation plan. Each year, the firm spends 15 percent of its pre-tax profit to buy company stock, which it distributes to employees from entry-level supervisors on up. "We have 25,000 owner-managers who have virtually every cent they own invested in stock of this company," says Nelson. "They knew that if we didn't change, somebody would, and there'd go your life savings."

Others within UPS are not as happy—or motivated. Relations have often been rocky between the company and the Teamsters union, which represents 165,000 drivers and package sorters. The union has long complained about how UPS treats its members; some drivers, for example, are told to make 15 deliveries or pickups an hour, no matter what the traffic conditions. Drawn-out contract negotiations and strikes loom as a long-term threat.

SKILL DEVELOPMENT EXERCISE

Kent Nelson and other UPS executives clearly recognized that they had a serious customer-service problem, but uncooperative drivers could damage corporate efforts to boost business. For each of the five primary cultural development mechanisms, suggest one thing the leaders of UPS should do to develop a more effective organizational culture that envelops all levels of UPS workers.

SOURCE: "After a U-Turn, UPS Really Delivers," *Business Week*, May 31, 1993, p. 92.

5. *Formal statements of organizational philosophy, creeds, or charters:* Explicit statements by leaders of organizations about their values are a means of shaping organizational culture.

Organizational leaders have devised a variety of methods for developing, maintaining, or changing organizational cultures. However, changing an organizational culture is a difficult task. If it is possible at all, it may require many years to complete. Continuation, routine, or limited strategy changes usually are implemented without changes to the organizational culture. Radical strategy changes and organizational redirections often require long-term changes in organizational culture.

SELECTING AN IMPLEMENTATION APPROACH

After evaluating the effect of culture on strategy implementations the manager must select an overall approach to implementing strategy based on an assessment of change, structure, and culture variables. Research on management practices at a number of companies has led David Brodwin and L. J. Bourgeois to suggest five fundamental approaches to implementing strategies.[15] These approaches range from simply telling employees to implement the strategy that has been formulated to developing employees who can formulate and implement sound strategies on their own. In each approach, the manager plays a somewhat different role and uses different methods of strategic management. Brodwin and Bourgeois call these five approaches the Commander approach, the Organizational Change approach, the Collaborative approach, the Cultural approach, and the Crescive approach. Table 5.3 presents an overview of these approaches; each is discussed below.

Commander Approach

Under this approach, the manager concentrates on formulating strategy, applying rigorous logic and analysis. The manager may either develop the strategy alone or supervise a team of strategists charged with determining the optimal course of action for the organization. Tools such as the growth–share matrix and industry and competitive analysis are commonly used by managers who employ this approach. After determining the best strategy, the manager passes it along to subordinates with instructions to execute it. The manager does not take an active role in implementing the strategy.

This approach has a serious drawback in the potential to reduce employee motivation; employees who feel that they have no say in strategy formulation are unlikely to be a very innovative group. However, the approach can work effectively in smaller companies within stable industries. It works best when the strategy to be implemented requires relatively little change.

Although the Commander approach can raise a number of problems, it is commonly advocated by certain business consultants and is used by many managers. Several factors account for its popularity. First, despite its drawbacks, it allows managers to focus their energies on strategy formulation. By dividing the strategic management task into two stages—thinking and doing—the manager reduces the number of factors that have to be considered simultaneously. Second, young managers, in particular, seem to prefer this approach because it allows them to focus on the quantitative, objective aspects of a situation rather than on qualitative, subjective behavioral interactions.

TABLE 5.3

Comparison of Five Approaches to Implementing a Strategy

Factor	Approach				
	Commander	**Change**	**Collaborative**	**Cultural**	**Crescive**
HOW ARE GOALS SET? Where in the organization (top or bottom) are the strategic goals established?	Dictated from top	Dictated from top	Negotiated among top team	Embodied in culture	Stated loosely from top, refined from bottom
WHAT SIGNIFIES SUCCESS? What signifies a successful outcome to the strategic planning/implementation process?	A good plan as judged on economic criteria	Organization and structure that fit the strategy	An acceptable plan with broad top management support	An army of busy implementers	Sound strategies with champions behind them
WHAT FACTORS ARE CONSIDERED? What kinds of factors, or types of rationality, are used in developing a strategy for resolving conflicts between alternative proposed strategies?	Economic	Economic, political	Economic, social, political	Economic, social	Economic, social, political, behavioral
WHAT TYPICAL LEVEL OF ORGANIZATION-WIDE EFFORT IS REQUIRED?					
During the planning phase	Low	Low	High	High	High
During the implementation phase	N/A	High	Low	Low	Low
HOW STRINGENT ARE THE REQUIREMENTS PLACED ON THE CEO IN ORDER FOR THE APPROACH TO SUCCEED?					
Required CEO knowledge: To what extent must the CEO be able to maintain personal awareness of all significant strategic opportunities or threats?	High	High	Moderate	Low	Low
Required CEO power: To what extent must the CEO have the power to impose a detailed implementation plan on the organization?	High	High	Moderate	Moderate	Moderate

SOURCE: David R. Brodwin and L. J. Bourgeois III, "Five Steps to Strategic Action." Copyright © 1984 by the Regents of the University of California. Reprinted from the *California Management Review,* Vol. 26, No. 3. By permission of The Regents.

(Many young managers are better trained to deal with the former than with the latter.) Finally, such an approach may make some ambitious managers feel powerful in that their thinking and decision making can affect the activities of thousands of people.

Organizational Change Approach

Whereas the manager who adopts the Commander approach avoids dealing directly with implementation, the Organizational Change approach (or simply the Change approach) focuses on how to get organization members to implement a strategy. Managers who follow the Change approach assume that they have formulated a good strategy; they view their task as getting the company moving toward new goals. The tools used to accomplish this task are largely behavioral, such as changing the organizational structure and staffing to focus attention on the organization's new priorities, revising planning and control systems, and invoking other organizational change techniques. The manager functions as an architect, designing administrative systems for effective strategy implementation.

Because the Change approach to implementation employs powerful behavioral tools, it is often more effective than the Commander approach, and it can implement more difficult strategies. However, the Change approach has several limitations that may restrict its use to smaller companies in stable industries. It doesn't deal well with politics and personal agendas that discourage objectivity among strategists. Also, because it calls for imposing strategy from the top down, it can cause the same motivational problems as the Commander approach.

Finally, this approach can backfire in uncertain or rapidly changing conditions. The manager sacrifices important strategic flexibility by manipulating the systems and structures of the organization in support of a particular strategy. Some of these systems (particularly incentive compensation) take a long time to design and install. Should a change in the environment require a new strategy, it may be very difficult to change the organization's course, which has been firmly established to support the now-obsolete strategy.

Collaborative Approach

In the Collaborative approach, the manager in charge of the strategy calls in the rest of the management team to brainstorm strategy formulation *and* implementation tactics. Managers are encouraged to contribute their points of view in order to extract group wisdom from multiple perspectives. The manager functions as a coordinator, using his or her understanding of group dynamics to ensure that all good ideas are discussed and investigated. For example, several years ago General Motors formed business teams that brought together managers from different functional areas. The teams were intended simply to bring out different points of view on strategic problems as they arose. Exxon's major strategic decisions are made by its management committee, which comprises all of Exxon's inside directors, led by the chairman of the board. Every committee member serves as a contact executive for the line managers of one or more of Exxon's 13 affiliates and subsidiaries.

The Collaborative approach overcomes two key limitations of the other two approaches we have evaluated so far. By capturing information contributed by managers closer to operations, and by offering a forum for the expression of many viewpoints, it can increase the quality and timeliness of the information incorporated in the strategy. To the degree that participation enhances commitment to the strategy, it improves the chances of efficient implementation.

Though the Collaborative approach may gain more commitment than the foregoing approaches, it has other problems. Negotiating strategy among managers with different points of view and, possibly, different goals may reduce management's chances of formulating and implementing superior strategies. For one thing, a negotiated strategy is likely to be less visionary and more conservative than one created by an individual or staff team. For another, gaming and empire building by various individual managers may skew a strategy toward a particular functional area, sacrificing an overall strategic perspective. Also, the negotiation process can take so much time that an organization misses opportunities and fails to react quickly enough to changes in the environment.

Finally, a fundamental criticism of the Collaborative approach questions whether it really amounts to collective decision making from an organizational viewpoint because upper-level managers often retain centralized control. In effect, this approach preserves the artificial distinction between thinkers and doers and fails to draw on the full human potential throughout the organization. When properly used, the Collaborative approach can increase commitment to a strategy and encourage effective implementation, yet it can also create political problems within the organization that can impede rapid and efficient strategy formulation and implementation.

Cultural Approach

The Cultural approach expands the Collaborative approach to include lower levels in the organization. In this approach, the manager guides the organization by communicating and instilling his or her vision of the overall mission for the organization and then allowing employees to design their own work activities to support this mission. Once the strategy is formulated, the manager plays the role of coach, giving general directions but encouraging individual decision making on the operating details of executing the strategy.

The implementation tools used in building a strong organizational culture range from such simple notions as publishing a company creed and singing a company song to much more complex techniques. These techniques involve what can be called *third-order control*. First-order control is direct supervision; second-order control involves using rules, procedures, and organizational structure to guide behavior. Third-order control is more subtle, and potentially more powerful. It seeks to influence behavior by shaping the norms, values, symbols, and beliefs on which managers and employees base day-to-day decisions.

The Cultural approach partially breaks down the barriers between thinkers and doers, because each member of the organization can be involved to some degree in both formulation and implementation of strategy. Hewlett-Packard is a well-known example of a company whose employees share a strong awareness of the corporate mission. They all know that the "HP way" encourages product innovation at every level. Matsushita, for its part, starts each work day with 87,000 employees singing the company song and reciting its code of values. The company creed at JCPenney is reprinted in Table 5.4.

The Cultural approach appears to work best in organizations that have sufficient resources to absorb the cost of building and maintaining suppor-

---

TABLE 5.4

JCPenney's Company Creed

JCPenney's company creed, called "The Penney Idea," was adopted in 1913. It consists of the following seven points:

1. To serve the public, as nearly as we can, to its complete satisfaction
2. To expect for the service we render a fair remuneration and not all the profit the traffic will bear
3. To do all in our power to pack the customer's dollar full of value, quality, and satisfaction
4. To continue to train ourselves and our associates so that the service we give will be more and more intelligently performed
5. To improve constantly the human factor in our business
6. To reward men and women in our organization through participation in what the business produces
7. To test our every policy, method and act in this wise: "Does it square with what is right and just?"

---

tive value systems. Often these are high-growth firms in high-technology industries.

While this approach has a number of advantages, not the least of which is dedicated, enthusiastic implementation of strategies, it also has limitations. First, it tends to work only in organizations composed primarily of informed, intelligent people. Second, its development consumes enormous amounts of time. Third, its strong sense of organizational identity can become a handicap; for example, bringing in outsiders at top management levels can be difficult because they aren't accepted by other executives. Fourth, companies with excessively strong cultures often suppress deviance, discourage attempts to change, and foster homogeneity and inbred thinking. To handle this conformist tendency, some companies (such as IBM, Xerox, and GM) have segregated their ongoing research units and their new product development efforts, sometimes placing them in physical locations far enough from other units to shield them from the corporation's dominant culture.

Crescive Approach

The manager who adopts the Crescive approach addresses strategy formulation and strategy implementation simultaneously. (*Crescive* means increasing or growing.) However, she or he does not focus on performing these tasks, but on encouraging subordinates to develop, champion, and implement sound strategies on their own. This approach differs from the others in several ways. First, instead of strategy falling downward from top management or a strategy group, it moves upward from the doers (salespeople, engineers, production workers) and lower middle-level managers and supervisors. Second, strategy becomes the sum of all the individual proposals that surface throughout the year. Third, the top-management team shapes the employees' premises, that is, the employees' notions of what would constitute supportable strategic projects. Fourth, the chief executive, or manager in charge of strategy, functions more as a judge evaluating the proposals rather than as a master strategist.

Brodwin and Bourgeois advocate the Crescive approach primarily for CEOs of large, complex, diversified organizations. In such an organization, the CEO cannot know and understand all the strategic and operating forces that affect each division. Therefore, to formulate and implement strategies effectively, the CEO must give up some control to spur opportunism and achievement. The 3M Corporation provides an example of this approach to strategy implementation. Top managers set a target for the percentage of each division's revenues that must come from new products. Division managers can then use whatever means they like to achieve these targets. One division manager, for example, restructured his divisions into cross-functional teams to bring new products to market more quickly.

This approach has several advantages. First, it encourages middle-level managers to work to formulate effective strategies and gives them opportunities to implement their own plans. This autonomy increases their motivation to make the strategy succeed. Second, strategies developed by employees and managers closer to strategic opportunities, as these are, often are operationally sound and readily implemented. However, this approach requires that the firm (1) provide funds for individuals to develop good ideas unencumbered by bureaucratic approval cycles, and (2) extend tolerance in the inevitable cases of failure despite worthy efforts. Furthermore, converting a centralized, top-down organization to the Crescive approach can be very difficult, expensive, and time consuming. Finally, the Crescive approach does not specify how managers should go about implementing the strategy. In sum, the Crescive approach is viable for complex organizations that compete in dynamic industries.

EVALUATING IMPLEMENTATION SKILLS FOR MANAGERS

By this stage, the manager has a clear idea of the level of strategic change to be implemented. In addition, analysis of the organization's structure and culture has developed an understanding of the factors within the organization that will facilitate or impede implementation. An implementation approach has been selected that promises the best job of capitalizing on the firm's strengths and overcoming, circumventing, or minimizing problems within the organization. The task at the last stage of implementation is to evaluate the implementation skills needed by managers.

Professor Thomas V. Bonoma of the Harvard Business School suggests that successful implementation of strategies requires four basic types of managerial skills.[16] These are shown in Figure 5.4 and discussed below.

Interacting skills are expressed in managing one's own and others' behavior to achieve objectives. Depending on the level of strategic change required to implement a strategy, managers may need to influence others both within and outside the organization. Bonoma suggests that, in general, managers who show empathy—the ability to understand how others feel—and have good bargaining skills are the best implementers.

Allocating skills influence managers' abilities to schedule tasks and budget time, money, and other resources efficiently. Able managers avoid putting too many resources into mature programs and recognize that new, riskier programs often demand investment of more resources.

Monitoring skills involve the efficient use of information to correct any problems that arise in the process of implementation. Good implementers have

FIGURE 5.4   Four Key Implementation Skills

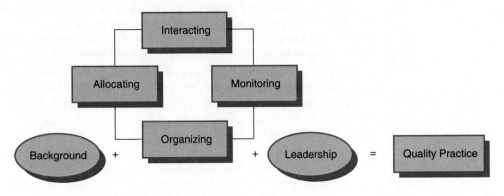

SOURCE: Adapted and reprinted with the permission of The Free Press, an imprint of Simon and Schuster from THE MARKETING EDGE: Making Strategies Work by Thomas V. Bonoma. Copyright 1985 by The Free Press.

efficient feedback systems to analyze progress toward strategy execution and any problems that occur. For example, one general manager of a company with 38 plants and 300,000 customers ran everything he considered crucial according to notations on two 3-by-5 index cards!

Organizing skills help the manager to create a new informal organization or to address each problem that occurs. Good implementers know people in every part of the organization (and outside it) who, by virtue of mutual respect, attraction, or some other tie, can and will help however they can. In other words, good implementers customize the informal organization to facilitate good execution.

Thus, implementation often depends on managers who possess particular skills tailored to overcoming obstacles and ensuring that tasks are performed efficiently. Managers must continuously evaluate how well the strategy is being executed and whether it is accomplishing organizational objectives. We focus on that topic, strategy control and evaluation, in the next chapter.

SUMMARY

In this chapter, we consider implementation as a critical part of the strategic management process that is too frequently undervalued. We develop a five-stage model of the strategy implementation process to draw attention to key facets.

First, it is important to analyze how much the firm itself will have to change in order to implement a proposed strategy successfully. Strategies can range from the no-change or stable strategy through routine strategy change, limited strategy change, and radical strategy change all the way to organizational redirection. This last step consists of sweeping transformations that a firm usually undergoes only when it enters a new industry or takes part in a merger or acquisition. We also consider the skills managers need in order to manage change effectively.

The next stage in the strategy implementation process is to analyze and manage both the formal and informal structures of the organization. A formal structure may be simple (an owner-manager and employees); the firm may be divided into functions (such as marketing, operations, and finance), divisions (handling different product lines, geographic areas, distribution channels, or the like), or groups of divisions known as *strategic business units*. In the matrix organizational structure, functional responsibility and project responsibility may overlap. In the network structure, core competencies provide the basis for reducing the number of functions held within a firm and increasing the number of functions performed by partner firms. Recognizing the linkage of structure to successful strategy implementation is always important.

Analyzing and managing organizational culture is important for implementing strategies. The organization culture consists of the values, beliefs, and attitudes toward the firm that employees share. Leader behaviors, criteria for recruiting and rewarding employees, rules and procedures, formal statements of company creeds, oft-told tales about important events and people in the history of the organization, and even the physical layout of the buildings—all of these can contribute to effective organizational cultures and help to shape employee attitudes and behavior. Once ingrained, organizational culture is persistent, and strategic changes that run counter to it are often doomed to failure.

Brodwin and Bourgeois suggested several different approaches to implement a given strategy. In the Commander approach, the manager formulates a strategy and simply instructs subordinates to implement it. The Organizational Change approach works by assuming that the strategy is good and marshaling behavioral approaches to change organizational structure to implement it. The Collaborative approach invites a management team to participate in both the formulation and the implementation of strategy. The Cultural approach democratizes the Collaborative approach to include lower levels of the organization. Finally, the Crescive approach encourages subordinates to develop, propose, and implement strategies of their own devising. We probed the merits and drawbacks of each approach and outlined the conditions under which each is most likely to be appropriate.

Finally, the implementation process hinges on managers' skills in interacting and empathizing with others, in allocating resources, in monitoring progress toward goals, and in organizing new informal networks. Managers who have such skills can oversee the implementation of strategy effectively and evaluate the implementation process as it unfolds, taking remedial action if necessary.

KEY TERMS

CHECK✓*LIST*   ## Analyzing Strategy Implementation in Problems and Cases

___ 1. Does the situation or case involve strategy implementation issues?

___ 2. Is the strategy implementation fulfilling all of its purposes?

___ 3. Has the strategy been successfully translated into action?

___ 4. Is it clear what level of strategic change is necessary and appropriate?

___ 5. Have the organization's formal and informal structures been well-analyzed prior to strategy implementation?

___ 6. Does the situation or case focus on how a structural type can be used to implement a strategy?

___ 7. Are various levels of management appropriately involved in the strategy implementation process?

___ 8. Have the implementation skills needed by managers been evaluated?

___ 9. Have each of the primary and secondary cultural-development mechanisms been assessed?

___ 10. Does the implementation plan focus on the correct approach?

Additional Readings

Egelhoff, William G. "Great Strategy or Great Strategic Implementation—Two Ways of Competing in Global Markets." *Sloan Management Review,* Winter 1993, p. 37.

Floyd, Steven, and Bill Wooldridge. "Managing Strategic Consensus: The Foundation of Effective Implementation." *Academy of Management Executive* 6, no. 4 (November 1992), pp. 27–39.

Hatch, Mary J. "The Dynamics of Organizational Culture." *Academy of Management Review* 18, no. 4 (October 1993), pp. 657–693.

Ketchen, David J., Jr., James B. Thomas, and Charles C. Snow. "Organizational Configurations and Performance: A Comparison of Theoretical Approaches," *Strategic Management Journal* 36, no. 6 (December 1993), pp. 1,278–1,313.

Marcoulides, George, and Ronald Heck. "Organizational Culture and Performance." *Organization Science* 4, no. 2 (May 1993), pp. 209–225.

Mezias, Stephen, and Mary Ann Glynn. "The Three Faces of Corporate Renewal: Institution, Revolution, and Evolution." *Strategic Management Journal* 14, no. 2 (February 1993), pp. 77–101.

Mintzberg, Henry, and Frances Westley. "Cycles of Organizational Change." *Strategic Management Journal* 13 (Winter 1992, Special Issue), pp. 39–59.

Venkatesan, Ravi. "Strategic Sourcing: To Make or Not to Make." *Harvard Business Review,* November/December 1992, p. 98.

CASE

FORD TEAM LOOKS TO PAST FOR FUTURE STRATEGY

The Ford Mustang may be an American icon, inspiration for romance and rock songs, but in the brutal global auto industry of the 1990s, romance takes a back seat to cash flow. When Ford Motor Co. executives first looked at a Mustang overhaul in late 1989, the $1 billion development price-tag looked far too expensive.

That's when a group inside Ford known as "Team Mustang" got together. The group of about 400 people spent three years reconciling the conflicting forces of finance and feeling.

The 1989 version of the Mustang was essentially unchanged from the dumpy 1979 incarnation, one of Ford's most trouble-plagued models. It bore little resemblance to the 1964 model that swept a generation off its feet. At the model's 1966 peak, 600,000 Mustangs were sold; by 1992, sales were down to just over 86,000. Japanese cars—even the Ford Probe, built by Ford partner Mazda Motor Corp.—were literally whizzing by in sales and popularity.

In August of that year, John Coletti and a small group of managers were assigned the task of saving the Mustang. They began with a six-month global tour of auto plants, to uncover how rivals brought out new cars for hundreds of millions less than Ford had been spending. They had the backing of Alex Trotman, executive vice president of Ford's North American automotive operations.

The "skunk works" development team fleshed out a plan to bring out a new Mustang in just three years, using a new product-development approach that put everyone from engineers to stylists to financial officers under one roof. The plan would give them unprecedented freedom to make decisions without waiting for approval from headquarters or other departments. The plan for managerial autonomy cut sharply against the grain of Ford's corporate culture. It called for breaching budgetary walls and persuading department heads to cede some control to their subordinates. Dia Hothi, the program's manufacturing chief, demanded—and got—veto power over changes to the Mustang body that would threaten his plans to build the car with many of the factory tools used for the old one. Trotman signed on to the project, and in September 1990, the group began work.

Engineers were grouped into "chunk teams," with responsibility for every aspect of a particular piece, or chunk, of the car. The new process disposed of the standard bidding procedure; Mustang team leaders simply picked the best available suppliers and asked them to join the process.

Time and money were saved by testing most of the convertible's designs on computer rather than by building actual cars. Still, initial test-drives of prototypes showed the need for major structural revisions. An eight-week blitz of reengineering work, computer manipulations, and budget discussions began. Although Trotman and other senior Ford executives were aware of the crisis, they kept their promise not to interfere.

Team Mustang made its September 1993 production start date; the aerodynamically designed car, styled along the lines of the original model, went on sale December 9. Its three-year overhaul at a cost of about $700 million is about 25 percent less time and 30 percent less money than for any new car program in Ford's recent history. The automaker used the savings to price the Mustang below the $13,999 starting price of its archrival, the Chevrolet Camaro. Ford executives hope the Mustang's low-cost salvation will inspire other Ford engineers.

DISCUSSION QUESTIONS

1. What type of strategic change did the Mustang redesign effort demand at Ford?

2. What was Ford's approach to managing the Mustang project? What structure and culture challenges did Ford's top managers face in supporting the Mustang team? How did they meet these challenges?

3. What would you recommend to Mr. Trotman about overall strategy implementation at Ford, based on the results (to date) of the Mustang project?

SOURCE: Joseph B. White and Oscar Suris, "How a 'Skunk Works' Kept Mustang Alive—on a Tight Budget," *The Wall Street Journal*, September 21, 1993, p. A1.

Notes

1. Thomas J. Peters and Robert H. Waterman, Jr., *In Search of Excellence* (New York: Harper & Row, 1982), pp. 13–14.

2. Henry Mintzberg, "Crafting Strategy," *Harvard Business Review*, July/August 1987, p. 66.

3. See Peter Petre, "What Welch Has Wrought at GE," *Fortune*, July 7, 1986, pp. 43–47; Marilyn A. Harris, Zachary Schiller, Russell Mitchell, and Christopher Power, "Can Jack Welch Reinvent GE?" *Business Week*, June 30, 1986, pp. 62–67; Stratford P. Sherman, "Inside the Mind of Jack Welch," *Fortune*, March 27, 1989, pp. 38–53; and Thomas A. Stewart, "GE Keeps Those Ideas Coming," *Fortune*, August 12, 1991, pp. 41–49.

4. David E. Whiteside, "Roger Smith's Campaign to Change the GM Culture," *Business Week*, April 7, 1986, pp. 84–85; and Alex Taylor III, "The Tasks Facing General Motors," *Fortune*, March 13, 1989, pp. 52–60.

5. See Anthony Bianco, "Jerry Tsai: The Comeback Kid," *Business Week*, August 18, 1986, pp. 72–80.

6. James Brian Quinn, *Strategies for Change* (Homewood, Ill.: Richard D. Irwin, 1980).

7. Michael Beer, Russell Eisenstat, and Bert Spector, *The Critical Path to Corporate Renewal* (Boston: Harvard Business School Press, 1991); Rosabeth M. Kanter, Barry Stein, and Todd Jick, *The Challenge of Organizational Change* (New York: Free Press, 1992).

8. Raymond E. Miles and Charles C. Snow, "Causes of Failure in Network Organizations," *California Management Review*, Summer 1992, pp. 53–72.

9. Peters and Waterman, *In Search*, p. 307.

10. R. Miles and C. Snow, "Fit, Failure, and the Hall of Fame," *California Management Review*, Spring 1984, pp. 10–28; R. Miles and C. Snow, "Organizations: New Concepts for New Forms," *California Management Review*, Spring 1986, pp. 62–73; Miles and Snow, "Causes of Failure"; C. Snow, R. Miles, and H. Coleman, "Managing 21st Century Network Organizations," *Organizational Dynamics*, Winter 1992, pp. 5–20.

11. Miles and Snow, "Causes of Failure," p. 55.

12. Ibid.

13. John Byrne, "Congratulations. You're Moving to a New Pepperoni," *Business Week*, December 20, 1993, pp. 80–81.

14. Edgar H. Schein, *Organizational Culture and Leadership* (San Francisco: Jossey-Bass, 1985), pp. 223–243; the discussion that follows is based on this work. Also see Guy S. Saffold III, "Culture Traits, Strength, and Organizational Performance: Moving beyond 'Strong' Culture," *Academy of Management Review* 13, no. 4 (1988), pp. 546–558; Bernard C. Reimann and Yoash Weiner, "Corporate Culture: Avoiding the Elitist Trap," *Business Horizons*, March/April 1988, pp. 36–44; and Mary Jo Hatch, "The Dynamics of Organizational Culture," *Academy of Management Review*, October 1993, pp. 657–693.

15. The discussion that follows is based on David R. Brodwin and L. J. Bourgeois III, "Five Steps to Strategic Action," *California Management Review*, Spring 1984, pp. 176–190. Also see Paul C. Nutt, "Selecting Tactics to Implement Strategic Plans," *Strategic Management Journal* 10 (1989), pp. 145–161.

16. This discussion is based on Thomas V. Bonoma, *The Marketing Edge* (New York: Free Press, 1985), pp. 112–121. See also Thomas V. Bonoma, "Making Your Marketing Strategy Work," *Harvard Business Review*, March/April 1984, pp. 69–76; and Thomas V. Bonoma and Victoria L. Crittenden, "Managing Marketing Implementation," *Sloan Management Review*, Winter 1988, pp. 7–14.

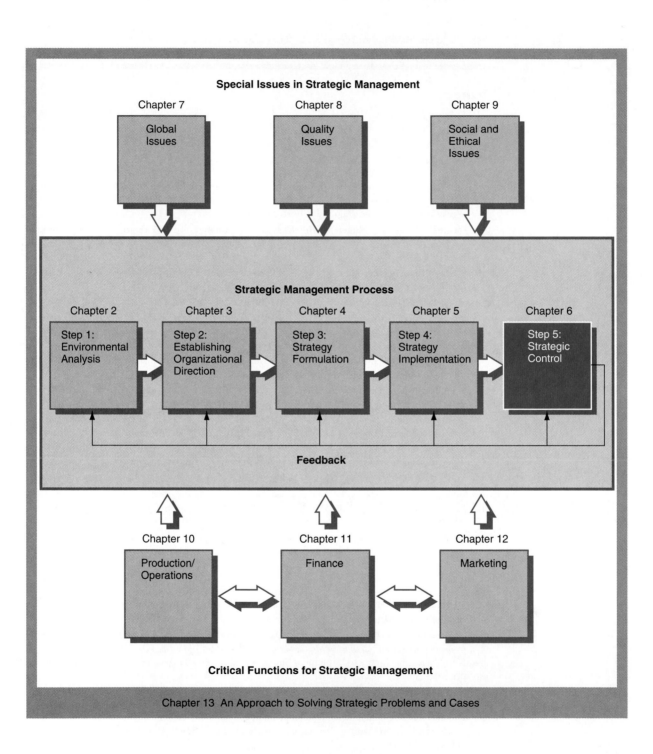

Special Issues in Strategic Management

Chapter 7

Global Issues

Chapter 8

Quality Issues

Chapter 9

Social and Ethical Issues

Strategic Management Process

Chapter 2

Step 1: Environmental Analysis

Chapter 3

Step 2: Establishing Organizational Direction

Chapter 4

Step 3: Strategy Formulation

Chapter 5

Step 4: Strategy Implementation

Chapter 6

Step 5: Strategic Control

Feedback

Chapter 10

Production/ Operations

Chapter 11

Finance

Chapter 12

Marketing

Critical Functions for Strategic Management

Chapter 13 An Approach to Solving Strategic Problems and Cases

CHAPTER

6

Strategic Control

Previous chapters in this section have discussed the strategic management process by focusing on the interrelated steps of conducting an environmental analysis, establishing an organizational direction, formulating strategy, and implementing strategy. This chapter emphasizes the last major step in the strategic management process, exerting strategic control. This consists of making certain that strategies unfold as intended, and taking corrective action, as needed. Much like the discussion of strategy implementation, we will see that strategic control is not the domain of one functional speciality; success requires a truly cross-functional effort.

First, we briefly examine the broader topic of organizational control in order to understand the context in which more specific strategic control issues develop. We then proceed to define *strategic control* and outline the purposes of the strategic control process.

The main part of the chapter covers the process of strategic control itself. We examine at length how a strategic audit can measure organizational performance, and we differentiate between qualitative and quantitative measures. We discuss ways to compare actual organizational performance to goals and standards, and we explain how to determine whether corrective action is appropriate.

Next, we explore the link between strategic control and management information systems. Finally, we examine the role of top management in making the strategic control process successful.

ORGANIZATIONAL CONTROL AND STRATEGIC CONTROL

Without an understanding of the broader issues involved in controlling an organization, it is impossible to appreciate the special issues that arise in strategic control. For this reason, we briefly discuss the broader topic of control at the organizational level before narrowing our focus to the specific issues involved in strategic control.

Broad View of Organizational Control

Controlling an organization entails monitoring, evaluating, and improving various activities that take place within an organization. We will first define the term *control,* and then we will outline the general characteristics of the control process.

Definition of *Control*

Control is a major part of every manager's job. **Control** consists of making something happen the way it was planned to happen.[1] For example, if an organization plans to increase net profit by 10 percent based upon accelerating product demand, control entails monitoring organizational progress and making modifications, if necessary, to ensure that net profit does, indeed, increase by 10 percent.

Effective control requires that managers have a clear understanding of the intended results of a particular action. Only then can they ascertain whether the anticipated results are occurring and make any necessary changes to ensure that the desired results do occur. Managers control to ensure that plans become reality, so they need a clear understanding of what reality is planned.[2]

General Characteristics of the Control Process

In practice, managers actually control by following a three-step procedure: measuring performance, comparing measured performance to standards, and taking corrective action to ensure that planned events actually materialize.

Keep in mind that these steps are broad recommendations for overall organizational control. More specific types of organizational control (such as production control, inventory control, strategic control, and quality control) are based on these same three steps, tailored to the demands of the specific type of control. Figure 6.1 shows a general model of how these broad steps of the control process relate to one another. This model implies that when performance measurements differ significantly from standard or planned outcomes, managers take corrective action to ensure that expected outcomes actually occur. On the other hand, when performance does measure up to standard or planned outcomes, no corrective action is necessary and work continues without interference.

FIGURE 6.1   General Model of the Control Process

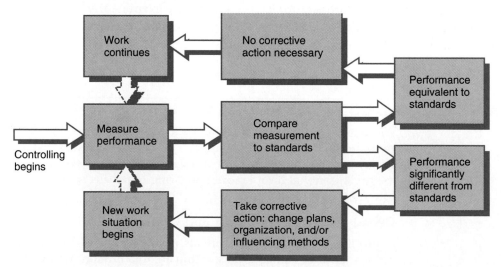

SOURCE: Samuel C. Certo, MODERN MANAGEMENT: Diversity, Quality, Ethics, and the Global Environment, 6 e., © 1994, p. 436. Reprinted by permission of Prentice Hall, Englewood Cliffs, New Jersey.

APPLICATION OF STRATEGIC CONTROL

Armed with a general understanding of control as managers apply it in organizations, we are now ready to discuss strategic control specifically. We will first define *strategic control*, then explain why strategic control is important, and finally trace the steps involved in the process of strategic control.

Definition of Strategic Control

Strategic control is a special type of organizational control that focuses on monitoring and evaluating the strategic management process to make sure that it functions properly. In essence, strategic control ensures that all outcomes planned during the strategic management process do, indeed, materialize. Although this definition oversimplifies strategic control and makes it sound somewhat mechanical, we will soon discover how challenging and intricate this process really is.

Purposes of Strategic Control

Perhaps the most fundamental purpose of strategic control is to help top managers achieve organizational goals by monitoring and evaluating the strategic management process. As we have seen, the strategic management process encompasses assessment of organizational environments (environmental analysis); establishment of organizational vision, mission, and goals (establishing organizational direction); development of ways to deal with competitors in order to reach these goals and fulfill the organization's mission (strategy formulation); and setting a plan to translate organizational strategy into action (strategy implementation). Strategic control provides feedback that is critical for determining whether all steps of the strategic management process are appropriate, compatible, and functioning properly.

PROCESS OF STRATEGIC CONTROL

Three distinct but related steps comprise the strategic control process within an organization. Because they constitute a special type of organizational control, these steps are closely related to the more general control model presented earlier. They include measuring organizational performance, comparing performance to goals and standards, and taking necessary corrective action.[3]

Step 1: Measure Organizational Performance

Before managers can plan actions to make the strategic management process more effective, they must measure current organizational performance. In order to understand performance measurements and how a manager can take such measurements, we need to introduce two important topics: strategic audits and strategic audit measurement methods.

Strategic Audit

A **strategic audit** is an examination and evaluation of organization operations affected by the strategic management process. Such an audit may be very comprehensive, emphasizing all facets of a strategic management process, or narrowly focused, emphasizing only a single part of the process, such as environmental analysis. In addition, the strategic audit can be quite formal, adhering strictly to established organizational rules and procedures, or quite informal, allowing managers wide discretion in deciding what organizational measurements to take and when. Whether it is comprehensive or focused, formal or informal, the strategic audit must work to integrate related functions. To satisfy this requirement, strategic audits are often carried out by cross-functional teams of managers.

No single method can be prescribed for performing a strategic audit, and each organization must design and implement its own audits to meet its own unique needs. Table 6.1 presents a worthwhile set of general guidelines on how to conduct a strategic audit.

Strategic Audit Measurement Methods

Managers measure organizational performance by several generally accepted methods. One way of categorizing these methods divides them into two distinct types: qualitative and quantitative methods. Although this scheme is useful for developing an understanding of strategic audit measurement methods, a few methods do not fall neatly into one or the other of these categories; instead, they combine both types.

Qualitative Organizational Measurements　These measurements give organizational assessments in the form of nonnumerical data that are subjectively summarized and organized before any conclusions are drawn on which to base strategic control action. Many managers believe that the best qualitative organizational measurements are simply answers to critical questions designed to reflect important facets of organizational operations. There is no universally endorsed list of such questions, but several that might be useful to the practicing manager appear in Table 6.2.

Seymour Tilles has written a classic article on the qualitative assessment of organizational performance.[4] This article discusses several important issues involving one small facet of organizational performance: organizational routines that result in organizational strategy. The Tilles article suggests several important questions to ask during qualitative organizational measurement that focuses on organizational procedures to develop strategy:

1. *Is organizational strategy internally consistent?* Internal consistency relates to the cumulative impact of various strategies on the organization. Do strategies serve conflicting purposes? According to Tilles, a strategy must be judged not only by its own effects, but also by its relationship to other organizational initiatives.
2. *Is the organization's strategy consistent with its environment?* Organizational strategy must make sense in light of what is happening outside the organization. Is organizational strategy consistent with pending or new government regulations, changing consumer tastes, or trends in the labor supply? Most organizational problems that arise from inconsistency between strategy and environment do not reflect extreme difficulty in matching these two variables. Rather, such problems crop up simply because organizations do not consciously work to match strategy to its environment.
3. *Is the organizational strategy appropriate, given organizational resources?* Without appropriate resources, organizations simply cannot make strategies work. Are the organization's resources sufficient to carry out a proposed strategy?

TABLE 6.1

How to Conduct a Strategic Audit

A strategic audit is conducted in three phases: diagnosis to identify how, where, and in what priority in-depth analyses need to be made; focused analysis; and generation and testing of recommendations. Objectivity and the ability to ask critical, probing questions are key requirements for conducting a strategic audit.

PHASE ONE: DIAGNOSIS

1. Review key documents such as:
   a. Strategic plan
   b. Business or operational plans
   c. Organizational arrangements
   d. Major policies governing matters such as resource allocation and performance measurement
2. Review financial, market, and operational performance against benchmarks and industry norms to identify key variances and emerging trends.
3. Gain an understanding of:
   a. Principal roles, responsibilities, and reporting relationships
   b. Decision-making processes and major decisions made
   c. Resources, including physical facilities, capital, management, and technology
   d. Interrelationships between functional staff members and businesses or operating units
4. Identify strategic implications of strategy for organization structure, behavior patterns, systems, and processes—define interrelationships and linkages to strategy.
5. Determine internal and external perspectives.
   a. Survey the attitudes and perceptions of senior and middle managers and other key employees to assess the extent to which they are consistent with the strategic direction of the firm. One way to accomplish this task is through carefully focused interviews and/or questionnaires to ask employees to identify and make trade-offs among the objectives and variables they consider most important.
   b. Interview a carefully selected sample of customers and prospective customers and other key external sources to understand their view of the company.
6. Identify aspects of the strategy that are working well. Formulate hypotheses regarding problems and opportunities for improvement based on the findings above. Define how and in what order to pursue each.

PHASE TWO: FOCUSED ANALYSIS

1. Test the hypotheses concerning problems and opportunities for improvement through analysis of specific issues. Identify interrelationships and dependencies among components of the strategic system.
2. Formulate conclusions as to weaknesses in strategy formulation, implementation deficiencies, or interactions between the two.

PHASE THREE: RECOMMENDATIONS

1. Develop alternative solutions to problems and ways of capitalizing on opportunities. Test these alternatives in light of their resource requirements, risks, rewards, priorities, and other applicable measures.
2. Develop specific recommendations to produce an integrated, measurable, and time-phased action plan to improve strategic results.

SOURCE: Adapted from A. J. Prager and M. B. Shea, "The Strategic Audit," in *The Strategic Management Handbook,* ed. K. J. Albert (New York: McGraw-Hill, 1983), pp. 8–14. Copyright © 1983. Reproduced with permission of McGraw-Hill.

TABLE 6.2

Sample Questions for Qualitative Organizational Measurement

- Are financial policies with respect to investments, dividends, and financing consistent with the opportunities likely to be available?
- Has the company defined the market segments in which it intends to operate specifically with respect to both product lines and market segments? Has it clearly defined the key capabilities it needs to succeed?
- Does the company have a viable plan for developing a significant and defensible superiority over competitors based on these capabilities?
- Will the business segments in which the company operates provide adequate opportunities for achieving corporate objectives? Do they appear attractive enough to draw an excessive amount of investment to the market from potential competitors? Is the company providing adequately for developing attractive new investment opportunities?
- Are the management, financial, technical, and other resources of the company really adequate to justify an expectation of maintaining superiority over competitors in key capabilities?
- Does the company have operations in which it cannot reasonably expect to outperform competitors? If so, can managers expect these operations to generate adequate returns on invested capital? Is there any justification for investing further in such operations, even just to maintain them?
- Has the company selected business segments that can reinforce each other by contributing jointly to the development of key capabilities? Do competitors combine operations in ways that give them superiority in the key resource areas? Can the company's scope of operations be revised to improve its chances against competitors?
- To the extent that operations are diversified, has the company recognized and provided for the special management and control systems this requires?

SOURCE: Milton Lauenstein, "Keeping Your Corporate Strategy on Track," **Journal of Business Strategy** 2, no. 1 (Summer 1981), p. 64. Reprinted by permission.

Without enough money, people, materials, or machines, it is senseless to pursue any strategy, however well-planned.

4. *Is organizational strategy too risky?* Together, strategy and resources determine the degree of risk the organization takes. Naturally, each organization must determine the amount of risk (or potential for losing resources) it wishes to incur. In this area, management must assess such issues as the total amount of resources a strategy requires, the proportion of the organization's resources that the strategy will consume, and the time commitment the strategy demands.

5. *Is the time horizon of the strategy appropriate?* Every strategy is designed to accomplish some organizational goal within a certain time period. Is the time allotted for implementing the strategy and for reaching the related organizational goals realistic and acceptable, given organizational circumstances? Managers must ensure that the time available to reach the goals and the time necessary to implement the strategy are consistent. Inconsistency between these two variables can make it impossible to reach organizational goals in a satisfactory way.

Qualitative measurement methods can be very useful, but applying them relies heavily on human judgment. Conclusions based on such methods must be drawn very carefully, because this subjective judgment, if exercised incorrectly, could easily render audit results invalid. Strategic control actions based on invalid audit results will certainly limit the effectiveness and efficiency of the strategic management process and could even become the primary reason for organizational failure.

Quantitative Organizational Measurements These measurements give organizational assessments in the form of numerical data that are summarized and organized before conclusions are drawn on which to base strategic control action. Data gathered via such measures are generally easier to summarize and organize than data gathered through more qualitative measurements. Still interpreting or making sense of quantitative measurements and the corrective actions they signal can be very difficult and highly subjective. Quantitative measurements can evaluate the number of units produced per time period, production costs, production efficiency levels, levels of employee turnover and absenteeism, sales and sales growth, net profits earned, dividends paid, return on equity, market share, and earnings per share.

In practice, each organization uses specially designed methods to measure its overall performance quantitatively. For an extended discussion of quantitative measures of organizational performance, see Chapter 10. Here, we will briefly discuss three measurements:

1. *Return on investment (ROI):* This is the most common measure of organizational performance. It divides net income by total assets to evaluate the relationship between the amount of income the firm generates and the amount of assets needed to operate the organization. Naturally, an ROI value for one year alone may not provide the manager with much useful information. Comparing ROI values for consecutive years or consecutive quarters, or to those of similar companies or competitors, usually generates a more complete picture of organizational performance in this area.

   Managers must keep in mind several advantages and limitations of ROI as a measure of organizational performance, as presented in Table 6.3. These limitations should not discourage managers from using ROI; it is an extremely useful measure. Rather, managers must thoroughly understand these limitations and supplement ROI with such other performance measures, as needed.
2. *Weighted Performance (Z) Score:* This common quantitative measure numerically weights and sums five performance measures to arrive at an overall score.[5] The score becomes a basis for classifying firms as healthy and unlikely to go bankrupt, or as sick and likely to go bankrupt. The formula is:

$$z = 1.2\, X_1 + 1.4\, X_2 + 3.3\, X_3 + 0.6\, X_4 + 1.0\, X_5$$

Here z is defined as an index of overall financial health. All other variables in the formula (X_1, X_2, etc.) are explained in Table 6.4. The z score typically ranges from 5.0 to 10.0. According to research, a score below 1.8 signals a relatively high probability of going bankrupt. Firms that score above 3.0 have relatively low probabilities of going bankrupt. Firms that score between 1.8 and 3.0 are in a gray area. Knowing and understanding the z score for a particular firm can give top management an idea of the financial health of the firm and insights into how to improve it.

TABLE 6.3

Advantages and Limitations of ROI Performance Measures

ADVANTAGES

1. ROI is a single comprehensive figure influenced by everything that happens in a firm.
2. It measures how well the division manager uses the assets of the company to generate profits. It is also a good way to check on the accuracy of capital investment proposals.
3. It is a common denominator that can be compared among many entities.
4. It provides an incentive to use existing assets efficiently.
5. It provides an incentive to acquire new assets only when doing so would increase the firm's return.

LIMITATIONS

1. ROI is very sensitive to depreciation policy. Variances in depreciation write-offs between divisions affect their ROI performance. Accelerated depreciation techniques reduce ROI, conflicting with capital budgeting discounted cash flow analysis.
2. ROI is sensitive to book value. Older plants with more fully depreciated assets have relatively lower investment bases than newer plants, increasing ROI. (Note also that inflation can skew asset values and ROI.) Managers might be tempted to hold down asset investment or dispose of assets in order to increase ROI performance.
3. In many firms that use ROI, one division sells to another, so transfer pricing affects the measure. Expenses incurred affect profit. Since, in theory, the transfer price should be based on the total impact on firm profit, some investment center managers are bound to suffer. Equitable transfer prices are difficult to determine.
4. If one division operates in favorable industry conditions and another division operates in an industry with unfavorable conditions, the former division will automatically look better than the other.
5. ROI reflects a short time span. The performance of division managers should be measured in the long run. This is top management's time-span capacity.
6. The business cycle strongly affects ROI performance, often despite managerial performance.

SOURCE: Excerpt from ORGANIZATIONAL POLICY AND STRATEGIC MANAGEMENT: TEXT AND CASES, Second Edition, by James M. Higgins, copyright © 1983 by The Dryden Press, reprinted by permission of the publisher.

3. *Stakeholders' audit:* Stakeholders are people who are interested in a corporation's activities because they are significantly affected by accomplishment of the organization's objectives.[6] Organizational stakeholders include (a) stockholders interested in the appreciation of stock value and dividends, (b) unions interested in favorable wage rates and benefit packages, (c) creditors interested in the organization's ability to pay its debts, (d) suppliers interested in retaining the organization as a customer, (e) government units, who see organizations as taxpayers contributing to the costs of running a society, (f) social interest groups, such as consumer advocates and environmentalists, and (g) the organization's customers.

Many managers believe that one very useful measure of organizational performance is a **stakeholders' audit,** a summary of the feedback generated

TABLE 6.4

Variables for z Score

X_1 = Working capital/Total assets

Frequently found in studies of corporate problems, this is a measure of the net liquid assets of the firm relative to its total capital. Working capital is the difference between current assets and current liabilities. This variable explicitly allows for liquidity and size characteristics. Ordinarily, a firm experiencing consistent operating losses will have shrinking current assets in relation to total assets.

X_2 = Retained earnings/Total assets

This measure of cumulative profitability over time relies on balance sheet figures. It implicitly considers the age of a firm. For example, a relatively young firm will probably show a low RE/TA ratio because it has not had time to build up its cumulative profits. Therefore, this analysis may seem to discriminate against the young firm, since its chance of being classified as likely to go bankrupt is relatively higher than another, older firm. This is precisely the situation in the real world, though. Failure is much more likely in a firm's earlier years; over 50 percent of firms that fail do so in the first five years of existence. Note, however, that the retained earnings account is subject to manipulation via corporate quasi reorganizations and stock dividend declarations. A bias could be created by a substantial reorganization or stock dividend.

X_3 = Earnings before interest and taxes/Total assets

In essence, this ratio measures the true productivity of the firm's assets, abstracting from any tax or leverage factors. Since a firm's ultimate existence is based on the earning power of its assets, this ratio appears to be particularly appropriate for studies dealing with corporate failure. Furthermore, insolvency occurs when total liabilities exceed a fair valuation of the firm's assets, with value determined by the earning power of the assets.

X_4 = Market value of equity/Book value of total liabilities

Equity is measured by the combined market value of all shares of stock, preferred and common, while liabilities include both current and long-term debt. Book values of preferred and common stockholders' equity may be substituted for market values. The substitution of book values, especially for the common stock component, should be recognized as a proxy without statistical verification, however, since the model was built using market values (Price × Shares outstanding). The measure shows how much the firm's assets can decline in value (measured by market value of equity plus debt) before the liabilities exceed the assets and the firm becomes insolvent. For example, a company with equity worth $1,000 and debt worth $500 could experience a two-thirds drop in asset value before insolvency. However, the same firm with $250 in equity would be insolvent after a drop of only one-third in value.

X_5 = Sales/Total assets

This capital-turnover ratio is a standard financial ratio that illustrates the sales-generating ability of the firm's assets. It is one measure of management's capability in dealing with competitive conditions.

Note that variables X_1, X_2, X_3, and X_4 should be inserted into the model as decimal fractions; for example, a Working capital/Total assets ratio of 20 percent should be written as 0.20. The variable X_5, however, is usually a ratio greater than unity; for example, where sales are twice as large as assets, the ratio is 2.0.

SOURCE: Adapted from Edward I. Altman and James K. LaFleur, "Managing a Return to Financial Health," **Journal of Business Strategy,** 2, no. 1 (Summer 1981), pp. 31–38. Reprinted by permission.

TABLE 6.5

Stakeholder Groups and Their Impact on Organizational Performance

Stakeholder Category	Near-Term Performance Measures	Long-Term Performance Measures
Customers	Sales (value and volume) New customers Number of new customer needs met	Growth in sales Turnover in customer base Ability to control price

Suppliers	Cost of raw material
	Delivery time
	Inventory
	Availability of raw materials
		Growth rates of
		  Raw materials costs
		  Delivery time
		  Inventory
		  New ideas from suppliers

Financial community	EPS[a] Stock price Number of "buy" lists[b] ROE[c]	Ability to sell strategy to Wall Street Growth in ROE
Employees	Number of suggestions Productivity Number of grievances	Number of internal promotions Turnover

Congress	Number of new pieces of legislation
	  that affect the firm
	Access to key members and staff
		Number of new regulations that
		  affect the industry
		Ratio of cooperative to competitive
		  encounters

Consumer advocates	Number of meetings
	Number of hostile encounters
	Number of coalitions formed
	Number of legal actions
		Number of changes in policy due to
		  consumer advocates
		Number of calls for help initiated by
		  consumer advocates[d]

Environmentalists	Number of meetings
	Number of hostile encounters
	Number of coalitions formed
	Number of Environmental Protection
	  Agency complaints
	Number of legal actions
		Number of changes in policy due to
		  environmentalists
		
		Number of calls for help initiated by
		  environmentalists

[a]Earnings per share.

[b]Lists from which financial brokers recommend stock purchases for their clients.

[c]Return on equity.

[d]Calls in which consumer advocates attempt to enlist others in action against a company.

SOURCE: Adapted from Strategic Management: A Stakeholder Approach, Boston: Pitman Publishing, 1984. © R. Edward Freeman.

by stakeholder groups. The tone and content of such feedback can be an extremely valuable indicator of organizational progress toward financial and non-financial goals. Table 6.5 lists several stakeholder groups and measures to assess both the short-run and long-run impact they may have on organizational performance. The Skills Module invites you to evaluate a stakeholder analysis at Nike.

Our discussions about the variety of ways to measure strategic performance, and the variety of environments in which firms operate, suggest that strategic control systems may differ from firm to firm. Goold and Quinn propose that these systems depend on the level of environmental turbulence (high or low)

SKILLS MODULE
Assessing Stakeholder Attitudes toward Nike

INTRODUCTION

Stakeholders are groups or individuals who are interested in a corporation's activities because they are significantly affected by the organization's accomplishment of its objectives. Review the following situation at Nike, and then complete the skill development exercise that follows to analyze the reactions of various stakeholder groups to organizational strategy.

SITUATION

Philip Knight, founder and chairman of Nike Corp., has made business moves smoother than the moves of the athletes who wear—and endorse— his shoes. He capitalized on the jogging craze of the 1970s and the aerobics boom of the 1980s; by last year, his Hood River, Oregon company was the world's biggest purveyor of shoes. In the 1990s, Nike is going after the outdoor shoe market, a hot-growth area that, even for Nike, has limits.

But there are doubts about the latest twist in Nike's overall strategy. After a six-year hot streak that quadrupled annual sales to $3.9 billion and profits to $365 million, Nike has stubbed its toe. Sales of its major line, basketball shoes, have plateaued at around $600 million annually; sales of other athletic shoes have also stalled. The company's stock is down 43 percent from a high of $90.25 a share in late 1992, and Knight predicts no more than single-digit profit growth for the rest of 1994.

In 1992, Nike sold $123 million of outdoor footwear, just a small part of the company's overall U. S. sales of $2 billion. The line's growth was nearly 100 percent, though, while Nike's other sneaker lines barely registered single-digit increases. Knight predicts that his company will sell as many outdoor shoes as basketball sneakers in another couple of years.

Many retailing experts doubt that Nike's renaissance is in outdoor footwear alone; after all, the company cannot capture the market with models named after sports icons. Even if Nike does win over the outdoor windsurfing, rock-climbing, and snow-boarding crowd, retailing experts say that outdoor shoes won't generate anywhere near the multiple sales that sneakers and basketball shoes do.

But Knight is pursuing other strategies, as well, which rivals say simply reflect his desire for control. In the next year, Nike expects to open as many as 80 new boutiques within larger retailing stores that are devoted solely to Nike's products. Knight also talks of transforming Cole-Haan, the upscale shoe unit he purchased in the late 1980s, into a billion-dollar powerhouse going toe-to-toe with Timberland Inc.'s successful outdoor-style boots.

"We can see ourselves broadening out beyond shoes and clothes," he adds. Knight has been conferring with Michael Ovitz, chairman of the Hollywood talent agency Creative Artists Agency, on how to capitalize on interactive television and cable's vastly expanded channel range. Nike itself is getting involved in the talent business, taking over total management of the careers of four young professional athletes, including pro football and baseball player Deion Sanders and the NBA's Alonzo Mourning.

SKILL DEVELOPMENT EXERCISE

Nike chairman Philip Knight is busy formulating strategy while maintaining control over its implementation. Obviously, with stock prices down and long-term outlook hazy, stockholders are intensely interested in how well the various strategies will work. Some will probably respond positively to some moves, negatively to others. Analyze Nike's strategies and explain the reactions of stakeholders to its moves. Given your analysis, is Knight correct to employ so many diverse strategies, or is he overextending his ability to control the company's fortunes?

SOURCE: Bill Richards, "Nike's Management Races to Remake Company's Image," *The Wall Street Journal*, September 14, 1993, p. B4.

and a firm's ability to specify and measure precise strategic objectives. Their framework, shown in Figure 6.2, results in four strategic control types. When turbulence is low and precise goals are easy to specify and measure, strategic control systems can be described as valuable. When turbulence becomes high, however, control systems need greater flexibility to stay valuable.

When firms have difficulty specifying and measuring precise strategic objectives, low environmental turbulence calls for strategic controls that track a number of less precise indicators of performance. When turbulence is high

FIGURE 6.2
Strategic Control in
Different Sorts of
Businesses

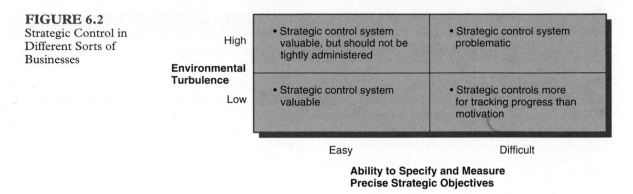

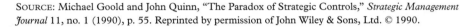

SOURCE: Michael Goold and John Quinn, "The Paradox of Strategic Controls," *Strategic Management Journal* 11, no. 1 (1990), p. 55. Reprinted by permission of John Wiley & Sons, Ltd. © 1990.

and precision difficult, strategic control, though still desirable, is problematic, due to changing external conditions that quickly make strategic control systems obsolete. For example, the biotechnology industry in the 1990s finds it difficult to specify precise objectives in a highly turbulent environment, because of both competitive conditions and the changing political climate with regard to health care.

This section has reviewed many different ways to measure organizational performance. Managers must establish and use whatever methods best suit their organization. One important guideline should govern this work, though. Organizations should measure, as best they can, performance in all critical areas targeted by goals, strategies, and plans.

Step 2: Compare Organizational Performance to Goals and Standards

After taking measurements of organizational performance, managers must compare them with two established benchmarks: goals and standards. Organizational goals are simply the output of an earlier step of the strategic management process.

Organizational standards are developed to reflect organizational goals; they are yardsticks that place organizational performance in perspective.[7] The specific standards that companies actually establish vary from firm to firm. As a rule, managers must develop standards in all performance areas that established organizational goals address. Developed many years ago at General Electric, the following standards are typical of those used by many firms in the 1990s.[8]

1. *Profitability standards:* These standards indicate how much profit General Electric would like to make in a given time period.
2. *Market position standards:* These standards indicate the percentage of a total product market that the company would like to win from its competitors.
3. *Productivity standards:* These production-oriented standards indicate various acceptable rates at which final products should be generated within the organization.

4. *Product leadership standards:* Innovation is critical for long-run organizational success. Product leadership standards indicate levels of product innovation that would make people view General Electric products as leaders in the market.
5. *Personnel development standards:* Development of organization members in all areas is critical to continued organizational success. Personnel development standards list acceptable levels of progress in this area.
6. *Employee attitude standards:* These standards indicate attitudes that General Electric employees should adopt. Not only are workers evaluated for the degree to which they project these attitudes, but managers are evaluated for the extent to which they develop them in their subordinates.
7. *Public responsibility standards:* All organizations have certain obligations to society. General Electric's standards in this area indicate acceptable levels of activity within the organization directed toward living up to social responsibilities.
8. *Standards reflecting balance between short-range and long-range goals:* General Electric, like most organizations, feels that both long-run and short-run goals are necessary to maintain a healthy and successful organization. Standards in this area indicate the acceptable long-range and short-range goals and the relationships among them.

The process of standard setting has attracted a great deal of interest in the 1990s with the popularity of the practice of **benchmarking.** In this control technique, a firm compares one of its functions, say product design, with that of another firm known for world-class excellence in that function, say 3M or Rubbermaid.

Step 3: Take Necessary Corrective Action

Once managers have collected organizational measurements and compared these measurements to established goals and standards, they should take any corrective action that is warranted. **Corrective action** is defined as a change in an organization's operations to ensure that it can more effectively and efficiently reach its goals and perform up to its established standards. Corrective action may be as simple as changing the price of a product or as complicated as a boardroom struggle, which ends in the firing of the CEO.

As the Company Example illustrates, strategic control can also result in changes as dramatic as modifying the products a company offers in the marketplace. In order to attract more customers, Radio Shack has taken corrective action to improve the design of its stores, its array of products (now to include IBM PCs), and the market appeal of its advertising campaign.

A thorough understanding of the steps of the strategic control process and their relationships to the major steps of the strategic management process should guide corrective action. Figure 6.3 summarizes the main steps of the strategic control process and illustrates its relationship with the major steps of the strategic management process.

Assume that a particular organization has failed to meet appropriate organizational goals and standards so that corrective action is necessary. As Figure 6.3 implies, this action might include attempting to improve organizational performance by focusing on one or more of the major steps of the strategic management process. Of course, this analysis could include improving the

FIGURE 6.3   Relationships between the Strategic Process and the Strategic Control Process

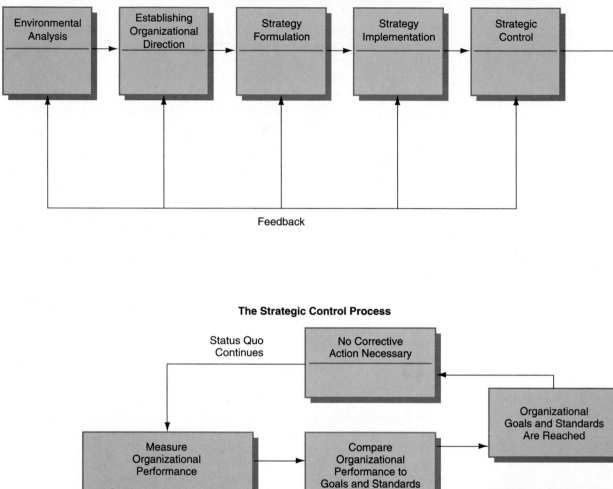

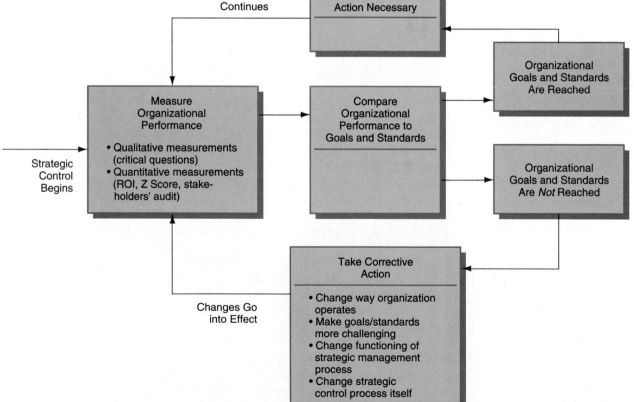

COMPANY EXAMPLE

Tandy Cedes Control and Label-Only Strategy

Change, more profound to the company's operating strategy than its new store floor plans and service offerings, more long-lasting than its new advertising campaign, was unveiled recently at Radio Shack.

Continuing its bid to revitalize the consumer-electronics store chain, parent company Tandy Corp. has abandoned its private-label-only strategy for personal computers, and says it will introduce name-brand products into its stores. In 500 Radio Shack stores that have previously recorded healthy sales of laptop computers, the chain will begin selling two IBM notebook computer models. The pilot program also includes test-marketing of IBM and AST Research Inc. desktop PCs, and possibly other brands.

Last year, the consumer-electronics giant sold its computer manufacturing business to AST, which continues to supply the Tandy label. The $175 mil-lion sale enabled Tandy to sell PCs from competing manufacturers.

Radio Shack dealers have complained about the company's lackluster products and weak computer brand name. Tandy's chairman, John V. Roach, doesn't disagree, acknowledging that Tandy was having a tough time keeping up with technological developments and recovering development costs. "With very short product cycles, you need very fast inventory turns," said Roach. "It makes sense to supplement the line with name-brand products."

Although Roach says that Radio Shack will increase its reliance on name-brand products, he says that no decision has been made on whether to offer IBM computers at all 6,500 Radio Shack stores.

SOURCE: "Tandy's Radio Shack, Changing Strategy to Offer IBM PC's," *The Wall Street Journal*, May 5, 1994, p. B7

strategic control process itself by enhancing the validity and reliability of organizational performance measures.

In most situations, corrective action is not necessary if the organization is reaching its goals and standards. However, management must not automatically assume that this is the case. Goals and standards may have been set too low, in which case corrective action should be taken to make them more challenging.

INFORMATION FOR STRATEGIC CONTROL

Successful strategic control requires valid and reliable information about various measures of organizational performance. Without such information, strategic control action will have little chance of consistently improving organizational performance. Reliable, timely, and valid information is the lifeblood of successful strategic control.

To gather this valid, reliable, and timely information, virtually every organization develops and implements some type of formal system. The following sections discuss two such systems: management information systems (MISs) and management decision support systems (MDSSs).

Management Information System (MIS)

A **management information system** is a formal, computer-assisted organizational function designed to provide managers with information to help their decision making. Although such information has many different uses, a significant portion of it supports strategic control.

As Figure 6.4 illustrates, operating an MIS is largely a matter of performing six related steps. We interpret these steps in the context of an MIS for strategic control.

Once managers decide what information they need for strategic control, they must collect and analyze appropriate data, and disseminate the information this analysis yields to appropriate organization members, usually upper management. Next, upper management must plan and implement strategic control activities in light of this information. Finally, continuing feedback on the effect of implementing these activities, and on the functioning of the MIS system itself, must guide efforts to meet the information needs of strategic control more effectively in the future.

MIS and Management Levels   Because managers at various levels of the organization perform different kinds of activities, the MIS should be flexible enough to provide various management levels with the information they need to carry out these activities. Table 6.6 summarizes typical activities performed by top, middle, and lower-level managers. This table illustrates that strategic control and other strategic management tasks are the primary focus of top management, but all management levels have some role in the strategic management process, and the MIS should provide them the supportive information they need.

FIGURE 6.4
Major Steps in
Operating an MIS

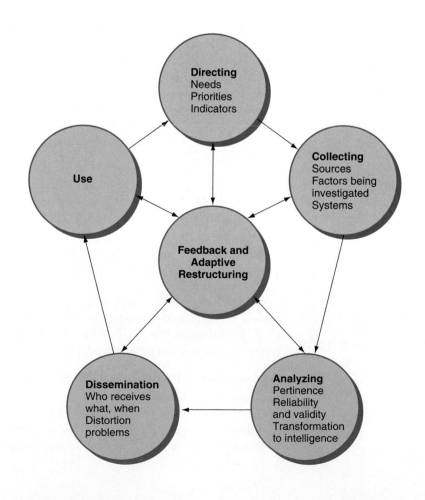

TABLE 6.6		

Typical Activities of Managers at Various Organizational Levels

Organizational Level	Characteristics of Activities	Sample Activities
Top management	Future oriented Significant uncertainty Significant subjective assessment Strategic management emphasis	Establishing organizational direction Performing environmental analysis Developing organizational strategies
Middle management	Somewhat future oriented (less than top-management activities) Emphasis on implementation of strategies	Making short-term forecasts Budgeting Human resource planning
Supervisory management	Emphasis on daily production Emphasis on daily performance that reflects organizational strategy and contributes to attaining long-term goals	Assigning jobs to specific workers Managing inventory Supervising workers Handling worker complaints Maintaining organizational procedures and rules

Symptoms of an Inadequate MIS   Because the effectiveness of the strategic control process depends largely on valid and reliable organizational performance measures, managers must continually assess MIS functioning to ensure that it meets strategic control needs. Most managers agree that they must constantly watch for signals that an MIS is not operating effectively. Naturally, once such symptoms are discovered, managers must take steps to solve whatever problems plague the MIS. Once these problems are eliminated, the symptoms of trouble should disappear.

Sensing MIS-related problems can be quite difficult, or it may be as simple as listening to the comments of strategic control decision makers. These individuals may complain that they have too much information of the wrong kind and not enough of the right kind, that information is so dispersed throughout the company that they must struggle to gather simple facts, that others sometimes suppress vital information for political reasons, that vital information frequently arrives too late to be useful, or that information often defies efforts to assess its accuracy and no one can provide confirmation. Managers may bluntly worry that the information they get may be moving them in the wrong strategic direction at full speed.[9]

Bertram A. Colbert, a principal of Price Waterhouse & Company, has indicated other kinds of symptoms that can also betray malfunctions in an MIS: (1) *operational symptoms,* which are related to the way an organization functions; (2) *psychological symptoms,* which reflect the feelings of organization members; and (3) *report content symptoms,* which affect the structures of reports generated by the MIS. Table 6.7 lists several organizational symptoms that fall in each of these three categories.

As soon as they become aware of symptoms of this sort, managers should take action to solve the MIS problems. In practice, however, it may be quite difficult to determine exactly what problems within an organization are

TABLE 6.7

Symptoms of a Malfunctioning MIS

Operational Symptoms	Psychological Symptoms	Report Content Symptoms
Large physical inventory adjustments	Surprise at financial results	Excessive use of large tables of numbers
Capital expenditure overruns	Poor attitude of executives about usefulness of information	Multiple preparation and distribution of identical data
Unexplained changes from year to year in operating results	Lack of understanding of financial information by nonfinancial executives	Disagreements among information from different sources
Uncertain direction of company growth	Lack of concern for environmental changes	Lack of periodic comparative and trend information
Unexplained cost variances	Excessive homework	Late information
No order backlog awareness		Too little or excess detail
No internal discussion of reported data		Inaccurate information
Insufficient knowledge about competition		Lack of standards for comparison
Purchasing parts from outside vendors that the firm could make itself		Failure to identify variances by cause and responsibility
Failure of investments in facilities, or in programs such as R&D and advertising		Inadequate externally generated information

SOURCE: Institute for Practitioners in Work-Study, Organization, and Methods, Middlesex, England, *Management Sciences* 4, no. 5 (September–October 1967), pp. 15–24. Reprinted by kind permission of the editor—Management Services.

hampering the effectiveness of the MIS. Answering five questions may help the manager to pinpoint strategic control problems related to the MIS:

1. Where and how do managers involved in the strategic control process get information?
2. Can managers involved in strategic control make better use of their contacts to get information?
3. In what strategic control areas is the knowledge of these managers weakest, and what information might help to minimize such weaknesses?
4. Do managers involved in strategic control tend to act before receiving enough information?
5. Do managers involved in strategic control wait so long for information that opportunities pass them by and they become bottlenecks?[10]

Management Decision Support System (MDSS)[11]

An MIS that gathers data and provides information to managers electronically is invaluable. This MIS assistance has been especially useful in areas where managers must make recurring decisions; the computer repeatedly generates the information they need. An example of such a structured decision might be using the computer to track cumulative population shifts in the market a firm serves. The computer may update environmental analysis reports automatically and even remind management to consider deploying additional salespeople when the number of target customers in a specified market area increases substantially.

Closely related to the MIS is the management decision support system (MDSS), sometimes referred to as an executive information system (EIS). A **management decision support system** is an interdependent set of decision aids that helps managers make relatively unstructured, perhaps nonrecurring decisions. The computer (in conjunction with software like *Lotus* spreadsheet) is the main element of the MDSS, functioning as an analytical tool to assist in judgment decisions. The MDSS, however, does not pretend to dictate the manager's decision or impose solutions to problems. Many managers use an MDSS to help them make strategic control decisions and other types of strategic management decisions. For example, a manager may consider how best to implement strategy within an organization by determining all the different costs of various implementation alternatives. The MDSS provides and organizes the information and the manager makes the decision based on it.

Stunning technological advances in microcomputers have made MDSSs feasible and available to virtually all managers. Continuing developments in information analysis software support more subjective decision making, contributing to the popularity of the MDSS. Figure 6.5 is a recent attempt to graphically portray the information needs of executives responsible for

FIGURE 6.5   Information, Executives, and Strategic Decision Making

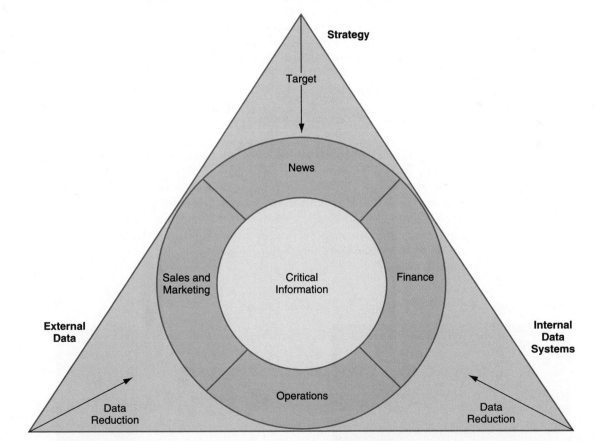

SOURCE: Reprinted with permission from *Long Range Planning* 25, no. 6 Robin Matthews and Anthony Shoebridge, "EIS—A Guide for Executives," (December 1992), p. 98, Elsevier Science Ltd., Pergamon Imprint, Oxford, England.

strategic control in their firms, and the internal functions responsible for finding, interpreting, and passing on critical information to top managers.

TOP MANAGERS AND STRATEGIC CONTROL

Because strategic management is primarily the responsibility of top managers, and because it is a critical ingredient of successful strategic management, top managers must understand strategic control and know how to take actions implied by the strategic control process. Top managers must make a solid and enduring commitment to establishing and using a strategic control system within the organization. Of course, they must commit organizational resources to support this activity.

Figure 6.6 illustrates the variables that are important to maintaining successful strategic control. According to this model, strategic control entails reaching either of two primary objectives: maintaining strategic momentum already achieved or leaping to a new strategy direction if and when it is appropriate.

According to this model, in order to reach either of these objectives, top managers must ensure that four interrelated organizational variables are consistent and complementary: (1) organizational structure, (2) reward systems, (3) information systems, and (4) organizational value systems or cultures. To maintain strategic momentum or leap to a new strategy, top management must ensure that:

1. Reward systems encourage appropriate behavior within the organization.
2. The organizational structure contributes to attainment of strategic objectives.
3. Values and norms that define the organizational culture are consistent with the firm's objectives.
4. The information support systems needed to track performance are in place.

SUMMARY

Organizational control entails monitoring, evaluating, and improving various types of activities within an organization in order to make events unfold as planned. Strategic control, a special type of organizational control, focuses on monitoring and evaluating the strategic management process to ensure that what is supposed to happen actually does happen. Although strategic control has many different purposes within an organization, the most fundamental one is to help managers achieve organizational goals via control of strategic management.

FIGURE 6.6   Variables Important to Maintaining Strategic Control

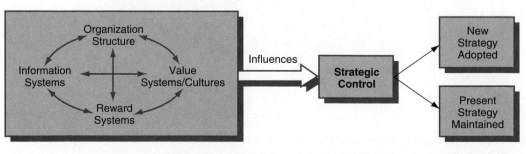

The strategic control process includes three basic steps. Step 1 measures organizational performance. Here management generally uses strategic audits to determine what is actually happening within the organization. Step 2 compares organizational performance to goals and standards. Here management builds a case to conclude whether or not what has happened as a result of the strategic management process is acceptable. Step 3 in the strategic control process is actually taking any corrective action necessary. If events are promoting organizational goals established within the strategic management process, no corrective action is necessary. If events are out of line with plans, however, some type of corrective action is usually appropriate.

Information that reflects valid and reliable measurements of organizational activities is a prerequisite for successful strategic control. Recognizing the importance of acquiring and applying such information, most organizations establish both management information systems (MISs) and management decision support systems (MDSSs). These systems typically use the computer in conjunction with specially tailored software to provide management with needed measures of organizational performance. Once established, information systems must be constantly monitored to ensure that they continue to work properly.

Top managers have an important role in making sure that strategic control is successful. Upper-level managers must design and implement the strategic control process to encourage appropriate strategic control behavior within the organization through organizational reward systems, an organizational structure consistent with strategic objectives, an organizational culture that supports strategic control, and necessary information.

KEY TERMS

control, p. 138
strategic control, p. 139
strategic audit, p. 139
stakeholders' audit, p. 144
organizational standard, p. 148
benchmarking, p. 149

corrective action, p. 149
management information system (MIS), p. 151
management decision support system (MDSS), p. 155

CHECKLIST   Analyzing Strategic Control in Problems and Cases

___ 1. Does the situation or case involve strategic control issues?

___ 2. Is the strategic control effort described in the case fulfilling all of its purposes?

___ 3. Does the case raise issues about the role and conduct of strategic audits?

___ 4. Have both qualitative and quantitative measures of organizational performance been appropriately employed?

___ 5. Are the interests of various stakeholder groups being considered?

___ 6. Are appropriate performance standards being set and compared to organizational performance?

___ 7. Is any necessary corrective action taken?

___ 8. Is a management information system (MIS) established and operating appropriately?

___　9.　Is a management decision support system (MDSS) working as it should?

___　10.　Are various levels of management appropriately involved in the strategic control process?

Additional Readings

Goold, M., and J. J. Quinn. "The Paradox of Strategic Controls." *Strategic Management Journal* 11, no. 1 (1990), p. 43.

Harrison, Jeffrey S., Ernest H. Hall, Jr., and Rajendra Norgundkar. "Resource Allocation as an Outcropping of Strategic Consistency: Performance Implications." *Academy of Management Journal*, October 1993, p. 1,026.

Hinterhuber, Hans H., and Wolfgang Popp. "Are You a Strategist or Just a Manager?" *Harvard Business Review*, January/February 1992, p. 105.

Julian, Scott. "Toward a Comprehensive Framework for Strategic Control," *Academy of Management Best Paper Proceedings*, ed. by Dorothy Moore (1993), p. 17.

Kovacevic, Antonio, and Nicholás Majluf. "Six Steps of IT Strategic Management." *Sloan Management Review*, Summer 1993, p. 77.

Lorange, P., M. Scott-Morton, and S. Ghoshal. *Strategic Control Systems*. St. Paul, Minn.: West, 1986.

Preble, J. "Toward a Comprehensive System of Strategic Control." *Journal of Management Studies* 29, no. 4 (1992), p. 391.

CASE

Benetton's Strategy for a New Era

Benetton, purveyor of brightly colored clothing in more than 7,000 shops in 110 countries, prides itself on confounding conventional wisdom. Despite the recession in its West European heartland, the Italian company's 1993 post-tax profits increased 12.6 percent on sales that were up 9.5 percent. It runs what many call tasteless advertisements—a priest kissing a nun, the bloodstained clothing of a Bosnian war victim—which offend some but bring the company a high public profile at a low cost. Benetton, still 70 percent family-owned, spends only 4 percent of sales revenue on marketing.

Now it intends to pose its greatest challenge to conventional wisdom—refuting the idea that all fashion retailers eventually go out of fashion.

Benetton has thrived through a unique organizational system and a philosophy that it is a clothing services company rather than a retailer or manufacturer. Its customers are its shops, which are owned by outsiders; unlike normal franchise systems, the shops pay no royalties and Benetton accepts no returned stock. The company's in-house responsibilities are similar; Benetton handles only those bits of manufacturing—design, cutting, dyeing, and packing—that it thinks crucial to maintain quality and cost-efficiency. The rest it contracts out to local suppliers, reducing Benetton's risk and allowing it the flexibility to respond to sales trends.

The formula has worked well; unlike most retailers, Benetton is debt-free. But there are drawbacks to the devolved structure. With little control or leverage over shop owners, Benetton has had problems encouraging them to expand and invest in larger quarters; only 5 percent have done so. Instead, the company is relying on price cuts of up to 40 percent to increase market share in Europe; volume is up 25 percent in some markets.

Luciano Benetton says that losing creativity is the biggest risk his company faces. He counters that possibility by building innovation into the corporate structure—the firm has 200 young designers and is setting up a new international design school. Nevertheless, most of Benetton's future profits depend on cut-and-dried business issues: diversification and cost-cutting. The company should soon formalize a joint venture for 300 shops in China, and it is fast expanding in Egypt, India, and South America. But progress abroad is not perfect. After breakneck expansion into the world's most competitive retail market—the United States—Benetton has only 150 stores, down from 800 in 1988.

Benetton maintains 80 percent of its clothing production in Europe; Luciano Benetton believes that the key to competing with Asia-based producers is computers, or what he calls "modern industrial production." In 1993, the company opened a 430,000-square-foot, high-tech cutting and packing plant for jeans. Plans for another plant were approved a few months later. Both will be linked by tunnels to a computerized warehouse, opened in 1986, that handles 30,000 boxes a day with a staff of 20. The company has also developed software for machine-knitted, seamless sweaters that require no hand finishing.

DISCUSSION QUESTIONS

1. How effectively has Benetton completed the three major steps in the strategic control process? Explain.

2. How can Luciano Benetton maintain strategic control within the company's structure? Will Benetton's structure be an impediment to future growth?

3. Identify the interrelationships among components of Benetton's strategic system. What are some alternative solutions to the company's problems and ways of capitalizing on opportunities?

SOURCE: *The Economist*, April 23, 1994, p. 68.

Notes

1. For a comprehensive discussion of the control function see Robert N. Anthony, *The Management Control Function* (Boston: Harvard Business School Press, 1988).

2. Robert L. Dewelt, "Control: Key to Making Financial Strategy Work," *Management Review*, March 1977, p.18. This link between planning and control is supported and illustrated in S. S. Cowen and J. K. Middaugh, "Designing an Effective Financial Planning and Control System," *Long Range Planning* 21 (December 1988), pp. 83–92. See also Robert Simons, "Strategic Orientation and Top Management Attention to Control Systems," *Strategic Management Journal* 12, no. 1 (1991), pp. 46–62.

3. For an excellent discussion of the strategic control process, see J. Preble, "Toward a Comprehensive System of Strategic Control," *Journal of Management Studies* 29, no. 4 (1992), p. 391.

4. Seymour Tilles, "How to Evaluate Corporate Strategy," *Harvard Business Review*, July/August 1963, pp. 111–121.

5. Edward I. Altman and James K. LaFleur, "Managing a Return to Financial Health," *The Journal of Business Strategy* 2, no. 1 (Summer 1981), pp. 31–38.

6. R. E. Freeman, *Strategic Management: A Stakeholder Approach* (Boston: Pitman, 1984), p. 25.

7. For insights regarding how to construct worthwhile performance indicators, see R. Kaufman, "Preparing Useful Performance Indicators," *Training and Development Journal* 42 (September 1989), pp. 80–83.

8. Robert W. Lewis, "Measuring, Reporting, and Appraising Results of Operations with Reference to Goals, Plans, and Budgets," in *Planning, Managing, and Measuring the Business: A Case Study of Management Planning and Control at General Electric Company* (New York: Controllership Foundation, 1955).

9. Daniel H. Gray, "Uses and Misuses of Strategic Planning," *Harvard Business Review,* January/February 1986, pp. 89–97.

10. Henry Mintzberg, "The Manager's Job: Folklore and Fact," *Harvard Business Review,* July/August 1975, p. 58. Some implications of this article from a strategic viewpoint are discussed in James Brian Quinn, Henry Mintzberg, and Robert M. James, *The Strategy Process: Concepts, Contexts, and Cases* (Englewood Cliffs, N. J.: Prentice-Hall, 1988), p. 21.

11. This section is based on Steven L. Mandell, *Computers and Data Processing: Concepts and Applications with BASIC* (St. Paul, Minn.: West, 1982), pp. 370–391.

PART III

Special Issues in Strategic Management

In Parts I and II of this text, we introduced and analyzed the strategic management process. The knowledge and skills you developed in your study of Chapters 1 through 6 can be successfully applied to a variety of strategic management problems and cases. However, dealing with certain situations that arise in strategic management may require additional, specialized knowledge of particular areas. In the following part, we discuss three such areas that strategic managers often need to be familiar with: international operations (Chapter 7), total quality management (Chapter 8), and social responsibility and ethics (Chapter 9). After carefully studying this part, you should understand the special problems that strategic managers confront when they deal with issues in these important areas.

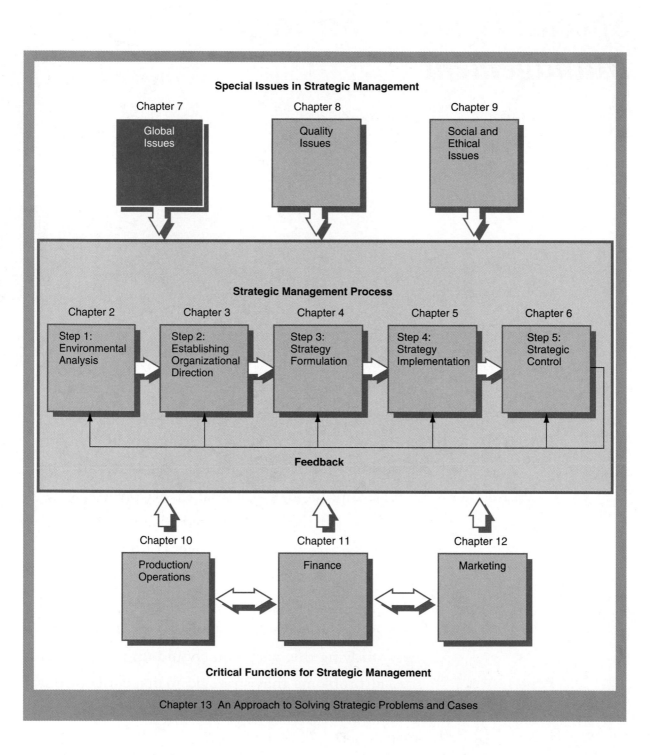

CHAPTER

7

Strategic Management of International Operations

This chapter explores the strategic management process for businesses that operate internationally. Over the last several years, businesses have increasingly crossed international borders in their operations. Since this trend is expected to continue, international issues are extremely important to the success of any effort to formulate and implement organizational strategy.

This chapter divides its discussion into four sections. First, we discuss some of the trends that drive the growth of international business in general. Second, we discuss the main international trade agreements that underlie all international business. We then discuss national industrial policies and how they facilitate or hinder an organization's progress toward its objectives. Finally, we trace the familiar steps in strategic management process, noting the special characteristics of international strategic management.

GROWING IMPORTANCE OF INTERNATIONAL MANAGEMENT

Before we can discuss the impact of international operations on the strategic management process, we must explain the meaning of the term *international management*. This leads to an overview of the growing importance of international issues in organizations.

International Management Defined

International management involves performing management activities across national borders. In other words, the organization seeks to accomplish its mission, at least partially, by conducting business in a foreign country. This could be as simple as selling a product in a foreign country or as complicated as collaborating with foreign partners to manufacture and sell products throughout the world.

Advances in transportation, technology, and communications, along with developments in the economic, political, and cultural components of the business environment, have helped organizations to cross international borders. An excerpt from the mission statement of General Motors' Asian Technical Center illustrates the extent of some U.S. firms' commitments to foreign investment:

Corporate support for further development of the market in Japan has resulted in the establishment of a technical center called the Asian Technical Center (ASTEC) in Akishima. The establishment of ASTEC is symbolic of the GM Automotive Components Group's commitment to sell automotive parts to Japanese companies. ASTEC's engineers are primarily Japanese who were trained in the United States so they can effectively communicate and provide timely responses to customers. Our sales achievement of $180 million in 1991 is an excellent base from which to move forward, and we intend to aggressively pursue a higher rate of growth. We remain committed to introducing new technology to the Japanese market as we continue to improve product quality and cost.[1]

Such strong commitments to growth and success in international markets compel managers to integrate international issues into their strategic planning and decision making. Before we examine how they do this, we must explore some important changes in the context of international business and trade.

Context of International Business

International issues are growing more important in organizations because international business is becoming more integrated around the globe. In 1993, the World Future Society sponsored its WORLD 2000 project to identify the forces that are integrating life around the earth into a coherent global order, as well as the forces that are creating disorder. This project began by reviewing research literature to identify a set of trends. A group of business executives then reviewed, evaluated, and summarized the trends. Although powerful forces drive disorder and disintegration, the overall trends seem to be leading in the direction of order, interdependence, and integration. Table 7.1 summarizes the findings of WORLD 2000.[2]

The movement toward order and interdependence shown in the table is also reflected in the growing interconnection between individuals' daily lives and events taking place around the globe. For example, two decades ago a place like Troy, a city of about 19,000 tucked away in southwestern Ohio, was considered heartland America.[3] Far removed and well-insulated from the bustle of international business and the aggravation of volatile exchange rates, the citizens of Troy could go about their daily routines without worrying about markets in China and business practices in Tokyo. Today, Troy still has the deceptive appearance of classic Americana: swings and American flags hang from inviting porches; mom-and-pop stores line Main Street; Lee's Family Restaurant promotes a $1.99 chicken gizzard dinner. Beneath this calm veneer, however, the inhabitants of Troy are plugged into a complex global network that brings events in Kuala Lumpur and Yokohama into their daily routines.

Mike Hines, a foreman in PMI Food Equipment Group in Troy, knows that at 1:30 p.m. each day, a truck picks up hand-assembled mixers from his factory to be exported to places like the United Arab Emirates, China, and Malaysia. Kay DeWeese, who farms 1,300 acres in Troy with her husband and son, regularly tracks commodity prices via a backyard satellite dish. Some of the corn and soybeans they grow are exported to Japan. "We want to see a strong enough Japanese economy to be able to buy our grain," she says. Jim Witmer, a Troy photographer, knows that the prices of Nikon cameras sold at B-K Photo Products have shot up twice during 1993. A new Nikon

TABLE 7.1

Trends That Drive the Emerging Global Order

TRAJECTORY TOWARD INTEGRATION

Trend 1. Stable population.
Worldwide population will stabilize at 10–14 billion by the mid-21st century
Trend 2. Wiring the globe.
Advances in information technology suggest the emergence of a single, worldwide communications network.
Trend 3. International culture.
The consolidation of economic blocs and political federations, combined with new information technology, hold the promise of an emerging international culture.
Trend 4. Universal standard of freedom.
The number of nations with political systems based on freedom and the recognition of human rights continues to grow.
Trend 5. Transcendent values.
People across the globe strive for quality of life, community, and self-fulfillment—higher-order values that transcend material needs.

OBSTACLES TO INTEGRATION

Issue 1. The transition to a uniform global order requires systems that integrate the world.
Issue 2. Individual-based capitalist systems (e.g., United States) clash with collaboration-based economic systems (e.g., Japan).
Issue 3. The conflict between growth and environmental protection must be resolved.
Issue 4. We have not yet invented the new institutions needed to manage this complex new world.
Issue 5. The economic disparity between the developed countries in the North and the less-developed countries of the South continues to grow.

300-millimeter lens that cost $750 at the beginning of the year soared to more than $1,000 by December because the yen grew stronger relative to the dollar.

The dollar's decline in value helped to induce foreign corporations to manufacture in the United States. Corporations like American Matsushita Electronics Corporation employ thousands of Troy residents at plants along nearby Interstate 75. In 1993, this unit of Japan's Matsushita Electric Industrial announced that it would bolster its local work force of 600 employees, who make picture tubes for Panasonic color television sets. Honda Motor Co. and Gokoh Corp. have offices and plants nearby. More than 50 Japanese executives and their families have settled in Troy. Troy's motor vehicle bureau offers the written driver's license exam in Japanese to make it easier for the executives and their wives to take the test.

Growth of International Trade

Like the citizens of Troy, modern managers operate in an increasingly international environment. This environment has emerged from a decade of continuous growth in international trade and a steady drop in the tariffs and duties that restrict international flows of goods and services. Tables 7.2 and 7.3 show the rates at which world trade has grown and tariffs have dropped.

As organizations scramble to stay in line with these emerging international trends, managers must evaluate and monitor the political and economic forces that drive the trends, and their influence on the strategic management process. An increasingly liberal international trade environment demands that managers evaluate threats from competitors across the globe. Lands' End hoped to pose such a threat to catalog retailers in Europe, as the Skills Module explains. Their environmental analysis must expand to encompass a number of international concerns:

- What institutional environment constrains competitors?
- What rules govern competitors' actions?

TABLE 7.2

Annual Percentage Change in International Trade

	World Merchandise Output	World Merchandise Trade
1982	−1.88%	−3.08%
1983	1.15	2.31
1984	5.77	8.08
1985	2.69	2.61
1986	2.69	4.61
1987	2.88	5.77
1988	4.92	8.84
1989	3.65	6.92
1990	1.92	5.00
1991	0.38	2.88
1992	0.96[a]	3.85[a]

[a]Figures for 1992 are preliminary estimates based on data available in March 1992.

SOURCE: Adapted from R. Scherer, "Seven Years Later: Deal Is Likely," *Christian Science Monitor,* December 10, 1993, p. 6.

TABLE 7.3

Average Tariffs on Imports to Industrial Nations

	Average Tariffs
1940	40.0%
1950	24.7
1960	16.7
1970	12.3
1980	8.0
1990	5.3
2000	2.7[a]

[a]Estimated.

SOURCE: Adapted from H. LaFranchi, "What's Next for World Trade?" *Christian Science Monitor,* December 23, 1993, p. 6.

SKILLS MODULE
Lands' End Seeks Global Future

INTRODUCTION

The impact of international operations on strategic management has become increasingly significant as trends toward domestic and bottom-line interests and global competition have become intertwined. Review the following situation at Lands' End, and then complete the skill development exercise that follows. This will help you to analyze the special considerations that affect the strategic management process on the international stage.

SITUATION

After years of growth in the United States, Lands' End Inc. decided to set sail for international markets. The Dodgeville, Wisconsin, seller of upscale apparel had enjoyed wide success with its domestic catalog sales of outdoor apparel and household goods. Like some of its U.S. competitors—including L. L. Bean, J. Crew, and Spiegel Inc.—the catalog merchant determined that its real growth opportunities lay overseas.

Although overseas sales accounted for less than 10 percent of its $870 million in overall sales, a company representative asserted that "international expansion will be a primary avenue of growth for us." William J. O'Neill, vice president, international for Lands' End, added that conditions made the environment ripe for success: two-worker families had increased, delivery service became quicker, and shopping by mail had become increasingly popular.

The U.S. mail-order industry was booming, with sales expected to increase 7 percent in 1994. In 1993, more than 8,000 catalog houses issued 12 billion catalogs in the United States. All of these small, specialty marketers competed on a level playing field; no company took more than a 6.4 percent share of the industry's $55 billion in total sales.

Still, the overseas market looked huge; in Japan alone, 1992 mail-order sales of $178 billion were more than triple U.S. sales. The situation among European catalogers was similar, and their businesses were just as dissimilar to those of their American counterparts. In Europe, huge catalog concerns published books up to 1,300 pages long to sell everything from clothing and furniture to consumer electronics and appliances. Their shares of the home-market, mail-order pie ranged from 20 percent to 35 percent.

The majority of U.S. firms that headed overseas specialized in basic work and leisure apparel—clothing that had the widest cross-cultural appeal. That's the basis of the Lands' End marketing strategy, said O'Neill. Men in Japan "wear white shirts and ties, and the women wear skirts and jackets, and we sell those things."

The Americans' skill at reproducing their marketing and distribution success overseas would decide their fate. They also had to adapt their operations to local constraints and outrun local competitors. One of France's giant catalogers had already battened down the hatches; to blunt the effect of J. Crew's arrival, it launched a new book offering clothing similar to the American company's.

Lands' End began testing the waters in 1991, mailing catalogs to customers in the United Kingdom. Two years later, it opened a distribution center there, reducing delivery time to three days from two weeks. It grew to mail 70-page versions of its standard, 160-page U.S. catalog 10 times a year in the United Kingdom. In late 1994, it planned a mass mailing to Japan.

SKILL DEVELOPMENT EXERCISE

As head of the Lands' End marketing department, outline how you can best ensure the company's success in differentiating its products and its image from both its American counterparts and its foreign competitors. Detail how you would anticipate the competition and respond to it, and trace the strategic management steps you would take to build a foundation for international success.

SOURCE: Gregory A. Patterson, "U.S. Catalogers Test International Waters," *The Wall Street Journal*, April 19, 1994, p. B1.

- What recourse is available to minimize damage from the actions of competitors?
- What government policies strengthen competitors?
- How can firms influence these government policies?
- What new markets and opportunities emerge as barriers to international trade continually shrink?

Answers to these questions are unique to specific organizations and industries. However, multilateral and regional trade agreements form a foundation for all international business operations.

INTERNATIONAL TRADE AGREEMENTS

The competitive environment varies significantly across international markets. An emerging nation like Uzbekistan may have no laws that protect the copyright of an American organization. Even when copyright protection is written into the local laws, in Thailand for example, the enforcement of the local laws may be lax. Walt Disney Co. has moved aggressively to stem the flood of pirated Disney products in Thailand. John Feenie, the head of Disney's consumer products division, hired an anticounterfeiting consultant, accumulated evidence against the pirates, staged raids to confiscate counterfeits, and burned entire consignments of counterfeit Donald Duck, Mickey Mouse, and Bambi dolls. To orchestrate his company's massive retaliation against counterfeiters in Thailand, Feenie operated within a complex web of international trade laws, economic agreements, and business regulations. This web includes broad multilateral economic agreements, as well as more narrowly focused regional arrangements. In this section we discuss the structure, intentions, and provisions of trade agreements that define the infrastructure within which managers like Feenie compete in global markets.

General Agreement on Tariffs and Trade (GATT)

The **General Agreement on Tariffs and Trade** is a broad, multilateral trade agreement designed to smooth the flow of goods between nations. Together, the 115 nations that subscribe to this treaty account for more than 90 percent of world trade. The treaty is administered by a Geneva-based bureaucracy that referees world trade. Its basic aim is to liberalize and promote world trade. Since 1948, GATT has functioned as the principal international forum for negotiating reductions in trade barriers and governing international trade relations. An abbreviated history of the GATT is provided in Table 7.4.

Although the actual GATT agreement is a long and complicated document, its provisions have emerged from a simple set of principles and aims.[4]

- Members are expected to engage in trade without discrimination. No country may give special trading advantages to another or discriminate against another. Exceptions to this rule are limited to certain special circumstances such as regional trading arrangements and trade with developing countries.
- Any protection to domestic industry must take the form of a customs tariff. This makes the extent of protection clear.
- Member nations must abide by negotiated tariff levels. This promotes stability in trade, with a provision for renegotiation of tariffs.
- When a country feels that its rights under the agreement are being denied or compromised, it may call on GATT for a fair settlement. Most of these

TABLE 7.4

History of GATT

1946–1947	The first proposal was made to form the International Trade Organization (ITO) as a special agency of the United Nations. The political climate that lingered after the protectionist trade policies of the 1920s and 1930s was not supportive. ITO was abandoned, but part of its charter was later salvaged as the General Agreement on Tariffs and Trade.
1948	GATT was established, joining 23 nations to try to liberalize world trade by eliminating tariffs. The agreement consisted of a set of articles that laid down the basic principles of trade. Member nations' trade laws had to conform with these articles.
1950–1959	The Annecy Round, the Torquay Round, and the Geneva Round, named for the cities in which the documents were signed, began seven rounds of multilateral negotiations to reduce trade barriers.
1960–1961	The Dillon Round was initiated in response to a proposal by some European nations to band together under a regional trade agreement, the European Economic Community. Steps were taken to ensure that world trade would not suffer as a result of such regional agreements.
1963–1967	The Kennedy Round was the first round to reduce tariffs comprehensively rather than product by product. Dumping—international sales of goods below cost—was recognized as a problem, and the first antidumping measures were passed.
1973–1979	The Tokyo Round was the first to recognize the importance of nontariff trade barriers such as quotas.
1986–1993	The Uruguay Round began with the goal of reducing tariffs by one-third. Additionally, it addressed the weak enforcement of GATT rules, increases in bilateral and unilateral actions, emergence of newly industrialized economies, trade in services, and protection of intellectual property rights. By this time, GATT had 115 member nations.
1994	GATT was renamed World Trade Organization.

SOURCE: Adapted from R. Scherer, "GATT's Conception and Progress," *Christian Science Monitor,* December 10, 1993, p. 6.

differences are settled directly between the countries concerned. Sometimes the GATT council appoints independent experts to facilitate the negotiations between member nations.

- A country may seek a waiver from a particular GATT obligation if special economic or trade circumstances warrant one.
- GATT generally prohibits quantitative restrictions on trade. An exception to this rule allows quantitative restrictions to deal with balance-of-payments difficulties.
- GATT permits **regional trade arrangements,** in which groups of countries agree to abolish or reduce barriers against imports from one another, as exceptions, providing they meet certain criteria. These rules are intended to ensure that the arrangements facilitate trade among the countries concerned without raising barriers to trade with the outside world.

The city of Stoke on Trent in England is the world capital of the fine tableware industry. The Dudson Group is a typical example of a local tableware manufacturer. This family-owned firm was founded in 1800 by Managing Director Ian Dudson's ancestors. In the Dudson Group's factory, workers busily mold and fire clay into fine china for customers the world over. GATT allows Ian Dudson to sell fruit bowls to a Canadian restaurant, soup dishes to roadside stalls on Italy's *autostrada,* teacups to the Belgian railway, and dinner plates to a Singapore hotel.[5]

GATT reassures Ian Dudson that his products will not suffer discrimination based on their country of origin, and it provides unambiguous information about the tariff structures and other protectionist barriers in member nations across the globe. (**Tariffs** are taxes levied on imported goods.) Italy can change its tariff on soup dishes only by renegotiating the existing tariff with all the member nations that are affected by the change. GATT gives companies like the Dudson Group a structure within which they can settle any differences that may arise out of their international trade.

Multilateral agreements such as GATT extend the economic benefits of increased world trade to all member nations. However, these economic benefits are not painless. Organizations that have thrived behind the protection of tariff barriers are usually ill-equipped to take on strong foreign competitors. Employees and organizations that face risks from more liberal world trade tend to exercise their political clout to gain protection. In fact, GATT's Uruguay Round lasted for seven years as the 115 member nations found it extremely difficult to balance these imperatives.

In summary, GATT is a multilateral trade agreement devoted to liberalizing world trade and reducing the tariffs that protect national markets from foreign competition. Although its aims are simple, finalizing the agreement is a complex political task that has required prolonged discussion and negotiation. GATT stabilizes world trade by providing a clear set of rules. Finally, when a country feels a threat to its rights, GATT provides a framework for consultation, conciliation, and settlement of differences.

Across the globe, smaller groups of nations have also tried to develop regional trade agreements to reap the benefits of liberalized regional trade. Regional agreements free nations from the horrendous complexity of appeasing the demands of hundreds of members. The North American Free Trade Agreement, the European Community, and the Asia–Pacific Economic Cooperation Forum are three of the most prominent regional trade agreements.

North American Free Trade Agreement (NAFTA)

The **North American Free Trade Agreement** (NAFTA) is designed to phase out tariffs among the United States, Canada, and Mexico over 15 years, and to liberalize investment rules in Mexico. Trade between the United States and Canada was promoted through a separate free trade agreement that predated NAFTA and was generally subsumed under NAFTA. Direct trade between Mexico and Canada is minimal, however, representing less than 3 percent of each country's exports and imports.

NAFTA will significantly affect trade between the United States and Mexico. Before NAFTA, Mexico's tariffs on U.S. goods averaged 10 percent while U.S. tariffs on Mexican goods averaged 4 percent. On January 1, 1994, the day NAFTA became effective, the United States eliminated tariffs on about half of Mexico's exports, and Mexico dropped its tariffs on about a third of U.S. exports.

Although the full text of NAFTA fills five volumes, the key provisions of the agreement can be summarized in terms of its effect on trade, investment, government spending, and two side agreements covering environmental protection and labor.[6]

Trade Provisions   U.S. and Mexican tariffs and quotas will be phased out over 15 years beginning in 1994. Goods made with material or labor from outside North America qualify for NAFTA treatment only if significant, value-added manufacturing activity takes place within the United States, Mexico, or Canada. NAFTA will reduce tariffs in different industries according to specific conditions. For example, in the automotive industry, NAFTA will eliminate a tariff after eight years only if 62.5 percent of a product's cost (50 percent for the first four years, 56 percent for the following four years) represents North American materials or labor. After 10 years, U.S. producers of automobiles need not produce in Mexico to sell there.

In the textile and apparel industries, strict rules eliminated tariffs only for goods made from North American spun yarn or from fabric made from North American fibers. In agriculture, NAFTA immediately eliminated about half of the tariffs and quotas that existed in 1993. However, tariffs on politically sensitive crops, such as U.S. corn sold to Mexico or Mexican peanuts, sugar, and orange juice sold to the United States, will be phased out over 15 years. By the end of 1999, NAFTA will lift limits on U.S. truckers driving cargo across the border. By the year 2000, U.S. companies will be allowed to buy stakes in Mexican trucking companies and by 2003 they will be allowed to own them entirely.

Investment Provisions   NAFTA places strict limits on foreign investment in Mexico's energy and railroad industries, the U.S. airlines and radio communications industries, and Canada's movie and television industries. Although Mexico will continue to restrict foreign ownership of certain land and forbid foreign investment in oil and gas exploration, it will open most petrochemical and electric-generation sectors to U.S. investment. For the first time, U.S. drilling companies will be allowed to share in the profits from oil found in Mexico. Limits on foreign investment in Mexican banks, insurers, and brokerage firms will be phased out over 7 to 15 years beginning in 1994.

Government Spending   NAFTA allows companies from all three nations to compete for government contracts. Mexico will phase out restrictions on purchases by its government-owned energy industry over 10 years beginning in 1994. The U.S. government will spend $90 million to retrain workers who lose their jobs because of NAFTA during the first 18 months of the agreement. The U.S. and Mexican governments will invest $225 million each to form a new North American Development Bank that will then borrow an additional $3 billion and lend the money to aid communities hurt by the agreement.

Side Agreements   The agreement will establish an agency in Canada to investigate environmental abuses in any of the three countries. Fines or trade sanctions could be imposed on countries that fail to enforce their own environmental laws. The U.S.–Mexico Border Environmental Commission will spend up to $8 billion on various environmental clean-up projects. An agency will be established in Washington to investigate labor abuses identified by two of the three countries. Fines or trade sanctions will be imposed if any of the countries fail to enforce worker-safety rules, child-labor laws, or minimum-wage standards.

Although it is called a *free trade agreement,* NAFTA contains special provisions designed to help specific industries or companies. These deals can make a tremendous difference in an organization's strategic management process. For example, regulations on Mexico's automotive industry will relax at a pace slow enough to block car makers from exporting there for a decade or so. This gives an advantage to companies like General Motors, Chrysler, Nissan, and Volkswagen, which were already manufacturing in Mexico before NAFTA. Similarly, Mexico is phasing out tariff controls on glass very slowly in order to benefit its big glass manufacturer, Vitro SA.

In summary, NAFTA is a regional trade agreement designed to reduce tariffs and to liberalize trade between the United States, Canada, and Mexico. Since freer trade relations between the United States and Canada predated NAFTA and direct trade between Mexico and Canada is minimal, NAFTA will affect trade relations primarily between the United States and Mexico. The agreement covers issues in trade, investment, government spending, environmental protection, and labor. NAFTA will phase out the tariffs and quotas that govern trade relations between the United States and Mexico over 15 years, beginning in 1994.

European Union (EU)

The organization that has become the **European Union** was first formed in 1951 by Belgium, France, West Germany, Italy, Luxembourg, and the Netherlands. Originally called the European Coal and Steel Community, it was designed to allow the free flow of coal, iron, steel, and scrap metal between member nations. In 1957 when the Treaty of Rome was signed, the European Economic Community was formally established and its objectives were modified. The new objectives called for the creation of a common market through elimination of internal trade barriers, creation of a common external tariff, and removal of all obstacles to the free movement of goods, services, and factors of production among member nations. Since 1957 the overall philosophy of the common market has remained the same, membership in the community has expanded, and the details of creating free trade have continued.

Original members of the European Union were Belgium, Denmark, France, Germany, Greece, Ireland, Italy, Luxembourg, the Netherlands, Portugal, Spain, and the United Kingdom. Austria, Finland, Norway, and Sweden were admitted as new members. Interest in EU membership has continued. Cyprus, Malta, Switzerland, and Turkey have applied, and applications are expected from the Czech Republic, Hungary, and Poland. The mission of the union is to weld the member states together into a single market.

The methods used to achieve the common market include:

• *Removing all frontier controls.* The elimination of passports, customs, and excise controls between member nations would eliminate border delays and reduce the size and cost of the state bureaucracy that was formerly used for these controls.

- *Establishing mutual standards.* Harmonizing the product standards of the member nations would simplify the task of competing in this market.
- *Competing for public contracts.* Companies from one member nation would be allowed to compete for the government contract from another member nation.
- *Broadening availability of financial services.* Insurance and retail banking companies in one member nation would be allowed to extend their services to other member nations.
- *Eliminating exchange controls.* All restrictions on foreign exchange transactions would be removed.
- *Relaxing freight transport regulations.* Foreign truckers could pick up and deliver goods within any member nation.

The significance of the European Union comes from its size. The population within the community totals 320 million people. Its gross domestic product is more than that of the United States. Its exports account for 33 percent of total world exports.[7]

By creating a common market, the EU's members hope to gain several benefits:

- The unified market's purchasing power would match that of the United States.
- Simplifying procedures would reduce the costs of operating within the market.
- Creating a single set of uniform standards would allow organizations to achieve economies of scale.

Whereas individual nations in Europe are relatively small, adding their markets together to form a common market would create a market with immensely attractive size and purchasing power. The complex, idiosyncratic border controls designed by individual nations waste time and raise costs for business transactions that cross national borders. Today, a French manufacturer would find that border controls make it very difficult to sell its products in Germany at cost competitive prices compared to German manufacturers. A uniform, simplified set of border controls would make it easier for manufacturers to compete effectively throughout Europe.

Also, Germany alone sets more than 20,000 product standards that govern everything from the purity of the ingredients in beer to the number of electronic scan lines on the picture tube of a color TV. France has 8,000 product standards of its own, and the French and German standards for the same product are significantly different. This makes it virtually impossible for a European manufacturer to efficiently mass produce an item; production runs have to be broken into small chunks to conform to the different product specifications in different national markets. Uniform standards would allow organizations to achieve economies of scale.

Moving beyond Maastricht   In December 1991, the European Council meeting in Maastricht marked another major step along the road to greater European unity. Concluding the work of two intergovernmental conferences on political, economic, and monetary union, the members agreed to a new Treaty on European Union.[8] They clarified old goals and attached deadlines to them. They also set some new aims with the clear intention of reinforcing the unity of the community.

However, negotiating details tends to be a complex political process. For example, the British government insisted that the word *federal* be removed from the preamble to the treaty. Plans to eliminate frontier passport checks for citizens of member nations were supposed to take effect on January 1, 1993, but they were postponed due to opposition from the United Kingdom and Denmark. Of the 219 laws called for in the blueprint for the single market, just 106 had been implemented with the necessary national legislation in all 12 original member nations by November 1993.[9] As the members of the European Union negotiate ways to make their common market work, companies across the globe are positioning themselves to benefit from the integration.

Prospecting the European Market   Some of the opportunities presented by the European Union are obvious. For example, elimination of border controls can cut the time to ship goods from Milan to London in half. Jeff Fettig, vice president for marketing at Whirlpool International BV in Comerio, Italy, considers this a boon. However, the overall success of Whirlpool Corp.'s strategy in Europe has been far from obvious.[10] In January 1989, U.S.-based Whirlpool Corp. formed a joint venture with Philips Electronics NV of Europe to manufacture white-goods when the Whirlpool name was virtually unknown in Europe. (White-goods is the term applied to washing machines, dryers, and other similar electrical appliances.) In 1991, Whirlpool bought full control of the venture and launched an aggressive campaign to court the Euro-consumer.

Several experts predicted disaster for Whirlpool's pan-European campaign. Despite all the progress toward European integration, the European nations retain fundamental differences. Not only do kitchen appliances differ from one country to another, but consumers also react differently to advertising messages. Careful market research taught Whirlpool that many of the differences in consumer products among European countries have little to do with consumer tastes. For example, experts used to argue that French consumers would not accept front-loading washing machines because they were used to the narrow, top-loading machines made by French manufacturers. Whirlpool discovered that consumers across Europe wanted an appliance that would get their clothes clean; that would be easy to use; that wouldn't use too much electricity, water, or detergent; and that had a record of trouble-free service. If it met all those criteria, other features—such as where the machine opened and its size—were less important. "We've discovered," said Alex Vente, Whirlpool's director of marketing communications, "that Europeans are a lot less set in their ways than many people believe."

Whirlpool's approach to advertising in Europe was equally meticulous. It prepared the ground with careful research and created a special team to evaluate more than 20 potential campaigns. The team agreed on a campaign that featured a cool, bluish dream world of dryers and dishwashers, emphasizing high technology and the universal desire for more free time. Apparently this campaign hit a pan-European chord. Whirlpool's polls began to show that more and more consumers had become aware of Whirlpool and had positive associations with its products. In 1991, when industrywide sales of major appliances were flat, Whirlpool increased its market share in Europe as a whole, and in Germany, France, and Britain in particular.

Asia–Pacific Economic Cooperation (APEC) Forum

On the night in 1989 when the Berlin Wall fell, Walt Rostow, an economic development expert at the University of Texas, surprised Ted Koppel on ABC's *Nightline* program by suggesting that something even more historic had happened that day: the **Asia–Pacific Economic Cooperation (APEC) forum** was founded. By the time the Berlin Wall actually fell, its collapse had become inevitable; it was a relic of the past. By contrast, East Asia's economies are gearing toward the future. They have been growing at roughly twice the rates common in western nations and are anticipated to continue to do so in the next decade.

Asia's biggest export market is America, which buys approximately one-third of the exports of Japan, Taiwan, South Korea, and China, and a quarter of Hong Kong's exports.[11] At the same time, U.S. exports to Asia are climbing steadily, creating high-wage manufacturing jobs while European markets are stagnant. Exports from the United States to developing countries and Asia's four **newly industrialized countries** (NICs)—Hong Kong, Singapore, South Korea, and Taiwan—grew 13.7 percent between 1991 and 1992 while exports to developed countries grew only 1.8 percent.[12] Businesses in the state of Washington see Asia as a booming market for Boeing jets, Microsoft computer software, Kenworth trucks, and numerous other local products.[13] In light of these trends and local successes, it is not surprising that in November 1993, President Clinton used the fifth annual meeting of the APEC forum in Seattle to bring American trade links with Asian nations into the limelight.

To boost APEC's stature, President Clinton traveled to Seattle and invited other heads of government to a meeting that is normally attended by foreign and economic ministers of the member nations. The 15-member APEC forum is not an international organization with established decision-making processes like NAFTA and GATT. Its mission is to provide a forum for discussion of economic cooperation issues among member nations. Clearly, the United States would like to see the APEC forum transformed into a body that actively promotes trade and investment liberalization within the region.

APEC's members include Australia, Brunei, Canada, China, Hong Kong, Indonesia, Japan, Malaysia, New Zealand, the Philippines, Singapore, South Korea, Taiwan, Thailand, and the United States. Mexico, Chile, and Papua New Guinea have applied for membership. Ten working groups within APEC discuss a variety of issues to promote cooperation among market-oriented Pacific Rim economies. The 15 member nations have a total population of more than 2 billion people, account for more than one-third of world trade, and have a combined gross domestic product of over $12 trillion, half the world total.[14]

With the economies of the United States, Europe, and Japan sputtering, smart American companies are moving quickly into the developing and newly industrialized nations of Asia and Latin America. Although Mexico has been the traditional focus of U.S. investment and attention, it is important to understand the emerging significance of Asian nations. Diebold Corporation is a $543 million manufacturer of banking equipment. When asked about the potential demand for his company's products in China, Diebold Chairman

Robert W. Mahoney said, "I hate to even contemplate it in strategy meetings, it gets me so excited. It's a staggering figure." In 1993, after just two weeks in China, a Diebold sales representative returned with orders for 93,000 bank safe-deposit boxes at about $1,000 a piece.[15] Since this is more than Diebold can churn out in a year, the company has had to expand its Ohio factory. In May 1993, Diebold went beyond exports in its quest to cash in on the banking boom that is taking place as Chinese citizens move savings from under their mattresses into bank accounts. It joined with Chinese partners to make automated teller machines in a new Shanghai factory.

Other Regional Trade Agreements

NAFTA, the EC, and APEC rank as critical international trading arrangements, and managers should understand them. In addition, however, other regional trade agreements have proliferated. The Association of Southeast Asian Nations (ASEAN) joined Brunei, Indonesia, Malaysia, the Philippines, Singapore, and Thailand in a cooperative organization in 1967. ASEAN has sought to foster free trade between the member nations and coordinate their industrial policies. Although some tariffs between ASEAN countries have fallen, in 1993 the intra-ASEAN trade that benefited from these reductions accounted for less than 6 percent of the total.

In 1988 Brazil and Argentina signed a free trade pact called MERCOSUR. This pact was perceived as instrumental in increasing trade between the two nations dramatically. In March 1990, it was expanded to include Paraguay and Uruguay. The long-term objective of the MERCOSUR pact is to form a free trade area by the end of 1994, and a common market soon afterward.

Since 1973 the English-speaking Caribbean nations have been trying to form a customs union called CARICOM. In 1991, these nations failed for the third time to meet a self-imposed deadline for fixing a common external tariff.

In summary, managers conduct international operations within a framework of several international trade agreements. GATT is a broad, multilateral agreement between 115 member nations aimed at worldwide reductions in tariff barriers. NAFTA is a narrowly focused regional arrangement to liberalize regional trade between three nations. Planning for international operations must include analysis of the opportunities and constraints presented by these trade agreements. For example, NAFTA allows oil companies based in the United States to bid for business from the government-owned Mexican oil companies. On the other hand, the formation of the European Union may require American beer manufacturers to meet stringent German quality standards before they can enter the vast European market.

Trade agreements can have a crucial impact on any analysis of international operations. National governments also act independently, however, to promote the success of their native firms. Usually, this action is part of a national industrial policy.

INDUSTRIAL POLICY

Industrial policy is government policy designed to promote economic growth. More detailed definitions can be either broad or narrow in scope. Broadly defined industrial policy includes a nation's macroeconomic policies, labor–

management relations, education and infrastructure, production technologies, and cultural patterns. In June 1994, Robert Reich, labor secretary in the Clinton administration, announced a nationwide program for worker training; this announcement launched a broad industrial policy initiative that was designed to spur economic growth. Training American workers to upgrade their skills would help them to work more effectively, increasing the productivity and competitiveness of American industries.

Narrowly defined, industrial policy specifies government action intended to improve a country's economic well-being by supporting particular industries. When the White House eased Cold-War era export restrictions on computers to open the door for $35 billion worth of high-tech exports each year, it launched an industrial policy initiative that focused on the computer industry.[16]

Any whisper of the term *industrial policy* used to set off alarm bells in the United States during the Reagan and Bush eras; any suggestion that government could play a key role in nurturing a worldwide economy risked charges of heresy in the Republican administrations. However, as U.S. companies compete in markets across the globe, they often encounter obstacles that can be traced to the industrial policies of other nations. For example, Boeing has found that the German government's stake in Airbus, the European aircraft manufacturing consortium, has made it almost impossible to sell U.S. aircraft in Germany. Similarly, experts suggest that companies such as AT&T have found few customers in Japan because that country's Ministry of International Trade and Industry (MITI) encourages Japanese companies to support local suppliers. Industrial policy creates opportunities or threats for organizations. By understanding how it works, managers can evaluate industrial policy as part of strategic analysis.

Effects of Industrial Policy

Industrial policy is not a recent invention. In the 19th century, the U.S. federal government backed the development of the transcontinental railroad by ceding huge tracts of land to its builders. The government has also sponsored a network of universities, extension services, and research to help U.S. farmers reap the riches of a fertile land. In today's knowledge-based economy, however, industrial policy does not require the government to pick winning and losing industries. Instead, industrial policy weaves a web of measures that support the creation and commercialization of ideas. Typical industrial policy measures have a range of effects:[17]

- *Spurring cutting-edge technology.* Sematech is one of the most prominent government–industry partnerships in the United States. The six-year-old consortium brings together a dozen of the largest U.S. makers of computer chips to conduct research in advanced fabrication technologies. Half of the $200 million annual cost is paid by the Advanced Research Projects Agency at the Department of Defense. Experts say the United States has recently caught up with Japan in worldwide sales of chips because of Sematech.
- *Diffusing new technology.* Some experts say that outdated manufacturing practices account for 85 percent of the problems of American firms. To help small companies compete, 23 state governments spend a total of $50 million a year supporting 27 technology extension centers. The Company Example illustrates one state's efforts. The federal government is pitching in several million dollars more. These amounts pale, however, in comparison

COMPANY EXAMPLE

Pennsylvania's Industrial Policy Guides Small Firm's Strategy

Not every company can be a GM, a Xerox, or a Microsoft. Industrial states are recognizing this fact as they rethink the economic importance of small, nuts-and-bolts manufacturers. After a decade spent chasing down high-tech and service jobs to replace losses from closed steel and auto plants, states are recognizing the resiliency of small industry.

In Pennsylvania, for example, steel plant closings played a big role in the 22 percent decline in factory jobs during the 1980s. The number of manufacturing jobs in the state actually increased by 5 percent during the decade, however, to more than 17,000.

Scheirer Machine Co., employer of 65, was among the companies that contributed to Pennsylvania's job growth in the 1980s. Scheirer typifies the kind of company Pennsylvania leaders had in mind in 1988 when they created a technical-assistance program for manufacturers. The state now leads the nation in developing local industrial policies geared toward preserving stable, high-paying factory jobs.

When the Pittsburgh maker of replacement parts for steel and mining equipment needed help to become more competitive, it turned to its local Industrial Resource Center, one of eight regional centers funded by a $9 million state outlay. For a $3,000 fee, Scheirer acquired the services of a three-person team of experts who helped the company reorganize its shop floor and raise productivity by about 15 percent in only six months. In addition, the center lent Scheirer $150,000 at 5 percent interest to buy a computerized lathe. Ongoing assistance helps the firm to further upgrade its technology.

Although some complain that funding limits focus the state's industrial policy on stable and credit-worthy firms, rather than struggling or adventurous newcomers, Pennsylvania's comprehensive program also nurtures startups, using state money under the decade-old Ben Franklin Partnership. Recently, the state started lending more low-interest money for modernization to companies that pay above-average salaries.

SOURCE: Michael Schroeder, "Small Business Has a Friend in Pennsylvania," *Business Week*, April 6, 1992, p. 75.

with the $500 million that the Japanese government spends to back 185 technology extension centers.

- *Creating a new infrastructure.* A communications infrastructure that can support information-intensive industries is a critical competitive tool for organizations in the 1990s. The U.S. government is making a massive commitment to build a communications conduit made of fiber-optic cables and high-speed digital switching equipment. This conduit, which is expected to cost billions of dollars, will make it easier to manipulate and transfer huge amounts of data at high speed.

- *Increasing free trade.* Although the U.S. government has made a tremendous effort to smooth the flow of goods and services across the globe through NAFTA and GATT, as earlier sections have described, U.S. companies routinely encounter impediments that hinder their expansion into foreign markets. Giddings & Lewis, America's largest machine tool builder and a fierce competitor, has not sold a machine in Japan since 1974. "And it's not for lack of trying," says Chairman William Fife, Jr.[18] U.S. industrial policy has long worked to open the doors of restricted markets such as Japan.

- *Investing in new technologies.* Organizations commit to new technology only when the climate for investment is correct. Research and investment tax credits can speed innovation and investment. Andrew Grove, chief executive of Intel Corp., says, "I'm not looking for a handout, but a turbocharge."[19]

STRATEGIC MANAGEMENT IN THE INTERNATIONAL ARENA

As firms position themselves to compete in the international arena, they will continue to seek external reinforcement of their efforts, such as international trade agreements and favorable national industrial policies already discussed. However, going global raises several internal issues that need to be successfully managed. The remainder of this chapter discusses multinational corporations and explores international operations from the strategic management perspective: analyzing the environment, establishing organizational direction, formulating strategy, implementing strategy, and exerting strategic control.

Multinational Corporations

Since its first appearance in 1975, the term **multinational corporation** has described an organization that has significant operations in more than one country. The organization that invests in international operations is called the *parent company;* the country in which the parent makes the investment is called the *host country*. The multinational corporation views its diverse activities as a whole and develops and implements a unified strategy to encompass all of them.

At the end of the Second World War, the United States was the most powerful industrial nation, and for the next 35 years, U.S. enterprises ranked among the biggest in the world. In 1975, 126 of the world's 260 multinational organizations were based in the United States, including 15 of the largest 25 multinationals. In the 1980s and 1990s, things began to change rapidly. Japanese, British, German, French, Dutch, Italian, and South Korean multinational organizations grew in strength and size and began challenging U.S. companies, even in the North American market.

Some organizations accomplish the transformation into multinational corporations in stages: their early foreign operations rely on exporting, and they progress gradually through licensing to direct investment. (These stages are discussed in detail in the later section on international strategy formulation.) Today, however, progress in technology and global interdependence has freed organizations that do not rank with corporations like General Electric or IBM to exploit the potential of international markets. For example, Laser Communications Inc. (LCI), based in Lancaster, Pennsylvania, found a way to replace telephone lines and ground cables with nonstop streams of airborne laser beams. LCI's technology zaps audio, video, and data transmissions through the air over distances up to one mile. Founded in 1983, LCI posts annual revenues of about $2.5 million and employs only 13, yet its technology is in more than 1,000 installations in 35 countries.[20] Organizations as small as LCI and as big as IBM all must perform the main steps of the strategic management process.

International Environmental Analysis

Recall that environmental analysis is the process of monitoring the conditions in which an organization operates to identify present and future strengths, weaknesses, opportunities, and threats (SWOT) that affect its progress toward its goals. This complicated process involves analyzing:

1. The general environment—social, economic, technological, ethical, and political/legal conditions

2. The operating environment—suppliers, competitors, customers, and labor conditions
3. The internal environment—conditions within the organization

Charles J. Fombrun and Stefan Wally suggest that the multinational corporation's operating environment is more complex than that of a purely domestic firm, due largely to changes in three forces:[21]

1. Worldwide infrastructure
2. Worldwide sociostructure
3. Worldwide superstructure

Figure 7.1 illustrates some of the relationships between the forces of change, emerging trends, and the issues that affect environmental analysis of international operations. For example, changes in sociostructure may lead to the emergence of regional trading blocs. In turn, each bloc implies a unique set of market changes, competitive changes, and regulatory changes that guide the organization's environmental analysis. This demands that the multinational organization acquire additional skills and expertise that the purely

FIGURE 7.1 Forces That Influence International Environmental Analysis

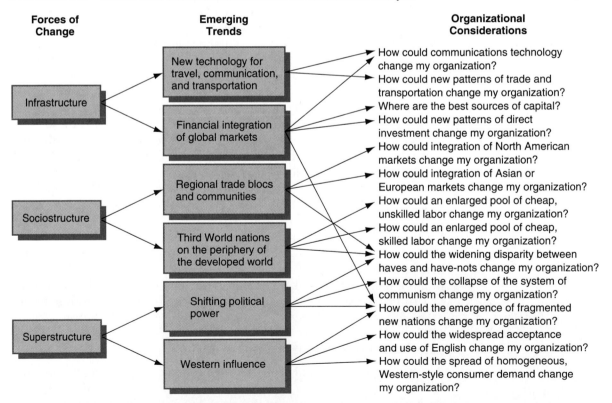

SOURCE: Adapted from C. J. Fombrun and S. Wally, "Global Entanglements: The Structure of Corporate Transnationalism," in V. Pucik, N. M. Tichy, and C. K. Barnett, eds., *Globalizing Management: Creating and Leading the Competitive Organization* (New York: John Wiley & Sons, 1993).

domestic organization does not need because it does not encounter these environmental complexities.

Within the general model for the links between the forces of change and emerging trends in Figure 7.1, several specific trends affect all multinational organizations' environmental analysis efforts. Michael Porter's analysis identifies several of these trends:[22]

- *Fewer differences among countries.* Differences in such areas as income, energy costs, marketing practices, and channels of distribution seem to be narrowing. In many industries, it is no longer meaningful to separate the German market from the American market or the Japanese market. Consumers are becoming increasingly alike. In a dark blue suit and Regal shoes, carrying a Casio pocket calculator in a Mark Cross wallet, frequenting a nearby sushi bar for lunch, and commuting in a Celica, the typical New York businessperson would not draw a second glance on the streets of Düsseldorf or Tokyo.[23]
- *More aggressive industrial policies.* The governments of such countries as Japan, Germany, and Taiwan have developed fiercely competitive attitudes toward international business. The future policies of these governments will probably make the international environment more and more competitive. For example, aggressive planning has moved Taiwan from an agricultural economy in the 1960s to worldwide economic power in the 1990s. This planning has brought so much success that in 1992, Taiwan had tangible assets worth $3.5 billion on the Chinese mainland; $5 billion in Malaysia; $3.4 billion in Thailand; $2.8 billion in Indonesia; and, as a good clue to the next century's star performer in the region, at least $500 million in Vietnam. In other words, pick any Asian country with cheap land and labor from the Philippines to Sri Lanka, and a Taiwanese business is probably putting up a factory there to make umbrellas, toys, wigs, or textiles for sale in markets across the globe.[24]
- *More vigorous protection for distinctive assets.* More and more countries seem to be focusing on determining their own unique assets and exploiting this uniqueness to best advantage. Perhaps the most obvious example is the formation of the oil cartel, the Organization of Oil Exporting Countries (OPEC). Although the effectiveness of this cartel has varied over time, its primary purpose is still clear: to protect the return its members can generate on a scarce natural resource, oil.
- *Emerging, large-scale markets.* New access to markets in countries such as India and Vietnam is establishing high-volume sales potential for successful products. For example, India is in the midst of a massive transition from a planned economy to a free-market economy. Some 40 million Indians—the "super-haves," as the local media call them—live in households with annual incomes of over 900,000 rupees, or $30,000; their purchasing power approximates a yearly income of $600,000 in the United States. These families travel and educate their children abroad and drink Coke, and they will storm the gates of McDonald's when it opens its first outlets in India within the next few years.[25] In line with this trend, a multinational corporation's environmental analysts should always watch for new markets to emerge.
- *Competition from developing countries.* Now more than ever before, smaller, developing countries are becoming competitors in international markets. Malaysia is the largest exporter of semiconductor chips in the world.

Environmental analysts for multinational corporations cannot stop after evaluating the larger, more established competitors; they must consider threats from developing countries, as well.

International Organizational Direction

The complexity of the international environment, magnified by several significant trends, affects the multinational firm's analysis of its environment. Based on this environmental analysis, managers must establish a direction for the organization that operates internationally.

Like the purely domestic organization, the multinational organization must carefully evaluate the results of environmental analysis and then develop an organizational vision and mission. Managers must decide on the type and extent of international involvement they want to pursue, because this decision guides the establishment of appropriate organizational goals.

The Mazda Motor Corp. provides an example of how an international emphasis can color a company's mission statement:

> Mazda is dedicated to developing vehicles for the world's motoring public that are distinctive and innovative. Mazda also seeks to meet the needs and values of motorists the world over with Mazda's latest and future technology. To accomplish this, Mazda has a global network of research and development bases: in Yokohama, Japan; Irvine, California and Ann Arbor, Michigan, U.S.A.; and Oberursel, near Frankfort, Germany.[26]

The goal of establishing and maintaining expensive research facilities in Europe and the United States emphasizes the significance of these markets to Mazda.

After clarifying a vision and defining a mission, managers provide further direction for a multinational organization by developing long-term and short-term goals. Naturally, these goals reflect the type and extent of international involvement outlined in the company mission statement. However, host countries often impose constraints that affect the goals of multinational organizations. These constraints can take many forms:

- A host country may require that a local person or firm maintain a major or controlling interest.
- Host countries commonly demand that their own citizens hold certain management and technology positions.
- Host countries normally require some level of training for all of their citizens employed by a foreign multinational.
- Host countries seek technology-based businesses and strive to raise the technology levels of multinational organizations within their borders.

International Strategy Formulation

Following the general model of the strategic management process, managers formulate a strategy that reflects organizational goals, which in turn reflect the organization's mission, the result of environmental analysis. Whether the organization limits itself to domestic operations or enters into international operations, the purpose of strategy is the same. Over the years many different companies have formulated and successfully implemented numerous international strategies. All of these specific strategies fall into three broad categories: exporting, licensing, and direct investment.

FIGURE 7.2
Strategies for Entering
Foreign Markets

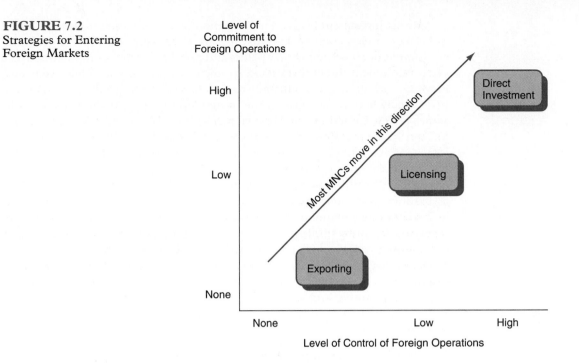

These strategies require different commitments from parent companies to foreign markets and offer parent companies varying levels of control over foreign operations (see Figure 7.2). Sometimes multinational organizations' first foreign operations involve exporting, and they progress gradually through licensing to direct investment. Regardless of the stage and the direction of a multinational corporation's progress, strategy formulation should involve an assessment of the level of commitment to and control of foreign operations that the organization's mission demands.

Exporting is selling goods or services to customers in a foreign country. This strategy leaves an organization's production facilities at home, from which it transfers products abroad. This strategy minimizes foreign investment, since the firm usually hires a foreign agent to act on its behalf, and products are often shipped directly to customers' warehouses. This strategy exposes the exporter to high transportation costs, however, and it must deal with government regulations and other operational and strategic issues from a distance.

A **licensing agreement** grants one company's right to its brand name, product specifications, and the like to another company, which sells the goods or services. The purchaser of the license hopes to profit from selling the products, whereas the seller of the license profits from the fee it charges for the license. At the international level, the purchaser and the seller of a license are from different countries, or the purchaser will sell the products in a country other than the one where it bought them. For example, all of the South Korean automobile manufacturers license technology from Japanese companies like Nissan and Toyota.

Franchising is a form of licensing that usually covers access to a wider range of rights and resources, perhaps including production equipment, managerial systems, operating procedures, advertising and trademarks. McDonald's is a good example of an MNC that sells franchises around the world.

A **direct investment** leads an organization to acquire and employ operating assets in a foreign country. This may involve purchasing existing factories and equipment or constructing new plants and purchasing new equipment. MNCs often implement direct investment strategies by entering into **joint ventures,** in which two companies contribute to the costs of creating a third business entity. Usually both firms share in the ownership of the joint venture and in its returns. New United Motor Manufacturing Inc. (NUMMI) is a joint venture formed by Toyota Motor Corporation and General Motors in Fremont, California. MNCs often form joint ventures to create synergy between the different sets of skills of the two parent companies. For example, it is commonly believed that NUMMI was formed because General Motors wanted to learn how to manufacture a high-quality, subcompact car and Toyota wanted to learn how to operate a manufacturing facility in the United States. When joint ventures are driven by this logic, the strategy formulation is guided by each parent company's desire to learn and internalize the skills of the other.[27]

Direct investment can also create a wholly owned subsidiary. An interesting example of this direct investment strategy has led American companies to start manufacturing and selling their products in Japan. Kodak, IBM, Procter & Gamble, and Motorola are examples of American companies that have successfully launched wholly owned subsidiaries in Japan.

International Strategy Implementation

After conducting an environmental analysis, establishing an appropriate organizational direction, and carefully formulating a strategy to take the firm in that direction, managers of international operations must implement the strategy they have devised. Implementing an international strategy is generally considered a much greater challenge than implementing a purely domestic strategy. Managers in multinational organizations have to design administrative systems for their employees across the globe.

The design of an administrative system is driven by two imperatives: the need to align the systems with the overall strategy of the organization, and the need to accommodate the cultural characteristics of each host country. Table 7.5 illustrates some inherent difficulties in trying to satisfy these imperatives. Although the table describes the cultural characteristics of only Japanese, North American, and Latin American managers, it demonstrates the complexities of designing systems to suit multiple host countries.

International Strategic Control

Controlling an international strategy must follow its implementation. Control ensures that the strategy is effective, given organizational conditions. Comparing this effectiveness to some predetermined standard and making any necessary changes are both part of strategic control.

Managers refer to the same financial standards at the international level to establish the appropriateness of performance as at the domestic level. Business people often mention return on investment as the most important financial measurement by which to evaluate the performance of foreign operations.

Applying such financial measurement is complicated, however, for operations in different countries. The comparison must take into account different currencies, different rates of inflation, and different tax laws, all of which contribute to this complexity. In the final analysis, comparing the financial

TABLE 7.5

Cultural Barriers to International Strategy Implementation

Japanese Values	North American Values	Latin American Values
Emotional sensitivity highly valued	Emotional sensitivity not highly valued	Emotional sensitivity valued
Restrained emotions	Straightforward or impersonal relations	Emotional passion
Subtle power plays; conciliation	Litigation; not as much conciliation	Overt power plays; exploitation of weakness
Loyalty to employer; employer taking care of employees	Lack of commitment to employer; breaking of ties by either, if necessary	Loyalty to employer (who is often family)
Group decision-making by consensus	Teamwork provides input to a single decision maker	Decisions handed down from one individual
Face-saving crucial; decisions often made simply to save someone from embarrassment	Decisions made on a cost–benefit basis; face-saving may not always matter	Face-saving crucial in decision making to preserve honor, dignity
Open special interest influence	Decision makers influenced by special interests, but often not considered ethical	Satisfying special interests expected, condoned
Nonargumentative stance; quiet when right	Argumentative when right or wrong, but impersonal	Argumentative when right or wrong; passionate
What is down in writing must be accurate, valid	Reliance on documentation as evidential proof	Impatient with documentation, seen as obstacle to understanding general principles
Step-by-step approach to decision making	Methodically organized decision making	Impulsive, spontaneous decision making
Good of group as ultimate aim	Profit motive or good of individual as ultimate aim	Good for group is good for the individual
Cultivate a good emotional social setting for decision making; get to know decision makers	Decision making impersonal; avoid involvements, conflicts of interest	Personalism necessary for good decision making

SOURCE: Courtesy of Pierre Casse, *Training for the Multicultural Manager: A Practical and Cross-Cultural Approach to the Management of People,* Washington, D.C., Copyright 1982, Society for Intercultural Education, Training and Research (SIETAR International).

performance of operations in different countries is very difficult and commonly somewhat subjective.

SUMMARY

Any organization that operates internationally must adjust the strategic management process to account for the complexities of cross-border transactions. International business has grown in importance in recent years, and this trend will only accelerate as national markets become more integrated and trade between them increases.

International trade agreements define much of the structural background for this trade. The General Agreement on Tariffs and Trade is a broad, multilateral system for negotiating reductions in tariffs and removal of other barriers to the smooth flow of products across national borders. Regional trade agreements function within the guidelines defined by GATT to promote trade between neighboring countries without excluding products from outside the region. The North American Free Trade Agreement, the European Union, and the Asia–Pacific Economic Cooperation forum are prominent regional trade agreements.

Within the provisions of these agreements, national governments develop and implement industrial policies to promote the competitive success of native organizations. These policies can seek to achieve broad, nationwide objectives or target specific industries for special attention.

Multinational corporations react to the pressures of international operations by adjusting their procedures for completing the strategic management process. Environmental analysis for such an organization must expand its scope to evaluate conditions and trends in distant, often idiosyncratic markets. Its vision and mission statements must guide later decisions about the appropriate type and extent of international involvement, given the results of the environmental analysis.

Managers then formulate strategies designed to move the firm in this chosen organizational direction, often following the traditional progression from exporting through licensing to direct investment in foreign operations. Implementing a previously formulated strategy becomes vastly more complex when it leads the firm across international borders; cultural differences can demand changes to the most successful strategy. Finally, strategic control of international operations faces problems to adjust familiar financial standards, especially return on investment, for differences in currencies, inflation levels, and tax laws, among other factors.

KEY TERMS

international management, p. 163
General Agreement on Tariffs and Trade (GATT), p. 168
regional trade agreement, p. 169
tariff, p. 170
North American Free Trade Agreement (NAFTA), p. 170
European Union (EU), p. 172
Asia–Pacific Economic Cooperation (APEC) forum, p. 175

newly industrialized countries (NICs), p. 175
industrial policy, p. 176
multinational corporation, p. 179
exporting, p. 183
license agreement, p. 183
franchising, p. 183
direct investment, p. 184
joint ventures, p. 184

CHECK✓LIST   **Analyzing International Operations in Problems and Cases**

___ 1. Does the case involve strategic management of international operations?

___ 2. Have decision makers assessed the impact of global/international issues on the strategic management process?

___ 3. Are the major steps of the strategic management process appropriately ordered and integrated?

___ 4. Have decision makers assessed the effects of industrial policy on the strategic management process?

___ 5. Is the strategy aimed at anticipating competitors' actions and responding to them?

___ 6. Does the strategy reflect organizational goals?

___ 7. Is the strategy appropriate, given the results of the international environmental analysis?

___ 8. Have decision makers evaluated future markets and opportunities created by lower trade barriers?

___ 9. Have decision makers considered the threat of global competition?

___ 10. Is the organizational mission clear to top managers in the various countries of operation?

Additional Readings

C. A. Bartlett and S. Ghoshal. *Managing across Borders.* Boston, Mass.: Harvard Business School Press, 1989.

J. Garland, R. N. Farmer, and M. Taylor. *International Dimensions of Business Policy and Strategy,* 2d ed. Boston, Mass.: PWS-Kent, 1990.

C. W. L. Hill. *International Business: Competing in the Global Marketplace.* Burr Ridge, Ill.: Richard D. Irwin, 1994.

C A S E

Lever Revamps Strategy to Standardize Products for the EU

Almost every large company operating in Europe has been affected by the effort to unite Europe politically and create one huge common market. As internal EU barriers fall, companies are trying to sell the same products in the same way across the continent, creating economies of scale to help them survive increasingly brutal marketing wars. Unfortunately, creating or selling a "Europroduct" is more than just difficult; the nuances of established markets, local consumer tastes, and decades-old marketing strategies are complicating standardization.

As Europe's borders began to blur in the late 1980s, Lever Europe, a subsidiary of Anglo-Dutch food and detergent maker Unilever, recognized the need to adjust its strategy. Its American arch-rival, Procter & Gamble, was introducing single products with single names across Europe.

Lever, despite being more established in Europe, has faced large-scale adjustment problems, both within its organization and among consumers. It sells hundreds of products under various brand names in different countries. Its fabric softener, for example, is known within Lever under two different brand names—Snuggle and Teddy Bear. The brand is sold in ten European countries under seven different names, often with different bottles, different marketing strategies, and sometimes even different formulas. The brands share only one thing: a picture of a teddy bear on the label.

The wide diversity of brand images is the legacy of what once seemed a shrewd strategy for many European consumer-product companies. Heavily decentralized, Lever left most product, manufacturing, and marketing decisions to powerful country managers. They, in turn, chose names that sounded appealing in the local language, designed packages to fit local tastes, manufactured the products in local factories, and sometimes tinkered with the formulas.

Lever began its attempts at unifying product lines in 1986, appointing a few European brand managers for its pan-European brands. It also began centralizing production, which required some painful plant closings. Today, Lever products like fabric softener, dishwasher soap, and skin cream are overseen across much of the continent by individual managers based in various European capitals. To stay close to local markets, though, Lever still distributes through its national marketing people. Other things have stayed the same, as well: To avoid tampering with success, the company has kept many of its established local brand names—and even some of the formula variations.

Changing those local formulas is a difficult step—one that Lever is taking gradually. Lever's strategy calls for introducing an environmentally friendly formula across the continent, which delights Lever workers in Sweden, where such a change is required by law, and in Germany, where consumers will pay premium prices for products that are gentle on lakes and rivers. But it creates problems in cost-conscious Spain; Lever's fabric softener has a quarter of the fast-growing market there, and the new strategy means higher costs for a price-sensitive product.

Lever figures that it will lose profits in the short run because of the switch, but managers remain convinced that its uniform, more advanced products will ultimately maximize profits across Europe.

Complexities continue to mount, however. For historical reasons, Lever sells its Teddy Bear and Snuggle fabric softeners in ten European countries, while it sells a creamier, more expensive product, Comfort, in seven others. To cut production costs and unify marketing, it is taking a first step toward merging the two, introducing identical bottles. To avoid alienating any loyal consumers, however, it will keep producing Comfort as a thicker liquid with a mother and child on its label while Teddy Bear features a bear. Selling fabric softener with a catalog of different brand names and at least two formulas ensures a worse cost position than P&G, which has one formula, one brand name, and one package.

DISCUSSION QUESTIONS

1. Do you agree with Lever's decisions about the pace of strategy implementation?

2. Is the strategy cost-effective? Explain.

3. How well-justified is Lever's decision to maintain dual production of Comfort and Teddy Bear?

4. How well does Lever's strategy reflect a thorough environmental analysis?

5. How can Lever maintain market share while more effectively centralizing its operations?

SOURCE: E. S. Browning, "In Pursuit of the Elusive Euroconsumer," *The Wall Street Journal,* April 23, 1992, p. B1.

Notes

1. "GM Asian Technical Center," General Motors brochure, 1992.

2. W. E. Halal, "Global Strategic Management in a New World Order," *Business Horizons,* November/December 1993, pp. 5–10.

3. V. Reitman, "Global Money Trends Rattle Shop Windows in Heartland America." *The Wall Street Journal,* November 26, 1993, p. A1.

4. "GATT: What It Is, What It Does," GATT Information Service Center brochure, 1991.

5. L. Ingrassia and A. Q. Nomani, "Firms Far and Wide Are Looking to GATT for Competitive Edge," *The Wall Street Journal,* December 7, 1993, p. A1.

6. "The Agreement's Key Provisions," *The Wall Street Journal,* November 18, 1993, p. A14.

7. "One Europe, One Economy," *The Economist,* November 30, 1991, pp. 53–54; and "A Touch of Eastern Promise," *The Economist,* March 26, 1994, p. 58.

8. M. Wise and R. Gibb, *Single Market to Social Europe: The European Community in the 1990s* (New York: Longman Scientific & Technical, 1993).

9. B. Javetski and P. Oster, "The Single Market Itself Is in Question," *Business Week,* November 1, 1993, p. 52.

10. M. M. Nelson, "Whirlpool Gives Pan-European Approach a Spin," *The Wall Street Journal,* April 23, 1992, p. B1.

11. "Balancing Act," *The Economist,* January 4, 1992, p. 30.

12. V. Reitman, "U.S. Firms Turn to the Developing World," *The Wall Street Journal,* August 4, 1993, p. A2.

13. M. Trumbull, "After the Vote: Clinton's Next Stop Is Seattle." *Christian Science Monitor,* November 16, 1993, p. 1.

14. M. Trumbull, "APEC at a Glance," *Christian Science Monitor,* November 16, 1993, p. 4.

15. Reitman, "U.S. Firms Turn."

16. J. Impoco, "President Clinton's Other Foreign Policy," *U.S. News & World Report,* November 1, 1993.

17. S. Pendleton, "Federal Labs Open Doors to Industry," *Christian Science Monitor,* May 11, 1993.

18. C. Farrell and M. S. Mandel, "Industrial Policy," *Business Week,* April 6, 1992, pp. 70–74.

19. Ibid.

20. B. W. Fraser, "Cost-Effective Laser Technology Makes Strides in Foreign Markets," *Christian Science Monitor,* June 7, 1994, p. 9.

21. C. J. Fombrun and S. Wally, "Global Entanglements: The Structure of Corporate Transnationalism," in V. Pucik, N. M. Tichy and C. K. Barnett, eds., *Globalizing Management: Creating and Leading the Competitive Organization* (New York: John Wiley & Sons, 1993).

22. M. E. Porter, "Changing Patterns of International Competition," in H. Vernon-Wortzel and L. H. Wortzel, eds., *Global Strategic Management: The Essentials* (New York: John Wiley & Sons, 1991).

23. K. Ohmae, "Becoming a Triad Power: The New Global Corporation," in H. Vernon-Wortzel and L. H. Wortzel, eds., *Global Strategic Management: The Essentials* (New York: John Wiley & Sons, 1991).

24. "A Survey of Taiwan," *The Economist,* October 10, 1992.

25. P. Fuhrman and M. Schuman, "Now We Are Our Own Masters," *Forbes,* May 23, 1994, pp. 128–138.

26. "Mazda in Brief," Mazda Motor Corp. brochure, 1992.

27. G. Hamel, "Competition for Competence and Interpartner Learning within International Strategic Alliances," *Strategic Management Journal* 12 (1991), pp. 83–103.

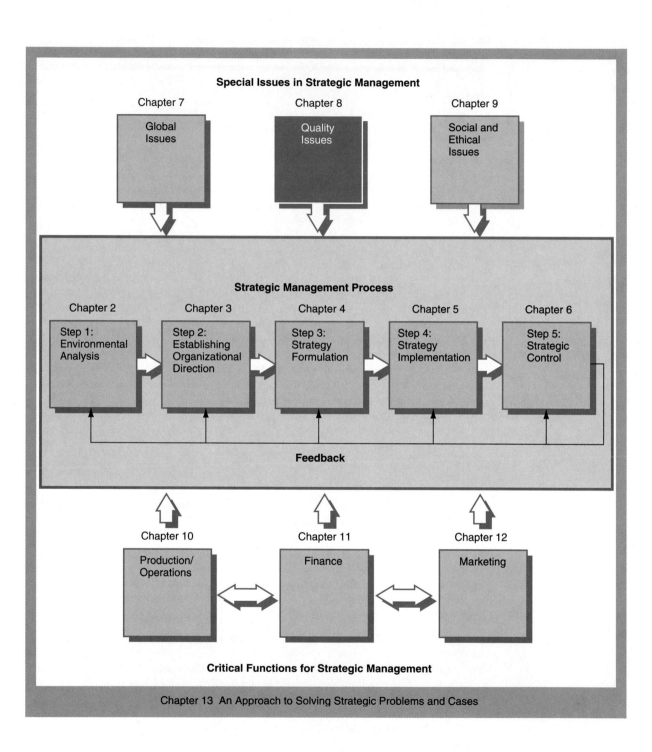

Special Issues in Strategic Management

Chapter 7

Global Issues

Chapter 8

Quality Issues

Chapter 9

Social and Ethical Issues

Strategic Management Process

Chapter 2

Step 1: Environmental Analysis

Chapter 3

Step 2: Establishing Organizational Direction

Chapter 4

Step 3: Strategy Formulation

Chapter 5

Step 4: Strategy Implementation

Chapter 6

Step 5: Strategic Control

Feedback

Chapter 10

Production/ Operations

Chapter 11

Finance

Chapter 12

Marketing

Critical Functions for Strategic Management

Chapter 13 An Approach to Solving Strategic Problems and Cases

8

Strategic Management and Total Quality Management

Armed with total quality management methods, Japanese organizations have won a long string of battles for market share throughout the world's markets. American and European firms have seen the power of this new competitive weapon, and they are scrambling to learn to use it themselves.

TQM offers powerful new insight into customers' needs and a firm's own operations. By making a thorough, committed, and vigorous effort to implement TQM, a firm can build a solid foundation for sustained competitive advantage.

Adopting a quality approach requires profound changes in organizations that practice it, though. Successful implementation of TQM affects every step of the organization's strategic management process, and it diffuses a consciousness of continuous improvement throughout the organization. Quality becomes the focus of every activity of the firm, rather than an isolated concern of a few specialists, as in early systems of quality control.

HISTORICAL DEVELOPMENT OF TOTAL QUALITY MANAGEMENT

The development of the quality movement began with a focus on inspection and post-production repairs to defective products. In a search for more proactive methods, several leaders shaped the **Total Quality Management (TQM)** movement. The impact of TQM becomes clear when one compares the competitive positions of organizations that have implemented TQM with varying degrees of success. The discussion of the basic characteristics of TQM and its impact on organizations has important implications for strategic management, as the last part of the chapter explains.

Quality in the 1960s and 1970s

Product quality has always been an important part of an organization's competitive success. In the 1960s and 1970s, however, few firms viewed quality as a responsibility of every employee. U.S. companies had developed a tradition of specialization, assigning **quality control** departments the narrow task of ensuring quality through a combination of final inspection and post-production rework and repair.[1] To ensure perfection in every product seemed impossible, so they could prevent defective products from reaching consumers only by inspecting them and repairing defective units.

This approach to quality management had three flaws. First, inspections themselves are not perfect: no human inspector can catch every flaw. Second, inspection can only correct the symptoms, rather than the cause, of the problem. For example, defects could be caused by low quality input, a poor design, adverse working conditions, badly maintained equipment, haphazard handling, or faulty storage. Inspection and repair leave these underlying causes to continue to create defects. Finally, inspection and repair separate the quality control function from such areas as planning, design, production, and distribution, which actually create the defects. This separation of quality control from the other functions of the organization allows most of the people in the organization to ignore their roles in ensuring the quality of the product.

In the three decades following the end of World War II, the U.S. economy produced unparalleled wealth and technological might. A tremendous worldwide demand clamored for American-made goods. Inspect-and-repair quality control served U.S. companies well in this era when competitors could not hope to challenge their technological superiority. In this environment, most U.S. companies spent the 1960s and the 1970s straining to meet the demand for their goods and services. Quality was important, but production output targets reigned supreme and inspect-and-repair techniques yielded products of adequate quality.

The environment of the 1980s and 1990s made the flaws of this approach painfully apparent. The quality levels achieved by U.S. companies began to compare unfavorably with those of their Japanese competitors. As managers and scholars studied how Japanese firms managed quality, they discovered the legacies of American leaders like Deming, Juran, and Crosby. The next section introduces these three individuals, who developed the basic concepts at the heart of the modern quality management method known as TQM.

In the last decade TQM has emerged as a coherent management system that focuses intensely on serving the needs of the customer quickly, efficiently, and effectively. To do this, the TQM method measures customers' needs, measures and evaluates customer satisfaction delivered by the product or service, and engages the organization in continuous improvement to stay tuned-in to changes in customers' needs.

Quality Gurus

The message of TQM spread across the globe, driven by the work of the "Big Three" of the quality management movement—W. Edwards Deming, Joseph M. Juran, and Philip B. Crosby. This section summarizes the contributions of these individuals and highlights the similarities and differences in their interpretations of quality management.

Deming   W. Edwards Deming, born in Sioux City, Iowa in 1900, earned his bachelor's degree in physics from the University of Wyoming and his doctorate in mathematical physics from Yale University. From 1928 to 1939, Deming worked as a mathematical physicist for the U.S. Department of Agriculture. This work first exposed Deming to the theories and practices of statistical control. From 1939 to 1945, Deming worked extensively with the Bureau of the Census and the U.S. weapons industry. During this period, he developed his basic quality management system. Table 8.1 summarizes Deming's views on the relationship between quality and management.

Deming recommended that every organization should promote continuous quality improvement by implementing his 14 steps. This requires breaking down all quality-related activities into four interlinked steps: **Plan-Do-Check-Act.** Repetitive completion of this cycle keeps the organization constantly moving on the path of continuous quality improvement, according to Deming.

By the end of World War II, the United States was one of the few developed countries in the world whose industrial capacity had not suffered devastation

TABLE 8.1

Deming's 14 Points for Management

1. **Create constancy of purpose for improvement of product and service.**[a] The shift from short-term thinking to planning for the long term requires dedication to innovation in all areas to most effectively meet the needs of the customer.
2. **Adopt a new philosophy in which defects are unacceptable.** Anything that can lead to a defect—shoddy materials, poor workmanship, defective parts, careless handling, and lax service—should be clearly identified as unacceptable.
3. **Cease dependence on mass inspection.** Focus on improving the process to eliminate defects. Inspection is too late, ineffective, and costly for effective quality management.
4. **End the practice of awarding business on price tag alone.** Price has no meaning without a measure of product quality. An organization's purchasing function and suppliers must understand specifications, but they must also know what the part does for production and final customers.
5. **Constantly and forever improve the system of production and service.** Reduce waste in every activity. Improvement comes from studying the production process. Most of the responsibility for process improvement rests with management.
6. **Institute modern methods of training on the job.** Restructure training around clearly defined criteria for acceptable work.
7. **Institute modern methods of supervising.** Supervisors must have the authority to inform top management about conditions that need correction.
8. **Drive out fear.** Workers must not be afraid to ask questions, report problems, or express ideas.
9. **Break down barriers between departments.** Individuals from research, design, purchasing, sales, production, and assembly must work together as a team to ensure the success of the organization as a whole.
10. **Eliminate numerical goals for the work force.** Instead of encouraging workers to meet numerical goals for productivity improvement, the organization as a whole must share a single goal: never-ending improvement.
11. **Eliminate work standards and numerical quotas.** Since quotas focus on quantity of production, not quality, work standards practically guarantee poor quality and high costs.
12. **Remove barriers that hinder the hourly workers.** Any barriers that hinder pride in work degrade quality. For example, a poor idea of the criteria for good work, supervisors motivated by quotas, off-gauge input parts, and out-of-order machines prevent hourly workers from identifying with their work and taking pride in it.

Continued

TABLE 8.1
Continued

13. **Institute a vigorous program of education and training.** Continuous improvement leads to continuous change in the number of people required in the different parts of the organization and their duties. People should be continually trained and retrained. All training must include basic statistical techniques.

14. **Create a structure in top management that will push everyday on the above 13 points.** The ultimate responsibility for implementing these principles lies with the top management of the organization. Top management should create a system that moves the organization to engage in continuous, daily improvement.

[a]Deming's words are in boldface type. The rest of each paragraph paraphrases Deming's discussions.

SOURCE: Adapted from A. March, "A Note on Quality: The Views of Deming, Juran, and Crosby," in Harry Costin, ed., *Readings in Total Quality Management* (New York: Harcourt Brace College Publishers, 1994), p. 143.

in the war. During the post-war period, strong pent-up demand combined with the worldwide shortage of production capacity to allow U.S. organizations to sell everything that they could produce. Deming's message fell on deaf ears in North America.

In contrast, the devastation of the war left Japanese managers to search for new ways to manage the organizations that they were rebuilding. They were anxious to learn from people like Deming. Deming first visited Japan in 1946 as a representative of the Economic and Scientific Section of the American Department of War. In 1950, the Union of Japanese Scientists and Engineers invited Deming back to offer classes on quality control. By August 1950, the top managers of most of Japan's largest companies had attended Deming's seminars at the Tokyo Chamber of Commerce. In 1951, the Japanese recognized this contribution by institutionalizing the pursuit of quality improvement through the creation of a quality award called the *Deming Prize*. In 1960, the Emperor of Japan rewarded Deming for his impact on the quality and competitiveness of Japanese products by presenting him with the Second Order Medal of the Sacred Treasure, the highest possible decoration the Japanese nation could bestow.

Juran   Joseph M. Juran's impact on Japanese quality management techniques is considered second only to Deming's. Like Deming, Juran was among the initial lecturers invited to Japan in the early 1950s. He enjoyed a varied and distinguished career that included stints as a business executive, government administrator, lecturer, writer, and consultant. In 1979, he established the Juran Institute to serve as a base for his seminars, consulting, and conferences. His U.S. clientele has included organizations like Texas Instruments, DuPont, Monsanto, and Xerox. Like Deming, Juran was awarded the Second Order Medal of the Sacred Treasure by the Japanese government.

Juran's approach to quality management shared many features in common with Deming's. For example, he recommended that an organization engage in a continuous cycle of three stages in improvement—quality planning, quality control, and quality improvement. This cyclical approach is analogous to Deming's Plan-Do-Check-Act cycle. However, Juran did make some distinctive contributions to TQM.

Juran defined quality as *fitness for use.* This definition proposes that the users of a product or service should be able to count on it to do what they needed or expected when they bought it.[2] For example, a manufacturer should be able to process a purchased material or component to meet the demands of its customers while achieving high yields and minimal downtime in production; a retailer should receive a correctly labeled product that is free from shipping damage and easy to handle and display; a consumer should receive a product that performs as claimed without prematurely breaking down.

Juran measured fitness for use in five ways:

- *Quality of design.* Every design activity that goes into building a Porsche is aimed at a different quality level than the design activities that go into building a Chevrolet. This dimension of fitness for use links the quality of the final product with the marketing, design, and engineering activities of the organization. Marketing activities affect design because design staff members depend on market research data to develop and refine the concept of the product.
- *Quality of conformance. Conformance* refers to the match between the actual product and the design intent. Conformance depends on the production process, ability to maintain tolerances, work force training, supervision, and test programs. This aspect of fitness for use links the quality of the final product with the manufacturing activities of the organization.
- *Availability.* The frequency and ease of repair affect product quality. Juran uses the term *availability* because a product that is in the process of being repaired is not available for normal use. This facet of fitness for use links the quality of the final product with the design, manufacturing, and after-sales service functions of the organization.
- *Safety.* Juran defines *safety* as the risk of injury due to product hazards. This links the quality of the product with its design features, the design of its instruction manual, and the quality of its component materials.
- *Field use.* The product's performance after it reaches the customer's hands has an important role in quality. This facet of fitness for use links the quality of the final product with its packaging, transportation, storage, and field service.

Juran saw connections between quality and every activity that the organization pursues during the product's entire life. This comprehensive approach sought to anchor quality firmly in the everyday activities of personnel throughout the organization, making a distinct departure from earlier quality control methods.

Juran's other major contribution to TQM was the concept of the cost of quality. Juran argued that the costs associated with quality fall into four categories:

- *Internal failure costs.* Quality affects costs associated with scrap, rework, downtime, and loss of efficiency when a product is identified as defective before shipment to the customer.

- *External failure costs.* Quality determines significant costs associated with complaints, returns, and warranty charges when defects become apparent after the product is shipped to the customer.
- *Appraisal costs.* Quality programs incur costs for inspection, testing, and testing equipment to evaluate the quality of raw materials and purchased components.
- *Prevention costs.* Quality programs generate costs associated with quality planning, training, gathering data, and analysis.

These concepts powerfully presented quality to top managers in a language that they understood—the language of money. No matter how complex products and processes became, no matter what esoteric demands quality management techniques placed on managers, Juran translated them into simple terms—the cost of quality is the cost of making, finding, repairing, or avoiding defective products. This helped top managers to focus on the task of minimizing the cost of quality.

Crosby   Philip B. Crosby began his career as a production line inspector. He worked his way up to corporate vice president of quality at ITT. In 1979, Crosby left ITT to found Philip Crosby Associates Inc. and the Crosby Quality College. By 1990, more than 70,000 executives and managers had attended Crosby's courses. General Motors acquired more than 10 percent of Crosby's stock and set up its own Crosby school for GM personnel. Other companies followed suit, including IBM, Johnson & Johnson, and Chrysler.

Crosby's approach to quality management borrowed many features from Juran and Deming. For example, he proposed his own 14 steps for quality improvement and four absolute laws of quality management that covered the same ground as Deming's 14 steps and Juran's cost of quality. Crosby continued Juran's effort to translate quality concepts into language that top managers could understand, but he went one step further. Crosby aimed to change top managers' perceptions and attitudes about quality. He tried to convince them that improved quality does not cost money; rather it saves money. As a result, an investment in a quality program will pay for itself by generating savings. This line of reasoning led Crosby to make the most dramatic statement associated with his doctrine—"Quality is free."

While Juran's statement of the cost of quality in financial terms was a powerful way of getting the attention of top managers, Crosby helped them to justify committing resources to quality improvement. These resources included management time and attention, as well as dollar investments for test equipment and employee training. If quality investments do pay for themselves, then quality programs need not compete with other resource allocation programs such as new market entries, new product introductions, and capital equipment purchases. The philosophy of continuous improvement slowly moved into the mainstream activities of American corporate giants such as General Motors, IBM, and Motorola.

Although Deming, Juran, and Crosby, the Big Three of the quality movement made distinct intellectual contributions, the practice of quality management in modern organizations usually mixes and matches their contributions. In fact, as Mike Hall's experience in the Skills Module demonstrates, employees rarely follow the sequential path from thinking about quality to solving quality problems. Instead they prefer to jump in and attack the quality

SKILLS MODULE
T. D. Williamson Takes TQM Abroad

INTRODUCTION

We have discussed the principles that led to the development of total quality management. Review the following situation at T. D. Williamson and then complete the skill development exercise that follows. This will help you better understand the practices behind the principles of TQM.

SITUATION

T. D. Williamson Inc., an oil-field equipment and service company based in Tulsa, Oklahoma, had enjoyed success in introducing its American work force to the principles of TQM. The company faced a challenge, however, teaching an American methodology and way of thinking in its Belgian factory.

Mike Hall, senior vice president and chief financial officer, heads Williamson's quality efforts. He remembers watching European employees listen to an explanation of Crosby's 14 points and other principles. Although the employees nodded courteously, no one was interested. Says Hall, "It was a waste of time."

But Williamson couldn't let the issue rest. Its European customers, the state-run oil and gas companies, insisted on high quality standards. Competitors there, mostly smaller niche players, were tough to beat. Williamson's managers began to focus on ISO 9000, a new quality standard, as a goal. They bypassed TQM theory and principle to focus on TQM practice and implementation. "We got people to measure critical aspects of the business, decide where there were problems, and work to solve them," says Hall.

It has worked. Welders once jumped from one hot project to another to meet a daily "hot list" of factory deadlines; today, they follow a simplified, better-planned, more flexible production system that allows priorities to change without disrupting the flow of work. Costs are lower; scrap rates have fallen; deadlines are being met.

SKILL DEVELOPMENT EXERCISE

Mike Hall determined that bypassing talk about Crosby's theories to put them directly into action works better abroad. If the cyclical approach to quality, such as Deming's Plan-Do-Check-Act sequence, is the lifeblood of a TQM program, how long-lived would you expect Williamson's quality program to be?

Create a TQM strategy for Williamson using the principles and ideas of Deming, Juran, and Crosby to create a workable, universal set of principles that *all* of the company's employees can understand.

SOURCE: Elizabeth Ehrlich, "The Quality Management Checkpoint," *International Business,* May 1993, p. 62.

problems and are often surprised to find themselves replicating the Plan-Do-Check-Act cycle or the cost of quality analyses proposed by the quality gurus.

TQM Today

TQM can be described in several ways. One way is to describe the philosophy that unifies all activities in an organization that embraces TQM. That philosophy demands *total dedication to the customer*. This abstract definition does not, however, provide any guidance about how to conduct company business. Another way to define TQM is to describe the outcomes that organizations should strive to achieve.[3] When an organization successfully implements TQM, it develops four characteristics:

- Customers are intensely loyal. They are more than satisfied because the organization meets their needs and exceeds their expectations.
- The organization can respond to problems, needs, and opportunities with minimal delays. It also minimizes costs by eliminating or minimizing tasks that do not add value. In minimizing costs, it enhances the quality of goods and services it gives to customers and the way it treats them.

- The organization's climate supports and encourages teamwork and makes work more satisfying, motivating, and meaningful for employees.
- The organization develops and nurtures a general ethic of continuous improvement. In addition, a method that employees understand leads them toward a state of continuous improvement.

To understand how managers design systems to achieve these outcomes, the next section explains the characteristics of TQM and the methods of organizations that apply TQM. This discussion reviews the criteria for the Malcolm Baldrige National Quality Award and the ISO 9000 certification process to set the stage for consideration of effective ways to configure the organization. This approach is particularly useful for two reasons: (1) When organizations compete for the Baldrige Award or apply for ISO 9000 certification, they use these criteria to guide changes in their management routines; (2) Many organizations do not apply for the award or the certification, but still design programs for continuous improvement based on the criteria. Additionally, the Baldrige Award and ISO 9000 certification have created a new set of hurdles for organizations to clear. To do business in the European Union, for example, they should now plan to become ISO 9000 certified. Motorola expects suppliers to its operations in the United States and Canada to go through the process of applying for the Baldrige Award.

APPLYING TQM METHODS

A review of the work of the quality gurus helps present the central concepts and philosophy of TQM. Still, it is important to see how these concepts can be applied to change organizations. This section identifies the characteristics that are common to all organizations that adopt TQM. The criteria for the Malcolm Baldrige National Quality Award and ISO 9000 certification provide some detail about these characteristics. Implementing these TQM methods has helped organizations achieve some impressive results.

Characteristics of TQM

Each organization applies TQM in a unique way. However, the TQM system can be defined in terms of five characteristics that are common to all organizations that have adopted TQM (see Table 8.2). Even though TQM first proved its worth in large, manufacturing organizations, many smaller organizations have found it very useful. Small organizations often find it easier to get close to their customers. Additionally, they can more easily generate the coordination, participation, and commitment that continuous improvement demands.

Malcolm Baldrige National Quality Award

In the 1980s the U.S. government decided to heighten national awareness of the characteristics and competitive significance of TQM. On August 20, 1987, President Reagan signed Public Law 100–107, the Malcolm Baldridge National Quality Improvement Act. This law established the **Malcolm Baldrige National Quality Award,** named for a former secretary of commerce. The award was designed to recognize U.S. companies that successfully implement TQM systems.

TABLE 8.2

Characteristics of TQM Organizations

CUSTOMER-DRIVEN DEFINITION OF QUALITY

TQM assumes that quality is driven by and defined by the customer. Goods and services with attributes that indicate quality to the customer will increase customer satisfaction and, ultimately, customer demand.

STRONG QUALITY LEADERSHIP

Only a strong leadership team focused on quality improvement can overcome inevitable inertia and resistance to change. Leaders make this change by creating clear quality goals and developing the systems and methods to achieve those goals.

CONTINUOUS IMPROVEMENT

TQM is driven by the quest to improve the efficiency on all business operations and work activities. Management systems must encourage identifying and seizing opportunities to improve.

RELIANCE ON FACTS, DATA, AND ANALYSIS

TQM demands careful decision making based on reliable information and analysis. Constant measurement of quality helps managers to identify and correct conditions that cause poor quality.

EMPLOYEE PARTICIPATION

All employees are accountable for quality, and all need tools and training to fulfill this responsibility. TQM assumes that the employee who is closest to daily operating procedures is in the best position to understand and improve the quality of those procedures.

SOURCE: Adapted from *Management Practices: U.S. Companies Improve Performance through Quality Efforts* (Washington, D.C.: United States General Accounting Office, May 1991), GAO/NSIAD–91–190.

Each year as many as six companies that pass rigorous examinations receive Baldrige Awards. As many as two prizes are awarded in each of three categories: manufacturing, services, and small business. The U.S. Department of Commerce's National Institute of Standards and Technology oversees the process, leaving its administration to a consortium that includes the American Society for Quality Control and the American Productivity and Quality Center.

The Baldrige Award is intended to improve American quality and productivity by:

- Stimulating organizations to produce excellent quality
- Recognizing outstanding organizations and using their experiences to teach others about quality
- Establishing guidelines by which other organizations can assess their own quality improvement efforts

These objectives form the basis of the evaluation process. Every applicant provides information on seven areas. The top scores in all examination categories

TABLE 8.3

Baldrige Award 1993 Examination Items and Point Values

1993 Examination Categories	Point Values
1.0 Leadership	95
1.1 Senior executive leadership	45
1.2 Management for quality	25
1.3 Public responsibility and corporate citizenship	25
2.0 Information and analysis	75
2.1 Quality and performance data	15
2.2 Competitive comparisons and benchmarking	20
2.3 Analysis and uses of company-level data	40
3.0 Strategic quality planning	60
3.1 Quality and company performance planning process	35
3.2 Quality and performance plans	25
4.0 Human resource development and management	150
4.1 Human resource planning and management	20
4.2 Employee involvement	40
4.3 Employee education and training	40
4.4 Employee performance and recognition	25
4.5 Employee well-being and satisfaction	25
5.0 Management of process quality	140
5.1 Design and introduction of quality goods and services	40
5.2 Process management: Production and delivery	35
5.3 Process management: Business and support services	30
5.4 Supplier quality	20
5.5 Quality assessment	15
6.0 Quality and operational results	180
6.1 Product and service quality results	70
6.2 Company operational results	50
6.3 Business process and support service results	25
6.4 Supplier quality results	35
7.0 Customer focus and satisfaction	300
7.1 Customer expectations: Current and future	35
7.2 Customer relationship management	65
7.3 Commitment to customers	15
7.4 Customer satisfaction determination	30
7.5 Customer satisfaction results	85
7.6 Customer satisfaction comparison	70
Total points	1,000

SOURCE: Adapted from M. M. Steeples, *The Corporate Guide to the Malcolm Baldrige National Quality Award* (Homewood, Ill.: Business One-Irwin, 1993).

total 1,000 points. These categories and their assigned weights are summarized in Table 8.3.

The numerous, detailed categories illustrate that applying for and winning the Baldrige Award is no easy undertaking. Category 1.0 of the examination requires the organization to describe its top managers' leadership style, personal involvement, and visibility in maintaining an environment for quality excellence. The application must demonstrate the linkage between quality and day-to-day leadership, management, and supervision activities in all organizational units. It must also document how the organization extends itself to the external community to promote public health, safety, and environmental protection. Category 2.0 of the application examines the scope, validity, use, and management of data and information that underlie the organization's quality improvement program. Applicants must show how they gather data and information and complete analysis to support a prevention-based approach to quality management. Category 3.0 examines the organization's planning process to assess how it achieves or retains quality leadership, and how it integrates quality improvement planning into its overall business planning. Category 4.0 examines how effectively the organization develops and exploits the full potential of its work force, including managers. Category 5.0 examines its statistical and procedural techniques for designing and producing goods and services. Category 6.0 examines the applicant's record of quality improvement based upon objective measures derived from analysis of customer requirements. Category 7.0 examines the organization's knowledge of its customers, overall customer service systems, responsiveness, and ability to meet customers' requirements.

Recent winners of the Baldrige Award include AT&T Network Systems (1992), Texas Instruments (1992), and Eastman Kodak Co. (1993) in the manufacturing organizations category; Granite Rock Co. (1992) and Ames Rubber Corp. (1993) in the small business organizations category; and AT&T Universal Card Services (1992) and The Ritz-Carlton Hotel Co. (1993) in the service organizations category.

ISO 9000

As the competitive significance of TQM caught the attention of the business world in the 1980s, scholars and consultants began recommending a variety of quality improvement methods, all of which judged quality in different ways. In 1987, the International Standards Organization's Technical Committee on Quality Assurance set out to develop an internationally accepted quality standard. This effort produced a set of standards commonly known as **ISO 9000.** ISO 9000 is not one standard, but a set of five documents (ISO 9000 to ISO 9004). The most commonly used standards appear in ISO 9001 to ISO 9003, divided by topic:

- ISO 9001 contains standards for engineering-based or construction-oriented organizations that design, develop, produce, install, and service products.
- ISO 9002 contains standards that are particularly relevant to chemical, process, and other related industries.
- ISO 9003 (the least frequently applied set of standards) concerns small shops and divisions within an organization (laboratories, for example).

ISO 9000 and ISO 9004 contain specialized standards for specific industrial applications.

Although ISO 9000 is often compared to the criteria for the Malcolm Baldrige National Quality Award, many important distinctions separate the two:[4]

1. Unlike the Baldrige Award, none of the ISO standard systems award points.

2. ISO standards do not pay much attention to human resource utilization and customer satisfaction.

3. When an organization applies for ISO 9000 certification, it requests that a team from an accredited registrar audit its overall quality system. At each stage, the auditors must determine whether or not the organization's quality management system conforms to ISO guidelines. The audit focuses on 20 features of this system, as summarized in Table 8.4.

Table 8.4 clearly shows that preparing for an ISO 9000 certification audit involves carefully examining every organizational activity that has an influence on the quality of the final product. The audit promotes continuous improvement by verifying that any organization that has an ISO 9000 certified quality management system in place has implemented all the organizational processes that TQM requires. The next section examines some of the obstacles and benefits associated with TQM.

Impact of TQM

None of the individual components of TQM is novel or revolutionary. Yet, implementing the entire system consistently over an extended period of time can yield startling results. One way to understand the benefits of TQM is to examine studies of organizations that have implemented it.

The most influential study of the impact of TQM reports on improvements in market share, profitability, customer satisfaction, quality, costs, and employee relations in 22 organizations.[5] These companies report that they have enjoyed an average annual market share increase of 13.7 percent after implementing TQM. Customer satisfaction has showed an average annual increase of 2.5 percent. Product reliability has improved by an annual average of 11.3 percent and the annual reduction in errors has averaged 10.3 percent. Employee relations, measured by the total number of suggestions for improvement submitted by employees, has showed an annual percentage increase of 16.6 percent.

Another way to understand the impact of TQM is to compare the characteristics of organizations in different areas where the system has been at

---

TABLE 8.4

Criteria for ISO 9000 Audit

1. *Management responsibility.* Someone in the top management of the organization must be responsible for ensuring effective management of the entire quality management system and that all goods and services delivered to customers meet or exceed their expectations.

2. *Quality system.* The organization must have a formal quality management system in place to ensure that it delivers all goods and services to customers' specifications.

3. *Contract review.* All contracts and orders accepted by the organization must go through a formal review process to verify agreement between what the marketing department sells and what the production system delivers.

4. *Design control.* All product designs must pass a formal, documented review process to verify that the design fulfills its intended use. The documentation tracks changes in the design of the product.

TABLE 8.4

Continued

5. *Document control.* The applicant must document unambiguously every bit of information needed to build, service, and maintain the product so that it is available for review.

6. *Purchasing.* The applicant must submit to a formal review of all systems that control the timing, quality, quantity, and types of purchases made by the organization. The review matches the purchases with the needs of the organization.

7. *Purchasing of supplied product.* Another review evaluates all systems for storage and maintenance of purchased components to ensure that the standards for identifying and correcting problems with purchased components are clearly articulated.

8. *Product identification and traceability.* All processes that identify, trace, and monitor parts within the production system are reviewed to determine how the organization ensures that its input components are identical to those in the design drawings.

9. *Process control.* The application process evaluates all methods to measure, control, and maintain quality in the production process to ensure valid uses of process control tools such as control charts, Pareto analysis, and cause and effect diagrams.

10. *Inspection and testing.* The process reviews all procedures designed to make sure that the product works as it should.

11. *Inspection, measuring, and testing equipment.* The application reviews all methods designed to maintain and test the accuracy of testing and inspection equipment.

12. *Inspection and test status.* Another review covers all the documentation that informs the customer that the product was tested.

13. *Control of nonconforming products.* Procedures that identify and test defective products must be reviewed.

14. *Corrective action.* Procedures used to correct identified defects must be reviewed.

15. *Handling, storage, packaging, and delivery.* Another evaluation focuses on procedures to handle, store, package, and deliver the product from the end of the manufacturing line to the hands of the customer. This review evaluates the firm's efforts to ensure that no product is damaged when it gets to the customer.

16. *Quality records.* All procedures to document the quality of products must also be reviewed. The records reviewed in this step span all activities from the raw material to the final product.

17. *Internal quality audits.* A review assesses all internal systems that help the organization to determine whether its production process is in control.

18. *Training.* An evaluation of all systems aimed at properly training employees focuses on both training methods and measures to determine whether or not a specific employee is properly trained.

19. *Servicing.* All systems to service a product after its release for use in the field must be reviewed.

20. *Statistical techniques.* All statistical techniques by which the firm maintains and controls quality must be reviewed. In addition to evaluating the proper use of these techniques, this review evaluates the training of the work force to use these techniques appropriately.

Source: Adapted from M. Breen, R. Jud, and P. E. Pareja, *An Introduction to ISO 9000* (Dearborn, Mich.: Society of Manufacturing Engineers, 1993).

work for different periods of time. Since continuous improvement programs yield their benefits over the long term, experts argue that organizations with longer track records applying TQM should enjoy higher benefits. The benefits of TQM extend beyond improved product quality to improve efficiency as measured by inventory and productivity levels. Accordingly, Japanese organizations should lead American and European organizations on measures of quality, inventory levels, and productivity levels because the Japanese have almost three decades of experience in applying TQM, whereas American and European organizations began applying these techniques in the mid-1980s.

Such an analysis can meaningfully compare organizations only if they operate in the same industry. Unfortunately, many of the organizational characteristics (for example defect rates and productivity) that would provide the most interesting insight into the results of TQM are measures of competitive strength of individual organizations. It is virtually impossible to obtain up-to-date information about such sensitive, proprietary issues. Table 8.5 presents some dated information (which is easier to obtain since it is no longer sensitive) to examine the impact of TQM in the automobile industry.

The two direct measures of quality in Table 8.5 are the number of assembly defects per 100 vehicles and the percentage of total assembly space devoted to post-production repair. Japanese organizations operating in Japan lead on both of these measures. American and European organizations lag significantly behind, while Japanese plants in America fall between the two extremes, at levels close to those of the Japanese organizations. Japanese firms' plants in America are usually headed by seasoned TQM veterans from Japan. These managers have raised the quality levels of their American operations to approximately the levels of their native Japanese counterparts. This

---

TABLE 8.5

TQM at Automobile Assembly Plants[a]

	Japanese Firms in Japan	Japanese Firms in America	American Firms	European Firms
Assembly defects per 100 vehicles	60	65	82	97
Repair area as percentage of assembly space	4.1	4.9	12.9	14.4
Inventory (days)[b]	0.2	1.6	2.9	2.0
Percentage of work force in TQM teams	69.3	71.3	17.3	0.6
Training of new workers (hours)	380	370	46	173
Productivity (hours per vehicle)	16.8	21.2	25.1	36.2

[a]Figures in this table are averages for plants in each region.
[b]For eight sample parts.
SOURCE: Adapted from "When GM's Robots Ran Amok," *The Economist,* August 10, 1991, pp. 64–65.

demonstrates that there is nothing peculiarly Japanese about the values, work ethic and teamwork required to apply TQM; the American workers in these plants have adopted TQM very successfully. Additionally, statistics on team organization and new worker training seem to indicate that American and European managers could profit from studying the methods of their Japanese counterparts.

In summary, Japanese-managed plants in Japan have reaped the most benefits from TQM. American and European plants seem to have gained significantly less because they have less experience in implementing the system. Japanese-managed plants in the United States seem to fall between these two extremes, indicating that even if top managers have intellectually grasped the TQM system, it takes time to move their organizations to positions to reap the complete benefits of TQM.

TQM IN THE STRATEGIC MANAGEMENT PROCESS

An understanding of the basic concepts of TQM and a review of some of the results that it can deliver lead to questions about how to introduce it to the strategic management process. This section discusses some of the issues managers face when they implement or maintain a TQM program in a company. The main steps of the strategic management process include environmental analysis, establishing an organizational direction, formulating strategy, implementing strategy, and exerting strategic control. This section returns to each step to highlight the kinds of issues that arise in implementing or maintaining a TQM program. Additionally, it examines TQM programs developed by organizations like AT&T, Corning, and Harley-Davidson, and it discusses some of the methods by which these firms have tried to generate the vision, teamwork, and cooperation that are critical components of any TQM program.

Environmental Analysis and TQM

The organizational environment includes all factors, both internal and external, that affect an organization's performance. Analysis of both internal and external environmental forces defines the context of the organization's overall strategy. A TQM program represents these factors as needs of external and internal customers. The **external customer** is well-known—the entity that buys the organization's good or service. Environmental analysis connects the specific needs of the external customer with the activities of the different parts of the organization. The concept of the **internal customer**—the next stage in the firm's internal value chain—develops specifically with the TQM system, as a later discussion will explain in detail.

External Customer   TQM usually visualizes the external customer as a collection of several dimensions of customer satisfaction. For example, the external customer may express satisfaction (or its opposite) with the availability of the product, its appearance, its safety, its reliability, and its user-friendliness. Any organization must identify specific internal activities that contribute to these dimensions of customer satisfaction. The matrix in Figure 8.1 shows how some companies choose to demonstrate how each business function relates to specific dimensions of customer satisfaction.

After charting the links between customer satisfaction and the organization's activities, managers design systems within each function to ensure

FIGURE 8.1   Departmental Contributions to External Customer Satisfaction

Dimensions of External-Customer Satisfaction

Department	Availability	Appearance	Safety	Reliability	User-friendly	Warranty
Design		+	=	+	=	+
Manufacturing	=	=	+	+		=
Marketing	=		+			
Sales	+				+	
Accounting						+

Key

(+) = Department plays a critical role in determining external customer satisfaction on this dimension.

(=) = Department plays a moderate role in determining external customer satisfaction on this dimension.

continued sensitivity to customers' needs. For example, if the sales staff plays a critical role in increasing the user-friendliness of the product, the managers may decide to tie sales people's pay and bonuses to customer survey data on user-friendliness. This sends the clear message that behavior and decisions should promote user-friendliness in the product. As a result, sales staff may pay greater attention to redesigning the instruction manual or clarifying their product demonstrations.

Organizations determine the needs of their external customers by a variety of methods. Market research firms use focus groups, customer opinion surveys, and face-to-face meetings to query customers about their perceptions of the utility of specific product features and their contributions to customer satisfaction. Many organizations use toll-free customer service phone lines to gather a wealth of information about customer concerns and product performance. The firm should channel every bit of information about the customers' needs, buying habits, preferences, and perceptions into refining the product to increase customer satisfaction.

Clearly, the customer satisfaction matrix for a product within a company is unique to that product-market at that particular point in time. The best companies measure external customer satisfaction continuously. This information helps managers plan the next set of improvements in the ceaseless Plan-Do-Check-Act sequence that is the heartbeat of a TQM program.

Internal Customer   Each organization activity must identify and work to satisfy its internal customer, the next stage in the firm's internal value chain. Within the organization, each division, department, and employee can be viewed as both a customer and a supplier to other divisions, departments, or employees. Figure 8.2 provides an example of an internal value chain in a manufacturing company. The market research department feeds the design department with information on the customer's needs. In this sense, the design department is an internal customer of the market research department;

FIGURE 8.2   Internal Value Chain of a Manufacturing Organization

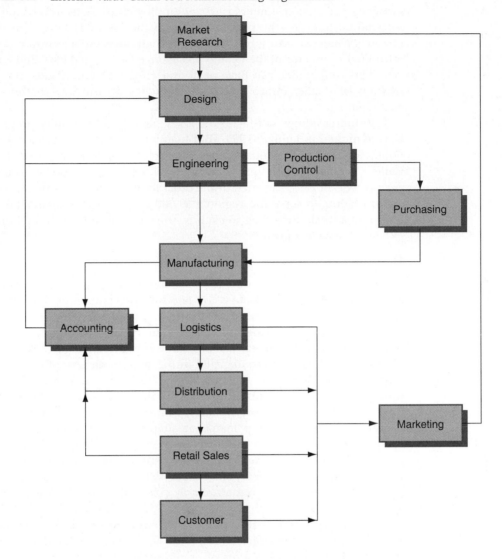

the design task cannot be completed effectively without the information from the market research department. The design department, in turn, processes the market research information and comes up with a product design, which it supplies to internal customers in the engineering department.

Each individual within the organization can identify the critical internal linkages that shape the quality of the final product by asking some simple questions: Who are my internal customers? Am I meeting their requirements? The organization can conduct an internal audit which includes a step-by-step examination of its value-adding process to identify the needs of internal customers. Experts suggest that meeting the needs of each internal customer effectively ensures that external customers will be satisfied with the product. In other words, excellent market research combines with excellence in design, which in turn combines with excellence at every stage in the internal value chain to give external customers a high-quality product.

For example, managers at AT&T believe that one of the first steps toward satisfying external customers is to get employees to focus inward and please internal customers—the people just down the assembly line or in the next office.[6] "Whatever your job is, you've got a supplier and a customer," says Edward Fuchs, director of the Quality Excellence Center at AT&T Bell Laboratories. This simple idea can have profound effects because it sets into motion a chain of quality improvement that reaches all the way to the external customer.

Internal customer satisfaction is a key element of a quality program that IBM launched in January 1990. IBM maintains a high-tech service desk at its Southeast Region headquarters in Research Triangle Park, North Carolina. Called *Solution Central,* this division guarantees a fast response to any manager or worker who is stymied by bureaucracy or needs help with a problem—any problem. To serve the region's 39,000 employees, 50 agents are on call 95 hours a week, including weekends, to reduce interference or hunt down experts that callers need.

Organizational Direction and TQM

To set an organizational direction managers evaluate their environmental analysis and craft appropriate vision and mission statements. They then specify organizational objectives to realize their vision and achieve their mission. When organizations change direction, leaders must change and renew the outmoded vision. In the early 1990s, large organizations such as Sears, IBM, Motorola, and AT&T were engaged in the mammoth task of their changing organizational directions. This involved redefining their goods or services, their technologies, their objectives, their philosophies, their self-concepts, and their public images. An organization's move toward continuous quality improvement begins with top managers shaping a new vision for the organization. A corporate vision can focus the collective energy of employees, and give external observers a better idea of where the organization is headed. Developing a vision that is truly shared across an organization is a difficult and time-consuming process, but absolutely essential to the success of any TQM initiative.

Top managers then define continuous, customer-focused improvement as a central part of the organization's mission. Quality-related themes recur throughout mission statements of organizations as diverse as Great Scot Supermarkets, Federal Express, and The Crummer School. These organizations' missions emphasize that quality and continuous improvement must drive every action of the organization.

However, crafting the mission statement does not complete top managers' role in directing the organization toward continuous improvement. Members of top management take personal responsibility for providing active, unwavering leadership over a long period of time. In this way, they keep the organization focused on meeting quality improvement objectives as part of a continuous and coherent system.

For example, James R. Houghton, chairman of Corning Inc., gives pretty much the same spiel 50 times a year at different Corning plants and offices.[7] Quality, quality, quality. World-class. Customer focus. Worker participation. At each site, he delivers a sermon for the employee ranks, then he conducts a nononsense performance review with local managers. Does Houghton get tired of this routine? Just a bit. He has been preaching this gospel since 1983, but he keeps at it. "After eight years if I stop talking about quality now, it would be a disaster," he says. The effort has paid off: Corning's operating profits are up 111 percent in five years.

Top management leadership and support is especially crucial because most organizations feel strong pressure to show financial results. TQM programs are hard to justify on the basis of short-term results; organizations have to work for a while before these programs begin to show benefits. Implementing a quality improvement program is a time-consuming process, usually prompted by severe competitive pressure. However strong the desire to demonstrate mastery of competitors, tenacious implementation over an extended time period is necessary for a successful TQM program.

For example, Modicon, a Massachusetts-based maker of industrial automation systems, threw itself into total quality management in the late 1980s. "Senior managers," says Dick Eppig, Modicon's vice president of quality, "tend to measure the firm's quality program against its short-term financial performance." They expect instant results, asking, "Has quality improved performance this quarter?" Such impatience makes doubtful positive results.[8]

Graham Sharman, a quality expert with McKinsey, reports, "Of those quality programs that have been in place in Western firms for more than two years, more than two-thirds simply grind to a halt because of their failure to produce the hoped for results." This short-term view ignores the scope and depth of TQM objectives. In the words of Glenn Eggert, vice president of operations at Allen-Bradley, "Before customers see the difference, quality must run through the company's blood."[9] Everybody from salespeople to shop-floor engineers must think about quality. Responsibility for quality has to reach down to the shop floor, organization structures have to be flattened, and barriers to cross-functional communications have to fall. This kind of change takes years.

Ron Hutchinson, head of customer service at Harley-Davidson, identifies another reason why TQM requires a long-term commitment. He says, "The continuous creeping shake-up that is needed to make quality improvements is a curious kind of goal." Human nature demands clearly defined targets, not the constantly shifting goals that lead a firm toward ever-higher quality. Maintaining the momentum of a quality program can make a manager feel like Sisyphus, the mythical laborer doomed to push a stone uphill forever. Yet, one glance at the statistics about the experience that companies have accumulated with TQM shows that a long slow effort is vital. In Japan, companies like Nippondenso, Honda, and Nissan have implemented TQM systems for more than 30 years. The Company Example presents a case of an unusually rapid implementation of a TQM program. In the United States, even exemplary practitioners like Motorola, Texas Instruments, and Xerox have implemented TQM for only 10 to 15 years. Their experience leaves them a long way from any claim to have internalized the discipline of TQM in a significant way.

Strategy Formulation and TQM

Formulating a strategy for an organization involves developing a cohesive plan to achieve objectives by adapting the organization to match its environment. Strategy formulation is primarily an analytical effort, supplemented by executive judgment and creativity. TQM injects the customer's perspective, the competitor's perspective, and the supplier's perspective into the process of formulating strategy.

COMPANY EXAMPLE

TQM at Toto

In 1984, two top officials at Toto Ltd. were converted to the cause of TQM. The change came when Toto, a maker of bathroom fixtures based on the Japanese island of Kyushu, failed to meet annual goals set out in its strategic plan.

First, Toto sent its board members to TQM seminars sponsored by the Japan Standards Association and other national organizations. It then gave five-day TQM courses to 550 of its middle managers. The structural change at Toto was supervised by the Total Quality Control Promotion Group, a task force led by a senior managing director and three board members.

To foster the TQM initiative, Toto's 8,200 employees were organized into 32 groups. The new system expected each of the 550 middle managers to uncover at least one quality problem twice a year to be solved over the next six months using the suggestions of the group. Within a period of six years, Toto had solved more than 900 quality problems ranging from missed sales quotas to misdirected deliveries.

By 1990, when Toto won its Deming Prize, the firm's culture had been transformed. The change in corporate and employee philosophy is apparent in even a quick walk through one of the company's factories. At the Kokura No. 2 plant, for example, every corridor has a quality-related name: Deming Cycle Street, Problem-Solving Street, Progressive Quality Street. The walls are covered with charts and diagrams used by the plant's 170 quality circles. In many departments, workers post their personal monthly goals, such as reducing the amount of time needed to set up a specific machine.

Toto's strategic commitment to total quality management is not confined to its factories and offices, according to Yasukazu Kitajima, general manager of the Kokura No. 2 plant. "Now, when I go out drinking with my colleagues, we spend more time talking about quality," he says.

SOURCE: R. Neff, "No. 1 and Trying Harder," *Business Week,* Special Issue on the Quality Imperative, October 25, 1991, pp. 20–24.

Strategy Formulation from the Customer's Perspective   One sees two kinds of smiles at Disneyland: the first displays the anticipation of people entering the park or boarding a ride; the second from the ride itself. The first might be a little easier to generate than the second; Disneyland consistently generates both. One secret of Disneyland's success is its consistent effort to incorporate the customer's perspective in formulating its strategy. The Disneyland handbook has the title, "We create happiness." One section reads, "Producing the Disneyland Show for our Guests requires the talents of a diverse group of people, more than 12,000 performing in more than 400 different roles. Although our individual jobs vary, we all work from the same script, speaking the same language."[10] Disneyland speaks the language of the customer.

For example, Dan Kent is manager of show quality standards for Walt Disney Imagineering. He is responsible for incorporating the customer's perspective into the design and appearance of the park and its attractions. Disneyland's commitment to customer satisfaction goes far beyond delivering safe, high-quality entertainment. The park must look right from the customer's perspective. Different attractions in the park must present a harmonious appearance. Splash Mountain, a heart-pumping water flume ride that opened in 1989, rests on a hill just north of Haunted Mansion, which opened 20 years earlier. Careful design and architectural decisions have ensured that the two attractions do not clash. "We want to make Splash Mountain look like it's been here since opening day," said Kent. "We don't want something to overshadow what's next to it."

Over time, Disneyland's commitment to satisfying customers has led it to invent a design technique called *forced perspective*. In other words, managers like Kent employ sophisticated techniques to deliver entertainment *and* to make it look just right. Sleeping Beauty Castle appears much larger than its real size because larger bricks at the base of the castle and smaller bricks at the top create an illusion. The design of buildings on Main Street is another symbol of this commitment to customer satisfaction. The distance between the Central Plaza (the hub of the park) and the Town Square (just inside the park) appears shorter from the Central Plaza end than it does from the Town Square end. That's because the Main Street buildings on the Central Plaza end are a little farther apart than the buildings on the Town Square end. This give the impression that the park is opening up to guests as they enter, and that the exit is a little closer as they leave. Disney has created a tradition of strategy formulation based on total customer satisfaction. Disney's top managers focus their analytical efforts on finding new ways to make the Disneyland experience satisfying in terms of its content and appearance. This dedication helps them identify and build the appropriate internal competencies. For example, Disney literally invented the forced perspective design technique by spending time and money to learn how to create the illusions that increase customer satisfaction.

Strategy Formulation from the Competitor's Perspective   Analysis of the effect of TQM on strategy formulation cannot ignore competitors. To think smart about an organization's future, top managers must seek sustainable advantage at the functional level, the business level, and the corporate level. The analytic effort is sharpened considerably through a systematic consideration of methods used by competitors. TQM depends on fact-based decision making aimed at continuous improvement. The facts that drive a continuous improvement strategy come from measurements of the organization's performance relative to the performance of its most successful competitor. An earlier chapter gave this analysis the name *benchmarking*. David Kearns, former president of Xerox Corporation, advocates "the continuous process of measuring products, services, and practices against the toughest competitors or those companies recognized as industry leaders."[11] The systematic search for successful methods used by other organizations can lead to valuable discoveries in the most unlikely places.

In the photocopier industry, they joke that a company can always be sure of two sales for a new model: to its own headquarters and to Xerox, which tests nearly all of its rivals' copiers. If another machine performs better, it becomes Xerox's benchmark, or goal for improvement. Xerox benchmarks more than copiers. For example, the corporation must quickly ship parts for its equipment to hundreds of thousands of customers around the world. Delays and mistakes make irate customers. To improve its logistics and distribution functions, Xerox turned to L. L. Bean. What can a copier manufacturer learn from a catalog sales firm? Xerox says plenty, since Bean may have the world's best small-item distribution system. Xerox recognized that Bean's system designed to move moccasins and tents could also move copy machine parts.

Strategy Formulation from the Supplier's Perspective   The effect of TQM on strategy formulation extends this analysis to consider maintaining and improving the quality of purchased parts, components, and raw materials. In the words of Noel Pooler, owner of Pooler Industries, "When large firms embrace TQM, it changes how everybody who deals with them does business. They reduce the number of suppliers that they have, they want long-term contracts, fewer and fewer suppliers, better and better quality."[12]

Japanese companies have pioneered supplier management methods that yield significant quality improvements. Davis Tool and Engineering Company's experience with Nissan is an example of how an organization can enrich its strategy formulation process by viewing it from the supplier's perspective.[13] Five years ago, Davis Tool bid to supply parts to the Nissan plant in Smyrna, Tennessee. Nissan sent engineers from Smyrna and Japan to examine the Davis Tool factory in Detroit before awarding the company a contract. Then, as it has done with two dozen suppliers across the United States, Nissan dispatched a pair of engineers from Smyrna for five days to help workers at Davis Tool's factory rethink their jobs. At this time five Davis employees were producing 200 oil pans per shift.

The results of Nissan's efforts astounded the managers at Davis Tool. At the end of five days, two workers were churning out 800 oil pans each shift. At Nissan's urging, Davis Tool assured its workers that efficiency gains would not cost them their jobs. Some of the changes seemed obvious, like raising parts bins to hip level so that workers no longer had to strain their backs bending over to reach the bins. The Nissan team broke down each worker's job, timing each activity to identify any waste. They then combined tasks to save time and space. Davis Tool had never before been prodded into such thorough scrutiny of its practices, explained Richard Davis II, president. The Japanese, he said, are "bringing these skills to their new supply base in America."

To help suppliers, Nissan has also created a training program in Smyrna. Managers from supplier companies visit to take courses that last about 16 days and range from problem solving to W. Edward Deming's techniques for improving quality. Nissan has divided its suppliers into regional groups. Suppliers from each region tour each other's factories to see how they have improved efficiency in everything from plant layout to lighting.

Strategy Implementation and TQM

Strategy implementation consists of managing change, organization structure, and culture to achieve strategic goals. TQM affects strategy implementation as the work force can be a source of tremendous competitive advantage, given the power to develop and implement new and better systems. For example, Exxon has two plants that make a tire ingredient in Houston and Baton Rouge, Louisiana. As part of a quality improvement program at these plants, top managers appointed Floyd, a drawling six-and-a-half footer, as an internal quality consultant in 1985. He taught himself the basics of quality management by studying Deming's books. He organized workers and managers into teams to find ways to streamline the plants. From 1988 to 1990, he says, the operation cut its working capital needs from 18 percent to 8 percent of its $400 million in yearly sales. In 1990, one of the plants won a national award for excellence in manufacturing administered by Utah State University.[14]

Strategic Control and TQM   To make certain that strategies unfold as intended, managers need yardsticks that can measure the organization's performance and provide the benchmarks for the strategic audit. After successful methods adopted by competitors and other organizations have been identified at the formulation stage, these methods have to be examined carefully and codified so that they can be used for strategic control.

To practice benchmarking, a firm continuously compares its processes with the same processes of the best competitors in the industry—including domestic and foreign firms; the comparison should also extend to the best firm outside the industry that has similar processes. The process of benchmarking consists of the following steps.[15]

- Learning how other organizations arrange their processes.
- Adapting the best-practice to the investigating organization.
- Taking action to improve the process to meet or exceed the standards of the best.

Benchmarking is a very systematic, intensive, and disciplined process that requires research about others' processes and a thorough understanding of one's own processes. This requires an investment of substantial time and resources, and it exposes the firm to a whole new world of shared experiences. Of course, competitors won't (and shouldn't) share their most important competitive secrets, but that leaves a very large number of processes about which competitors can share information.

Compaq and Apple, two highly competitive computer companies, have shared benchmarking information about certain processes with one another. IBM, Motorola, AT&T, and Xerox have benchmarked the designs of their training programs for employees. Xerox, Varian, Sun Microsystems, and Solectron have joined forces to study their methods to increase customer satisfaction. Competitors are often willing to share information (and legally they can do so under antitrust laws) provided they specify up front the areas to cover, the kind of information to exchange, and the uses of the results.

Benchmarking has become an important part of the strategic control efforts in many organizations. In 1992, the American Productivity and Quality Center released the results of a survey in which 98 percent of the respondents said they would be doing much more benchmarking over the next five years, and 80 percent agreed that companies will have to employ the technique to survive in the globally competitive world of the future.

SUMMARY

Business managers have always recognized that poor product quality could threaten customer satisfaction and perhaps even the survival of their organizations. Historically, they have tried to solve quality problems by implementing inspection and post-production repair systems. Modern organizations have developed more proactive methods of assuring quality, spurred by the teachings of W. Edwards Deming, Joseph M. Juran, and Philip B. Crosby, along with the competitive success of Japanese firms that have embraced and refined their methods.

The principles of total quality management guide unique changes in every organization's operations, but all firms that practice TQM share five characteristics: a customer-driven definition of quality; strong quality leadership; emphasis on continuous improvement; reliance on facts, data, and analysis; and encouragement of employee participation. The Malcolm Baldrige National Quality Award and ISO 9000 certification encourage organizations to embody these characteristics.

A total quality management initiative affects every step in the strategic management process. It focuses the firm's environmental analysis on the needs of external and internal customers. TQM fills the organization's vision and mission with images of continuous improvement in customer satisfaction, keeping objectives tied securely to customer's needs. TQM requires strategy formulation to develop a plan that considers customers', competitors', and suppliers' perspectives. TQM adds power to strategy implementation by tapping the potent force of employees' experience and insight into the organization's operations and to strategic control through benchmarking competitive products.

KEY TERMS

total quality management (TQM), p. 191

quality control, p. 191

Plan-Do-Check-Act, p. 193

Malcolm Baldrige National Quality Award, p. 198

ISO 9000, p. 201

external customer, p. 205

internal customer, p. 205

CHECKLIST Analyzing Total Quality Management in Problems and Cases

___ 1. Does the problem or case involve quality issues?

___ 2. Has the organization developed a basic system or strategy for quality management?

___ 3. Has it fully explicated and adapted the principles of TQM to its own organizational characteristics?

___ 4. Are all employees appropriately involved in the TQM process and strategy?

___ 5. Does the organization's TQM philosophy focus on outcomes that the company should strive to achieve?

___ 6. Is the TQM system defined in terms of the five characteristics common to all organizations that have adopted the method?

___ 7. Does TQM improve production and quality?

___ 8. Does an internally accepted quality standard apply to the problem or case?

___ 9. Has the organization evaluated the impact of quality issues on its strategic management process?

Additional Readings

Ciampa, D. *Total Quality: A User's Guide for Implementation.* Reading, Mass.: Addison-Wesley, 1992.

Dean, J. W., Jr., and J. R. Evans. *Total Quality: Management, Organization, and Strategy.* Minneapolis, Minn.: West Publishing, 1994.

Logothetis, N. *Managing for Total Quality: From Deming to Taguchi and SPC.* Hertfordshire, U.K.: Prentice-Hall International, 1992.

Rabbit, J. T. and P. A. Bergh. *The ISO 9000 Book.* White Plains, N. Y.: Quality Resources, 1993.

The Road to Total Quality. New York: Conference Board, 1990. Research Bulletin No. 239.

Steeples, M. M., *The Corporate Guide to the Malcolm Baldrige National Quality Award.* Homewood, Ill.: Business One-Irwin, 1993.

C A S E

Philips's Strategy Falls on Deaf Ears

It was supposed to be a triumphant moment at Philips Electronics' annual shareholders meeting. CEO Jan D. Timmer had done everything right; he had revived the world's third-largest consumer electronics company, coaxing healthy 1993 profits from a weakened giant that had lost $2.3 billion in 1990 and dipped into the red again in 1992.

Timmer had done it the hard way, slashing 70,000 jobs and axing businesses that were losing money. Despite a flat market, Philips had rebounded from a $486 million loss in 1992 to a profit of $1.06 billion in 1993. Still, shareholders held copies of an annual report that projected a sales increase of only 1 percent in 1993 and reported that $600 million of Philips's profit was nonrecurring income from divestitures. They wanted to know why new products were selling so slowly.

Timmer acknowledged that he'd really only finished half of the job—the easy half. Keeping up with the Joneses of global electronics—Sony Corp. and Matsushita Electric Industrial Co.—meant finding new products and new industries to fuel growth. It was a theme Timmer had been pounding home to his employees for three years.

Timmer admitted that a number of obstacles complicated his plans to get Philips moving, but he asserted that the company would conquer them. He planned to unveil a new strategy in mid-June that sources said would accelerate the Dutch company's move into software, services, and multimedia, where Timmer hoped to generate 30 percent to 40 percent of revenues by 2000, compared with just 20 percent currently.

It was a bold plan, but was it fast enough? "We can't continue to restructure," said Henk Bodt, a board member in charge of consumer electronics. "We have to develop new initiatives." Philips was poised to make a major acquisition, probably a leading U.S. interactive-software company.

Many of Philips's thrusts into multimedia aren't designed to produce profits until the end of the decade, however, and Timmer grappled with a number of immediate problems, especially in the all-important consumer-electronics division.

To speed the transformation, Timmer had already shaken up the top ranks at the inward-looking company. He brought in a number of non-Dutch managers, many with strong international and marketing backgrounds. Although he sensed a change in attitude, Timmer clearly faced an uphill battle. He was stunned at a company colloquium when employees asked where Philips was headed and why. He was astonished that the company's troops had failed to comprehend the plan he had been promoting for more than three years. In a fresh attempt at communicating Philips's strategy, Timmer planned to ask all 236,000 employees about the progress they had seen under his program of renewal, dubbed Operation Centurion. "It's an invitation for people to be very critical, even about people in charge," he said. "We must encourage entrepreneurial behavior at all levels."

DISCUSSION QUESTIONS

1. In what ways could TQM help Philips achieve its manufacturing and marketing goals?

2. How effective could a TQM strategy be when the company's strategy has remained so unclear to employees?

3. Write a mission statement for Philips, focusing on potential contributions from the principles of Deming, Juran, and Crosby that could help the company achieve its sales and marketing goals.

SOURCE: "Philips Needs Laser Speed," *Business Week,* June 6, 1994, pp. 46–47.

Notes

1. *Management Practices: U.S. Companies Improve Performance through Quality Efforts* (Washington, D.C.: United States General Accounting Office, May 1991), GAO/NSIAD–91–190.

2. A. March, "A Note on Quality: The Views of Deming, Juran, and Crosby," in Harry Costin, ed., *Readings in Total Quality Management* (New York: Harcourt Brace College Publishers, 1994), p. 143.

3. D. Ciampa, *Total Quality: A User's Guide for Implementation* (Reading, Mass.: Addison-Wesley, 1992).

4. J. Lamprecht, "The ISO 9000 Certification Process: Some Important Issues to Consider," *Quality Digest,* August 1991, pp. 61–70.

5. B. Stratton, "The Value of Implementing Quality," *Quality Progress,* July 1991, p. 70.

6. O. Port and J. Carey, "Questing for the Best," *Business Week,* Special Issue on the Quality Imperative, October 25, 1991, pp. 8–16.

7. K. H. Hammonds and G. DeGeorge, "Where Did They Go Wrong?" *Business Week,* Special Issue on the Quality Imperative, October 25, 1991, pp. 34–38.

8. "The Cracks in Quality," *The Economist,* April 18, 1992, pp. 67–68.

9. Ibid.

10. B. Stratton, "How Disneyland Works," *Quality Progress,* 24, no. 7 (1991), pp. 17–31.

11. D. Wilkerson, A. Kuh, and T. Wilkerson, "A Tale of Change," *Total Quality Management,* July/August 1992, pp. 146–151.

12. M. Barrier, "Small Firms Put Quality First," *Nation's Business,* May 1992, pp. 22–30.

13. J. Bennet, "Detroit Struggles to Learn Another Lesson from Japan," *New York Times,* June 19, 1994, p. 5.

14. T. Peterson, K. Kelly, J. Weber, and N. Gross, "Top Products for Less than Top Dollar," *Business Week,* Special Issue on the Quality Imperative, October 25, 1991, pp. 66–68.

15. C. J. Grayson, Jr., "Worldwide Competition," *Total Quality Management,* July/August 1992, pp. 134–138.

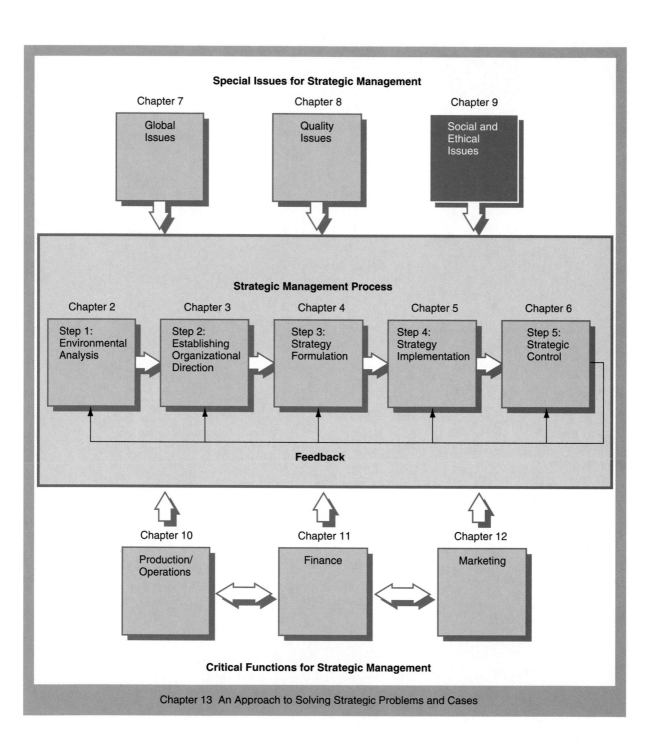

Strategic Management: Social and Ethical Dimensions

A **stakeholder** of an organization is an individual or group who has a stake in the consequences of management decisions and can influence those decisions. The managers of a successful corporation have obligations to many different stakeholders.[1] For example, they are responsible to:

- The *stockholders* or *owners* of the corporation, to attempt to increase the value of the firm
- The *suppliers* of materials and *resellers* of products, to deal fairly with them
- *Lenders* of capital, to repay them
- *Government agencies* and society, to abide by laws
- *Interest groups*, to consider their arguments
- *Employees* and *unions*, to provide safe work environments and recognize their rights
- *Consumers*, to provide safe products and market them efficiently
- *Competitors*, to avoid practices that restrain trade
- *Local communities* and *society at large*, to avoid practices that harm the environment

Some analysts argue that one or another of these obligations is most important, but we believe that all of them must be considered. Successful business firms are powerful forces in society; because of their power, they incur certain responsibilities. For example, consider this list of the rights of businesses (sellers) relative to consumers:[2]

- Sellers have the right to introduce any products in any sizes, styles, colors, or shapes, so

long as they meet minimum health and safety requirements.
- Sellers have the right to price their products as they please so long as they avoid certain discriminatory forms of pricing that undermine competition.
- Sellers have the right to promote their products using any amount of resources, any media, and any messages so long as they commit no deception or fraud.
- Sellers have the right to introduce any buying schemes they wish so long as they avoid discriminatory practices.
- Sellers have the right to alter product offerings at any time.
- Sellers have the right to distribute products in any reasonable manner.
- Sellers have the right to limit product guarantees or post-sale services that they offer.

Although this list is not exhaustive, it does serve to illustrate the power that businesses wield. Consumers, on the other hand, are generally accorded four basic rights: the right to safety, the right to be informed, the right to choose, and the right to be heard. These rights depend on the ability and willingness of consumers to be highly involved in purchases, and many consumers are neither able or willing to become so involved. For example, young children, a number of the elderly, and many uneducated consumers lack the experience or cognitive capacity to process information well enough to protect themselves. Further, consumers' rights leave broad gray areas that require managerial judgment and interpretation. For example, how safe do consumers have a right to expect a product to be? How much information can they expect? What do consumers have a right to know about gas tank designs of the automobiles they purchase?

A singular focus on the rights of businesses in relation to those of consumers and other stakeholders may, however, cause business leaders to overlook the ever-present companions of rights—responsibilities. While legal rights and protections may serve as theoretical boundaries for business decision making and action, **ethical responsibilities** may define roles more strictly than the minimum requirements of law and industry practice. In fulfilling such roles, an organization expresses its character and managerial values, and it can also enhance its competitive advantage over rivals. Organizations as diverse as Merck, Levi-Strauss, Johnson & Johnson, The Body Shop, Tom's of Maine, Ben & Jerry's, and Herman Miller have developed reputations for ethical, responsible

actions. These firms have recognized that, in the words of one New York executive, "The only sustainable competitive advantage any business has is its reputation."[3] Of course, a good reputation requires far more than statements of good intentions and self-serving press releases. Without question, the firms named above have enhanced their competitive positions by emphasizing traditional strengths like excellent product quality and service. Part of this kind of competitive strength rests on strong, ethical organizational cultures and self-images of "doing good while doing well."

In this chapter, we investigate the responsibility of business to society. In the first part of the chapter, we review arguments against and arguments in favor of businesses performing activities that might be termed *socially responsible*. We then discuss a number of specific questions that arise about social responsibility, and we investigate four influences on the social responsibility of business: legal, political, competitive, and ethical influences. Finally, we suggest a model for analyzing social responsibility issues from a strategic management viewpoint.

SOCIAL RESPONSIBILITY DEBATE

Consensus on the meaning of the term **social responsibility,** and on obligations of businesses to society will always remain elusive. These issues defy neat, final resolutions in a dynamic society; new answers continually emerge from the ongoing dialogue about business's informal contract with the society of which it is a part.[4] For the purposes of this text, however, we define *social responsibility* as the degree to which the activities of an organization protect and improve society beyond the extent required to serve the direct legal, economic, or technical interests of the organization. In other words, social responsibility involves performing activities that may help society, even if they do not directly contribute to the firm's profits.

A major debate rages in the strategic management literature, and throughout society, over whether firms should undertake activities primarily to live up to social responsibilities. The classical view denies that businesses should seek to promote social welfare, whereas the contemporary view affirms that they should. We shall discuss and compare these two views.

Classical View of Social Responsibility

The **classical view** holds that a business should not assume any social responsibility beyond making as much money as possible for its owners. The managers of an organization are employees of the stockholders, the argument runs, and have obligations only to them. The noted economist Milton Friedman, a proponent of this view, argues that

> there is one and only one social responsibility of business—to use its resources and engage in activities designed to increase its profits so long as it stays within the rules of the game, which is to say, engages in open and free competition, without deception or fraud. . . . Few trends could so thoroughly undermine the very foundations of our free society as the acceptance by corporate officials of a social responsibility other than to make as much money for their stockholders as possible. This is a fundamentally subversive doctrine.[5]

In the classical view, the role of managers is to produce and market goods efficiently, that is, in a way that gives the owners of the firm the greatest economic profits. Any other social responsibility activity is seen as disturbing fundamental economic relationships, and eroding profits.

Contemporary View of Social Responsibility

The **contemporary view** claims that businesses, as important and influential institutions in society, have a responsibility to help maintain and improve the society's overall welfare. A strong advocate of corporate social responsibility, Keith Davis, has elaborated on this view.[6] It can be summarized in terms of the following five propositions:

- *Proposition 1: Social responsibility arises from social power.* This proposition is built on the premise that business has a significant amount of influence or power over such critical social issues as minority employment and environmental pollution. In essence, the collective action of all businesses determines the proportion of minorities employed and much of the prevailing condition of the environment. Thus, because business has power over society, society can and must hold business responsible for social conditions affected by the use of this power.

- *Proposition 2: Business shall operate as a two-way open system with open receipt of inputs from society and open disclosure of its operations to the public.* Business must be willing to listen to social representatives concerning actions to improve social welfare. Davis suggests that continuing, honest, and open communications between business and social representatives is critical to maintaining or improving the overall welfare of society.

- *Proposition 3: Both the social costs and the social benefits of an activity, good, or service shall be thoroughly calculated and considered in order to decide whether or not to proceed with it.* Technical feasibility and economic profitability are not the only factors that should influence business decision making. Business should also consider both the long-term and short-term social consequences of all business activities before undertaking them.

- *Proposition 4: Social costs related to each activity, good, or service shall be passed on to the consumer.* Business cannot be expected to finance all activities that are economically disadvantageous, but socially advantageous. The cost of maintaining socially desirable activities within business should be passed on to consumers through higher prices for the goods or services that are directly related to those socially desirable activities.

- *Proposition 5: As citizens, business institutions have the responsibility to become involved in certain social problems that are outside their normal areas of operation.* If a business possesses the expertise to solve a social problem with which it may not be directly associated, it should accept responsibility for helping society solve the problem. Business will eventually receive increased profits from a generally improved society, so business should share in the responsibility of all citizens to improve that society.

Table 9.1 summarizes the major arguments for and against businesses accepting social responsibilities.

TABLE 9.1

Summary of Major Arguments for and against Social Responsibility for Business

FOR SOCIAL RESPONSIBILITY

1. It is in the best interest of a business to promote and improve the communities where it does business.
2. Social actions can be profitable.
3. It is the ethical thing to do.
4. It improves the public image of the firm.
5. It increases the viability of the business system. Business exists because it gives society benefits. Society can amend or take away its charter. This is the "iron law of responsibility."
6. It is necessary to avoid government regulation.
7. Sociocultural norms require it.
8. Laws cannot be passed for all circumstances. Thus, business must assume responsibility to maintain an orderly legal society.
9. It is in the stockholders' best interest. It will improve the price of stock in the long run because the stock market will view the company as less risky and open to public attack and therefore award it a higher price–earnings ratio.
10. Society should give business a chance to solve social problems that government has failed to solve.
11. Business is considered by some groups to be the institution with the financial and human resources to solve social problems.
12. Prevention of problems is better than cures—so let business solve problems before they become too great.

AGAINST SOCIAL RESPONSIBILITY

1. It might be illegal.
2. Business plus government equals monolith.
3. Social actions cannot be measured.
4. It violates profit maximization.
5. The cost of social responsibility is too great and would increase prices too much.
6. Business lacks social skills to solve societal problems.
7. It would dilute business's primary purposes.
8. It would weaken the U.S. balance of payments because price of goods will have to go up to pay for social programs.
9. Business already has too much power. Such involvement would make business too powerful.
10. Business lacks accountability to the public. Thus, the public would have no control over its social involvement.
11. Such business involvement lacks broad public support.

SOURCE: R. Joseph Monsen, Jr., "The Social Attitudes of Management," in Joseph W. McQuire, ed., *Contemporary Management* (Englewood Cliffs, N.J.: Prentice-Hall, 1974), p. 616. Reprinted by permission of R. Joseph Monsen.

Comparison of the Two Views

The classical view conceives of businesses as strictly economic entities, whereas the contemporary view conceives of businesses as members of society. Although business organizations clearly are both, recognizing this dual role does not answer the question of how much companies should incorporate social responsibility into their activities. In many cases, both views lead to the same conclusion about whether a firm should engage in a particular activity. For example, both views recognize the need to perform legally required activities. Also, in situations in which the activity enhances profits, both approaches support it.

The two views diverge when an activity (1) is not required by law *and* (2) is not profitable in the short term. Here the classical view would argue against performing the activity, but the contemporary view would argue in favor of performing the activity, if the costs were not too great.

One observer of this ongoing debate, Archie Carroll, proposes a **pyramid of corporate social responsibility,** shown in Figure 9.1, to clarify these issues. In general, economic and legal responsibilities form the base of the pyramid; the organization must fulfill these requirements to survive and continue to operate.

FIGURE 9.1
Pyramid of Corporate
Social Responsibility

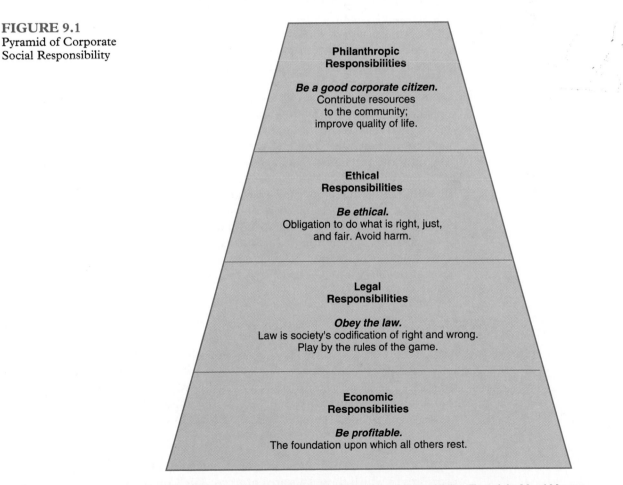

Philanthropic
Responsibilities

Be a good corporate citizen.
Contribute resources
to the community;
improve quality of life.

Ethical
Responsibilities

Be ethical.
Obligation to do what is right, just,
and fair. Avoid harm.

Legal
Responsibilities

Obey the law.
Law is society's codification of right and wrong.
Play by the rules of the game.

Economic
Responsibilities

Be profitable.
The foundation upon which all others rest.

SOURCE: Archie Carroll, "The Pyramid of Corporate Social Responsibility: Toward the Moral Management of Organizational Stakeholders." Reprinted from *Business Horizons,* July-August 1991, p. 42. Copyright 1991 by the Foundation for the School of Business at Indiana University. Used with permission.

Ethical and philanthropic responsibilities to stakeholders become critical when a firm begins to make a profit within the rules laid down by the broader society. Of course, in some industries (such as professional services, pharmaceuticals, or health care), an image of integrity and trust is critical to an organization's profitability. This forces ethical responsibilities much closer to the base of the pyramid.

Overall, we believe that the degree to which a firm seeks to advance social objectives depends on many factors, including the values of top executives, the size of the firm, its ability to invest in social programs, the structure of its industry, and the consequences of acting or not acting. Furthermore, these decisions depend on the specific problem and kind of action involved.

SPECIFIC AREAS OF SOCIAL RESPONSIBILITY

Questions have been raised about the social responsibility of business in many areas. Table 9.2 lists four of the more commonly discussed areas of concern and several specific questions related to each. As you review these questions, keep two points in mind.

First, business firms are considered socially responsible entities to the degree that they *voluntarily* act to maintain or increase social welfare without coercion by government regulations or laws. For example, a socially responsible firm would voluntarily remove a product from the market when it suspected tampering, rather than being forced to do so.

Second, managers can rely on few precise standards for socially responsible actions. In some cases, a firm's social responsibility activities can be compared with those of other firms in the same industry. However, this does not always yield a good measure. For example, consider the issue of product safety. Some might argue that only completely safe products should be allowed on the market, but imposing such a standard would be impractical. Bicycles often head the list of the most hazardous products, and every year many consumers are injured while riding them, yet few would argue that bicycles should be banned from the market. Much of the problem in resolving product safety issues involves the question of whether the harm done results from an inherent lack of product safety or from unsafe use by the consumer. Similarly, answers to many of the questions listed in Table 9.2 depend on social judgments, which differ depending on who makes the judgment, rather than on precise standards of business conduct.

INFLUENCES ON BUSINESS PRACTICES

As noted, business firms have considerable power and can powerfully influence society. However, our social system includes a number of checks and balances that guard against misuse of business power. Figure 9.2 illustrates four major influences that can inhibit the inappropriate use of business power: legal, political, competitive, and ethical influences.

Legal Influences

Legal influences consist of federal, state, and local laws and the agencies and processes by which these laws are enforced. The Company Example illustrates the threat that legal forces can pose.

TABLE 9.2

Areas of Social Responsibility Concern

CONCERN FOR CONSUMERS

1. Are products safe and well-designed?
2. Are products priced fairly?
3. Are advertisements clear and not deceptive?
4. Are customers treated fairly by salespeople?
5. Are credit terms clear?
6. Is adequate product information available?

CONCERN FOR EMPLOYEES

1. Are employees paid a fair wage?
2. Are employees provided a safe work environment?
3. Are workers hired, promoted, and treated fairly without regard to sex, race, color, or creed?
4. Are employees given special training and educational opportunities?
5. Are handicapped people given employment opportunities?
6. Does the business help rehabilitate employees with physical, mental, or emotional problems?

CONCERN FOR THE NATURAL ENVIRONMENT

1. Is the environment adequately protected from unclean air and water, excessive noise, or other types of pollution associated with manufacturing?
2. Are products and packages biodegradable or recyclable?
3. Are any by-products that pose a safety hazard to society (such as nuclear waste or commercial solvents) carefully handled and given proper treatment or disposal?

CONCERN FOR THE COMMUNITY

1. Does the firm support minority and community enterprises by purchasing from them or subcontracting to them?
2. Are donations made to help develop and support education, art, health, and community development programs?
3. Is the social impact of any plant location or relocation considered by the managers who make the decision?
4. Is appropriate information concerning business operations made public?

Table 9.3 lists several bills enacted by Congress that influence business practices. Some of this legislation is designed to control business practices in specific industries, such as toys or textiles; other laws are aimed at functional areas, such as packaging or product safety.

Units of government make laws that control business activity for a variety of reasons. Some laws reflect the collective sense of society that the business sector has not acted responsibly; these laws seek to establish tighter controls and to specify acceptable behavior (e.g., drug safety, workplace safety, and product safety laws). Such laws may result from alarming news reports such as pollution at Love Canal or accidents at unsafe factories. Other laws grow out of joint business–government efforts to equalize competitive conditions in certain industries. For example, the International Trade Commission protects U.S. firms from dumping (sales at artificially low prices) by non-U.S. competitors.

COMPANY EXAMPLE

Ethical Standards Sour at Stew Leonard's

Stew Leonard thought it important to pass along his values to his staff. With his folksiness and integrity, he became known as the Mister Rogers of food retailing.

His Norwalk, Connecticut, supermarket, Stew Leonard's, is listed by Ripley's "Believe It or Not" as the world's biggest dairy store. Leonard's animated megamarket includes dancing milk cartons, a petting zoo of live geese and goats, and employees in duck costumes waddling down the aisles. Leonard himself was often at the door, sometimes in a cow suit, greeting some of the 200,000 customers who flocked to his two stores every week.

But Stew Leonard is no longer greeting customers. The one-time milkman, called a marketing genius by Wall Street and a folk hero by his customers, is today called a criminal by the Internal Revenue Service. Leonard and executives of his $200 million business have pleaded guilty to what has been called the largest criminal tax case in Connecticut history, as well as the biggest computer-driven tax-evasion scheme in the nation.

Over the years, Leonard has been hailed for his adherence to the values of an old-fashioned family enterprise. According to the IRS, however, Leonard also had one foot in the future, pulling off "a crime of the 21st century."

Using a customized software program, Leonard was able to reduce item-by-item sales data and skim $17 million in cash, mostly during the 1980s. Computer tapes containing the real financial figures were destroyed, and the company's auditors were given the understated books. Leonard was able to divert even more money by requiring customers to pay cash for gift certificates.

Each day, say prosecutors, cash was emptied from the registers into a "money room," where it was counted, then placed in bags and dropped down a chute into the "vault room." Most of this cash was carried to the Caribbean, where Leonard owns a second home. Leonard's brother-in-law, an executive at the store, kept nearly $500,000 hidden behind a false panel in his basement.

Leonard has agreed to pay $15 million in restitution, and he faces up to five years in prison. In addition, his store is accused of short-weighing hundreds of food packages.

Yet neither the charges nor his confession of guilt has hampered business, which remains steady. "We were packed today. Our customers are extremely supportive and sympathetic," claims Stew Leonard, Jr.

SOURCE: Richard Behar, "Skimming the Cream," *Time,* August 2, 1993, p. 49.

FIGURE 9.2
Influences on Business
Practices

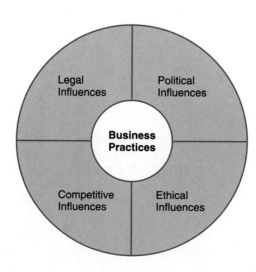

TABLE 9.3	

Examples of Federal Legislation Affecting Business Practices

Legislation	Major Provisions
Family and Medical Leave Act	Allows employees to take job-protected unpaid leaves because of family situations or their own illness
Americans with Disabilities Act	Facilitates equal access for individuals with disabilities in all major life activities, including employment
Toxic Substances Control Act Amendment	Provides adequate time for planning and implementation of school asbestos management plans
Federal Food, Drug, and Cosmetic Act Amendment	Bans reimportation of drugs produced in the United States; restricts distribution of drug samples; bans certain resales of drugs by health care facilities
Truth in Mileage Act	Amends the Motor Vehicle Information and Cost Savings Act to strengthen, for the protection of consumers, the provisions respecting disclosure of mileage when motor vehicles are transferred
Petroleum Overcharge Distribution and Restitution Act	Provides for distribution to injured consumers of escrow funds remaining from oil company settlements of alleged price allocation violations under the Emergency Petroleum Allocation Act of 1973
Superfund Amendments and Reauthorization Act	Extends and amends the Comprehensive Environmental Response Compensation and Liability Act of 1980; authorizes appropriations for and revises the EPA Hazardous Substance Response Trust Fund program for financing cleanup of uncontrolled hazardous waste sites
Anti-Drug Abuse Act	Amends the Food, Drug, and Cosmetic Act to revise provisions on regulation of infant formula manufacture
Processed Products Inspection Improvement Act	Amends the Meat Inspection Act to eliminate USDA continuous inspection requirements for meats, poultry, and egg processing plants for a six-year trial period
Emergency Response Act	Amends the Toxic Substances Control Act to require the EPA to promulgate regulations pertaining to inspections, development of asbestos management plans, and response actions
Safe Drinking Water Act Amendments	Amends the Safe Drinking Water Act; authorizes appropriations for and revises EPA safe drinking water programs, including grants to states for drinking water standards enforcement and groundwater protection programs
Drug Export Amendments Act	Amends the Food, Drug, and Cosmetic Act to remove restrictions on exports of human and veterinary drugs not yet approved by FDA or USDA for use in the United States and establishes conditions governing exports of such drugs

SOURCE: Partially based upon John R. Nevin, "Consumer Protection Legislation: Evolution, Structure and Prognosis," Working paper, University of Wisconsin–Madison, Wis., August 1989.

A variety of government agencies work to enforce these laws and investigate business practices. In addition to state and local agencies, a number of federal agencies are empowered to regulate particular areas of business activity. Table 9.4 presents a capsule summary of the activities of several federal regulatory agencies.

Table 9.4 shows clearly that federal agencies have broad and diverse powers to influence business practices, and they can impose a variety of remedies for

TABLE 9.4	

Some Important Federal Regulatory Agencies

Agency	Responsibilities
Federal Trade Commission (FTC)	Enforces laws and develops guidelines regarding unfair business practices
Food and Drug Administration (FDA)	Enforces laws and develops regulations to prevent the distribution and sale of adulterated or misbranded foods, drugs, cosmetics, and hazardous consumer products
Consumer Product Safety Commission (CPSC)	Enforces the Consumer Product Safety Act, which covers any consumer product not assigned to other regulatory agencies
Federal Communications Commission (FCC)	Regulates interstate wire, radio, and television
Environmental Protection Agency (EPA)	Develops and enforces environmental protection standards in such areas as water, air, and noise pollution
Office of Consumer Affairs	Handles consumer complaints
Equal Employment Opportunity Commission (EEOC)	Investigates and conciliates employment discrimination complaints that are based on race, sex, or creed
Office of Federal Contract Compliance Programs	Insures that employers that hold federal contracts grant equal employment opportunities to people regardless of race or sex
Occupational Safety and Health Administration (OSHA)	Regulates safety and health conditions in nongovernment workplaces
National Highway Safety Administration (NHSA)	Attempts to reduce traffic accidents through the regulation of transportation-related manufacturers and products
Mining Enforcement and Safety Administration	Attempts to improve conditions for mine workers by enforcing mine safety and equipment standards

improper business conduct. For example, the Federal Trade Commission has dealt with **deceptive advertising**—advertising that misleads consumers—by requiring firms to run corrective ads to clear up any misconceptions fostered by previous ads. The FTC has identified advertising for several products as misleading; classic examples include:

- Profile Bread's advertising misled consumers to believe it was effective in weight reduction.
- Domino Sugar's advertising misled consumers to believe it was a special source of strength, energy, and stamina.
- Ocean Spray Cranberry Juice Cocktail misled consumers about food energy.
- Sugar Information, Inc. misled consumers about the benefits of eating sugar.

The FTC required these firms to run ads with text that would correct these false impressions.[7]

Profile Bread   This text had to run in 25 percent of the brand's advertising for one year:

Hi, (celebrity's name) for Profile Bread. Like all mothers, I'm concerned about nutrition and balanced meals. So, I'd like to clear up any misunderstanding you may have about Profile Bread from its advertising or even its name.

Does Profile have fewer calories than any other breads? No. Profile has about the same per ounce as other breads. To be exact, Profile has seven fewer calories per slice. That's because Profile is sliced thinner. But eating Profile will not cause you to lose weight. A reduction of seven calories is insignificant. It's total calories and balanced nutrition that count. And Profile can help you achieve a balanced meal because it provides protein and B vitamins as well as other nutrients.

How does my family feel about Profile? Well, my husband likes Profile toast, the children love Profile sandwiches, and I prefer Profile to any other bread. So you see, at our house, delicious taste makes Profile a family affair.

Amstar   This statement had to run in one of four Domino ads for one year:

Do you recall some of our past messages saying that Domino Sugar gives you strength, energy, and stamina? Actually, Domino is not a special or unique source of strength, energy, and stamina. No sugar is, because what you need is a balanced diet and plenty of rest and exercise.

Ocean Spray   This text had to appear in one of four ads for one year:

If you've wondered what some of our earlier advertising meant when we said Ocean Spray Cranberry Juice Cocktail has more food energy than orange juice or tomato juice, let us make it clear: we didn't mean vitamins and minerals. Food energy means calories. Nothing more.

Food energy is important at breakfast since many of us may not get enough calories, or food energy, to get off to a good start. Ocean Spray Cranberry Juice Cocktail helps because it contains more food energy than most other breakfast drinks.

And Ocean Spray Cranberry Juice Cocktail gives you and your family Vitamin C plus a great wake-up taste. It's . . . the other breakfast drink.

Sugar Information, Inc.   This text had to run for one insertion in each of seven magazines:

Do you recall the messages we brought you in the past about sugar? How something with sugar in it before meals could help you curb your appetite? We hope you didn't get the idea that our little diet tip was any magic formula for losing weight. Because there are no tricks or shortcuts; the whole diet subject is very complicated. Research hasn't established that consuming sugar before meals will contribute to weight reduction or even keep you from gaining weight.

Legal influences and the power of government agencies to regulate business practices grew dramatically during the 1970s. However, the 1980s and 1990s have witnessed declines in many regulatory activities. In fact, deregulation of business has become a major trend, and many government agencies have considerably reduced their control of business practices.

Political Influences

Political influences include pressure exerted by **special-interest groups** in society to control business practices. These groups use a variety of methods to influence business, such as lobbying to persuade various government agencies to enact or enforce legislation and working directly with employees or consumers. Table 9.5 lists a few organizations that are designed to serve consumer

---

TABLE 9.5

Political Groups Concerned with Business Practices

BROAD-BASED, NATIONAL GROUPS

Consumer Federation of America
National Wildlife Federation
Common Cause

SMALLER, MULTI-ISSUE ORGANIZATIONS

National Consumer's League
Ralph Nader's Public Citizen

SPECIAL-INTEREST GROUPS

Action for Children's Television
American Association of Retired Persons
Group against Smoking and Pollution

LOCAL GROUPS

Public-interest research groups
Local consumer protection offices
Local broadcast and newspaper consumer action lines

SOURCE: Based on Paul N. Bloom and Stephen A. Greyser, "The Maturing of Consumerism," *Harvard Business Review,* November/December 1981, pp. 130–139.

---

interests. One tally found over 100 national organizations and over 600 state and local groups involved in consumer advocacy.[8]

Consumerism is a movement to augment the rights of consumers in dealing with business. Paul Bloom and Stephen Greyser argue that consumerism has reached the mature stage of its life cycle and that its impact has been fragmented.[9] Still, they believe that consumerism will continue to have an impact on business, and they suggest three strategies for coping with it. First, businesses can try to accelerate the decline of consumerism by *reducing demand* for it. This could be done by improving product quality, expanding services, lowering prices, and/or toning down advertising claims.

Second, businesses can *compete* with consumer advocacy groups by offering consumer education and assistance in seeking redress of grievances through active consumer affairs departments. Alternatively, businesses can fund and coordinate activities designed to promote deregulation and other probusiness causes.

Third, businesses can *cooperate* with consumer advocacy groups by providing financial and other support. All of these strategies would likely further reduce the impact of political influences on business's approach to social responsibility. However, to the degree that following these strategies leads business firms to step up their social responsibility activities in the long run, consumers and other stakeholder groups could benefit.

Competitive Influences

Competitive influences are the actions that competing firms take to affect each other and, thus, business practices in an industry. These actions can take many forms. For example, one firm might sue another or publicly allege that it engaged in illegal activities. Johnson & Johnson has frequently gone to court to prevent competitors from showing its Tylenol brand of pain relievers in comparative ads. Burger King has publicly accused McDonald's of overstating the weight of its hamburgers. Computer software firms regularly accuse one another of copyright infringement.

Competitors also influence one another by diluting each other's political, economic, and market power. For example, in a business environment with many competitors, a single firm usually cannot dominate the flow of information to consumers. Conflicting competitive claims and price deals offered by various firms may help consumers resist the influence of a single firm.

Society may also benefit from better, safer, more efficient products and services, which are often spawned by competitive pressure. In fact, some firms focus their strategies on a receptive and growing segment of consumers who are especially interested in product safety features. Michelin tires, Volvo automobiles, and certain chainsaw manufacturers have built viable competitive positions by selling safety to consumers. Overall, then, competition may help balance business power within an industry and stimulate the development of more responsible business practices.

The Skills Module invites you to evaluate the balancing effect of the competitive influence on social responsibility.

Ethical Influences

The last type of influence on business practices that we will discuss involves ethical decision making and self-regulation of business conduct. Many businesses follow rigorous codes of ethics; some firms establish offices specifically to handle employee whistle-blowing and consumer complaints.

Efforts to evaluate the ethical influences on business practice are complicated by the lack of a single, universal standard for judging whether a particular action is ethical. Gene Laczniak summarizes five ethical standards that have been proposed:[10]

1. *The Golden Rule:* Act in the way you would expect others to act toward you.
2. *The utilitarian principle:* Act in a way that results in the greatest good for the greatest number.
3. *Kant's categorical imperative:* Act in such a way that the action you take could be a universal law or rule of behavior under the circumstances.
4. *The professional ethic:* Take actions that a disinterested panel of professional colleagues would view as proper.
5. *The TV test:* Ask, "Would I feel comfortable explaining to a national TV audience why I took this action?"

As part of top executives' leadership role, they must choose the standards for their organizations to follow. One analyst proposes that three forces shape ethical decision making in an organization. Figure 9.3 shows these forces and the separate elements of each. The personal ethical perspective of an organization depends on the personal beliefs and values of its top managers or founders, often shaped by religion and early parental influences, combined with the level of their moral development and the particular ethical framework (e.g., utilitarian principle, Golden Rule, categorical imperative, etc.) that they favor. The closely related factors of organizational culture and the systems through which this culture is sustained and transmitted throughout the firm make up the other two building blocks of ethical decision making. Culture and systems may work either to constrain or to support the top managers' ethical perspective.

SKILLS MODULE
Price Cuts Undermine Fleet Street Ethos

INTRODUCTION

This chapter's discussion of social responsibility considers competitive influences and their role in controlling the power of businesses. Review the following situation and then complete the skill development exercise that follows to develop your ability to analyze this influence.

SITUATION

The owners of Britain's two most prestigious newspapers, Rupert Murdoch of *The Times* and Conrad Black of the *Daily Telegraph,* are locked in a savage circulation battle.

Murdoch's News International launched the price war in September, just as the country was coming out of a recession and advertising revenues could be expected to rise. The initial price cut lowered the price of *The Times* to 30 pence from 45 pence (45 cents from 68 cents) and the price of the tabloid *Sun* to 20 pence from 25 pence (30 cents from 37). It was an unheard-of strategy; in the country with the world's highest newspaper readership levels, publishers tend to raise prices above the inflation rate, but declining circulation throughout the industry—and *The Times*'s long-term failure to make a profit—was the catalyst to cut prices in an effort to boost circulation and attract the advertising that would make the newspaper profitable.

The price cut was a huge and immediate success: circulation rose 88,000 in one month, climbing from an average of 354,280 a day in August 1993 to 524,270 the following June. The *Sun*'s circulation rose to 4.16 million from 3.83 million.

Judging from losses from the move, reportedly in the $60 million to $75 million range, competitors initially thought the price cut would be short-lived. The *Daily Telegraph,* whose million-papers-a-day circulation made it the leader among serious newspapers, finally became alarmed when sales fell below seven figures, reaching a 40-year low of 993,395 in May. In June, the *Telegraph* responded to the new environment and cut its prices to 30 pence (45 cents) from 48 pence (72 cents). News International shot back, slashing the price of *The Times* to 20 pence (30 cents), making it cheaper than many tabloids.

While a full-page ad in the *Telegraph* still costs more than three times as much as the same ad in *The Times,* the former's ability to charge premium rates might disappear if the challenger can reach a circulation of 600,000. Indeed, *The Times* reported an increase in ad revenue of 50 percent, or $30 million, in 1994.

Black of the *Telegraph* views the battle as a war for survival: "He is trying to kill us."

Murdoch, who has been quoted as saying that the British newspaper industry would be reduced in the next century to three titles—*The Times,* the *Sun,* and the *Daily Mail*—denies that his purpose is to kill other newspapers. Still, the price war has affected them all, knocking huge sums off the stock-market values of all major newspaper companies in Britain; it already threatens the viability of many properties. The perennially unprofitable *Guardian* has lost circulation; other casualties include the *Daily Mirror,* the *Daily Express,* and the *Daily Mail.*

Worst hit is the long-troubled *Independent,* which in the fall had raised its price to 50 pence (75 cents) from 45 pence (68 cents). Circulation plummeted by nearly 50,000, to 277,377 in June, and the paper is struggling for survival. The *Independent* has complained to the government's Office of Fair Trading about alleged predatory pricing by News International; despite a preliminary inquiry, intervention appears unlikely.

SKILL DEVELOPMENT EXERCISE

The price war initiated by News International threatens to put other newspapers out of business, while also hurting its own bottom-line performance. Prepare a detailed argument either supporting or disputing the idea that Murdoch and *The Times* are competing unfairly. Taking the point of view of a *Times* stakeholder, determine whether the paper's possible long-term gains justify the short-term costs of its strategy.

SOURCE: Ray Moseley, "London Papers' Price War Being Reported in Red Ink," *Chicago Tribune,* July 29, 1994, Sec. 3, p. 1.

FIGURE 9.3
Forces That Shape
Managerial Ethics

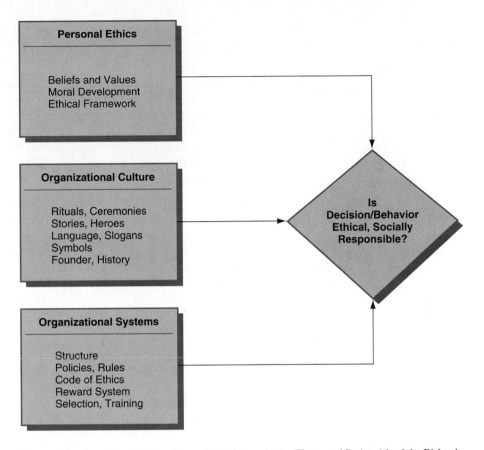

SOURCE: Reprinted by permission from p. 328 of *Organization Theory and Design*, 4th ed. by Richard Daft; Copyright © 1992 by West Publishing Company. All rights reserved.

As implied throughout this chapter, a firm best shapes its ethical standards, and its entire approach to social responsibility issues, through a cross-functional undertaking. Top managers or founders may try to set a certain climate in a firm, but managers and employees throughout the firm, by their actions and decisions, also affect that climate. In addition, different functional specialists contribute information about their functions, with their own professional ethics, codes, or standards, to the efforts of top managers. This information may help to shape the organization's internal ethical climate, as well as its externally focused approach to social responsibility. For example, managers from the marketing function may offer information about advertising codes, pricing standards and regulations, or pressures from environmentalists about product design and packaging. Accounting professionals bring a long tradition of professional ethics and accepted standards. Production managers who operate within a specific industry may have their own professional codes of conduct regarding safety, quality control, or relations with purchasing agents from supplier firms. This information, considered collectively across the several functions, can help top managers shape an organization's basic approach to social and ethical matters.

Applying diverse standards can result in different interpretations for ethical decisions or actions. Defining ethical decisions and actions in the context of international operations, with the added complexity of the diverse cultural and religious backgrounds of managers and employees, can be especially challenging. A few business scenarios may help to illustrate the practical problem of defining appropriate ethical conduct.[11]

Scenario 1 The Thrifty Supermarket Chain has 12 stores in the city of Gotham, U.S.A. The company's policy is to maintain the same prices for all items at all stores. However, the distribution manager knowingly sends the poorest cuts of meat and the lowest-quality produce to the store located in the low-income section of town. To justify this action, the manager explains that this store has the highest overhead due to factors such as employee turnover, pilferage, and vandalism. *Is the distribution manager's economic rationale sufficient justification for this allocation method?*

Scenario 2 The Independent Car Dealers of Metropolis, U.S.A. have undertaken an advertising campaign headlined by the slogan: "Is your family's life worth 45 MPG?" The ads admit that while its subcompacts are not as fuel efficient as foreign imports and cost more to maintain, they are safer according to government-sponsored crash tests. The ads implicitly ask if responsible parents, when purchasing a car, should trade off fuel efficiency for safety. *Is it ethical for the dealers association to use a fear appeal to offset an economic disadvantage?*

Scenario 3 A few recent studies have linked the presence of the artificial sweetener subsugural to cancer in laboratory rats. While the validity of these findings has been hotly debated by medical experts, the Food and Drug Administration has ordered products containing the ingredient banned from sale in the United States. The Jones Company sends all of its sugar-free J. C. Cola (which contains subsugural) to European supermarkets because the sweetener has not been banned there. *Is it acceptable for the Jones Company to send an arguably unsafe product to another market without waiting for further evidence?*

Scenario 4 The Acme Company sells industrial supplies through its own sales force, which calls on company purchasing agents. Acme has found that giving small gifts to purchasing agents helps cement cordial relationships and creates goodwill. Acme follows the policy that bigger orders justify bigger gifts to purchasing agents. The gifts range from sporting event tickets to outboard motors and snowmobiles. Acme does not give gifts to personnel at companies with known explicit policies prohibiting the acceptance of such gifts. *Assuming no laws are violated, is Acme's policy of providing gifts to purchasing agents morally proper?*

Scenario 5 The Buy American Electronics Company has been selling its highly rated System X Color TV sets (21, 19, and 12 inches) for $700, $500, and $300, respectively. These prices have been relatively uncompetitive in the market. After some study, Buy American substitutes several cheaper components (which engineering says may slightly reduce the quality of performance) and passes on the savings to the consumer in the form of a $100 price reduction on each model. Buy American institutes a price-oriented promotional campaign that neglects to mention that the second-generation System X sets are different from the first. *Is the company's competitive strategy ethical?*

MANAGING SOCIAL RESPONSIBILITY

Many managers have accepted the idea that corporate social responsibility is an integral part of a company's overall strategy. The key elements of integrating social responsibility into an organization's strategic management process are discussed below.

Environmental Analysis and Organizational Direction

Like every element of strategy development, social responsibility begins with environmental analysis. Managers analyze both problems and opportunities in the environment that affect their firm's impact on society and then decide what areas require further investigation. Organizational vision, mission, and core values guide the determination of areas of social responsibility or social involvement that raise special concerns.

Strategy Formulation

Once areas of concern about social responsibility have been identified and studied, strategy formulation for social action begins. The object is to develop appropriate responses to issues, choosing among many alternatives. For example, a firm could deal with problems associated with poor product performance by improving guarantees, installing consumer complaint hotlines, offering more detailed label information, removing products from the market, and modifying products.

Strategy Implementation

Implementation puts a formulated strategy into action, which entails assigning responsibility to individuals or groups, providing adequate information, and establishing controls to make sure the strategy is implemented efficiently. For example, Procter & Gamble developed its own consumer service department to handle consumer complaints and requests for information. In a recent year, it received over 670,000 mail and telephone contacts about its products. The consumer service department employs 75 people—30 to answer calls and the rest to answer letters and analyze data. Clearly, implementing this strategy entailed considerable expense and effort. P&G managers consider the system a very effective "distant, early warning signal" of product problems.[12]

Strategic Control

Strategic control activities help a firm to fulfill its social responsibility by measuring the results of the implemented strategy and changing it, if necessary. The specific areas in which individual companies actually take such measurements vary with their specific social objectives, but firms should probably consider four general areas:[13]

1. *Economic functional area.* A measurement should indicate whether or not the organization is producing goods and services that people need, creating jobs, paying fair wages, and ensuring worker safety. This measurement gives some indication of the organization's economic contribution to society.
2. *Quality-of-life area.* In this area, measurement should focus on determining whether the organization is improving or degrading the general quality of life in society. Producing high-quality goods, dealing fairly with employees and customers, and making an effort to preserve the natural environment could all help to assure the organization that it is upholding or improving the general quality of life. As an example, some people brand cigarette companies as socially irresponsible because they produce goods that damage the health of society overall.
3. *Social investment area.* This area deals with the degree to which the organization is investing both money and human resources to solve community social problems. The socially responsible organization might assist community organizations that promote education, charities, and the arts.

4. *Problem-solving area.* Measurements in this area should focus on the degree to which the organization deals with social problems themselves, as opposed to the symptoms of those problems. Such activities as participating in long-range community planning and conducting studies to pinpoint social problems would generally be construed as dealing with social problems rather than merely addressing their symptoms.

An organization may conduct a **social audit,** or use other reporting mechanisms, to take social responsibility measurements such as those we have listed. The basic steps in a social audit are monitoring, measuring, and appraising all aspects of an organization's social responsibility performance. The audit itself can be performed either by organization personnel or by outside consultants.

One aspect of social responsibility is public accounting on environmental issues. Table 9.6 is an excerpt from an environmental report prepared by

---

TABLE 9.6

A section of the 1994 General Motors Corporation Environmental Report (Detroit: Environmental and Energy Staff Communications 1994, p. 5).

ENVIRONMENTAL PROFESSIONALS

Currently, over 500 environmental professionals are employed at GM in the stationary source field. In addition, over 100 scientists are engaged in research and development activities. Thousands of our designers and engineers have responsibility for emissions control, fuel economy, and/or vehicle recycling as basic elements of their jobs. GM encourages professional development by offering a variety of training and educational opportunities:

- A specialized co-op program has been initiated in 1994 with four major universities for stationary source training. Mobile source environmental professionals have participated in GM's co-op programs for many years.
- GM's tuition assistance program pays eligible expenses for courses leading to most associate, undergraduate or graduate degrees from accredited institutions. Eligible expenses are also covered for course fees for job-related and certain professional development seminars.
- Corporate contracts have been established with various suppliers and learning institutions for specialized training and regulatory updates.
- GM has developed in-house training programs covering subjects such as wastewater treatment technologies, asbestos removal, chlorofluorocarbon handling, vehicle emissions, and fuel economy.

GM environmental professionals are updated on environmental initiatives and corporate policies through a variety of mechanisms:

- The first annual GM Environmental Engineers Conference was held in 1993 and included presentations regarding GM environmental initiatives and policies. Workshops were structured around pertinent environmental issues.
- Regulatory/legislative direction meetings provide in-depth updates on pertinent issues for all media including air, water, waste, remediation, and toxic substances. Summary updates are provided to environmental engineers through various internal communications. For example, GM's quarterly *Waste Watch* newsletter communicates waste minimization initiatives/projects and recommended waste management practices.

Employees are encouraged to submit suggestions for improvement in all company operations including environmental issues through the Quality Network Suggestion Program. In addition, the corporation's waste reduction program encourages the establishment of teams at each facility whereby employee suggestions for pollution prevention and waste management can be evaluated and incorporated into facility operating plans. In 1993, GM established the "GM Awareline," a 24-hour hotline that employees are encouraged to use to anonymously report actions contrary to corporate policy, possible criminal wrongdoings, and emergency or life-threatening situations.

SOURCE: Courtesy of General Motors Corporation.

General Motors Corporation. As you can see, the table focuses on company involvement with environmental professionals. Overall, the General Motors environmental report covers many other topics, including workplace hazards, pollution standards, waste management, and use of energy. The format of environmental reports vary from company to company according to management judgments regarding how best to present data and specific responsibility issues facing a company.

SUMMARY

In this chapter, we examined the social and ethical dimensions of strategic management. First, we outlined the classical view that companies should not assume any responsibility beyond their obligation to make a profit, and the contemporary view that businesses do have a responsibility to maintain and advance the welfare of society at large. We found that many businesses' activities are supported by both viewpoints and that the degree to which a firm should seek to achieve purely social objectives depends on many considerations. Then we noted several areas in which firms can exhibit social responsibility, such as concern for consumers, for employees, for the environment, and for society in general.

Next we investigated four major influences on businesses that shape their perspectives on social responsibility and curb the inappropriate use of their considerable power. These include legal influences, such as laws and government regulatory agencies; the political pressure brought to bear by various groups such as consumer advocates; the controls that competing firms exert on one another; and the ethical influences that are exhibited in many firms' self-regulation of their business conduct. We also identified three major factors—personal ethics, culture, and systems—that collectively shape the ethical climate of a firm.

Finally, we analyzed the effect of managing social and ethical issues on the strategic management process, offering examples of ways in which social responsibility can be taken into account in the course of conducting an environmental analysis, setting an organizational direction, and formulating, implementing, and controlling strategy. We examined the social audit and environmental report as effective means of appraising an organization's social responsibility performance.

KEY TERMS

stakeholder, p. 219
ethical responsibility, p. 220
social responsibility, p. 220
classical view of social responsibility, p. 220
contemporary view of social responsibility, p. 221

pyramid of corporate social responsibility, p. 223
deceptive advertising, p. 228
special-interest group, p. 229
consumerism, p. 230
social audit, p. 236

CHECKLIST

Analyzing Social Responsibility in Problems and Cases

__ 1. Does the problem or case involve social responsibility as an important concern?

— 2. Does any legislation require the organization to perform in a socially responsible manner?

— 3. Would performing social responsibility activities be economically profitable to the firm in the long run?

— 4. Can the organization afford to engage in social responsibility activities, and would they result in goodwill or other noneconomic benefits from one or more stakeholder groups?

— 5. What specific stakeholders and area(s) of social responsibility does the problem or case address?

— 6. Are any political forces attempting to change the firm's activities? If so, do they have sound arguments?

— 7. Do any competitive influences merit consideration?

— 8. Does the problem or case involve an ethical dilemma that requires a decision?

— 9. Does the organization have a well-developed program for dealing with social responsibility issues?

— 10. Would a social audit be useful for identifying problems and suggesting appropriate solutions?

Additional Readings

Dickson, Reginald. "The Business of Equal Opportunity." *Harvard Business Review,* January/February 1992, p. 46.

Nichols, Nancy A. "Profits with a Purpose: An Interview with Tom Chappell." *Harvard Business Review,* November/December 1992, p. 86.

Pearsall, A. E. "Corporate Redemption and the Seven Deadly Sins." *Harvard Business Review,* May/June 1992, p. 65.

Smith, N. Craig. *Morality and the Market: Consumer Pressure for Corporate Accountability.* London: Routledge, 1990.

Stark, Amber. "What's the Matter with Business Ethics?" *Harvard Business Review,* May/June 1993, p. 38.

Steidlmeier, Paul. *People and Profits: The Ethics of Capitalism.* Englewood Cliffs, N.J.: Prentice-Hall, 1992.

Velasquez, Manuel. *Business Ethics,* 3d ed. Englewood Cliffs, N.J.: Prentice-Hall, 1992.

CASE

ECONOMICS VERSUS SOCIAL POLICY AT STRIDE RITE

Public-service plaques line the walls of Stride Rite's Cambridge, Massachusetts, headquarters. Harvard University has honored the firm for "improving the quality of life" in its community and the nation. The shoe company has contributed 5 percent of its pre-tax profits to a charitable foundation, sent 100,000 pairs of sneakers to strife-torn Mozambique, paid Harvard graduate students to work in a Cambodian refugee camp, given scholarships to inner-city youths, permitted employees to tutor disadvantaged children on company time, and pioneered on-site facilities for day-care and elder-care.

While doing good, Stride Rite has done well. It has posted profits, usually at record levels, for the past 32 quarters. In 1993, its sales were expected to top $625 million, more than double the company's 1986 level. Its stock price has increased sixfold since then, making it a favorite of the New York Stock Exchange and socially conscious investors.

Just a few blocks away from its new headquarters, however, Stride Rite's old corporate office building sits surrounded by the empty lots and crumbling streets of Boston's tough Roxbury neighborhood. Here, 2,500 people once made Keds sneakers and Sperry Top-sider shoes; today, it houses 175 workers whose jobs will be gone by next summer. Stride Rite is closing this warehouse and one other to move its distribution operations to Kentucky. With local unemployment near 30 percent, Stride Rite's citations for good works ring hollow.

In the past decade, Stride Rite has prospered, in part, by closing 15 factories, mostly in the Northeast and several in depressed areas, and moving most of its production to various low-cost, Asian countries. The company still employs 2,500 workers in the United States, down from a peak of about 6,000.

Boston officials met frustration trying to retain Stride Rite's blue-collar jobs. They argue that good deeds are not enough; they want Stride Rite to meet the basic need of providing jobs in depressed areas, even at the expense of profits. "The most socially responsible thing a company can do is to give a person a job," says Donald Gillis, executive director of Boston's Economic Development and Industrial Corp.

"Putting jobs into places where it doesn't make economic sense is a dilution of corporate and community wealth," argues Stride Rite Chairman Ervin Shames. The company says that it could hardly avoid pulling out of Roxbury—and the rest of New England—over the past two decades to shift most of its production overseas. As much as they wish to link their corporate and social responsibilities, the company's directors concede that their primary obligation is to their stockholders. If Stride Rite cannot compete, say executives, it cannot afford its social programs, and it may not even survive. "It was a difficult decision," admits Shames. "Our hearts said, 'stay,' but our heads said, 'move.'"

Shames adds that the company will save millions by moving its distribution to the Midwest—a central location near most of its customers. The new distribution center in Louisville will eliminate 800 to 1,200 miles on some truck routes, speeding delivery by two and one-half to four days.

DISCUSSION QUESTIONS

1. Describe and evaluate Stride Rite's strategic reactions to changes in its competitive environment.

2. Does Stride Rite's dilemma and its resolution prove that the classical view of social responsibility is winning over the contemporary view?

3. Should company stakeholders demand further accountability from Stride Rite regarding its social responsibility activities?

SOURCE: Joseph Pereira, *The Wall Street Journal,* reprinted as "Split Personality," in *Utne Reader,* September/October 1993, pp. 61–66.

Notes

1. Portions of this chapter are based on Samuel C. Certo, *Modern Management: Diversity, Quality, Ethics, and the Global Environment,* 6th ed. (Boston: Allyn & Bacon, 1994), Chap. 3; and J. Paul Peter and Jerry C. Olson, *Consumer Behavior and Marketing Strategy,* 3d ed. (Homewood, Ill.: Richard D. Irwin, 1993), Chap. 21.

2. Philip Kotler, "What Consumerism Means for Marketers," *Harvard Business Review,* May/June 1972, pp. 48–57.

3. Susan Caminiti, "The Payoff from a Good Reputation," *Fortune,* February 10, 1992, p. 74.

4. Manuel Velasquez, *Business Ethics,* 3d ed. (Englewood Cliffs, N.J.: Prentice-Hall, 1992).

5. Milton Friedman, *Capitalism and Freedom* (Chicago: University of Chicago Press, 1962), p. 133, as reported in George A. Steiner and John F. Steiner, *Business, Government, and Society* (New York: Random House, 1985), p. 236.

6. Keith Davis, "Five Propositions for Social Responsibility," *Business Horizons,* June 1975, pp. 19–24. Also see Peter F. Drucker, "The New Meaning of Corporate Social Responsibility," *California Management Review,* Winter 1984, pp. 53–63; Jerry W. Anderson, "Social Responsibility and the Corporation," *Business Horizons,* July/August 1986, pp. 22–27; Jean B. McGuire, Alison Sundgren, and Thomas Schneeweis, "Corporate Social Responsibility and Firm Financial Performance," *Academy of Management Journal* 31 (December 1988), pp. 854–872; and Richard J. Klonski, "Foundational Considerations in the Corporate Social Responsibility Debate," *Business Horizons,* July/August 1991, pp. 14–28.

7. William L. Wilkie, Dennis L. McNeill, and Michael B. Mazis, "Marketing's 'Scarlet Letter': The Theory and Practice of Corrective Advertising," *Journal of Marketing,* Spring 1984, p. 13. Reprinted from *Journal of Marketing,* published by the American Marketing Association.

8. Ann P. Harvey, *Contacts in Consumerism 1980–1981* (Washington, D.C.: Fraser/Associates, 1980).

9. Paul N. Bloom and Stephen A. Greyser, "The Maturing of Consumerism," *Harvard Business Review,* November/December 1981, pp. 130–139.

10. Gene R. Laczniak, "Framework for Analyzing Marketing Ethics," *Journal of Macromarketing,* Spring 1983, pp. 7–18. Also see Harvey C. Bunke, "Should We Teach Business Ethics?" *Business Horizons,* July/August 1988, pp. 2–8; LaRue Tone Hosmer, "Adding Ethics to the Business Curriculum," *Business Horizons,* July/August 1988, pp. 9–15; Bruce H. Drake and Eileen Drake, "Ethical and Legal Aspects of Managing Corporate Cultures," *California Management Review,* Winter 1988, pp. 107–123; and R. Edward Freeman and Jeanne Liedtka, "Corporate Social Responsibility: A Critical Approach," *Business Horizons,* July/August 1991, pp. 87–99.

11. Gene R. Laczniak, "Framework for Analyzing Marketing Ethics," *Journal of Macromarketing,* Spring 1983, p. 8. Reprinted by permission of the publisher, Business Research Division, University of Colorado, Boulder.

12. "Customers: P&G's Pipeline to Product Problems," *Business Week,* June 11, 1984, p. 167. Also see Brian Dumaine, "P&G Rewrites the Marketing Rules," *Fortune,* November 6, 1989, pp. 34–48.

13. Frank H. Cassell, "The Social Cost of Doing Business," *MSU Business Topics,* Autumn 1974, pp. 19–26.

PART IV

Critical Functions for Strategic Management

We have emphasized from the start that effective strategic management is essentially a cross-functional process, relying on a variety of interdependent skills to create viable organizations by formulating and implementing innovative and defensible strategies. In this section, we explore three of those critical functions—operations (Chapter 10), finance (Chapter 11), and marketing (Chapter 12)—and the concepts and techniques that each contributes to the strategic management process. Students who have recently completed courses in these areas should approach the next three chapters as a focused review, or refresher course, on these topics.

Students should always treat strategic management, either in real time on the job or in a case analysis, as an integrative process, drawing on every skill and technique available to a manager. The concepts and tools discussed in Part IV are essential building blocks; these chapters certainly cannot cover everything a manager needs to know about the critical functions of operations, marketing, and finance.

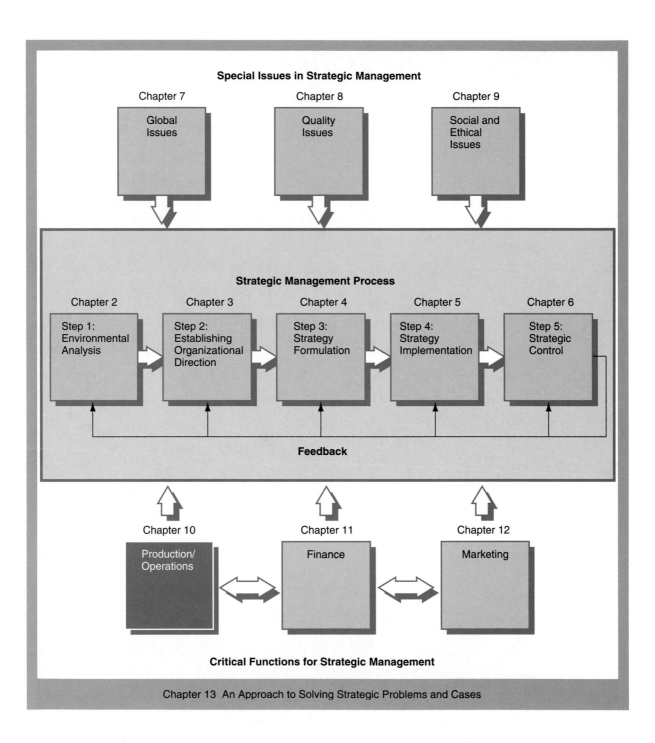

Special Issues in Strategic Management

Chapter 7

Global Issues

Chapter 8

Quality Issues

Chapter 9

Social and Ethical Issues

Strategic Management Process

Chapter 2

Step 1: Environmental Analysis

Chapter 3

Step 2: Establishing Organizational Direction

Chapter 4

Step 3: Strategy Formulation

Chapter 5

Step 4: Strategy Implementation

Chapter 6

Step 5: Strategic Control

Feedback

Chapter 10

Production/ Operations

Chapter 11

Finance

Chapter 12

Marketing

Critical Functions for Strategic Management

Chapter 13 An Approach to Solving Strategic Problems and Cases

CHAPTER 10

Operations and Strategic Management

This chapter covers the operations function, one of the major functional areas of organizations.[1] In the first part of the chapter, we explain what the operations function does. We examine its context by briefly reviewing its place among the other functions in the organization, and describe the various operations systems that have evolved to produce goods or provide services in manufacturing and non-manufacturing settings.

The second part of the chapter addresses the relationship of operations to strategic management. We note the vital association between marketing strategy and the operations function, for example, and the importance of considering the firm's operations capabilities when formulating any corporate strategy. Next we discuss strategy decisions for the operations function itself, focusing especially on the choice of which production characteristics the operations function will emphasize. Finally, we analyze the effect on operations strategy of product design.

Readers will notice the thematic relation of Chapter 10 to the discussion in Chapter 8 of quality issues. However, in Chapter 10 we extend the range of techniques and issues we consider to encompass the entire operations function.

ESSENTIALS OF ORGANIZATIONAL OPERATIONS

Operations Function

The **operations function** is performed by members of an organization who produce the goods or provide the services that it offers to the public. The operations function, also called the *production function,* is one of three primary functions within a business, the other two being finance and marketing. In a typical business, however, the operations function employs the greater number of people and uses the greatest portion of the firm's controllable assets. Clearly, operations is a very important function, and one that certainly merits detailed study. Our purpose in this chapter is to discuss the various activities within the operations function and to explore how these activities can affect strategic management.

Other Functions

The operations function is only one part of a larger system—the entire organization. It is interrelated with other functions in the organization, so its plans and actions must mesh across functions for the total organization to achieve its full potential. Before we discuss the operations function in greater detail, let us briefly review the other business functions—marketing and finance—as well as some secondary or supporting functions.

Marketing   The **marketing function** consists of organizational activities that focus on discovering or developing a need or demand for the company's goods and services. Marketing personnel seek to maintain a responsive working relationship with consumers or potential consumers. Profit-seeking companies cannot long survive without markets for their goods or services. Not-for-profit organizations, such as government agencies, may survive without genuine needs or demands for their services, but such situations represent a misapplication of a society's resources. A nonbusiness enterprise performs marketing activities when it determines the extent and location of the need for its services and when it makes the availability of its services known to the public. The marketing function is discussed in detail in Chapter 12.

Finance   The **finance function** consists primarily of organizational activities aimed at obtaining funds for planned activities and guiding the wise use of those funds. The finance function in nonbusiness enterprises may include lobbying for government support or seeking public contributions through the efforts of volunteers. The finance function includes efforts to budget and allocate funds to the various subdivisions of the firm and review of their expenditures. The finance function is discussed in detail in Chapter 11.

Supporting Functions   As explained in the discussion of value chain analysis in Chapter 4, functions other than operations, marketing, and finance exist within organizations, and they receive varying emphasis, depending on the organization's purposes, its external environment, and the persons within the organization who shape responses to the environment. If a company produces a tangible product, it must perform some research and development, design, and engineering functions. Nonmanufacturing companies must perform similar functions to decide what services to offer and how to provide them. A restaurant, for example, must decide whether to provide food for patrons through service at tables or at self-service cafeteria counters.

Because organizations require human effort, they must recruit personnel, train them, and distribute benefits to them so that they may share in the profits generated by the organization's work. The human resource function is critically important to the organization, in general, and to the operations function, in particular. Additional information on the human resource function and its relationship to strategic management is integrated throughout this text.

Interdependence of Functions   Public relations are important to all primary and secondary functions. Public attitudes can affect the success of attempts to sell stock or to borrow money. The public's attitude also affects the company's ability to sell its product and recruit competent employees to produce its goods and services.

Public relations activities illustrate some of the interrelationships among functions within businesses. Strategists may divide a company into smaller units, each with boundaries that recognize the human capacity to understand and supervise, but the parts still are only *parts*. They must work together, across functions, to make the total organization work properly.

The three major functions within a business are interdependent. Sufficient financial resources and operations to produce a product are of little value if the product finds no market. Sufficient financial resources and a market for a product are of little value if one cannot provide the product. The ability to produce a product and a market for the product are not sufficient if the organization lacks the necessary capital to employ personnel, buy raw materials, and put the other capabilities into action. All of the functions in an organization both contribute to the whole and depend on contributions from the remainder of the organization. For this reason, many firms in the 1990s are busily experimenting with new ways to integrate the work of the critical functions more efficiently. For example, they often establish cross-functional teams to develop, produce, and market new products rapidly, to improve and accelerate strategic decision making and enhance performance.

In this section, we consider each function separately as a manageable unit, but it is important to keep in mind that the other functions are necessary to, and dependent on, the function being studied. Figure 10.1 shows the interrelationships of business functions.

Today's Broader View of the Operations Function

The operations function is sometimes called the *production function,* or the *production and operations function.* In the past, the term *production* sometimes connoted only manufacturing of tangible items; later the term *operations* was added, or substituted, to include nonmanufacturing operations. Today the term *production* often has a broader meaning, referring to the production of goods or of services. Our earlier definition stated that the operations function is responsible for producing goods or providing services. In this chapter the terms *production, operations,* and *production and operations* all refer to the function in either manufacturing or nonmanufacturing settings.

Manufacturing operations perform some physical or chemical processes such as sawing, sewing, machining, welding, grinding, blending, or refining to convert some tangible raw materials into tangible products. All other operations that do not actually make goods can be called *nonmanufacturing* or **service operations.** Customers deal with some of these nonmanufacturing companies to obtain purely intangible services such as advice or instruction; they

FIGURE 10.1
Critical Functions
within Organizations

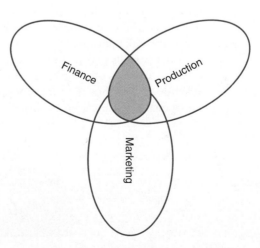

may seek help in completing tax forms, for example. Customers deal with other nonmanufacturing companies, such as wholesalers or retailers, to obtain goods, but these companies do not make the goods. These companies primarily serve their customers by transporting, packaging, storing, and the like, rather than by performing manufacturing processes. Thus, our major criterion for classifying operations depends on whether these operations manufacture goods or provide some type of service operation, even though they may provide tangible goods or some less tangible service to customers.

Operations: Providing a Product or Service   When viewed at a general or conceptual level, all types of production operations have some common characteristics. The most obvious common ground is the system's purpose or function; the production system creates the goods or services offered by the organization. The production system must transform some set of inputs into a set of outputs. All production systems share this element, illustrated schematically in Figure 10.2. The types of inputs, transformations, and outputs vary among operations.

Manufacturing operations transform or convert such inputs as raw materials, labor skills, management skills, capital, and sales revenue into some product, which the organization then sells. Other outputs are wages that flow into the economy, environmental effects, social influences, and other, even less obvious factors. The production system is a part of a larger system—the company. The company is a part of a larger system—the community. As the system boundaries expand, it becomes more difficult to determine all of the inputs, outputs, and transformations.

Service operations also transform a set of inputs into a set of outputs. A restaurant uses such inputs as meat, potatoes, lettuce, the chef's skills, servers' skills, and many others. Some of the transformation processes involve storing supplies, blending ingredients into desirable combinations, and altering the form of the inputs by cooking, freezing, heating, and transporting them to the proper tables at the proper times. Less tangible operations involve providing a pleasant atmosphere, perhaps even including entertainment. The organization hopes that its outputs include satisfied patrons. Other outputs include wages and purchase payments sent into the economy and refuse sent into the refuse collection system (which is yet another service system).

Educational institutions use such inputs as books, students, and instructional skills to produce knowledgeable and skilled individuals as output. Hospitals use scientific equipment, professional skills, and tender loving care to transform sick people into well ones. Repair shops use repair parts, equipment, and worker skills to transform malfunctioning inputs into properly functioning outputs. All types of operations, then, transform inputs into outputs.

When the output is a tangible product, the transformations performed by the operations function are intended to increase the utility of the inputs by

FIGURE 10.2
Conceptual Diagram
of a Production System

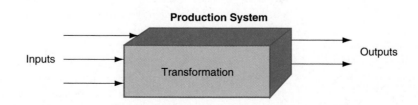

changing either the physical form of the inputs or the time or place at which the outputs are available. Operations that change the physical form of the input include factories, landscapers, restaurants, upholstery shops, ice cream shops, and laundries. Some operations provide access to special skills or improve convenience as part of their services to customers. Operations such as wholesalers, retailers, transporters, and the postal system provide materials-handling operations to change the places at which their outputs are available. Banks, public warehouses, and cold-storage plants for food or fur storage perform inventory functions to make outputs available at different times. Even though the inputs, transformations, and outputs may vary, the general characteristic of transforming inputs into more usable outputs holds true for all operations.

Manufacturing Operations   The production facilities and methods that a manufacturing company uses are sometimes referred to as its production system. A company often devises a production system to match the way it conducts its business. More specifically, this system's design is related to the stage at which the company plans to hold inventory in order to serve its customers more quickly than they could purchase all of the materials and convert them into the final product themselves. At the time a customer's order is received, the firm might hold the items to fill that order (1) as finished goods, (2) as standard modules waiting to be assembled, or (3) as basic inputs without any prior processing. The terms presented in the following paragraph characterize the degree of processing that is done after the customer's order is received.

Some companies are **make-to-stock producers** that complete products and place them in stock prior to receipt of the customer's order. The end item is shipped from finished-goods inventory after receipt of a customer order. In contrast, a **make-to-order producer** completes the end item after receipt of the customer's order. For a unique, custom-designed item, the customer will probably have to wait for the manufacturer to purchase many of the materials and perform the production work because the producer cannot anticipate what each customer might want and have the necessary raw materials and components on hand to shorten the production lead time. If it uses some components or materials frequently, however, the producer may keep some of them in stock—particularly if the lead time to purchase or produce these items is long.

The Skills Module discusses such a balancing act by a manufacturer of outdoor apparel. When a company produces standard-design, optional modules ahead of time and assembles a particular combination of these modules after the customer orders, the business is said to be an **assemble-to-order producer**.[2] An example of an assemble-to-order producer is an automobile factory that, in response to a dealer's order, provides an automatic or manual transmission, air conditioner, sound system, interior options, and specific engine options as well as a specified body style and color. The auto manufacturer would already have ordered many of the components or started them into production when the dealer placed the order. Otherwise the lead time to deliver the automobile would be much longer. With these terms in mind, we will now discuss the two major categories of production facilities and methods.

Continuous Production   A **continuous production system** arranges equipment and work stations in a sequence according to the steps to convert

SKILLS MODULE
Sport Obermeyer, Accurate Response and Product Design

INTRODUCTION

We have presented both product design and production systems as integral operations and strategy issues. Review the following situation, and then complete the skill development exercise that follows to help you develop your ability to appropriately manage product design within a production system as a component of overall strategy.

SITUATION

For more than 30 years, Sport Obermeyer's design-and-sales cycle was relatively straightforward. Production commitments for its fashion skiwear were based on firm orders, and fall delivery dates provided ample time for efficient manufacturing. The process began in March: design the product, make samples, and show the samples to retailers; in March and April, after receiving retail orders, place production orders with suppliers; in September and October, receive goods at the Denver distribution center and ship the goods immediately to retail outlets.

But the company's success and growing volume made its system obsolete by the 1980s. Unable to reserve sufficient production slots during the critical summer months, Sport Obermeyer began booking production the previous November—about a year before the goods would be sold—based on speculation about what retailers would order.

In addition, pressured by the need to reduce manufacturing costs and increase variety, the company developed a more complex supply chain. It sourced fabric and findings from three countries to be sewn in a fourth and finally delivered in the United States. This process greatly increased lead times just as earlier delivery had become paramount for dealers carrying Sport Obermeyer's new children's line; sales in the booming category were particularly strong in August, during the back-to-school season.

To deal with these problems—lengthening supply chains, limited supplier capacity, and retailers' demands for early delivery—Sport Obermeyer began a variety of quick-response initiatives to reduce lead times. The company introduced computerized systems that could process orders and compute raw-material requirements, halving the time that it had previously spent on these activities. The difficulty of reducing lead times to obtain raw materials led the company to an operational turnaround; it began to anticipate its materials requirements and preposition stocks in a warehouse in the Far East. With materials in place, Sport Obermeyer was able to begin manufacturing as soon as it received orders.

As delivery due dates approached, the company relied on air freight to expedite delivery from the Far East to Denver. By 1990, those changes had reduced delivery lead times by more than a month.

In February, Sport Obermeyer invited 25 of its largest retail customers to Aspen to preview the new fall line; persuading them to place orders earlier gave the company valuable, early insight on the likely popularity of specific styles and colors. Every year since the "Early Write" program began, its orders have accounted for about 20 percent of Sport Obermeyer's total sales.

SKILL DEVELOPMENT EXERCISE

Sport Obermeyer has successfully reduced its manufacturing and delivery lead times and solicited firm, early orders. What positive or negative effect could this strategy, especially anticipating materials needs, have on product design? If the most effective time to consider how to manufacture a product is during the design process, what role can Sport Obermeyer's product design department play to further reduce lead time?

SOURCE: Marshall L. Fisher, Janice H. Hammond, Walter R. Obermeyer, and Ananth Raman, "Making Supply Meet Demand in an Uncertain World," *Harvard Business Review*, May/June 1994, pp. 87–90.

the input raw materials into the desired component or assembly. The route of jobs are fixed, and the setup of the equipment seldom changes from one product to another. Materials flow relatively continuously during the production process. This type of production, sometimes called *repetitive manufacturing*, produces high volumes of discrete units, usually with a fixed sequence of material flow. Since the material flow path and processing steps are fixed, this type of production frequently turns out standard make-to-stock products.

Examples are production lines or assembly lines for the production of radios, televisions, refrigerators, or other products that may be produced and stocked in perhaps a few standard models. The customer selects a particular standard model. Continuous production might turn out items that are made to order or assembled to order if the volume is sufficient to justify a fixed, special-purpose production system.

Some continuous production operations produce products that blend together in bulk rather than being sold as discrete units. Some products of this type of operation include petroleum products, flour, cement, and liquid chemicals. The industries that produce these types of products are sometimes called **process industries,** particularly if some physical or chemical reaction is used. (Chemical processing can also produce batches of more specialized material; this is sometimes called *batch-process production.*)

Intermittent or Job Shop Production   An **intermittent production system** or *job shop* differs greatly from the continuous system in that it is designed to provide much more flexibility. This type of production system groups and organizes production equipment or work stations according to the functions or processes they perform. Different types of products flow in batches corresponding to individual orders. Each batch or lot might follow a different route through the functional work centers, depending on the requirements of the type of product being made. Products could be made for stock or to order, but generally this type of production is associated with make-to-order businesses.

Continuous and intermittent production systems represent opposite ends of a continuum that measures the degree of specificity of a production system (see Figure 10.3). At one end of the continuum are production facilities designed specifically to produce one particular standard item and optimized for the materials movement and production steps required to make that item. Near the other end of the continuum are job shops; they are not ideal for any single product, but are capable of producing wide varieties of items. Many production facilities embody features of both of these production approaches. They lie somewhere on the continuum between a job shop and a continuous production operation.

Lying at the flexible end of the continuum is the low-volume type of operation often referred to as a **project.** Usually, projects have relatively long durations, and the same personnel often are assigned to a project for a significant part of this time. In the manufacturing category, projects include such items as ships, bridges, buildings, and large, specialized machines.

Nonmanufacturing Operations   Nonmanufacturing operations, or service operations, do not produce tangible outputs. Like manufacturing operations,

FIGURE 10.3
Degree of Specificity
of Production Systems

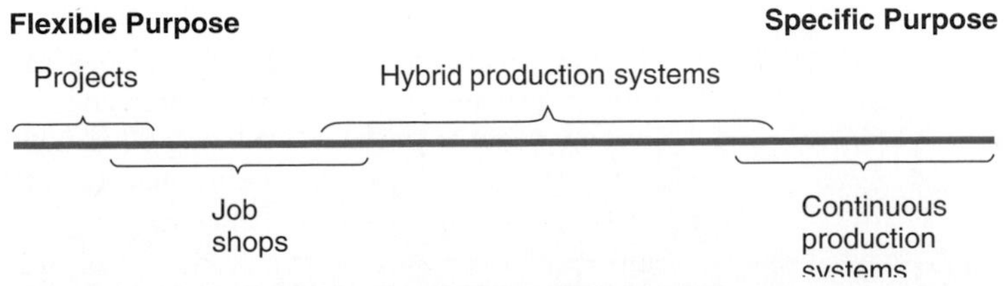

nonmanufacturing operations can be subdivided according to the degree of standardization of their outputs—that is, whether they are **standard services** or **custom services**—and/or the processes they perform. Some nonmanufacturing activities resemble projects because they involve the activities of teams of people over periods of time. A nonmanufacturing project might be a software package or a training program. Table 10.1 displays a classification system for manufacturing and nonmanufacturing operations based on the degree of standardization of their output.

TABLE 10.1

Classification of Types of Operations

Types of Operations	Manufacturing, or Goods-producing, Operations	Nonmanufacturing, or Service, Operations
Project: activity of long duration and low volume	Building a bridge, dam, or house; preparing for a banquet	Research project, development of software
Unit or batch: activity of short duration and low volume, producing custom goods or services	Job shop: making industrial hardware; printing personalized stationery; making drapes	Custom service: offering charter air or bus service; cleaning carpets; repairing autos; providing health care or counseling services; providing hair care; translating a foreign-language book for a publisher; designing costumes for a theatrical production; public warehousing; providing special-delivery mail service
Mass production: activity of short duration and high volume, producing standard goods or services	Continuous operation: making light bulbs, refrigerators, television sets, automobiles	Standard service: providing fast food, standard insurance policies, scheduled air or bus service, dry cleaning, personal checking accounts, regular mail service, distribution and wholesaling of standardized products; processing photographic film
Process industry: continuous processing of a homogeneous material	Continuous operation: processing chemicals, refining oil, milling flour, manufacturing paper	

Nonmanufacturing operations can be divided into categories according to another classification scheme that provides useful insights into the management issues they raise. Some nonmanufacturing operations deal primarily with tangible outputs, even though these operations do not manufacture the items. These types of operations, such as wholesale distributors and transportation companies, can utilize many of the same materials management principles and techniques that a manufacturing operation might use. The vital ideas of materials handling are also important in some operations that deal with tangible items.

Other nonmanufacturing operations deal in intangible products, or services, as their primary outputs. One should recognize that these service operations do not necessarily provide *only* services or *only* goods. Facilitating goods may be provided with services, and facilitating services may be provided with goods. For example, customers can obtain the same goods (although in different forms) from a grocery store or a restaurant. A grocery store seems primarily like a provider of goods. Restaurant customers primarily want services like selecting, preparing, and serving food, which is actually a tangible good. "Servicing" a car may include installation of some parts. The service is provided by someone who knows which parts to replace and how to replace them, and who spends time to perform this service.

Operations that deal primarily in services can be further divided according to the degree to which the customer participates in the process. Many services are custom services, so the customer often has some contact with the service provider. The customer does not have to be present, however, during the process for some types of services, such as having clothes laundered or watches repaired. Professor Richard Chase states that systems with more customer contact are more difficult to understand and control.[3] Table 10.2 displays a classification of nonmanufacturing operations, with some examples of each type of operation.

TABLE 10.2

Classification of Nonmanufacturing Operations

Nonmanufacturing Operations		
Providers of Tangible Products	**Providers of Services**	
Mail service	Services in which the customer is not a participant.	Services in which the customer is a participant.
Library services		
Wholesale and retail distribution	Examples:	Examples:
Examples:	Preparing tax forms	Health care
Television sets	Architectural design	Hair care
Radios	Landscaping	Travel
Watches	Cleaning clothes	Legal advice
Refrigerators	Repairing watches, automobiles, appliances, etc.	Financial advice
Air conditioners		Marriage counseling
	Rating and issuing insurance	

OPERATIONS AND STRATEGIC MANAGEMENT

Different Operations, Different Strategies

A company's overall strategy addresses many broad issues, perhaps even including plans for social responsibility, stockholder relations, and employee relations. One important aspect of the overall direction of a firm is its competitive strategy. At a very general level, one can identify some characteristics of strategies that are often associated with the types of operations functions previously introduced in this chapter. The strategy of a company with a custom product will tend to differ from that of a company with a more standardized product. Table 10.3 shows some general features of strategies for various types of operations.

Generally, companies can compete based on three primary features of their goods or services:

1. *Quality*   Do all of the characteristics of a product make it suitable and reliable for the customer's intended use?
2. *Price*   Is the cost to the customer over the life of the product affordable? Does it seem reasonable when compared to the quality of the product and other quality-to-price ratios available in the marketplace?
3. *Availability*   Can the product be obtained within a reasonable and competitive time?

To succeed in the marketplace, a product must be judged at least adequate on all three measures.

Operations: A Vital Element in Strategy

The operations function has great value as a competitive weapon in a company's strategy. Because it is the part of the firm that must produce the goods or provide the services that the consumer buys, the operations function plays an important role in implementing strategy. The operations function establishes the level of quality as a product is manufactured or as a service is provided. The operations function often encompasses the largest part of a company's human and capital assets. Thus, much of a product's cost is incurred within operations, and this cost affects the price that the firm charges and the profit margin it achieves. Finally, the ability of the operations function to perform determines to a great extent the ability of the company to have sufficient products available to meet delivery commitments.

It is clear, then, that the operations function has a critical influence on the cost, quality, and availability of the company's goods or services. In this way, operations strengths and weaknesses can have a great impact on the success of the company's overall strategy. Therefore, the capabilities of operations must be carefully considered when corporate strategy is formulated, and operations decisions must be consistent with corporate strategy so that the full potential of operations' resources can be harnessed in pursuit of the company's goals.

Strategy Decisions for Operations

Positioning Decisions   Strategy decisions at the top-management level and within the operations function affect how well the operations function contribute to the competitive effectiveness of a company. One broad strategy decision that is important in guiding and coordinating the actions of operations

TABLE 10.3

Strategies Associated with Various Types of Operations

Type of Operation	Type of Product	Typical Process Characteristics	Typical Characteristics of Strategy
Service Project Job shop	Make to order as customer specifies	Use of broadly skilled workers and general-purpose equipment; emphasis on good initial planning of work, quality, flexibility	Selling diversity of capabilities and ability to provide features customers desire, ability to perform a quality job, ability to achieve reasonable delivery times
Continuous Process	Make for inventory a product designed to have features desired by many potential customers	Use of workers with narrower skills, specialized equipment, perhaps automation; emphasis on efficiency and cost control; good distribution system to make items readily available	Selling the desirability of features that are already designed into the product plus the desirability of the price, availability, service. Market research is important to ensure that product features are appropriate for the market.

is related to positioning. **Positioning** establishes the extent to which the production system will emphasize certain characteristics in order to achieve the greatest competitive advantage. Regardless of how desirable it may sound, no product can simultaneously be lowest in cost, highest in quality, and instantly available in abundance at numerous, convenient locations. Professor Steven Wheelwright recommends that a manufacturing company explicitly establish relative priorities for the four performance characteristics: cost efficiency, quality, dependability, and flexibility.[4] These performance characteristics can be briefly described as follows:

- *Cost efficiency*   A company that emphasizes cost efficiency will keep its capital, labor, and other operating costs low relative to those of other, similar companies.
- *Quality*   A company that emphasizes quality will consistently strive to provide a level of quality that is significantly superior to those of its competitors, even if it has to pay extra to do so. The Company Example tells how Motorola revised its operations to improve quality.

COMPANY EXAMPLE

Motorola Reverses Manufacturing Trends

Motorola tries to measure every task performed by every one of its 120,000 employees. The company calculates that this effort saved it $1.5 billion by reducing defects and simplifying processes last year.

Some of Motorola's factories have achieved such high quality that they've stopped counting defects per million units and starting working on defects per *billion*. Overall, the company's goal is to reduce its error rate tenfold every two years and to cut its cycle time tenfold every five years.

Motorola's Land Mobile Products factory in Plantation, Florida, had a long way to go back in 1990. The plant took as long as ten days to turn out a finished radio. To decide which models to make, the company's analysts churned out elaborate forecasts of consumer demand, which were rarely on target. In an effort to cut costs, Motorola began building components at a feeder plant in Malaysia, where labor costs are low, and shipping them to Plantation for final assembly.

Times have changed. Today, the plant no longer relies on forecasts or a feeder plant. Workers on Plantation's Jedi line (named after the Star Wars characters) can make a specific radio for a specific customer in just two hours. They juggle more than 500 variations.

A number of manufacturing innovations are credited for the plant's turnaround. Among them, palettes marked with binary codes now surround the U-shaped assembly line that carries the radios; the codes give instructions to the robots and the workers who monitor them. Even more important, a newly invented, computer-controlled soldering process eliminates the need for costly and time-consuming tool changes.

Motorola is now converting the two-way radio plant in Malaysia, as well as its other major operation in Ireland, into clones of Plantation's "focused flexible factory."

SOURCE: Ronald Henkoff, "Keeping Motorola on a Roll," *Fortune*, April 18, 1994, pp. 67–78.

- *Dependability*   A company that stresses dependability can be relied on to have its goods available for customers or to deliver its goods or services on schedule, if at all possible.
- *Flexibility*   A company that emphasizes flexibility will work to respond quickly to changes in product design, product mix, or production volume.

Positioning might be visualized as selecting a particular spot within the pyramid shown in Figure 10.4, and consistently operating within that area. The pyramid defines the relative priorities that can be assigned to each of the four performance characteristics. However, the portion of the pyramid that the company seeks to occupy is a strategic decision that must rest with the top management. If each part of a company tries to move in its own direction to respond to competitors' moves in that area, then the company's overall money, talents, and efforts will not be effectively expended. By trying to move in several directions simultaneously, such a company would fail to demonstrate a distinctive competence that would attract and retain customers, and customers could not rely on it for consistent treatment.

Although a company cannot simultaneously reach all corners of the pyramid shown in Figure 10.4, it can expand the range of the pyramid that it covers. This is quite different from bouncing inconsistently from one location to another within the pyramid. Expanding the range within the pyramid that a company consistently covers amounts to shortening one or more legs of the

FIGURE 10.4
Possible Positions of an
Operations Function

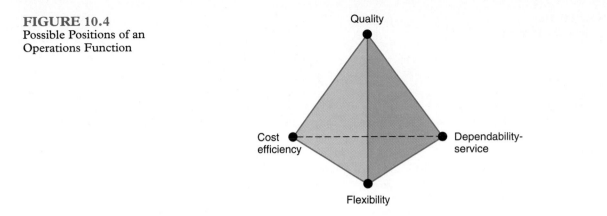

pyramid or making the pyramid smaller. A company can then cover a larger percentage of its pyramid than its competitors and leave less space for a competitor to develop a distinctive competence.

An example of shrinking the pyramid can be found in the operation of numerous Japanese companies. Through very careful and diligent efforts, these companies have controlled processes to prevent defects and have achieved superior quality. These actions have reduced the cost of screening and repairing defective work in the factory and the cost of warranty work in the field. In effect, these companies have simultaneously improved quality and cost so that they can cover a larger portion of the cost–quality leg of their pyramid. This effectively reduces the length of the cost–quality leg of the pyramid, as shown in Figure 10.5(a). Many Japanese manufacturers have also provided extensive training and cross training of their workers to develop multiskilled workers. This versatile work force, coupled with plant arrangements and equipment that can easily change over from one product to another, provides greater flexibility without a significant increase in cost. This shortens the flexibility–cost leg of the pyramid, as shown in Figure 10.5(b). Companies can employ these or other means to shrink various legs of their pyramids. Resourceful companies that succeed in shrinking their pyramids can serve their markets well, and leave their competitors few spots in which to try to establish their own distinctive competences.

Table 10.4 shows the four performance characteristics we have mentioned and some of the supporting features that are desirable in the operations function of a manufacturing company to help achieve a particular performance characteristic. Comments in the third column of the table indicate the degree to which each feature might also be appropriate to support the performance characteristic in a nonmanufacturing company.

Other Decisions   Once a company has selected its intended position and internally communicated this intention, all parts of the company can make more consistent decisions, that is, decisions that are more consistent with the company's overall decisions, and with decisions made in other parts of the company. The company will stand a better chance of achieving its strategic objectives when all of its divisions work in concert to support these objectives in all of their decisions and activities.

FIGURE 10.5
Shrinking the Pyramid

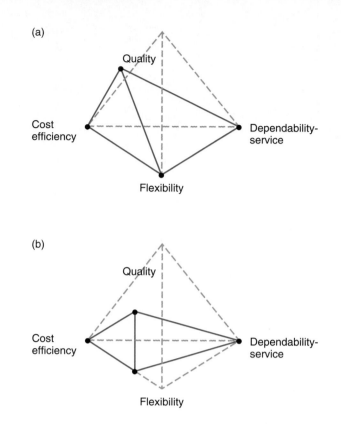

Numerous decisions within the operations function are related to the positioning decision, and to each other. Robert Hayes and Steven Wheelwright present eight major categories of strategy decisions for a manufacturing company, as shown in Table 10.5.[5] The first four categories are normally recognized as long-term decisions that are difficult to reverse and therefore more likely to be considered strategic. The last four categories appear to deal with tactical matters, that is, with more day-to-day, operating issues. It is important to recognize, however, that even these matters have long-run strategic impacts.

Product Design: An Important Strategic Factor

One of a company's basic decisions is what goods or services it will offer in the marketplace. Identifying the general type of product helps narrow the search for a niche in the market where the company might stimulate sufficient demand to achieve success. Beyond the broad question of what business it will be in, the company must address many details regarding what specific product or service it will offer and how. Decisions about the product's design specifications affect the selection of process technology (one of the decision categories in Table 10.5), which, in turn, affects the company's expenditures for equipment and facilities. Product design also affects the ease with which the product can be fabricated and assembled, so it affects operating costs. Design also affects the ease with which a product can be produced with few defects, and this influences market acceptance and the customer's perception of the company. Product design, then, has serious implications for the

TABLE 10.4

Operations Features that Support Particular Performance Characteristics

Performance Characteristic to be Emphasized	Features that Manufacturing Operations Might Provide	Applicability to Service Operations
Cost efficiency	Low overhead	Yes
	Special-purpose equipment and facilities	Yes
	High utilization of capability	Yes
	Close control of materials	Maybe
	High productivity	Yes
	Low wage rates	Yes
Quality	Skilled workers	Yes
	Adequate precision of equipment	Maybe
	Motivation for pride of workmanship	Yes
	Effective communication of standards or job requirements	Yes
Dependability	Effective scheduling system	Yes
	Low equipment failure	Yes
	Low absenteeism, low turnover, no strikes	Yes
	High inventory investment	Maybe
	Commitment of personnel to perform as required	Yes
Flexibility	Dependable, rapid suppliers	Yes
	Reserve capacity	Yes
	Multiskilled workers who can be shifted	Yes
	Effective control of work flow	Yes
	Versatile processing equipment	Yes
	Low setup time and cost	Maybe
	Integration of design and production	Maybe

TABLE 10.5

Categories of Strategy Decisions in Manufacturing Operations

1. **Capacity**—amount, timing, type
2. **Facilities**—size, location, specialization
3. **Technology**—equipment, automation, linkages
4. **Vertical integration**—direction, extent, balance
5. **Work force**—skill level, wage policies, employment security
6. **Quality**—defect prevention, monitoring, intervention
7. **Production planning materials control**—sourcing policies, centralization, decision rules
8. **Organization**—structure, control/reward systems, role of staff groups

company's long-range success, and therefore it has considerable strategic importance. The relationship between design and operating decisions differs for manufacturing and nonmanufacturing operations.

Product Design in Nonmanufacturing Operations   The product, or output, desired from the operations system of a nonmanufacturing firm will certainly affect the type of inputs it needs and the capabilities it needs to transform the inputs into the desired goods or services. The processing technology and kinds of skills that must be available in the operations function may be significantly affected, even by apparently small differences in the characteristics of the product or its delivery.[6] The decision of a food establishment to provide buffet meals rather than cafeteria-style service, for example, would reduce its need for people behind the counter to serve patrons. It would also, however, require the establishment to routinely prepare extra food, or be able to do so quickly, because management would no longer be able to control the size of each portion.

Levitz Furniture Corporation operated for years with cavernous 170,000-square-foot buildings that were combination warehouse–showrooms located near rail sidings in large cities. Customers could select furniture and haul it home. More recently, the company has added a chain of satellite stores that serve only as showrooms for warehouses located about 25 miles away. This change in merchandising strategy forced the company to keep better inventory records so the people at the showrooms would know what was available at various locations. The company also needed a more extensive fleet of vehicles and personnel to move products between locations and make deliveries to the customers.

To take another example of the operating implications that result from product design, consider a decision by the Wendy's Old-Fashioned Hamburgers chain. Wendy's had the choice of serving fresh or frozen french-fried potatoes. Serving fresh potatoes would have required each location to select, purchase, store, peel, store again, then cook and serve the potatoes. Offering preprocessed and frozen potatoes would have required each location only to store, then cook and serve the potatoes. Preprocessed potatoes also provided a more uniform product. Therefore, the chain decided to serve preprocessed, frozen french fries reducing the number of employees and the amount of space required at each location and reducing quality control and waste-disposal problems at each location.

Product Design in Manufacturing Operations   A manufacturing firm must balance the need to make its product marketable with the need to produce it economically. Product design can affect appearance, so the designer must work for an appealing look. Because some aspects of the product design may necessitate particular processes and production equipment, the best time to begin a cost-reduction program is while the product is on the drawing board. As the product is designed, managers should perform a cost–benefit evaluation, taking into account the kind and amount of materials, labor, and processing equipment that each alternative design will require. The company must also recognize that the potential consumer will also perform some sort of cost–benefit evaluation before deciding whether to purchase the product. Some processes and materials are more expensive and should be used only if the functions of the product make them necessary or the aesthetic appeal of the results justifies the expense.

Myriad alternative designs for a product are usually possible, and managers may have to choose among alternative production methods even after the product is designed. Production engineers often advise designers, helping them develop product designs that are reasonably economical to produce. A brief discussion of product design ideas will provide some appreciation of the complex nature of this topic. In selecting the raw material for a product, the designer must consider such properties as hardness, wear resistance, fatigue strength, tensile strength, weight, transparency, and ductility. Although a designer might consider the use of an inexpensive raw material, a more expensive material such as a free-machining alloy might result in a net saving when the processing costs are considered. After the material is selected, other design parameters must be evaluated. Economy can result from such ideas as:

- Using a different process to achieve a basic shape—for example; casting instead of machining.
- Requiring machined surfaces only where necessary
- Requiring close tolerances only when necessary
- Ensuring that surfaces are easily accessible to the types of processes to be used
- Considering less costly ways of joining materials, such as spot welding rather than riveting
- Requiring thinner materials or less severe bends so that light-capacity machines can be used for forming operations

As indicated earlier, the most effective time to consider how to manufacture a product is while the product is being designed. Close coordination between the design and manufacturing departments is desirable if a company wants to develop economical and effective designs. One characteristic that was found to be common during a comparison of some of America's best-managed factories was a close linkage between design and manufacturing departments, allowing them to rapidly develop easily producible designs. (Other similarities included superior ability to "build in quality, make wise choices about automation, get close to the customer, and handle their work forces."[7])

Overall, managers must keep in mind that making decisions about product design in manufacturing, as well as nonmanufacturing, situations is an extremely important aspect of strategic management. The appropriateness of such decisions a manager makes will rely heavily on his or her understanding of issues, such as how the operations function fits within an organization, how operations relates to strategic management, and how product positioning relates to product design.

SUMMARY

The operations function is performed by the people in an organization who produce the goods or services that the firm offers in the marketplace. The operations function must be compatible and consistent with other important organizational functions, such as marketing and finance, in order for any organization to succeed. Our discussion of the operations function distinguished manufacturing functions from nonmanufacturing, or service, functions. We further characterized manufacturing firms as make-to-stock, make-to-order, or assemble-to-order producers and differentiated between firms with continuous and intermittent production processes. Turning to nonmanufacturing operations, we drew a distinction between those that deal in tangible outputs that they do not manufacture and those that deal in intangible outputs, or services.

Because a firm's competitive strategy is such an important part of its overall direction, managers must understand the relationship between their operations function and their strategy. Strategy decisions determine which production characteristic(s)—cost efficiency, quality, dependability, or flexibility—the operations function will emphasize. This can also be crucial to the firm's success. Product design is a key strategy factor. It affects the selection of process technologies, the cost of equipment and facilities, the ease with which the product can be produced, the quality of the product, and hence the customer's perception of the firm.

KEY TERMS

operations function, p. 243
marketing function, p. 244
finance function, p. 244
manufacturing operations, p. 245
service operations, p. 245
make-to-stock producer, p. 247
make-to-order producer, p. 247
assemble-to-order producer, p. 247

continuous production system, p. 247
process industries, p. 249
intermittent production system, p. 249
project, p. 249
standard services, p. 250
custom services, p. 250
positioning, p. 253

CHECKLIST   Analyzing Operations in Problems and Cases

___ 1. Does the case or problem involve true production or operations issues?

___ 2. Is the operations function in the case or problem appropriately integrated with other important business functions, such as finance and marketing?

___ 3. Is the organization involved in producing goods or services? Is this fact of particular significance in the case or problem?

___ 4. If the organization is involved in manufacturing, is the production process that is used appropriate for the situation?

___ 5. If the organization is involved in a nonmanufacturing operation, is the production process that is used appropriate for the situation?

___ 6. Are the strategies employed in the case or problem consistent with the type of production function that exists?

___ 7. Is enough emphasis placed on using operations as a critical element of strategy?

___ 8. Do product positioning decisions take the operations function into account?

___ 9. Are decisions concerning such issues as capacity, facilities, technology, vertical integration, the work force, quality, production planning and materials control, and organization consistent with product positioning?

___ 10. Is product design as a strategic factor appropriately linked to operations?

Additional Readings

Belohlav, James A. "Quality, Strategy, and Competitiveness." *California Management Review,* Spring 1993, p. 55.

Garvin, David A. "Manufacturing Strategic Planning." *California Management Review,* Summer 1993, p. 85.

Harmon, Roy L., and Leroy D. Peterson. *Reinventing the Factory: Productivity Breakthroughs in Manufacturing Today.* New York: Free Press, 1989.

Hayes, Robert H., Steven C. Wheelwright, and Kim B. Clark. "The Power of Positive Manufacturing." *Across the Board,* October 1988, pp. 24–30.

Peters, Tom. "Rethinking Scale." *California Management Review,* Fall 1992, p. 7.

Schonberger, Richard J. *Japanese Manufacturing Techniques: Nine Hidden Lessons in Simplicity.* New York: Free Press, 1982.

———. *The World Class Company.* New York: Free Press, 1990.

C A S E

Redner's Upends Operations

In the five years since Redner's converted from a conventional supermarket operation to a warehouse store format, sales at the Reading, Pennsylvania, company have tripled to the current level of $230 million. That's an average store-for-store increase from $100,000 to roughly $300,000 a week.

President Dick Redner has a bullish prediction that the company will be a billion-dollar operation by the end of the century and have 100 stores by 2010.

Redner's was a healthy company, its nine stores reporting industry-average sales trends and good profits. Executive interest was piqued, however, by the success of wholesalers, who sell huge volumes with hardly any advertising. One of Redner's stores was a likely prospect for a test conversion: Its 38,000-square-foot Palmyra store was the fourth operation in the small town. Even after Redner's cut its losses in half, business had not increased beyond what the previous owner had done—$90,000 to $100,000 a week. Conversion was a no-lose proposition: Operating on only a two-year lease, the chain could test the warehouse concept and, if it failed, close the store and walk away.

The transformation was completed in three days, and business immediately doubled. Despite the good customer reception, Redner's managers were troubled. "A lot of guys said, 'You know, it's not broke, so let's not fix it,'" says Dick Redner. "But as we noted the results, we just felt we couldn't be a dual operator. We were either going to stay a conventional operator or we were going all the way with the warehouse concept."

The chain converted the rest of its stores within a year, with identical results: business doubled and the sizes of the stores followed suit. As business has tripled, Redner's has built new stores, bringing its total to 15. Construction is concluding on a new 120,000-square-foot warehouse to feed the rapid growth in the company's direct-buying program, part of a drive to increase margins with the increase in volume in all departments. Other moves included eliminating sales games, gimmicks, and double coupons.

Dick Redner says the formula is simple—no deviation from the program to become a price leader in the marketplace. Everything is discounted, from produce to meat to deli products to health and beauty aids. That message is pounded home with the phrase *WAREHOUSE MARKET* printed on everything from store signs to management business cards. Redner's warehouse concept is an egoless operational philosophy that takes priority over everything, including family identity—a departure from the traditional supermarket strategy of stressing a family name and involvement.

DISCUSSION QUESTIONS

1. Which materials management principles and operations features commonly used by manufacturing operations could best be applied to Redner's service operation?

2. How much leverage has Redner's allowed itself with its low-price positioning strategy?

3. Write an operational mission statement for Redner's, focusing on how the company can best compete on quality, price, and product availability.

SOURCE: Bob Ingram, "Redner's 'Racks' Up the Volume," *Supermarket Business,* March 1994, pp. 53–56.

Notes

1. This chapter is based on Chapter 1 ("Zeroing in on Operations") and Chapter 2 ("Operations Strategy") in James B. Dilworth, *Production and Operations Management: Manufacturing and Non-manufacturing* (New York: Random House, 1986). This book is available in a 1992 version from McGraw-Hill Book Company. The authors would like to express their sincere appreciation to Professor James B. Dilworth for his important contribution to this text.

2. These terms are defined in accordance with Thomas F. Wallace, *APICS Dictionary,* 5th ed. (Falls Church, Va.: American Production and Inventory Control Society, 1984).

3. Richard B. Chase, "Where Does the Customer Fit in a Service Operation?" *Harvard Business Review,* November/December 1978, p. 138.

4. Steven C. Wheelwright, "Reflecting Corporate Strategy in Manufacturing Decisions," *Business Horizons,* February 1978, pp. 57–66.

5. Robert H. Hayes and Steven C. Wheelwright, *Restoring Our Competitive Edge* (New York: John Wiley & Sons, 1984), p. 31.

6. Dan R. E. Thomas, "Strategy Is Different in Service Businesses," *Harvard Business Review,* July/August 1980, pp. 158–165.

7. Gene Bylinsky, "America's Best-Managed Factories," *Fortune,* May 28, 1984, pp. 16–24.

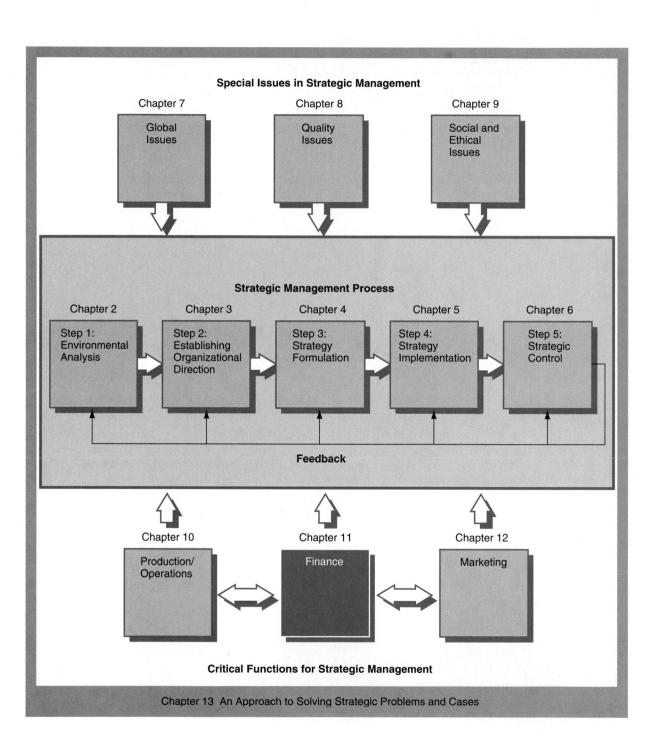

Special Issues in Strategic Management

Chapter 7

Global
Issues

Chapter 8

Quality
Issues

Chapter 9

Social and
Ethical
Issues

Strategic Management Process

Chapter 2

Step 1:
Environmental
Analysis

Chapter 3

Step 2:
Establishing
Organizational
Direction

Chapter 4

Step 3:
Strategy
Formulation

Chapter 5

Step 4:
Strategy
Implementation

Chapter 6

Step 5:
Strategic
Control

Feedback

Chapter 10

Production/
Operations

Chapter 11

Finance

Chapter 12

Marketing

Critical Functions for Strategic Management

Chapter 13 An Approach to Solving Strategic Problems and Cases

The Finance Function and Strategic Management

Many types of financial analyses provide useful aids for strategic decision making. In this chapter, we investigate several tools that are commonly used in analyzing strategic management problems and cases.[1] First, we discuss financial ratio analysis, which is a useful starting point for investigating the financial condition of an organization. Next, we examine break-even analysis, a simple financial tool for investigating the potential value of an investment. Finally, we describe net present value analysis, a method of examining investment alternatives.

Financial analysis is useful, most obviously, in the strategic control stage of the strategic management process, when top managers assess the bottom-line financial results of their earlier strategic decisions. However, financial tools can provide powerful help at other stages of the process. During environmental analysis, financial tools can contribute to SWOT analysis, as top managers attempt to quantify and evaluate the strengths and weaknesses of their firm in relation to those of its competitors, and to assess market opportunities and threats. At the strategy formulation stage, financial tools such as break-even and net

present value analysis help managers to assess the comparative merits of different potential strategies. The Company Example illustrates the effect of financial constraints on one firm's strategic decisions.

During strategy implementation, early-stage financial analysis can often signal the need for corrective action or change. In addition, the finance function provides essential analytical tools to the other core functions—marketing and operations. In marketing, for example, financial analysis helps drive decisions about alternative distribution channels or packaging. In operations, assessments of alternative investments in plant and equipment draw upon net present value analysis and similar techniques.

These points underscore the importance of viewing an organization's operations through a cross-functional lens. In the 1990s the speed of strategic actions is critical, and a firm can enjoy great benefits if it effectively integrates its functional specialists in the strategic management process and resists outdated notions about keeping functions separated, each behind its own wall.

COMPANY EXAMPLE

Start-up Financing at Highland Energy Group

After teaming with a vendor of energy-efficient lighting to assemble a lease package for a large company, Tom Stoner says he determined that the energy savings on a five-year deal amounted to more money than the lease payments on the equipment. He decided to start a firm specializing in alternative energy. "I knew that with utilities having been a monopoly there was an opportunity to create efficiencies in this market. And where you can create efficiencies, profits can be made."

In order to sell the company to investors and customers, Stoner decided that his New England–based Highland Energy Group would not only design customized programs for conversion to energy-efficient technology but guarantee the results to large-scale energy users.

Buoyed by a friend's initial investment of more than $1 million, Stoner leveraged additional funds by structuring financing deals with architectural and engineering firms with which he worked on specific projects. A public offering put out to accumulate more capital had no takers until the company won some bids. Investors now own 70 percent of the business.

In 1992, Highland Energy sold products worth $5 million; today, it has secured utility contracts that should generate more than $20 million in revenue over the next three years. "Before, we needed capital to execute bids and set up systems, but now we need the capital to grow," says Stoner. "The dollar amount gets larger, and you always need twice as much as you think. It's like guessing the moon."

While managing growth has been a concern, the decisions to sustain that growth are the most difficult. "You could go one way and get cash-flow positive or you could get bigger, better, and more credible," he says. "Do you hire a bookkeeper at $20,000 a year or a chief financial officer at $80,000? You have to plot your commitment day in and day out, but it's like plotting a course in a vacuum."

SOURCE: Margaret Kaeter, "Buddy, Can You Spare a Million?" *Business Ethics*, May/June 1994, pp. 27–28.

FINANCIAL RATIO ANALYSIS

A useful starting point in analyzing an organization's financial condition is to perform a financial ratio analysis. A **financial ratio analysis** is based on information provided in the organization's balance sheet and income statement. These two financial statements are frequently included in strategic management cases, and performing a financial ratio analysis is a convenient way to gain insight into the condition of the firm. In this section, we first review the balance sheet and income statement and then propose a four-step process for performing a financial ratio analysis.

Table 11.1 presents the balance sheet for the MoPower Robotics Company, a manufacturer of specialized industrial robots. The **balance sheet** is a summary of the assets of an organization and the claims against its assets at a particular time. Actually, Table 11.1 represents a **comparative balance sheet,** stating the assets and liabilities of MoPower for more than one time. Note that two types of assets are shown. **Current assets** are those that the firm expects to convert to cash within one year, whereas **fixed assets** are those that it expects to hold for a longer time. Similarly, **current liabilities** are amounts of money that it owes and expects to pay out within one year; other obligations are longer term in nature.

Table 11.2 presents MoPower's income statement. The **income statement** shows the financial results of an organization's operations during an interval

TABLE 11.1

MoPower Robotics Company Balance Sheet ($000)

ASSETS	Dec. 31, 1994	Dec. 31, 1995
Cash	$ 30	$ 25
Marketable securities	40	25
Accounts receivable	200	100
Inventories	430	700
Total current assets	$ 700	$ 850
Plant and equipment	1,000	1,500
Long-term investments	500	900
Other assets	200	250
Total assets	$2,400	$3,500

LIABILITIES AND NET WORTH		
Trade accounts payable	$ 150	$ 200
Notes payable	100	100
Accruals	25	100
Provision for federal taxes	40	50
Total current liabilities	$ 315	$ 450
Bonds	500	1,000
Debentures	85	50
Stockholders' equity	1,500	2,000
Total liabilities and stockholders' equity	$2,400	$3,500

TABLE 11.2

MoPower Robotics Company Income Statement for the Year Ending December 31, 1995 ($000)

Sales		$3,600
Cost of goods sold		2,700
Gross profit		$ 900
Less operating expenses		
Selling	$40	
General and administrative	60	100
Gross operating revenue		$ 800
Less depreciation		250
Net operating income (NOI)		$ 550
Less other expenses		50
Earnings before interest and taxes (EBIT)		$ 500
Less interest expense		200
Earnings before taxes (EBT)		$ 300
Less federal and state income taxes (40%)		120
Earnings after taxes (EAT)		$ 180

of time, usually one year. The income statement lists net sales (sales minus returns and allowances) at the top and then proceeds to subtract various amounts to determine earnings after tax (net income). The amounts subtracted from net sales on this income statement include cost of goods sold, operating expenses, depreciation, other expenses, interest, and taxes. Various organizations may have different entries and labels, but these two financial statements represent common reporting procedures.

Financial statements contain a tremendous amount of useful information for strategic managers. However, it is very difficult, based on a simple look at the statements, to determine how well the organization is doing. For example, is MoPower currently in a solid financial position, or do these financial statements suggest that the company has problems? In order to answer this question, we need a method of comparing MoPower's financial situation over time with the situations of other firms of similar size in the same industry, and with industry averages. These comparisons are the basis for financial ratio analysis.

Performing a financial ratio analysis can be divided into four steps: (1) choosing appropriate ratios, (2) calculating the ratios, (3) comparing the ratios, and (4) checking for problems and opportunities. We will discuss each of these steps in turn.

Choosing Appropriate Ratios

The many types of financial ratios include liquidity ratios, leverage ratios, activity ratios, profitability ratios, growth ratios, and valuation ratios. All have important uses in evaluating the financial well-being of an organization. Though strategic managers may use all of these types of ratios, some of them are very specialized, and applying them in a meaningful way requires an extensive financial management background.[2] However, there are several types of financial ratios that should be applied routinely in analyzing *any* strategic management case that includes financial statements. These types—the liquidity, activity, and profitability ratios—are especially useful for uncovering symptoms of problems in cases and for supporting both arguments about the major issues in the cases and proposed solutions. Each of these types includes many ratios; we will discuss only a few of the most useful ones.

Liquidity Ratios   One of the first financial considerations to consider when analyzing a strategic management case is the liquidity of the organization. *Liquidity* refers to the ability of the organization to pay its short-term obligations. If the organization cannot meet its short-term obligations, it can do little else until it corrects the problem. In other words, a firm that cannot meet its current financial obligations must resolve the problem before long-term strategic planning can be effective.

The two most commonly used ratios for investigating liquidity are the current ratio and the quick ratio (or acid test ratio). The **current ratio** is found by dividing current assets by current liabilities. It measures the overall ability of an organization to meet its current obligations. A common rule of thumb is that the current ratio should be about 2:1, although what is acceptable depends greatly on the industry and the situation.

The **quick ratio** is determined by subtracting inventory from current assets and dividing the result by current liabilities. Because inventory is the least liquid current asset, the quick ratio gives an indication of the degree to which an organization has funds readily available to meet short-term obligations. A common rule of thumb is that the quick ratio should be at least 1:1, although, again, the appropriate level depends on the industry and the situation.

Activity Ratios   Activity ratios, also called *asset management ratios,* investigate how well the organization handles its assets. For strategic management purposes, two of the most useful activity ratios measure inventory turnover and total asset utilization.

Inventory turnover is determined by dividing sales by inventories. If the firm is not turning over its inventory as rapidly as it has in the past, or as rapidly as other firms in the industry, it may have a problem. Perhaps it is tying up too much money in unproductive or obsolete inventory, or it is not marketing its products as well as it has in the past.

A second useful activity ratio is total asset utilization. **Total asset utilization** is calculated by dividing sales by total assets. It measures how productively the firm has used its assets to generate sales. If this ratio is well below the industry average, management may not be using company assets effectively.

Profitability Ratios   The profitability of an organization is an important measure of its effectiveness. Although financial analysts suggest that a firm's goal is to maximize shareholder wealth, profitability is a common yardstick for measuring success. Two key profitability ratios are profit margin on sales and return on investment (ROI). **Profit margin on sales** is calculated by dividing earnings before interest and taxes (EBIT) by sales. Serious questions about an organization should be raised if this figure is declining over time or is well below the figures for other firms in the industry.

Return on investment is calculated by dividing earnings after taxes (EAT) by total assets. This ratio is also called *return on assets,* and earnings after taxes are sometimes referred to as *profit after taxes, net profit,* or *net income.* This ratio gives an indication of how productively the organization has acquired, used, and managed assets. Return on investment is a commonly discussed measure of corporate performance.

Calculating Ratios

The next step in ratio analysis is to calculate the ratios. Below we have calculated each of the six ratios we have discussed, using data derived from the financial statements for the MoPower Robotics Company, for the year 1995.

Liquidity Ratios

$$\text{Current ratio} = \frac{\text{Current assets}}{\text{Current liabilities}} = \frac{850}{450} = 1.89$$

$$\text{Quick ratio} = \frac{\text{Current assets} - \text{Inventory}}{\text{Current liabilities}} = \frac{150}{450} = 0.33$$

Activity Ratios

$$\text{Inventory turnover} = \frac{\text{Sales}}{\text{Inventory}} = \frac{3,600}{700} = 5.14$$

$$\text{Total asset utilization} = \frac{\text{Sales}}{\text{Total assets}} = \frac{3{,}600}{3{,}500} = 1.03$$

Profitability Ratios

$$\text{Profit margin on sales} = \frac{\text{EBIT}}{\text{Sales}} = \frac{500}{3{,}600} = 0.14$$

$$\text{Return on investment} = \frac{\text{EAT}}{\text{Total assets}} = \frac{180}{3{,}500} = 0.05$$

Comparing Ratios

We cannot overemphasize the statement that no single ratio has meaning by itself. In other words, comparing ratios is critical for effective financial ratio analysis. Ratios can be compared across time for the same firm, compared with those of similar firms in the industry, or compared with industry averages. The following examples illustrate each of these different types of comparisons.

First, suppose that in 1994 MoPower had sales of $3,300,000, earnings before interest and taxes of $600,000, and earnings after taxes of $200,000. With this information, and the balance sheet information for December 31, 1994 (supplied in Table 11.1), we can compute the ratios for 1994 and then compare them with those for 1995 to investigate trends. Table 11.3 summarizes this comparison.

To compare an organization's ratios with those of similar firms in the industry or with industry averages, the analyst must look up the industry information. Sources of industry information include:[3]

1. *Annual Statement Studies.* Published by Robert Morris Associates, this work includes 16 financial ratios computed annually for over 150 lines of business. Each line of business is divided into four size categories.
2. Dun & Bradstreet provides 14 ratios calculated annually for over 100 lines of business.
3. *The Almanac of Business and Industrial Financial Ratios.* This work, published by Prentice-Hall, Inc., lists industry averages for 22 financial ratios. Approximately 170 businesses and industries are listed.
4. *The Quarterly Financial Report for Manufacturing Corporations.* This work, published jointly by the Federal Trade Commission and the Securities and Exchange Commission, contains balance-sheet and income-statement information by industry groupings and by asset-size categories.
5. Trade associations and individual companies often compute ratios for their industries and make them available to analysts.

Table 11.4 compares MoPower's 1995 ratios with those of firms of similar size in the industry and with the industry medians. (Financial sources often report the industry median rather than the mean to avoid the distorting effects of outliers, or values that lie far beyond the area where most tend to cluster.) Once the analyst has prepared comparative statements such as those shown in Table 11.3 and Table 11.4, it is time to interpret what all of the information means. This is the final step in ratio analysis.

TABLE 11.3

Comparison of Financial Ratios for MoPower Robotics Company, 1994 and 1995

	1994	1995
LIQUIDITY RATIOS		
Current ratio	2.22	1.89
Quick ratio	0.86	0.33
ACTIVITY RATIOS		
Inventory turnover	7.67	5.14
Total asset utilization	1.38	1.03
PROFITABILITY RATIOS		
Profit margin on sales	0.18	0.14
Return on investment	0.08	0.05

TABLE 11.4

Comparison of Financial Ratios for MoPower with Industry Figures

	MoPower Company	Industry Firms, Assets $1–10 Million	Industry Median
LIQUIDITY RATIOS			
Current ratio	1.88	1.80	1.80
Quick ratio	0.33	0.90	1.00
ACTIVITY RATIOS			
Inventory turnover	5.14	7.80	7.90
Total asset utilization	1.03	1.70	1.80
PROFITABILITY RATIOS			
Profit margin on sales	0.14	0.13	0.15
Return on investment	0.05	0.15	0.16

Checking for Problems and Opportunities

The comparisons between ratios shown in Tables 11.3 and 11.4 suggest that MoPower is not in a strong financial position and that its position has declined since the previous year. Although MoPower's liquidity was in good shape in 1994, its position in 1995 was not favorable. Particularly, given the quick ratio of 0.33, MoPower could be in serious trouble if its creditors were to demand quick payment. What appears to have happened is a large inventory buildup. This may mean that MoPower's products have been superseded in a market experiencing the effects of rapid technological change; they may not be selling well. Alternatively, MoPower may be building inventory for an expected increase in demand. In either case, its liquidity position needs to be improved.

The buildup in inventory is also reflected in the decrease in activity ratios. Inventory turnover and total asset utilization have slipped and are now well below industry averages. Perhaps MoPower has also accumulated some other unproductive or outdated assets that it should divest.

In terms of profitability, although profit margin on sales has decreased from 18 percent to 14 percent, it is still above the standard for firms of similar size in the industry. However, the company's return on investment is far below industry figures and has shrunk significantly. This could be a very important problem for MoPower, particularly if it is trying to attract new investors. However, much depends on other factors, such as whether MoPower is a new company that is expected to have a large increase in future earnings.

What should be clear from the foregoing analysis is that ratios offer a convenient way to investigate the financial well-being of an organization. Calculating various ratios and comparing them can alert analysts to areas that strategic managers should investigate more fully. However, financial ratios only indicate symptoms of problems; the real problems are the *reasons* for poor financial performance. To discover these underlying causes, carefully consider other information contained in a case or strategic management situation.

Finally, even when a firm's financial ratios appear to conform to industry averages, this does not mean that the firm has no financial or other strategic management problems. For example, perhaps the firm is neglecting to exploit a clear differential advantage by which it could far outstrip average industry performance. Alternatively, perhaps the firm's finances look good at the moment, but a serious competitive threat could wipe it out in the near future. In short, financial ratio analysis is a very useful tool for analyzing strategic management cases, but it cannot replace other types of analysis and careful consideration of the issues in the case.

BREAK-EVEN ANALYSIS

Break-even analysis is a simple method for investigating the potential value of a proposed investment. It is useful in the analysis of three important types of strategic management decisions:

1. In *new product decisions,* break-even analysis can help determine how much of a new product a firm must sell to achieve profitability.
2. Break-even analysis can be used as a broad framework for studying the effects of a general *expansion* in the level of a firm's operations.
3. When the firm is considering *modernization* and *automation* projects where it invests in more equipment in order to reduce variable costs, particularly the cost of labor, break-even analysis can help managers analyze the consequences of the action.[4]

The **break-even point** is the level of sales, stated in either units or dollars, at which a firm covers all costs of investing in a project. In other words, it is the level at which total sales revenue just equals the total costs necessary to achieve those sales.

In order to compute the break-even point, an analyst must obtain three values. First, the analyst needs to know the selling price per unit of the product (*SP*). For example, after extensive market analysis, MoPower Robotics Company plans to sell its new, multifunction industrial robot for $5,000.

Second, the analyst needs to know the level of fixed costs (*FC*). Fixed costs are all costs relevant to the project that do not change regardless of how many units are produced and sold. For example, whether MoPower produces and sells 1 robot or 10,000, MoPower must pay executives their salaries, purchase machinery, and construct a plant. Other fixed costs include interest payments, lease payments, and sinking fund payments. MoPower has tallied all of its fixed costs to produce the new robot and estimates the total to be $10 million.

Third, the analyst needs to know the variable costs per unit produced (VC). Variable costs, as the name implies, are those that vary directly with the number of units produced. For example, for each robot produced, MoPower must pay for electrical and mechanical components, labor to assemble the robot, and machine costs such as electricity. MoPower estimates that for each robot produced, the variable costs will be $3,000.

Armed with this information, the analyst can determine the break-even point by dividing total fixed costs by the contribution margin. The **contribution margin** is simply the difference between the selling price per unit and the variable costs per unit. Algebraically,

$$\text{Break-even point (in units)} = \frac{\text{Total fixed costs}}{\text{Contribution margin}}$$

$$= \frac{FC}{SP - VC}$$

Substituting the MoPower estimates:

$$\text{Break-even point (in units)} = \frac{10,000,000}{5,000 - 3,000}$$

$$= \frac{10,000,000}{2,000}$$

$$= 5,000 \text{ units}$$

In other words, MoPower must sell 5,000 robots in order to break even—to make its total sales equal its total costs. This is a very useful number. It informs the analyst that if sales projections at this price level are less than 5,000 units, the project may not be viable.

Alternatively, the analyst may want to know the break-even point in terms of total sales dollars rather than units. Of course, if the preceding analysis has been done, one can simply multiply the break-even point in units by the selling price: 5,000 units × $5,000 = $25 million. However, the break-even point in dollars can be computed directly with the following formula:

$$\text{Break-even point in dollars} = \frac{FC}{1 - \dfrac{VC}{SP}}$$

$$= \frac{10,000,000}{1 - \dfrac{3,000}{5,000}}$$

$$= \frac{10,000,000}{1 - 0.6}$$

$$= \$25 \text{ million}$$

Thus, MoPower must produce and sell 5,000 robots, which equals $25 million in sales, just to break even on this project. Of course, MoPower does not want to break even, but to make a profit. The logic of break-even analysis can easily be extended to include profits (P). For example, suppose that MoPower decides that a 20 percent return on fixed costs is the minimum that the project would have to generate to make it worth investing. MoPower would need 20 percent of $10 million, or $2 million in additional income to make the project worth the investment. To calculate how many units MoPower must sell to achieve this level of profits, add the profit figure to fixed costs in the foregoing formulas:

$$\text{Break-even plus profits} = \frac{FC + P}{SP - VC}$$

$$= \frac{10,000,000 + 2,000,000}{5,000 - 3,000}$$

$$= \frac{12,000,000}{2,000}$$

$$= 6,000 \text{ units}$$

In terms of the formula for sales dollars:

$$\text{Break-even plus profits} = \frac{FC + P}{1 - \dfrac{VC}{SP}}$$

$$= \frac{10,000,000 + 2,000,000}{1 - \dfrac{3,000}{5,000}}$$

$$= \frac{12,000,000}{1 - 0.6}$$

$$= \$30 \text{ million}$$

MoPower must produce and sell 6,000 robots, which equals $30 million in sales, to achieve its minimum acceptable profit level. This is a very useful figure to calculate, because it invites the analyst to consider the probability of obtaining this level of sales. For example, if the entire market were 10,000 units, is it likely that MoPower could obtain a 60 percent market share, given the competition? If so, the project would be worth investing. If not, MoPower should seek other opportunities or change its strategic plan. If the firm were to reduce the price of the robots, for example, sales increases might result in economies of scale and a profitable project.

Graphs can present a clear overall picture of break-even analysis. Figure 11.1 is a graph of our MoPower break-even example. Such a graph provides an easy-to-understand, visual representation of the various relationships among sales, fixed costs, and variable costs, and it illustrates levels of losses and profits under various conditions. The Skills Module offers you an opportunity to perform a break-even analysis.

Although break-even analysis is a useful tool, it does have limitations. For example, a whole series of break-even analyses are necessary if the analyst

FIGURE 11.1   Graphical Presentation of Break-Even Analysis

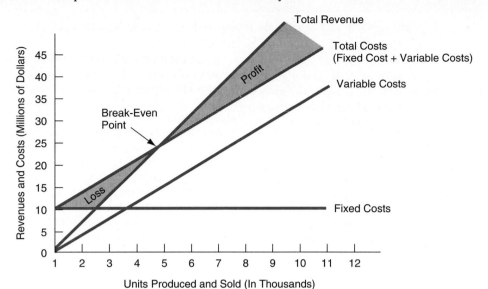

wishes to consider different price levels or different estimates of fixed or variable costs. Similarly, many costs are likely to change at different volume levels. For example, at higher volume levels, more employees may have to be hired and more machines may have to be purchased, which would change the various cost curves. Break-even analysis is useful (and in some cases, it is the only technique that can be applied), but more detailed analyses are often recommended for probing investment alternatives. One of these is net present value analysis.

NET PRESENT VALUE ANALYSIS

A detailed treatment of net present value analysis is beyond the scope of this text. Even so, we should review, in general terms, its use in strategic management analysis. **Net present value analysis** can be used to investigate the value of a proposed investment to an organization or to compare alternative investments to determine which is better from a financial point of view.

This analysis is based on the idea that money has a time value. For example, $10 today is worth more than $10 one year from today because it could be invested for the year. If the $10 were put in a money market account to earn 6 percent interest, it would be worth $10.60 a year from today. Thus, a financial analyst who is considering cash inflows and outflows that will occur in the future can use net present value analysis to discount them—that is, to reflect their value in today's dollars.

In order to calculate the net present value of an investment, the analyst needs several figures. First, the total initial cost of the investment must be determined. This includes all payments made today to begin the project. Second, the firm's cost of capital must be estimated. The cost of capital is often given in cases for which net present value analysis is appropriate. If not, one can estimate using methods suggested in financial management texts.[5] Third, the project's expected life must be determined. Fourth, the net cash flows

SKILLS MODULE

Break-Even Analysis at Sylvan Learning Systems

INTRODUCTION

We have discussed break-even analysis in some detail. Review the following situation and then complete the skill development exercise that follows to help you develop this important skill.

SITUATION

Although the partners who run Sylvan Learning Systems Inc. want to build the company into a huge enterprise, they have their work cut out for them. The Columbia, Maryland, company reported a loss of $363,833 last year on revenue of $18.1 million. Now, instead of cutting their losses, the partners are trying to avoid stagnation by branching out in a new direction.

Sylvan's main business is franchising tutoring centers where parents pay between $1,200 and $1,800 to boost their children's study skills. The company's success in that field has plateaued, however; with nearly 500 franchised units operating in the United States and Canada, there are limited desirable sites for additional franchisees.

The company is counting on two new areas to shore up its growth and improve its bottom line: computerized testing and remedial-skills contracts. The business of running remedial reading and math classes for students and employees in their schools or work sites has taken off in Baltimore. There, public school officials are using the program in eight schools under a $3.7 million program supported by federal funds targeted at disadvantaged students.

Computerized testing is the bigger growth arena. In many of its tutoring centers, Sylvan has installed electronic equipment to deliver computerized versions of standardized tests for graduate school admissions and professional licensing and certification exams. Sylvan's thrust into a new niche is having some success: its computerized tests are now mandatory for all candidates for licensing as practical nurses in the United States. The company says that it has contracts in the offing with the nonprofit Educational Testing Service to deliver computerized tests in the United States and more than 170 other countries within five years.

Sylvan recently announced that ETS had invested $1.5 million in newly issued Sylvan stock and taken options to invest another $4 million. Public investors are also high on Sylvan's strategy.

SKILL DEVELOPMENT EXERCISE

Assume that Sylvan's computerized tests have a variable cost of $15 each and that total fixed costs for its computerized testing contracts amount to $8 million. If Sylvan and its franchisees mark up the testing fee 50 percent, what is the break-even point for the test? How many computerized tests or contracts would Sylvan have to sell to make a profit of $1 million.

SOURCE: Jeffrey A. Tannenbaum, "Sylvan Learning, to Avoid Stagnation, Acts to Diversify," *The Wall Street Journal*, April 26, 1994, p. B2.

---

from the project must be estimated. **Net cash flows** are the net amounts (cash inflows minus cash outflows) that the firm receives from the project each year; they include earnings after taxes (net income) and depreciation.

The basic equation for calculating net present value is:

$$NPV = \frac{NCF_1}{(1 + k)^1} + \frac{NCF_2}{(1 + k)^2} + \ldots + \frac{NCF_n}{(1 + k)^n} - I$$

where

NPV = net present value
NCF = net cash flows each year of the project's life
I = total initial investment
k = cost of capital

This equation states that the net present value of an investment is equal to the net cash flows discounted at the cost of capital, minus the initial investment outlay. For example, suppose that MoPower is deciding whether to get into the market for home robots and has gathered the following financial information for the project:

Initial investment in equipment	$1,500,000
Useful life of equipment	10 years
Depreciation	10 percent per year
Salvage value	$200,000
Net income per year	$150,000
Cost of capital	10 percent

Because financial management texts include net present value tables, actually solving for the net present value is much easier than working through the formula. Table 11.5 presents the net cash flows—net income ($150,000 per year) plus depreciation ($150,000 per year) equals $300,000 and an additional $200,000 in year ten for salvage value, the appropriate discount factors for a cost of capital of 10 percent, and the present value of these cash flows. The present value of the net cash flows is $1,920,450; subtracting the initial investment of $1,500,000 results in a net present value of $420,450. The net present value is positive, so MoPower should invest in entering the home robot market.

Because the net cash flows for the first nine years are the same, it would be much easier to calculate the present value by treating these nine years as an annuity and multiplying by the total of the discount factors for nine years—that is, $300,000 \times 5.7590 = $1,727,700$. Adding the figure for the tenth year ($500,000 \times 0.3855 = $192,750$) to this amount makes it easier to obtain the present value of $1,920,450.

Net present value analysis is a useful method for examining investment alternatives. Employing it requires some background in financial management,

TABLE 11.5

Present Value Calculations for the MoPower Robotics Company

Year	Net Cash Flow	10% Discount Factor	Present Value
1	$300,000	0.9091	$ 272,730
2	300,000	0.8264	247,920
3	300,000	0.7513	225,390
4	300,000	0.6830	204,900
5	300,000	0.6209	186,270
6	300,000	0.5645	169,350
7	300,000	0.5132	153,960
8	300,000	0.4665	139,950
9	300,000	0.4241	127,230
10	500,000	0.3855	192,750
			$1,920,450

TABLE 11.6

Selected Present Value Discount Factors

Year	8%	10%	12%	14%	16%	18%
1	0.9259	0.9091	0.8929	0.8772	0.8621	0.8475
2	0.8573	0.8264	0.7972	0.7695	0.7432	0.7182
3	0.7938	0.7513	0.7118	0.6750	0.6407	0.6086
4	0.7350	0.6830	0.6355	0.5921	0.5523	0.5158
5	0.6806	0.6209	0.5674	0.5194	0.4761	0.4371
6	0.6302	0.5645	0.5066	0.4556	0.4104	0.3704
7	0.5835	0.5132	0.4523	0.3996	0.3538	0.3139
8	0.5403	0.4665	0.4039	0.3506	0.3050	0.2660
9	0.5002	0.4241	0.3606	0.3075	0.2630	0.2255
10	0.4632	0.3855	0.3220	0.2697	0.2267	0.1911

but net present value analysis should be applied to strategic management cases when the required information is available or can be estimated. Table 11.6 presents some commonly used present value discount factors; again, complete tables can be found in most financial management texts.

SUMMARY

This chapter investigated three financial tools that are useful for strategic management. We discussed ratio analysis and examined three types of financial ratios: liquidity, activity, and profitability ratios. We suggested that these types of ratios should be applied routinely to strategic management situations that include balance sheet and income statement information. We then discussed break-even analysis as a method for investigating the potential value of an investment to an organization. It enables the firm to determine at what level of sales the total revenue generated by a product just equals the costs incurred to achieve those sales. It can be extended to include desired profit levels. Finally, we presented net present value analysis as a sophisticated but useful method for analyzing investment alternatives. It enables the firm to determine the value in today's dollars of cash flows that will occur in the future.

KEY TERMS

financial ratio analysis, p. 266
balance sheet, p. 266
comparative balance sheet, p. 266
current assets, p. 266
fixed assets, p. 266
current liabilities, p. 266
income statement, p. 266
current ratio, p. 268
quick ratio, p. 268

inventory turnover, p. 269
total asset utilization, p. 269
profit margin on sales, p. 269
return on investment, p. 269
break-even analysis, p. 272
break-even point, p. 272
contribution margin, p. 273
net present value analysis, p. 275
net cash flows, p. 276

CHECKLIST

Analyzing Finances in Problems and Cases

___ 1. Does the problem or case include financial statements to provide information for ratio analysis?

___ 2. Would ratio analysis contribute to a better understanding of the firm and its problems?

___ 3. What is the financial condition of the company? That is, how does it compare with other firms in the industry in terms of such measures as liquidity, activity, and profitability ratios? What are the implications for alternatives that would solve the firm's problems?

___ 4. Does the problem or case include the information needed to perform a break-even analysis?

___ 5. Would a break-even analysis help to evaluate a proposed project for the company?

___ 6. Given a break-even point, is the firm likely to be able to sell enough units to reach that point and be profitable?

___ 7. Does the problem or case include information for a net present value analysis?

___ 8. Would a net present value analysis contribute to an analysis of the firm's investment opportunities?

___ 9. Given a positive net present value, is there any reason why the firm should not invest in the project?

___ 10. If the analyst lacks enough information to perform a break-even or net present value analysis, could such analyses be performed based on a few reasonable assumptions? For example, could one assume a cost of capital in order to perform the analysis?

Additional Readings

Brealey, Richard A., and Stewart C. Myers. *Principles of Corporate Finance*, 4th ed. New York: McGraw-Hill, 1991.

Brigham, Eugene F., and Louis C. Gapenski. *Financial Management: Theory and Practice*, 7th ed. Fort Worth, Dryden Press, 1994.

Dickerson, Bodil, B. J. Campsey, and Eugene F. Brigham. *Introduction to Financial Management*, 4th ed. Fort Worth, Dryden Press, 1995.

Rappaport, Alfred. "CFOs and Strategists: Forging a Common Framework." *Harvard Business Review*, May/June 1992, p. 84.

CASE

Financial Analysis for Polaroid Corporation

The Polaroid Corporation designs, manufactures, and markets a variety of products primarily in instant image-recording fields. These include instant cameras and films, magnetic media, light-polarizing filters and lenses, and diversified chemical, optical, and commercial products. The principal products of the company are used in amateur and professional photography, industry, science, medicine, and education. Selected financial data for 1985 include the following (in millions):

Current assets	$1,035.7	Sales	$1,295.2
Inventory	335.0	EBIT	62.5
Total assets	1,384.7	EAT	36.9
Current liabilities	337.9		

Some of Polaroid's major products are cameras that focus and control exposure automatically. These cameras use advanced computerlike circuitry to make more than 30 complex focusing and exposure decisions within fifty-thousandths of a second. The cameras, film, accessories, and services involved are collectively called the Spectra System. This system was Polaroid's major product innovation for 1986.

DISCUSSION QUESTIONS

1. Calculate the current ratio, quick ratio, inventory turnover, total asset utilization, profit margin on sales, and return on investment for Polaroid for 1985.

2. Compare Polaroid's ratios with the following industry averages. What conclusions about Polaroid's financial condition do these comparisons suggest?

Current ratio	2.2	Total asset utilization	1.1
Quick ratio	1.0	Profit margin on sales	0.067
Inventory turnover	4.3	Return on investment	0.039

3. Suppose Polaroid were considering the development of an even more technologically advanced camera system. Say the total investment required was to be $2.5 million, and net cash flows were expected to be $750,000 for the first year, $1,500,000 for the second year, and $2,000,000 for the third year. Because the technology would be superseded after the third year, the project would end then and there would be no salvage value. If Polaroid's cost of capital were 12 percent, what would be the net present value of this investment?

SOURCE: Based on *1985 Polaroid Corporation Annual Report.*

Notes

1. This chapter is based in part on J. Paul Peter and James H. Donnelly, Jr., *Marketing Management: Knowledge and Skills,* 4th ed. (Burr Ridge, Ill.: Irwin, 1995), Section 3.

2. For cases that require detailed ratio analyses of issues such as leverage, growth, and evaluation, consult J. Fred Weston and Eugene F. Brigham, *Essentials of Managerial Finance,* 10th ed. (Fort Worth: Dryden Press, 1993), pp. 48–64.

3. This list is from James C. Van Horne, *Financial Management and Policy,* 7th ed. © 1986, pp. 767–768. Reprinted by permission of Prentice-Hall, Inc., Englewood Cliffs, New Jersey.

4. Based on Weston and Brigham, *Essentials of Managerial Finance,* p. 330.

5. Ibid., Chapter 15.

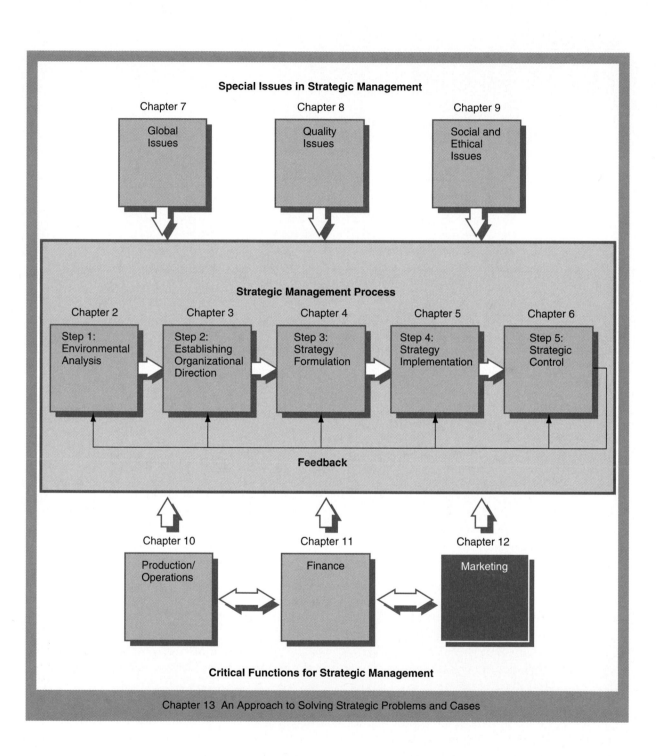

Special Issues in Strategic Management

Chapter 7

Global Issues

Chapter 8

Quality Issues

Chapter 9

Social and Ethical Issues

Strategic Management Process

Chapter 2

Step 1: Environmental Analysis

Chapter 3

Step 2: Establishing Organizational Direction

Chapter 4

Step 3: Strategy Formulation

Chapter 5

Step 4: Strategy Implementation

Chapter 6

Step 5: Strategic Control

Feedback

Chapter 10

Production/ Operations

Chapter 11

Finance

Chapter 12

Marketing

Critical Functions for Strategic Management

Chapter 13 An Approach to Solving Strategic Problems and Cases

C H A P T E R

12

The Marketing Function and Strategic Management

The marketing function facilitates exchanges between an organization and either industrial buyers or end users.[1] It is obviously an important function; profit-seeking organizations must develop and retain customers in order to generate sales and profits.[2] Nonprofit organizations also develop marketing strategies to attract donations of time, money, and other resources in order to maintain their operations and achieve their objectives.

Many of the strategic management issues that we have discussed in this text contribute to the creation of successful strategies for the marketing function, or marketing strategies. Environmental analysis is a critical aspect of marketing strategy development, because changes in an organization's environment can lead to both marketing opportunities and constraints on successful marketing. In particular, changes in the marketing strategies of competitors very directly affect the marketing opportunities available to an organization.

An organization's mission and objective statements provide a framework and guidance for designing marketing objectives and strategies. For example, if a firm adopts an organizational objective of increasing net profits by 15 percent per year, this goal has important implications for its efforts to develop new products and market existing products.

Finally, the development of marketing strategies involves strategic management functions such as planning, analysis, implementation, and control. Although there is no clear distinction between some aspects of strategic management and marketing strategy, marketing strategy focuses primarily on knowing, adapting to, and influencing consumers in an effort to achieve organizational objectives. Marketing strategies are usually designed to increase sales and market share in order to increase long-run profits.

In this chapter, we investigate the process of developing successful marketing strategies. We focus on those issues that are most commonly considered marketing tasks and avoid many of the more general strategic management issues discussed previously in the text. Figure 12.1 provides an overview of this process and outlines the contents of the chapter. We begin by discussing the analysis of consumer/product relationships, a critical aspect of the development of marketing strategy. Next we consider the different ways in which it is possible to segment a market, or divide it into groups of similar consumers. We then investigate the process of designing a marketing mix strategy. Finally, we examine the implementation and control of the firm's marketing strategy.

FIGURE 12.1   Strategic Marketing Process

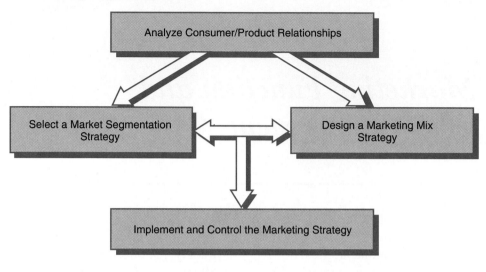

ANALYZING CONSUMER/PRODUCT RELATIONSHIPS

The first step in preparing a marketing strategy is to analyze consumer/product relationships. This analysis entails investigating why consumers buy a particular product, what the product means to them, what consequences they expect from using the product, how much they become involved in purchasing the product, and in what situations they purchase and use the product. Test marketing and primary market research may help answer these questions, and one can often gain considerable insight by investigating secondary sources of information and studying general buying habits.

In performing this analysis, it is useful first to classify products as either consumer or industrial products. **Consumer products** are those that are purchased by the final user, whereas **industrial products** are purchased to aid in the production of other products or services. Each of these types of products can be divided into the categories shown in Table 12.1. Consumer goods are commonly classified as convenience, shopping, or specialty goods on the basis of the degree of involvement consumers have with the product and how much time and effort they invest in purchasing it. Industrial goods are divided into five basic categories based on their roles in the production process. Table 12.1 also suggests some of the basic characteristics of these products and some considerations to take into account when marketing them. Simply classifying a product in this way provides some useful direction for developing marketing strategy.

Classifying products is a useful starting point in analyzing consumer/product relationships, but researching and studying the consumers of the product are critical. Consider a simple product such as toothpaste. What are some reasons why consumers buy this product? It seems clear that different consumers seek different benefits from the product. Decay prevention, fresh breath, sex appeal, whiter teeth, and plaque removal may have varying levels of importance to various consumers. Similarly, performance, economy, status, and styling vary in importance across groups of car buyers. Analysis of

TABLE 12.1

Categories of Products and Marketing Strategy Considerations

Characteristics and Marketing Considerations	Type of Product		
	A. Consumer Products		
	Convenience	Shopping	Specialty
CHARACTERISTICS:			
1. Time and effort devoted by consumer to shopping	Very little	Considerable	Cannot generalize; consumer may go to nearby store and buy with minimum effort or may have to go to distant store and spend much time and effort
2. Time spent planning the purchase	Very little	Considerable	Considerable
3. How soon want is satisfied after it arises	Immediately	Relatively long time	Relatively long time
4. Are price and quality compared?	No	Yes	No
5. Price	Low	High	High
6. Frequency of purchase	Usually frequent	Infrequent	Infrequent
7. Importance	Unimportant	Often very important	Cannot generalize
MARKETING CONSIDERATIONS:			
1. Length of channel	Long	Short	Short to very short
2. Importance of retailer	Any single store is relatively unimportant	Important	Very important
3. Number of outlets	As many as possible	Few	Few; often only one in a market
4. Stock turnover	High	Lower	Lower
5. Gross margin	Low	High	High
6. Responsibility for advertising	Manufacturer's	Retailer's	Joint responsibility
7. Importance of point-of-purchase display	Very important	Less important	Less important
8. Advertising used	Manufacturer's	Retailer's	Both
9. Brand or store name important	Brand name	Store name	Both
10. Importance of packaging	Very important	Less important	Less important

Continued

TABLE 12.1
Continued

B. Industrial Products

Characteristics and Marketing Considerations	Type of Product				
	Raw Materials	Fabricating Parts and Materials	Installations	Accessory Equipment	Operating Supplies
Example	Iron ore	Engine blocks	Blast furnaces	Storage racks	Paper clips
CHARACTERISTICS:					
1. Unit price	Very low	Low	Very high	Medium	Low
2. Length of life	Very short	Depends on final product	Very long	Long	Short
3. Quantities purchased	Large	Large	Very small	Small	Small
4. Frequency of purchase	Frequent delivery; long-term purchase contract	Infrequent purchase, but frequent delivery	Very infrequent	Medium frequency	Frequent
5. Standardization of competitive products	Very much; grading is important	Very much	Very little; custom-made	Little	Much
6. Limits on supply	Limited; supply can be increased slowly or not at all	Usually no problem	No problem	Usually no problem	Usually no problem
MARKETING CONSIDERATIONS:					
1. Nature of channel	Short; no intermediaries	Short; intermediaries only for small buyers	Short; no intermediaries	Intermediaries used	Intermediaries used
2. Negotiation period	Hard to generalize	Medium	Long	Medium	Short
3. Price competition	Important	Important	Not important	Not main factor	Important
4. Presale/postsale service	Not important	Important	Very important	Important	Very little
5. Demand stimulation	Very little	Moderate	Sales people very important	Important	Not too important
6. Brand preference	None	Generally low	High	High	Low
7. Advance buying contract	Important; long-term contracts	Important; long-term contracts	Not usually	Not usually	Not usually

SOURCE: Based on William J. Stanton, Michael J. Etzel, and Bruce J. Walker, *Fundamentals of Marketing*, 9th ed. (New York: McGraw Hill, 1991), pp. 171, 174.

SKILLS MODULE
MCI Dials Marketing Success

INTRODUCTION

Analysis of consumer/product relationships is an important starting point for developing sound marketing strategies. Review the following situation and then complete the skill development exercise to help you develop this important skill.

SITUATION

Early in 1993, MCI Communications decided to explore the untapped potential of the collect-call market. The company recognized that AT&T had all but cornered the $3-billion-a-year market by signing long-term contracts with stores, airports, and hotels with pay phones. The industry leader also benefited from its dialing formula—a simple 0 for operator and the number the caller wanted to contact.

MCI's perceptive marketing strategy to win some of the collect-call business took 11 weeks from conception to implementation. It was based on market research results that collect-calling costs were high because more than half such calls came from pay phones under long-term contracts with AT&T or other carriers. A ten-minute phone call could cost twice as much as a direct-dial call, ranging from $4.00 to $6.25, depending on where and when the call was made.

MCI research cast doubt on the assumption that the caller didn't care about the cost because the other person was paying for it. The company found that of the 300 million collect calls placed annually, 24 percent were from military personnel calling home, 33 percent were from children calling home, and 70 percent of the callers were under 30. Those findings suggested that families might encourage relatives to use a discount plan.

MCI Chairman Bert C. Roberts, Jr., approved the idea the day it was presented. The next job for MCI's marketing staff, and the most vital one, was to find an easy alternative to dialing 0 and the number. They came up with a number that is easy to recall and bypasses carriers that have contracts with pay-phone owners—1–800–COLLECT.

In addition, MCI set rates at up to 44 percent off AT&T's operator-assisted rates. Ads targeted young audiences—biplanes pulling 1–800–COLLECT banners flew over beaches and TV ads starred familiar faces from late-night television.

But the masterstroke was MCI's decision not to mention its name, so that the potential users of the service wouldn't think that only MCI subscribers could use it. The anonymity of 1–800–COLLECT bled calls from AT&T, whose research showed that half of those calling the MCI number had assumed it was run by AT&T. After the phone giant set up its own 1–800–OPERATOR number in an attempt to counter MCI's surge, it discovered that many callers needed spelling lessons; they were misdialing and punching in 1–800–OPERATER. That number was an MCI toll-free number, part of MCI's shrewd comeback in the face of AT&T's retaliatory strike. As a result, MCI handled a few hundred thousand dollars in mistaken calls. By March 1994, AT&T had started over with 1–800–CALL–ATT.

In 1993, AT&T held 75 percent of the collect-call market, MCI had 11 percent, and Sprint had 5 percent. MCI says that 18 million U.S. homes received at least one collect call through the 1–800–COLLECT program in its first year, up from 4.5 million collect calls in the prior year.

SKILL DEVELOPMENT EXERCISE

MCI was clearly successful in introducing its collect-calling campaign. 1–800–COLLECT was the result of consumer research that upended conventional wisdom about who made collect calls. Explain how you would analyze the consumer/product (or in this case, consumer/service) relationships for collect-calling services. Devise a marketing strategy for AT&T detailing where and how the company should direct its marketing efforts; include a synopsis of MCI's probable strategic response.

SOURCE: Mark Lewyn, "MCI Collects on 1-800 C-O-L-L-E-C-T," *Business Week*, June 13, 1994, p. 78.

consumer/product relationships may yield some initial idea of the appropriate market segments an organization should seek to satisfy with its products.

The Skills Module invites you to try your hand at analyzing consumer/product relationships.

SELECTING A MARKET SEGMENTATION STRATEGY

The logic of market segmentation is quite simple: it is based on the idea that a single product does not usually appeal to all consumers. Individual consumers' purchasing goals, product knowledge, involvement, and purchase behavior vary. For this reason, marketing strategists typically focus their marketing efforts on specific groups of consumers rather than on the whole population. **Market segmentation** is the process of dividing a market into groups of similar consumers and selecting the most appropriate group(s) for the organization to serve. Markets are selected on the basis of size, profit potential, and how well they can be defined and served by the organization.

Markets can be segmented on a variety of dimensions, or bases. Table 12.2 lists some of the more common dimensions for segmenting consumer and industrial markets. Often a number of these dimensions are used together to segment markets and develop profiles of the consumers in them. Typically, considerable market research is done to define particular markets very carefully. We will briefly describe four market segmentation techniques; geographic, demographic, psychographic, and benefit segmentation.

Geographic Segmentation

For many products, **geographic segmentation** offers a useful basis for initially defining markets. For example, the markets for such products as snowmobiles, ice fishing equipment, engine block heaters, and snow skiing equipment are concentrated in northern areas. Fast-food restaurants such as McDonald's and Burger King use information on population size and density to help them select restaurant locations. Because geographic data are available from public sources, collecting such information is an inexpensive way to explore market potential.

Demographic Segmentation

Demographic segmentation uses population characteristics to segment markets. Many products are designed for groups defined on the basis of sex (clothes, cosmetics), age (toys), or income (automobiles). Demographic variables are also used in conjunction with other segmentation techniques to describe particular markets more thoroughly. For example, a major market for light beer consists of men in their thirties who are eager to stay healthy and trim. In this market profile, both sex and age are demographic variables, and concerns about health and weight are psychographic variables.

Psychographic Segmentation

Psychographic segmentation, also called *lifestyle segmentation,* involves the study of consumers' activities (such as work, hobbies, and vacations), interests (such as family, job, and community), and opinions (about such things as politics, social issues, and business). Consumers are grouped together by empirical analysis of the similarity of their responses to research instruments into various lifestyle groups. A well-known psychographic segmentation system was developed at SRI International in California. This system, called VALS™ for "values and lifestyles," divided consumers in the United States into nine groups. However, while this segmentation system was commercially successful, it tended to place the majority of consumers into only one or two groups and

TABLE 12.2

Useful Segmentation Bases for Consumer and Industrial Markets

Consumer Markets	
Segmentation Base	**Base Categories**

GEOGRAPHIC SEGMENTATION

Region	Pacific, Mountain, West North Central, West South Central, East North Central, East South Central, South Atlantic, Middle Atlantic, New England
City, county, or SMSA size	Under 5,000, 5,000–19,999, 20,000–49,999, 50,000–99,999, 100,000–249,999, 250,000–499,999, 500,000–999,999, 1,000,000–3,999,999, 4,000,000 or over
Population density	Urban, suburban, rural
Climate	Warm, cold

DEMOGRAPHIC SEGMENTATION

Age	Under 6, 6–12, 13–19, 20–29, 30–39, 40–49, 50–59, 60+
Sex	Male, female
Family size	1–2, 3–4, 5+
Family life cycle	Young, single; young, married, no children; young, married, youngest child under 6; young, married, youngest child 6 or over; older, married, with children; older, married, no children under 18; older, single; other
Income	Under $5,000, $5,000–$7,999, $8,000–$9,999, $10,000– $14,999, $15,000–$24,999, $25,000–$34,999, $35,000 or over
Occupation	Professional and technical; managers, officials, and proprietors; clerical, sales; trades, supervisor, operatives; farmers; retired; students; housewives; unemployed
Education	Grade school or less, some high school, graduated high school, some college, graduated college, some graduate work, graduate degree
Religion	Catholic, Protestant, Jewish, other
Race	White, black, oriental, other
Nationality	American, British, French, German, Italian, Japanese, and so on

Continued

TABLE 12.2

Continued

Consumer Markets	
Segmentation Base	**Base Categories**

PSYCHOGRAPHIC SEGMENTATION

Social class	Lower-lower, upper-lower, lower-middle, upper-middle, lower-upper, upper-upper
Lifestyle	Traditionalist, sophisticate, swinger
Personality	Compliant, aggressive, detached

COGNITIVE AND BEHAVIORAL SEGMENTATION

Attitudes	Positive, neutral, negative
Benefits sought	Convenience, economy, prestige
Readiness stage	Unaware, aware, informed, interested, desirous . . . intention to purchase
Perceived risk	High, moderate, low
Innovativeness	Innovator, early adopter, early majority, late majority, laggard
Involvement	Low, high
Loyalty status	None, some, total
Usage rate	None, light, medium, heavy
User status	Nonuser, ex-user, potential user, current user

Industrial Markets	
Segmentation Base	**Base Categories**

Source loyalty	Purchase from one, two, three, four, or more suppliers
Size of company	Small, medium, large relative to industry
Average size of purchase	Small, medium, large
Usage rate	Light, medium, heavy
Product application	Maintenance, production, final product component, administration
Type of business	Manufacturer, wholesaler, retailer; SIC categories
Location	North, East, South, West; sales territories
Purchase status	New customer, occasional purchaser, frequent purchaser, nonpurchaser
Attribute importance	Reliability of supply, price, service, durability, convenience, reputation of supplier

SRI felt a need to update it to reflect changes in society. Thus, SRI developed a new typology called VALS 2™.[3]

VALS 2 is based on two national surveys of 2,500 consumers who responded to 43 lifestyle questions. The first survey developed the segmentation system, and the second validated it and linked it to buying and media behavior. The

FIGURE 12.2   Eight American Lifestyles in VALS 2™

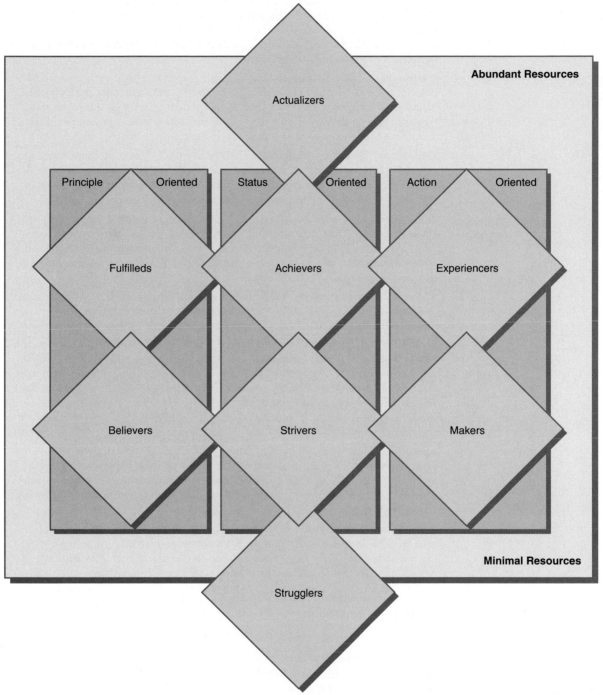

Continued

questionnaire asked consumers to agree or disagree with statements such as "My idea of fun at a national park would be to stay at an expensive lodge and dress up for dinner" and "I could stand to skin a dead animal." Consumers were then clustered into the eight groups shown and described in Figure 12.2.

FIGURE 12.2 *Continued*

Actualizers. These consumers have the highest incomes and such high self-esteem and abundant resources that they can indulge in any or all self-orientations. They are located above the rectangle. Image is important to them as an expression of their taste, independence, and character. Their consumer choices are directed toward the finer things in life.

Fulfilleds. These consumers are the high resource group of those who are principle-oriented. They are mature, responsible, well-educated professionals. Their leisure activities center on their homes, but they are well-informed about what goes on in the world and they are open to new ideas and social change. They have high incomes but are practical consumers.

Believers. These consumers are the low resource group of those who are principle-oriented. They are conservative and predictable consumers who favor American products and established brands. Their lives are centered on family, church, community, and the nation. They have modest incomes.

Achievers. These consumers are the high-resource group of those who are status-oriented. They are successful, work-oriented people who get their satisfaction from their jobs and families. They are politically conservative and respect authority and the status quo. They favor established products and services that show off their success to their peers.

Strivers. These consumers are the low-resource group of those who are status-oriented. They have values very similar to Achievers but have fewer economic, social, and psychological resources. Style is extremely important to them as they strive to emulate people they admire and wish to be like.

Experiencers. These consumers are the high-resource group of those who are action-oriented. They are the youngest of all the segments with a median age of 25. They have a lot of energy, which they pour into physical exercise and social activities. They are avid consumers, spending heavily on clothing, fast foods, music, and other youthful favorites—with particular emphasis on new products and services.

Makers. These consumers are the low-resource group of those who are action-oriented. They are practical people who value self-sufficiency. They are focused on the familiar—family, work, and physical recreation—and have little interest in the broader world. As consumers, they appreciate practical and functional products.

Strugglers. These consumers have the lowest incomes. They have too few resources to be included in any consumer self-orientation and are thus located below the rectangle. They are the oldest of all the segments with a median age of 61. Within their limited means, they tend to be brand-loyal consumers.

SOURCE: Martha Farnsworth Riche, "Psychographics for the 1990s," *American Demographics,* July 1989, pp. 24–26.

The VALS 2 groups are arranged in a rectangle measured on two dimensions. The vertical dimension represents resources, which include income, education, self-confidence, health, eagerness to buy, intelligence, and energy level. The horizontal dimension represents self-orientations and includes three different types. **Principle-oriented consumers** are guided by their views of how the world is or should be; **status-oriented consumers** are guided by the actions and opinions of others; **action-oriented consumers** are guided by a desire for social or physical activity, variety, and risk taking.

Each of the VALS 2 groups represents from 9 to 17 percent of the United States adult population. Marketers can buy VALS 2 information for a variety of products and can have it tied to a number of other consumer databases.

Benefit Segmentation

Underlying **benefit segmentation** is the concept that the benefits that people seek in consuming a given product are the real reasons for the existence of market segments. This approach attempts to measure consumer value systems and perceptions of various brands in a product class. The classic example of benefit segmentation is drawn from the toothpaste market.[4] As shown in Table 12.3, four basic segments were identified: the Sensory, Sociable, Worrier, and Independent segments.

The segments shown in Table 12.3 have important implications for many aspects of marketing strategy, including the selection of advertising copy and media, length of commercials, packaging, and new product design. For example, colorful packages might be appropriate for the Sensory segment, aqua packages (to indicate fluoride) for the Worrier group, and gleaming white packages for the Sociable segment because of their interest in white teeth. Benefit segmentation is a useful approach for investigating the meaning and value of products and brands to consumers.

Table 12.4 lists several questions that can help in analyzing consumer/product relationships and segmenting markets.

TABLE 12.3

Benefit Segmentation in the Toothpaste Market

	Sensory Segment	Sociable Segment	Worrier Segment	Independent Segment
Principal benefit sought	Flavor and product appearances	Brightness of teeth	Decay prevention	Price
Demographic strengths	Children	Teens, young people	Large families	Men
Special behavioral characteristics	Users of spearmint-flavored toothpaste	Smokers	Heavy users	Heavy users
Brands disproportionately favored	Colgate	Macleans, Ultra Brite	Crest	Cheapest brand
Lifestyle characteristics	Hedonistic	Active	Conservative	Value-oriented

SOURCE: Based on Russell I. Haley, "Benefit Segmentation: A Decision-Oriented Research Tool," *Journal of Marketing*, July 1968, pp. 30–33. From J. Paul Peter and James H. Donnelly, Jr., *Marketing Management: Knowledge and Skills*, 4th ed. (Burr Ridge, Ill.: Irwin, 1995), p. 84. Reprinted by permission.

TABLE 12.4

Some Questions to Ask When Analyzing Consumer/Product Relationships and Segmenting Markets

1. Why do consumers purchase this product?
2. What does this product mean to consumers, and how important to them is its purchase?
3. What does the product do for consumers in a functional, organizational, or social sense?
4. In what situations is the product purchased and used?
5. What are the appropriate dimensions for segmenting the market for this product?
6. Is market segmentation research necessary? If so, what are its costs and benefits?
7. Is this market segment large enough for the firm to serve profitably?
8. Can this market segment be reached efficiently, given the organization's resources?
9. Is competition too strong for the organization to attract consumers in this target market?
10. What are the implications of this analysis for marketing strategy?

DESIGNING A MARKETING MIX STRATEGY

The **marketing mix** consists of product, price, promotion, and channels of distribution (or place). These four elements are the controllable variables that organizations use to adapt to or influence market segments that they target. Organizations must develop strategies to synchronize all four of these elements so they work together to achieve the same objectives. We will discuss each of these elements in some detail, since they are the primary techniques that organizations use to obtain sales, profits, and market share.

Product Strategy

The survival of many organizations depends on developing and marketing successful new products and managing them throughout the product life cycle. In this section, we explain the process of developing and marketing new products in terms of a seven-stage **product life cycle.** This life cycle includes both stages that precede and stages that follow introduction of the product to the market. We then discuss several product characteristics that influence the success of new or existing products.

Stages in a Product's Life   The life of a successful product can be divided into seven stages, as shown in Figure 12.3. The stages from concept generation and screening to commercialization/introduction represent the process of new product development; the stages from commercialization/introduction to market decline/product deletion represent the phases of the traditional product life cycle. We will briefly describe each of these seven stages.

Concept Generation and Screening   New products start as ideas or concepts. Thus the first step in new product development involves generating concepts and screening out those that have little potential. New product concepts can come from a variety of sources, including consumers, competi-

FIGURE 12.3
Stages in a Product's
Life Cycle

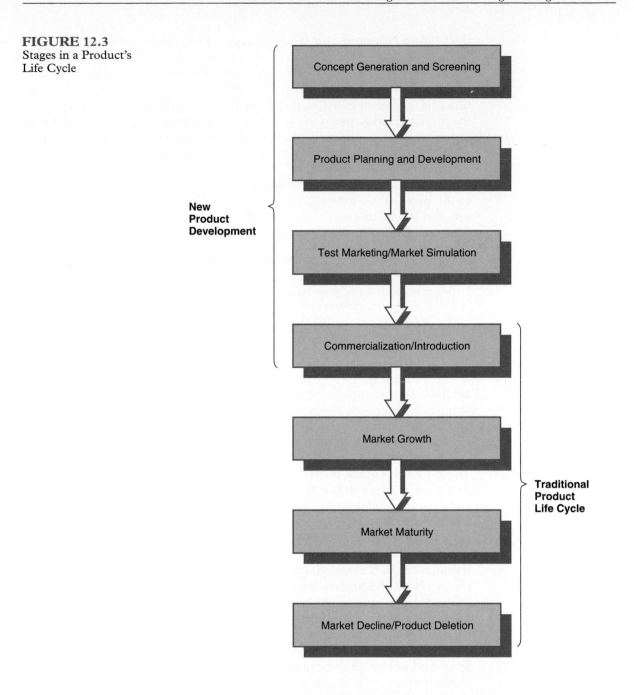

tors, salespeople, and the firm's own research and development department. Typically, the industry a firm is in determines the types of products it seeks to develop for consumers.

Some evidence suggests that firms are becoming more efficient at concept generation and screening. Research on 13,000 new product introductions has revealed that in 1968 it took an average of 58 ideas to generate one product. In 1981, however, it took only 7 ideas to generate a product. This is partly because firms are spending more money in the earlier phases of product development, up from 10 percent to 21 percent of their total new-product dollars.[5]

Product Planning and Development   This stage involves further evaluation, planning, and development of product concepts that have passed the initial screening. These concepts are formalized into a product plan that includes cross-functional collaboration and analysis of production, marketing, financial, and competitive factors, as well as the results of prototype testing. If the product plan supports the feasibility of producing the product and results in favorable sales and profit estimates, then it is time to investigate consumer reactions to the product. This is commonly done through test marketing or market simulation.

Test Marketing/Market Simulation   In this stage, consumer reactions to the product are investigated. Traditionally, products have been test marketed in particular cities to determine their sales potential. However, as one analyst explains, there are a number of problems with test marketing:

> While a test market . . . sounds realistic, in fact almost everything can go wrong to mess up the findings. Competitors can distort the results of a test by slashing prices in the test city, promoting their brand[s] heavily, or even buying up all the items put out for the test sale, which is what happened some years ago when General Foods tried to test frozen baby food. Gerber, Libby, and Heinz bought it all. And though tests may not always be realistic, they're always expensive. They can cost up to $1.5 million.[6]

For these reasons, some firms have purchased or developed simulated market tests. Such a test is based on a small sample of the public. Members of this sample are shown ads and promotions for a variety of products, including the one being tested. The shoppers are then taken to a mock-up store or a real store where their purchases are recorded. The behavior of shoppers and their willingness to rebuy the item are then analyzed via computerized models. These models consist of sets of equations designed to simulate the market. This service ranges in cost from about $35,000 to $75,000 and can be run in eight weeks without giving competitors a look at the product. Some of these models have been credited with making very accurate predictions of product successes and failures, but their overall accuracy is sometimes disputed.

Commercialization/Introduction   If test market results and other determinations of business planning are favorable, the product is introduced to the market. This is the last stage of the new product development process and the first stage of the traditional product life cycle. The main objectives at this stage are to make consumers aware of the product and to get them to try it. Figure 12.4 shows a typical sales curve generated as a product passes through the traditional product life cycle. The tabular portion of this figure shows how several other characteristics and strategies change as the product ages.

Many estimates of the percentage of new products that fail after introduction have been offered; they range from 33 to 90 percent. However, an extensive review of this question found that about 30 to 35 percent of new consumer products fail to meet the expectations of their developers.[7]

Market Growth   In this stage, sales of the product begin to increase rapidly and the product may become profitable. The market may expand because of increased repurchases by original buyers and a large set of new buyers who have been influenced by them. As shown in Figure 12.4, a major objective at this point is to establish a strong position with distributors and users of the product.

FIGURE 12.4

Elements of Marketing
Strategy in the Product
Life Cycle

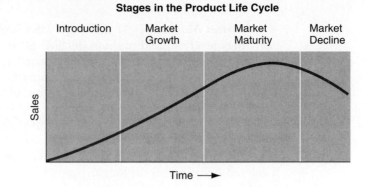

Stages in the Product Life Cycle

| Introduction | Market
Growth | Market
Maturity | Market
Decline |

Time ⟶

	Introduction	Market Growth	Market Maturity	Market Decline
Competition	None of importance	Some emulators	Many rivals competing for a small piece of the pie	Few in number with a rapid shakeout of weak members
Overall strategy	Market establishment; persuade early adopters to try the product	Market penetration; persuade mass market to prefer the brand	Defense of brand position; check the inroads of competition	Preparations for removal; milk the brand dry of all possible benefits
Profits	Negligible because of high production and marketing costs	Reach peak levels as a result of high prices and growing demand	Increasing competition cuts into profit margins and ultimately into total profits	Declining volume pushes costs up to levels that eliminate profits entirely
Retail prices	High, to recover some of the excessive costs of launching	High, to take advantage of heavy consumer demand	What the traffic will bear; need to avoid price wars	Low enough to permit quick liquidation of inventory
Distribution	Selective, as distribution is slowly built up	Intensive; employ small trade discounts since dealers are eager to store	Intensive; heavy trade allowances to retain shelf space	Selective; unprofitable outlets slowly phased out
Advertising strategy	Aim at the needs of early adopters	Make the mass market aware of brand benefits	Use advertising as a vehicle for differentiation among otherwise similar brands	Emphasize low price to reduce stock
Advertising emphasis	High, to generate awareness and interest among early adopters and persuade dealers to stock the brand	Moderate, to let sales rise on the sheer momentum of word-of-mouth recommendations	Moderate, since most buyers are aware of brand characteristics	Minimum expenditures required to phase out the product
Consumer sales and promotion expenditures	Heavy, to entice target groups, with samples, coupons, and other inducements, to try the brand	Moderate, to create brand preference (Advertising is best suited to do this job.)	Heavy, to encourage brand switching, hoping to convert some buyers into loyal users	Minimal, to let the brand coast by itself

SOURCE: Adapted from William Zikmund and Michael D'Amico, *Marketing*, 3d ed. (New York: John Wiley & Sons), Copyright © John Wiley & Sons, Inc. Reprinted by permission of John Wiley & Sons, Inc. and the authors.

Market Maturity   At this stage, sales begin to grow less rapidly; eventually they level off, and perhaps decline. Most of the consumers who are ever going to purchase the product have tried it and are either continuing to purchase it or have abandoned it. Competition becomes most intense at this stage and some competitors are forced out of the market or merge with other firms. As Figure 12.4 suggests, a major objective at this point is to maintain and strengthen customer loyalty to the firm's products.

Market Decline/Product Deletion   At this stage, the product has run its normal course and sales begin to decline rapidly. Eventually, the product is deleted because it is no longer profitable to maintain it. Of course, attempts can be made to revitalize the product. These attempts may include seeking new markets for the product, finding new uses for the product, or adding new features to the product. However, if opportunities to revitalize a product do exist, they should be considered long before a product is under consideration for deletion.

Reasons for Product Success   Why do some products have long, profitable lives while others are expensive failures? There is no simple answer to this question, but several factors contribute to product acceptance by consumers. Two of the most important are competitive differential advantage and product symbolism.

Competitive Differential Advantage   In marketing strategy, competitive differential advantage derives from the characteristics of a product that make it superior to competitive products. We believe that competitive differential advantage is a most important reason for product success and should be considered in any product strategy analysis.

In some situations, a competitive differential advantage can be obtained through technological developments. For example, at the product class level, RCA introduced the videodisc player that showed programs on any TV set. The disc player cost half as much as cassette machines, and the discs were cheaper than videocassettes. However, videocassettes had a competitive differential advantage over the disc player: Cassette machines could record programs and disc players could not. RCA assumed that recording ability was not an important factor to consumers—and lost more than $500 million learning otherwise.

At the brand level, however, it is often difficult to maintain a competitive differential advantage based on superior technology because competitors promptly copy new or improved technology. For example, Sony pioneered the Betamax system of videotape recorders and, in 1975, had the entire VCR market. Yet by 1982 Sony held only 14 percent of the market and was fighting for survival as competitors simply copied the technology and, having spent little on R&D, could sell at lower prices. Thus, although competitive differential advantage is a critical element of profitable marketing strategies, for such an advantage to be sustained, it often must derive from something other than technology or product modifications. One important source of sustainable competitive differential advantage is product symbolism.

Product Symbolism   Product symbolism is what the product means to consumers and what consumers experience in purchasing and using it. At the brand level, it refers to the image that a particular item evokes in the minds of consumers. Marketing researchers recognize that products have symbolic importance and that consumption of some goods may depend more on their social meaning than on their functional utility.

For many product classes, the products and brands offered are relatively homogeneous in the functions they perform for the consumer, yet these products and brands differ widely in market share. For example, it is well-known that few consumers can differentiate among the tastes of various brands of beer. Yet market shares vary dramatically, partly because of the brand images that have been created. Similarly, brands of jeans such as Levi's, Lee, and Wrangler are very similar in appearance, price, and quality. Yet it seems clear that these brand names have important meanings for consumers and symbolize different values, resulting in differences in market share. Guess? jeans obtained sales of $200 million in the first three years. A large portion of the market for these jeans consisted of teenagers who may have sought to present an identity different from that of wearers of traditional brands, such as their parents. Thus, the differential advantage of this brand of jeans may have been that Guess? products were a symbol of new generation of jeans wearers.

Product symbolism and appropriate brand images can actually be more important than technological superiority. For example, the IBM personal computer was not the fastest, most advanced PC on the market and its keyboard layout was criticized. IBM was not the first in the PC market and had little experience in marketing consumer goods. IBM dominated the PC market, however, perhaps because it had a superior company image as a computer manufacturer. IBM *meant* computers to many consumers.

Table 12.5 lists several questions that can help in analyzing product strategies. Product symbolism and brand images are often created by other elements of the marketing mix, including pricing, promotion, and channels of distribution. We will now discuss strategy in terms of each of these elements.

TABLE 12.5

Some Questions to Ask When Analyzing Product Strategies

1. What process does the organization use to develop new products?
2. How are new products evaluated?
3. What previous success has the organization had in developing new products?
4. What is the product's stage in the product life cycle?
5. What consumers make up the target market, and what are their reactions to the product?
6. What is the competitive differential advantage of this product?
7. Can this competitive differential advantage be sustained, or can it easily be copied by competitors?
8. Is product symbolism or brand image an important factor in the market, and what is the image of the organization's product among consumers?
9. What product strategies are competitors using, and how successful are they?
10. What changes in product characteristics could be made to improve the sales, profits, and market share of this product?

Pricing Strategy

Pricing strategy comes into play in three situations: (1) when an organization is introducing a new product and establishing its initial price; (2) when an organization is considering a long-term price change for an existing product; and (3) when an organization is considering a short-term price change, usually a decrease to stimulate demand. Three important influences on pricing strategy are consumer characteristics, organization characteristics, and competitive characteristics.

Consumer Characteristics   The nature of the target market and its expected reactions to a given price or price change are major considerations in pricing strategy. For some products, consumers may use price as an indicator of quality, so a low price does *not* stimulate demand. For many products, price is used to segment consumers into prestige, mass, and economy markets. Price is also used for creating product and brand images. For example, Old Milwaukee beer was promoted as tasting just as good as Budweiser at a lower price. Thus, it is positioned as a bargain for the consumer. Other products, such as Chivas Regal scotch, Cadillac automobiles, and Gucci handbags, are positioned as prestige products partly on the basis of their high prices.

Organization Characteristics   Several organization characteristics influence pricing strategies. First, the variable cost for a product usually sets the lower limit on its price. The price of a product must at least cover the variable costs of production, promotion, and distribution and should provide some profit. Second, the objectives of the organization influence pricing strategy. A common pricing objective is to achieve a target return on investment consistent with the organization's objectives. Third, the nature of the product influences pricing strategy. Distinctive products often have higher prices, for example, and perishable products must often be priced lower to promote faster sales.

Finally, the stage of the product life cycle that a product has reached may influence pricing strategy. A **skimming pricing strategy** involves setting a relatively high price early in the product life cycle and then gradually decreasing the price when competitors enter the market. Generally, skimming is used when the organization has a temporary monopoly and when demand for the product is not very sensitive to price. A **penetration pricing strategy** involves setting a relatively low price early in the product life cycle in anticipation of raising it at a later stage. Penetration is used when the firm expects competition to move in rapidly and when demand is strongly influenced by price. Penetration is also used to obtain large economies of scale and to create a large market rapidly.

Competitive Characteristics   Competitors—their number, size, cost structures, and past reactions to price changes—influence pricing strategy. An organization can price at, below, or above the competition, depending on such factors as its own cost structure, competitive differential advantage, and financial and marketing abilities.

Table 12.6 lists several questions that can help in analyzing pricing strategies.

Promotion Strategy

Designing promotion strategies involves selecting the appropriate mix of promotion tools to accomplish specific objectives. Four types of promotion tools

---

TABLE 12.6

Some Questions to Ask When Analyzing Pricing Strategies

1. How important is price to the target consumers of this product?
2. Do consumers of this product use price as an indicator of quality?
3. How will various prices affect the product or brand image?
4. What are the variable costs of the product, and will consumers pay a price that will cover them plus the desired level of profit?
5. What are the organization's objectives, and what price must be charged to obtain these objectives?
6. Is the product distinctive or perishable to the degree that pricing strategies are affected?
7. What is the product's life cycle stage, and what influence does this have on pricing strategy?
8. Do conditions warrant a penetration or skimming pricing strategy?
9. What are the prices of competitive products?
10. How will competition react to the initial price or to the price change contemplated?

---

can be used to inform, persuade, and remind consumers or industrial buyers:

1. **Advertising** is any paid form of nonpersonal presentation and promotion of ideas, goods, or services by an identified sponsor. (Examples include TV and radio commercials and magazine and newspaper ads.)
2. **Sales promotion** is a short-term incentive to encourage the purchase or sale of a product or service. (Examples include contests, games, premiums, and coupons.)
3. **Publicity** is any unpaid form of nonpersonal presentation of ideas, goods, or services. (An example is the discussion of a new product on a TV talk show.)
4. **Personal selling** is direct, face-to-face communication between sellers and potential buyers for the purpose of making an exchange.

As shown in Table 12.7, each of these promotion tools has a variety of advantages and disadvantages. No single method is always superior, and promotion mix decisions depend on several factors. For example, although sales of complex products such as insurance and computers are influenced by advertising, some personal selling is usually required to close sales.

Simpler products such as cereal and shampoo can be marketed to consumers via advertising and sales promotion, but salespeople are often required for selling the product to retailers. In general, designing promotion strategies involves three steps: determining promotion objectives, formulating the promotion plan, and developing promotion budgets.

Determining Promotion Objectives   Table 12.8 lists some general objectives of promotion. Which of these promotion objectives (or others) is appropriate depends in part on the results of the company's earlier analysis of consumer/product relationships. There are, of course, many possible relationships between consumers and products, and they lead to different promotion objectives. For example, consider the following situations:

TABLE 12.7

Advantages and Disadvantages of Major Promotion Tools

Advantages	Disadvantages
ADVERTISING	
Can reach many consumers simultaneously	May waste promotion dollars if it reaches consumers who are not potential buyers
Offers relatively low cost per exposure	Is a major target of marketing critics because of high visibility
Is excellent for creating brand images	Offers very brief exposure time for advertising message
Offers high degree of flexibility and variety of media choices; can accomplish many different types of promotion objectives	Can be quickly and easily screened out by consumers
SALES PROMOTION	
Can stimulate demand by short-term price reductions	May influence primarily brand-loyal customers to stock up at the lower price and result in few new customers
Offers a large variety of tools to choose from	May have only short-term impact
Can be effective for changing a variety of consumer behaviors	May hurt brand image and profits by overuse of price-related sales promotion tools
Can be easily tied in with other promotion tools	If effective, may be easily copied by competitors
PUBLICITY	
Can be positive and stimulate demand at no cost as "free advertising"	Content of messages cannot be completely controlled
May be perceived by consumers as more credible because it is not paid for by the seller	Not always available
	Seldom a long-term promotion tool for brands, since messages are repeated only a limited number of times
May be paid more attention because messages are not quickly "screened out," as many advertisements are	Can be negative and hurt sales as well as company, product, and brand images
PERSONAL SELLING	
Can be the most persuasive promotion tool, since salespeople can directly influence purchase behaviors	Is high in cost per contact
Allows two-way communication	Can be expensive and difficult since it involves training and motivation
Is often necessary for technically complex products	Has a poor image as a career, making recruitment difficult
Allows direct one-on-one targeting of promotional effort	Can hurt sales as well as company, product, and brand images if done poorly

TABLE 12.8

Some General Objectives of Promotion Strategies

1. Increase brand awareness
2. Increase consumer knowledge of product and brand
3. Change consumer attitudes about company
4. Change consumer attitudes about brand
5. Increase short-term sales
6. Increase long-term sales
7. Build corporate image
8. Build brand image and positioning
9. Announce a price reduction
10. Inform consumers of place of sale
11. Develop brand loyalty
12. Reassure consumers of brand quality
13. Close a sale
14. Prospect for customers
15. Obtain product trial
16. Inhibit purchase of competitive brands
17. Inform consumers of favorable credit terms
18. Increase store patronage and store loyalty
19. Reduce dissonance
20. Inform, persuade, and remind consumers

- *Situation 1: Consumers are unaware of a brand but have a need for the product.* In this situation, an appropriate promotion objective is to inform consumers of the existence of the brand and demonstrate its benefits and uses. Companies promoting new products frequently employ advertising and free samples to accomplish this objective. Promotion objectives in this situation are stated in terms of a particular percentage increase in awareness of a product.
- *Situation 2: Consumers are aware of a brand but purchase a competing brand.* In this situation, an appropriate promotion objective is to demonstrate the superiority of the firm's brand. For example, Burger King employed a series of comparative ads emphasizing the merits of flame broiling to attract McDonald's customers. Promotion objectives in this situation may be stated in terms of increases in market share or changes in consumer behavior.
- *Situation 3: Consumers are aware of a brand and purchase it, but they sometimes purchase competing brands also.* In this situation, a primary promotion objective may be to develop a higher degree of brand loyalty. For example, cereal manufacturers frequently enclose cents-off coupons in packages to encourage repeat purchases of the same brand.
- *Situation 4: Consumers are aware of a brand and purchase it consistently.* In this situation, a primary promotion objective may be to reinforce purchases via reminder advertising or phone calls. For example, automobile salespeople frequently call past customers to encourage them to rebuy the same brand. Similarly, promotion can be used to inform consumers of new uses of the product. For example, Arm & Hammer dramatically increased sales of its baking soda by demonstrating its use in freshening refrigerators and carpets.

These brief sketches of a few possible situations and appropriate promotion objectives illustrate three important points. First, objectives depend on the relationships between consumers and various products and brands. Second, promotion tools vary in their effectiveness for achieving specific objectives. Advertising is more effective for achieving awareness in a mass market, yet sales promotion and personal selling may be more effective for closing sales and developing brand loyalty. Third, promotion objectives change over time to reflect changes in consumers, competitors, and other elements of the environment. The Company Example illustrates how strategy drives the choice of promotion methods.

Formulating the Promotion Plan   At this stage, decisions are made concerning the desired structure of the promotion mix, and a promotion plan is developed. These decisions and plans are based on the objectives determined in the previous stage, which in turn depend on the analysis of consumer/product relationships.

As we have noted, the promotion mix consists of advertising, sales promotion, publicity, and personal selling. The task at this stage is to determine to what degree and in what situations each of these tools will be used. In addition, appropriate promotion messages, media choices, and schedules are formulated on the basis of the firm's promotion objectives for the product, the nature of the product, and the purchasing habits and media preferences of target consumers.

Many of these decisions depend on whether the product is new or has reached a later stage of the life cycle. If the product is new, managers must decide whether to field a sales force, what its size should be, and what territories it should cover. They must also address compensation and management issues. Similarly, for new products, they must develop appropriate brand images and appeals.

This does not mean that management of the sales force or advertising decisions can be ignored for existing products. The structure and sales organization that are already in place should be reviewed. Similarly, for an existing product, many decisions about the appropriate messages, media, and scheduling for other forms of promotion usually require careful consideration. Decision making in this situation involves investigating alternative promotion methods that could boost the efficiency of the promotion mix.

Developing Promotion Budgets   Managers establish promotion budgets by many methods. For example, some firms use the **affordable method,** which amounts to allocating to promotion as much as the firm can afford. Other firms use a **percentage of sales method,** allocating some particular percentage (such as 5 percent) of current or anticipated sales to promotion. Still others use a **competitive parity method,** setting the promotion budget to match competitors' outlays. Each of these methods has its advantages and disadvantages, but most promotion experts argue for what is called the **task method,** or *objective and task method.*

The task method takes a three-stage approach that corresponds to the three stages outlined in this section. A firm that uses the task method first determines its promotion objectives, then it formulates a promotion plan detailing the specific promotion tasks that it must perform to achieve its promotion

COMPANY EXAMPLE

Thor-Lo's Product Does the Marketing

Just as Nike and Reebok took the sneaker and re-designed it into a specialized sport shoe, Thor-Lo Inc. created sports-specific socks. Its low-key marketing—the virtues of the socks are reported mostly by word-of-mouth—helped the company earn $30 million in revenues in 1991.

Thor-Lo's foot equipment includes socks designed for 18 different sports, including tennis, aerobics, and basketball. Extra, high-density padding is placed in the areas where the foot takes the most pounding.

The socks were the brainchild of James Throneburg, the son of Thor-Lo's founders. The company, founded in 1953, was a private-label maker of socks for FootJoy, Izod, and other name-brand manufacturers. The decision in the mid-1980s to market the new, innovative socks under the company name garnered yawns from store owners. Their indifference changed when they realized how much more lucrative it was to sell a pair of Thor-Lo Padds than a competitor's socks. At about $7.50 a pair, Thor-Los are almost double the price of standard athletic socks. Using the standard markup, that placed nearly $4 in retailers' pockets on every pair of Thor-Los they sold.

Today, most stores carry wall displays of Thor-Lo's different socks so shoppers can feel the difference between the company's high-end, padded products and their competitors.

Throneburg's innovation created an entirely new market. Sports-specific socks are now a $150-million-a-year retail business. Thor-Lo's share of that market was almost 50 percent in 1991; recognizing the success of its brand image, it discontinued all of its private-label manufacturing. During that time, the company spent just $47,000 on promotional advertising. That figure does not include Thor-Lo's one concession to modern sports marketing—hiring a celebrity spokesperson. But its use of tennis pro Martina Navratilova arose from her pursuit of the company, and she accepted far less than she could have earned from another sock endorsement.

SOURCE: Gretchen Morgenson, "The Foot's Friend," *Forbes*, April 13, 1992, pp. 60–62.

objectives. In the third step, it estimates the costs of performing all of the promotion tasks that it has selected. The sum of these costs represents the appropriate promotion budget. Of course, if the resulting figure is more than the organization can afford, or more than management is willing to invest, some reduction must be made in the planned promotion strategy.

Table 12.9 lists several questions that can help in analyzing promotion strategies.

Channel Strategy

A **channel of distribution** is the combination of institutions through which a seller markets products to industrial buyers or ultimate consumers. In **direct channels,** manufacturers sell directly to end users. In **indirect channels,** manufacturers use one or more intermediaries to sell to end users. Table 12.10 lists some of the types of marketing intermediaries that make up channels of distribution.

Manufacturers use intermediaries because intermediaries can perform marketing functions more efficiently than manufacturers or because manufacturers lack the financial resources or expertise to market directly to consumers. Table 12.11 lists the major functions performed in channels of distribution. It is important to note that, whether the manufacturer or one or more intermediaries perform these functions, all of them must usually be assumed

TABLE 12.9

Some Questions to Ask When Analyzing Promotion Strategies

1. What is the target market for this product, and what sources of product information do these consumers use?
2. What are the overall promotion objectives, and what are the specific objectives of each promotion tool?
3. What is the appropriate promotion mix of advertising, sales promotion, publicity, and personal selling?
4. Who is responsible for planning, organizing, implementing, and controlling the promotion strategy?
5. What should the various forms of promotion communicate about the product?
6. What are the appropriate types and combinations of personal and nonpersonal media to use? Consider salespeople, television, radio, billboards, magazines, newspapers, and direct mail.
7. How long should the firm use this promotion strategy before changing its focus or methods?
8. What is the appropriate schedule for sales calls, advertisements, sales promotions, and publicity releases?
9. How much should be spent on each of the various forms of promotion, and how much should be spent in total?
10. How will the effectiveness of promotion be measured?

by someone. Thus distribution requires that managers decide who will do which of these tasks.

From the consumer's viewpoint, channels provide form, time, place, and possession utility. To create **form utility** is to convert raw materials into finished goods and services that consumers seek to purchase. Creating **time utility** means making products available when consumers want to buy them. In creating **place utility,** channels make products available where consumers can purchase them. In creating **possession utility,** channels facilitate the transfer of ownership of products from manufacturers to consumers.

Given the variety of types of intermediaries, distribution functions, and types of utility provided to consumers by channels, the task of selecting and designing a channel of distribution may at first appear overwhelming. However, in many industries all competitors use essentially the same channel structure and the same types of intermediaries. In these industries, a manufacturer may *have* to use the traditional channels in order to compete in the industry. For example, nationally branded consumer food products are typically sold in a variety of grocery stores, and automobiles are typically sold through franchised dealers. These channels are likely to be highly efficient and thus appropriate for a manufacturer. In addition, no other types of intermediaries may be available to market the product. This is not to say that channel design allows no room for innovation. For example, health and beauty aids are commonly sold in a variety of retail stores. Yet Mary Kay Cosmetics sells such products door-to-door, often very profitably.

The four major concerns in designing channels of distribution are dis-

TABLE 12.10

Major Types of Marketing Intermediaries

Intermediary—independent business concern that operates as a link between producers and ultimate consumers or industrial buyers.

Merchant intermediary—intermediary who buys goods outright and takes title to them.

Agent—a business unit that negotiates purchases, sales, or both but does not take title to the goods in which it deals.

Wholesaler—merchant establishment operated by a concern that is primarily engaged in buying, taking title to, and usually storing and physically handling goods in large quantities, then reselling the goods (usually in smaller quantities) to retailers or to industrial or business users.

Retailer—merchant intermediary who is engaged primarily in selling to ultimate consumers.

Broker—intermediary that serves as a go-between for the buyer or seller; assumes no title risks, does not usually have physical custody of products, and is not looked upon as a permanent representative of either the buyer or the seller.

Sales agent—independent channel member, either an individual or a company responsible for the sale of a firm's products or services but does not take title to the goods sold.

Distributor—wholesale intermediary, especially in lines where selective or exclusive distribution is common at the wholesale level in which the manufacturer expects strong promotional support; often a synonym for *wholesaler*.

Jobber—intermediary who buys from manufacturers and sells to retailers; a wholesaler.

Facilitating agent—business firm that assists in the performance of distribution tasks other than buying, selling, and transferring title (i.e., transportation companies, warehouses, etc.).

SOURCE: Based on Peter D. Bennett (ed.), *Dictionary of Marketing Terms* (Chicago: American Marketing Association, 1988).

tribution coverage, channel control, total distribution cost, and channel flexibility.

Distribution Coverage   Because of the characteristics of the product, the environment needed to sell the product, and the needs and expectations of potential buyers, different products call for varying intensity of distribution coverage. Distribution coverage varies on a continuum from intensive through selective to exclusive distribution. **Intensive distribution** involves selling the product through as many wholesalers and retailers as possible. Intensive distribution is appropriate for most convenience goods because of their low unit value and high frequency of purchase. **Selective distribution** involves selling through a limited number of intermediaries in a particular geographic area. Appliances and home furnishings are usually distributed selectively, on the basis of the reputation and service quality of particular retailers. **Exclusive distribution** involves selling through only one intermediary in a particular territory and is commonly employed to increase the selling effort for a manufacturer's product. Automobile dealerships and beer distributors are examples of exclusive distribution arrangements.

TABLE 12.11

Marketing Functions Performed in Channels of Distribution

Buying—purchasing products from sellers for use or for resale.

Selling—promoting the sale of products to ultimate consumers or industrial buyers.

Sorting—function performed by intermediaries in order to bridge the discrepancy between the assortment of goods and services generated by the producer and the assortment demanded by the consumer. This function includes four distinct processes: sorting out, accumulating, allocating, and assorting.

Sorting out—sorting process that breaks down a heterogeneous supply into separate stocks which are relatively homogeneous.

Accumulating—sorting process that brings similar stocks from a number of sources together into a larger, homogeneous supply.

Allocating—sorting process that consists of breaking a homogeneous supply down into smaller and smaller lots.

Assorting—sorting process that consists of building an assortment of products for use in association with each other.

Concentrating—process of bringing goods from various places together in one place.

Financing—providing credit or funds to facilitate a transaction.

Storing—maintaining inventories and protecting products to provide better customer service.

Grading—classifying products into different categories on the basis of quality.

Transporting—physically moving products from where they are made to where they are purchased and used.

Risk-taking—taking on business risks involved in transporting and owning products.

Market research—collecting information concerning such things as market conditions, expected sales, consumer trends, and competitive forces.

SOURCE: Based on Peter D. Bennett (ed.), *Dictionary of Marketing Terms* (Chicago: American Marketing Association, 1988).

Channel Control　One important influence on the design of distribution channels is the amount of control an organization wants over the marketing of its products. Typically, a more direct and exclusive channel gives a manufacturer more control. Often, however, a channel is controlled by an intermediary rather than the manufacturer. For example, a large retailer such as Sears, Roebuck may control small manufacturers who produce Sears-labeled products.

Total Distribution Cost　The concept of total distribution cost suggests that channels should be designed to minimize costs, other things being equal. Thus, if a system of wholesalers and retailers can distribute a product more cheaply than marketing directly to consumers, such a system should be selected, other things equal. However, it is also important to consider the effects of a particular channel on sales, profits, the total marketing mix, and the level of consumer service that is needed to make the product successful.

Channel Flexibility　One reason why a channel strategy must be chosen so carefully is that it usually involves a long-term commitment to a particular

TABLE 12.12

Some Questions to Ask When Analyzing Channel Strategies

1. What is the target market for this product, and where do these consumers usually purchase?
2. What is the nature of the product, and what problems and opportunities does this information suggest for distribution?
3. How do competitors distribute products like this, and how successful have they been?
4. What are the total distribution costs of various channel alternatives?
5. What degree of market coverage is needed to reach the target market?
6. How competent is the organization to manage various types of channels?
7. How much control over the channel does the organization want?
8. Are appropriate intermediaries available and willing to distribute and market the product?
9. What is the relative market power of the manufacturer versus different types of intermediaries?
10. Can the manufacturer afford to perform all of the marketing functions, and can it do so efficiently?

course of action. Channels are typically not changed as frequently as other elements of the marketing mix. For example, long-term leases for retail store space and long-term agreements with wholesalers limit the flexibility of an organization. In general, more uncertainty in the environment makes channel alternatives that involve long-term commitments less favorable.

Table 12.12 lists several questions that can help in analyzing channel strategies.

IMPLEMENTING AND CONTROLLING THE MARKETING STRATEGY

Implementing a marketing strategy involves putting it into action according to a predefined schedule. Even the most carefully developed strategies often cannot be executed with perfect timing. Thus, the organization must closely monitor and coordinate implementation. In some situations, the basic strategy may need adjustments because of changes in the environment. For example, a competitor's introduction of a new product may make it desirable to speed up or delay implementation. The reaction of the market to the withdrawal of the original-formula Coke certainly required a change in planned marketing strategies for the Coca-Cola Company. In almost all situations, some fine-tuning is necessary.

Controlling the marketing strategy involves three steps. First, the results of the implemented strategy are measured. Second, the results are compared with the objectives of the strategy. Third, managers determine whether the strategy is achieving its stated objectives. If so, they must decide whether some change in strategy would improve results. If not, they must decide whether the objectives were unrealistic or the strategy is simply not effective. If the strategy is judged ineffective, a new one must be developed.

Measuring the effects of a particular strategy can involve considerable market research. For example, measuring the effects of a strategy designed to "increase awareness of the product by 25 percent" usually involves primary market research on members of the target market to estimate changes in awareness. However, marketing strategies designed to achieve other objectives, such as increases in sales, profits, or market share, can often be evaluated by examining secondary information, such as the organization's sales records.

SUMMARY

This chapter investigated the marketing function and its role in strategic management. The first step in preparing a marketing strategy is to analyze consumer/product relationships. Classifying goods as either consumer or industrial products is often helpful. Consumer products can be further divided into convenience, shopping, and specialty goods on the basis of how much trouble and expense the consumer will go to in order to purchase them. Similar classification schemes exist to help firms market industrial goods. Any research that sheds light on the reasons why consumers buy certain products can help businesses understand their target markets better.

Market segmentation is the process of dividing a market into groups of similar consumers and selecting the most appropriate group or groups to serve. For some products geographic segmentation is best. For others, the most effective segmentation is based on a demographic variable such as sex, age, or income. Segmentation based on lifestyle, or the psychographic characteristics of a market, is sometimes appropriate, as is segmentation in terms of the benefits people seek in consuming a given product.

The marketing mix consists of product, price, promotion, and channels of distribution. The product's position in the seven-stage product life cycle (from concept generation through deletion) profoundly affects the way it is marketed. Other significant factors include any competitive differential advantage that can be established either functionally or through product symbolism. Pricing strategy is influenced by consumer characteristics, organization characteristics, and competitive characteristics. Some cases call for low prices and sometimes high prices are best. The major approaches to promoting products are advertising, sales promotion, publicity, and personal selling. All suit different objectives and work best under different conditions. Choosing one or more promotion techniques is a key part of the marketing mix decision. Selecting a channel of distribution—that is, the combination of intermediaries through which the firm markets products to the consumer—is another crucial decision. Channels convert products into the forms consumers want, they make products available where and when consumers want to buy them, and they facilitate the transfer of ownership of products from manufacturers to consumers. The intermediary can sometimes be eliminated, but the functions it performs cannot.

In the course of implementing a marketing strategy, it is important to work to keep a plan on schedule and to be flexible enough to adjust it if changes in the environment make it advisable to do so. Controlling the marketing strategy involves measuring the results of the strategy, determining whether it is achieving its objectives, and then deciding what changes are needed to correct an ineffective strategy or (perhaps) to improve a successful one.

KEY TERMS

consumer product,
p. 284
industrial product,
p. 284
market segmentation,
p. 288
geographic segmenta-
tion, p. 288
demographic segmen-
tation, p. 288
psychographic seg-
mentation, p. 288
principle-oriented con-
sumer, p. 292
status-oriented con-
sumer, p. 292
action-oriented con-
sumer, p. 292
benefit segmentation,
p. 293

marketing mix, p. 294
product life cycle,
p. 294
skimming pricing strat-
egy, p. 300
penetration pricing
strategy, p. 300
advertising, p. 301
sales promotion,
p. 301
publicity, p. 301
personal selling, p. 301
affordable promotion
budgeting method,
p. 304
percentage of sales
promotion budgeting
method, p. 304
competitive parity pro-
motion budgeting

method, p. 304
task promotion bud-
geting method, p. 304
channel of distribu-
tion, p. 305.
direct channels, p. 305
indirect channels,
p. 305
form utility, p. 306
time utility, p. 306
place utility, p. 306
possession utility, p.
306
intensive distribution,
p. 307
selective distribution,
p. 307
exclusive distribution,
p. 307

CHECKLIST   **Analyzing Marketing in Problems and Cases**

____   1. Does the problem or case involve relationships between an organization and consumers of the organization's product(s)?

____   2. Why should consumers purchase the organization's product(s) rather than competitive offerings? That is, what is the organization's competitive differential advantage from the consumer's point of view?

____   3. What are the appropriate market segments for the organization's products, and has the firm identified them?

____   4. Are these market segments large enough to serve profitably, and can the organization serve them efficiently?

____   5. What are the strengths and weaknesses of the organization's current marketing strategy?

____   6. Are all elements of the marketing strategy consistent and designed to achieve the organization's objectives?

____   7. Which elements of marketing strategy are of greatest concern in this problem or case? That is, is this a very general problem concerning the development and implementation of a marketing strategy, or is it focused on a particular type of decision?

____   8. Does the organization have good marketing skills, and is it capable of formulating and implementing a sound marketing strategy?

____   9. How would the marketing strategy have to change to achieve the organization's objectives?

____   10. What is the probable long-term impact on the organization of following the current or suggested marketing strategy?

Additional Readings

Churchill, Gilbert A., Jr., and J. Paul Peter. *Marketing: Creating Value for Customers.* Burr Ridge, Ill.: Austen Press/Irwin, 1995.

Cravens, David, and Shunnon Shipp. "Market-Driven Strategies for Competitive Advantage." *Business Horizons,* January/February, 1991, pp. 54–66.

Kotler, Philip. *Marketing Management: Analysis, Planning, and Control,* 8th ed. Englewood Cliffs, N.J.: Prentice-Hall, 1994.

McCarthy, E. Jerome, and William D. Perrault. *Basic Marketing.* 11th ed. Homewood, Ill.: Irwin, 1993.

Peter, J. Paul, and James H. Donnelly, Jr. *Marketing Management: Knowledge and Skills,* 4th ed. Burr Ridge, Ill.: Irwin, 1995.

Treacy, Michael, and Fred Wiersema. "Customer Intimacy and the Other Value Disciplines." *Harvard Business Review,* January/February, 1993, p. 84.

C A S E

Niche Marketing by Boston Beer

During the past decade, Jim Koch has built Boston Beer Co. into a $50 million company and the largest specialty brewer in the United States. Boston Beer has won market share by hammering away at the key weaknesses of imports— lengthy shipping times and less hearty, made-for-export formulations—while touting its own quality ingredients and brewing processes.

Indeed, Koch's beer, Samuel Adams Boston Lager, has won a number of industry awards. On four separate occasions at the Great American Beer Festival, it has been voted the Best Beer in America; it also has received six gold medals at the festival's blind tastings.

Consumer response has been strong. Sales jumped 63 percent in 1992 when the company went national and placed its beer in the bars and restaurants of 48 states.

Initially, however, Koch's marketing challenge was deceptively simple: create sales in a market that focuses as much on the image of the consumer who drinks the product or the fantasy world it creates. He had created a full-bodied beer to compete against premium imports in the high end of the beer market. Koch believed that the quality of his product would be his best sales tool.

While other microbrewers aimed their marketing at more sophisticated beer consumers, however, Koch was determined to sell directly against the imports. Koch based his marketing approach on his product, using a recipe for a pre-Prohibition beer that was heavier in taste and more full-bodied than Budweiser or Miller. His compliance with Germany's strict beer-purity laws and use of "noble" hops was aimed at attracting a select group of beer drinkers past their college days who could pay premium prices for good-tasting beer.

With only $240,000 in start-up capital, Koch hired a brewery to brew his beer; besides saving the $10 million it would cost to build a state-of-the-art brewery from scratch, this move gave Koch access to superior facilities and skills. The downside was that the beer would retail at $20 a case, roughly 15 percent more than premium imports such as Heineken. "It was a marketing nightmare," he says.

He began the slow process of convincing retailers—bars, restaurants, supermarkets, and package stores—as well as consumers to try his beer and to pay the higher price. He relied on persistent personal sales calls, occasionally visiting a potential customer 15 times before winning an agreement to carry the product. Many told him: "My customers don't drink the beer; they drink the advertising."

He responded in 1986 with a $100,000 marketing and advertising campaign that sold the beer rather than the lifestyle. No beaches, bikinis, or funny dogs were featured. Instead, print ads proclaimed that imported versions of Heineken, Beck's, and St. Pauli Girl did not pass Germany's purity standards because they contained corn starch or sugar. In addition, Koch appealed to drinker's patriotism by playing up Samuel Adams' domestic origins: "Declare your independence from foreign beer."

The brashness of the campaign garnered media attention and further established Samuel Adams' brand-name recognition. In addition, Koch redefined point-of-sale marketing. Samuel Adams table tents feature more than the Boston Beer logo. They also include the bar's name and a listing of all its beverages.

While ensuring that Boston Beer had the production capacity to supply each new market as the company expanded, Koch began hiring sales reps. In 1989, the firm had fewer than a dozen; today it has 70 across the nation—about the same as beer giant Anheuser-Busch. Highly personalized selling is still the company's hallmark; the sales force calls on 1,000 accounts a week, and each salesperson carries a supply of hops to be able to offer a sample.

DISCUSSION QUESTIONS

1. What is Boston Beer's competitive differential advantage?
2. How are environmental factors contributing to the company's success?
3. What are the marketing limits of Boston Beer's reliance on premium pricing to differentiate its product?

SOURCE: Jenny C. McCune, "Brewing Up Profits," *Management Review,* April 1994, pp. 16–20.

Notes

1. This chapter is based on J. Paul Peter and James H. Donnelley, Jr., *Marketing Management: Knowledge and Skills,* 4th ed. (Burr Ridge, Ill.: Irwin, 1995), Section 1; and J. Paul Peter and Jerry C. Olson, *Consumer Behavior and Marketing Strategy,* 3d ed. (Homewood, Ill.: Irwin, 1993), Section 5.
2. Theodore Levitt, *The Marketing Imagination* (New York: Free Press, 1983), p. 5.
3. This discussion is based on Martha Farnsworth Riche, "Psychographics for the 1990s," *American Demographics,* July 1989, pp. 24–26 ff.
4. See Russell I. Haley, "Benefit Segmentation: A Decision-Oriented Research Tool," *Journal of Marketing,* July 1968, pp. 30–35. Also see Russell I. Haley, "Benefit Segmentation—20 Years Later," *Journal of Consumer Marketing,* no. 1 (1983), pp. 5–13.
5. Jeremy Main, "Help and Hype in the New-Products Game," *Fortune,* February 7, 1983, pp. 60–64. Also see C. Merle Crawford, *New Products Management,* 4th ed. (Burr Ridge, Ill.: Irwin, 1994).
6. Ibid., p. 64.
7. See C. Merle Crawford, *New Products Management,* 4th ed. (Burr Ridge, Ill.: Richard D. Irwin, 1994).

PART V

Framework for Strategic Analysis

This part of the text explains a detailed approach to analyzing strategic management problems and cases. It is designed primarily to address analysis of comprehensive problems and cases, although the general logic of the approach can also help students to identify and analyze more specialized issues. Skilled case analysts think flexibly and adapt this approach to specific problems or cases. You will find the approach helpful when you analyze the cases in this text and when you set out to solve the actual strategic management problems you will face as a practicing manager.

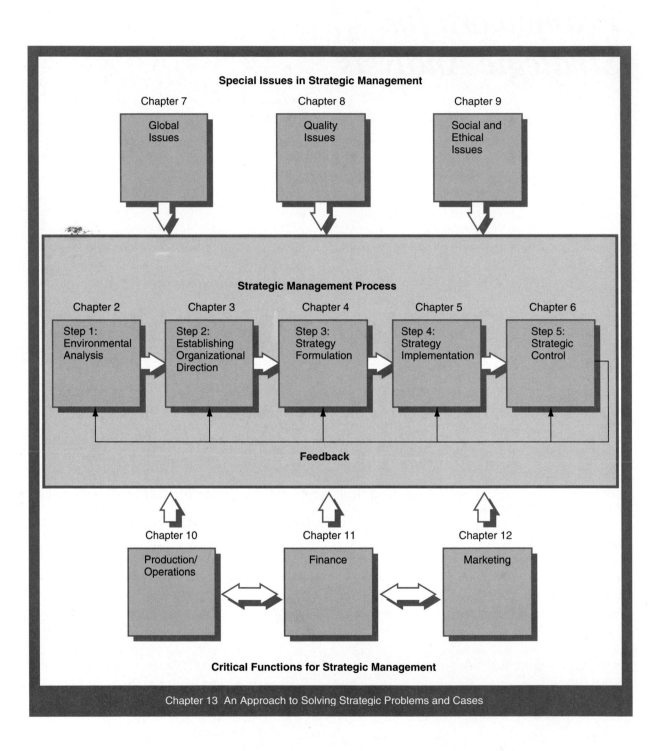

Special Issues in Strategic Management

Chapter 7

Global Issues

Chapter 8

Quality Issues

Chapter 9

Social and Ethical Issues

Strategic Management Process

Chapter 2

Step 1: Environmental Analysis

Chapter 3

Step 2: Establishing Organizational Direction

Chapter 4

Step 3: Strategy Formulation

Chapter 5

Step 4: Strategy Implementation

Chapter 6

Step 5: Strategic Control

Feedback

Chapter 10

Production/ Operations

Chapter 11

Finance

Chapter 12

Marketing

Critical Functions for Strategic Management

Chapter 13 An Approach to Solving Strategic Problems and Cases

Comprehensive Approach to Analyzing Strategic Problems and Cases

Since its development at the Harvard Business School in the 1920s, case analysis has become a major tool of management education. **Cases** are detailed descriptions or reports of strategic management problems. They are often written by trained observers who were actually involved with the organizations and problems or issues described in the cases. Cases usually include both qualitative and quantitative data that students must analyze in order to determine appropriate alternatives and solutions.

Since managers encounter many different types of strategic management problems, students encounter many different types of cases. Some cases involve large, diversified companies; others involve small, single-product companies. Some cases involve very successful companies seeking to maintain industry leadership; others focus on failing companies working to avoid bankruptcy. One case may involve a complicated mixture of strategic management problems; another may focus on a single issue.

A primary advantage of the case method is that it introduces a measure of realism into strategic management education. Rather than emphasizing concepts, the case method stresses the *application* of concepts and sound logic to real-world problems. In this way students learn to bridge the chasm between abstraction and application and to appreciate the value of both.

The purpose of this chapter is to outline a general approach to the analysis of strategic problems and cases. In addition, we suggest some common pitfalls to avoid in case analysis and some approaches to presenting cases. Remember, however, that although the approach offered here is a logical and useful way to develop sound analyses, no single approach can be applied routinely or mechanically to all cases. Cases differ widely in scope, context, and amount of information available. Analysts must always be ready to customize this approach to the particular situations they face.

For example, our approach offers a number of worksheets to assist analysts in various stages of case analysis. These worksheets are designed for broad, general cases and may have to be adapted to more specialized cases and problems. In short, there is no magic formula to guarantee an effective case analysis, and there is no substitute for logical, informed thinking on the part of the case analyst.

A major reason instructors use the case method is that analyzing cases helps students develop and improve their skills at identifying

This chapter is based on J. Paul Peter and James H. Donnelly, Jr., *A Preface to Marketing Management*, 6th ed. (Burr Ridge, Ill.: Irwin, 1994), pp. 328–342.

TABLE 13.1

A Case for Case Analysis

Cases help to bridge the gap between classroom learning and the so-called *real world* of strategic management. They provide us with an opportunity to develop, sharpen, and test our analytical skills at:

- Assessing situations
- Sorting out and organizing key information
- Asking the right questions
- Defining opportunities and problems
- Identifying and evaluating alternative courses of action
- Interpreting data
- Evaluating the results of past strategies
- Developing and defending new strategies
- Interacting with other managers
- Making decisions under conditions of uncertainty
- Critically evaluating the work of others
- Responding to criticism

SOURCE: Adapted from David W. Cravens and Charles W. Lamb, Jr., *Strategic Marketing: Cases and Applications,* 4th ed. (Burr Ridge, Ill.: Richard D. Irwin, 1993), p. 95. Reprinted by permission.

---

problems and creating sound solutions to them. If this process required nothing more than routinely plugging information into a formula, there would be no need for strategic managers! Managers are paid to recognize problems and to formulate and implement sound solutions to them. Having a successful career in management depends on developing these skills. Table 13.1 lists some of the skills that case analysis helps student analysts develop.

CASE ANALYSIS FRAMEWORK

The basic approach to case analysis that we propose is shown in Figure 13.1. This four-stage process suggests that analysts first clearly define the problem or issue to be resolved. Second, they should formulate reasonable alternatives that could potentially solve the problem. Third, analysts should evaluate each of the alternatives and compare them to find an effective solution. Finally, the alternative judged to be most effective and efficient should be selected and implemented to solve the problem.

When this process is carried out in a real situation, an additional step is included. Analysts would evaluate the effects of implementing the alternative to determine whether the problem had been solved. If so, they would continue to monitor the situation to ensure the sustained effectiveness of the alternative. If not, they would go back to the problem definition and begin the whole process again to continue the search for an effective solution.

This problem-solving approach to case analysis is the approach we advocate. However, for students who are not experienced in the analysis of strategic problems and cases, this basic framework may be inadequate and oversimplified because it does not explain how to approach each of these tasks.

FIGURE 13.1
Stages in Case Analysis

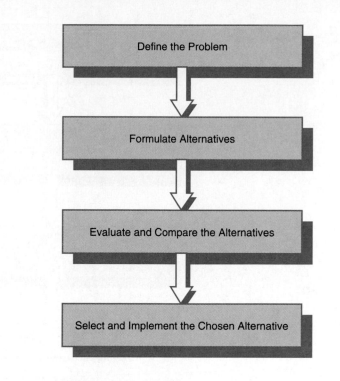

For example, consider the first stage, problem definition. What is desired here is a clear, unambiguous statement of the major problems or issues that define the case. Yet, just as in real situations that confront practicing managers, few cases offer direct statements of these pivotal problems. In fact, after initially reading a case, students often conclude that the case is no more than a description of events that present no problems or important issues for analysis. Even in cases that do include direct statements about problems or issues, the problem is almost always deeper or more complex than first meets the eye, and much more analysis must be done.

For these reasons we have developed the more detailed framework for case analysis shown in Figure 13.2. This framework is designed to help students recognize case problems and issues and sequentially devise appropriate solutions to them.

Analyze and Record the Current Situation

Whether the analysis of a strategic problem is conducted by a manager, a student, or an outside consultant, the first step is to analyze and record the current situation. This does not mean writing up a history of the organization or rewriting the case material. It involves the type of environmental analysis described in the following paragraphs.

Analyzing and recording the current situation is critical for three reasons. First, until the analyst has developed a clear understanding of the current situation, it is impossible to determine appropriate courses of action. In other words, one has no basis for deciding how to improve a situation until one knows what that situation is.

Second, the major purpose of this stage of the analysis is to investigate the current and potential problems involved in the case. By sequentially analyzing

FIGURE 13.2
Expanded Framework
for Case Analysis

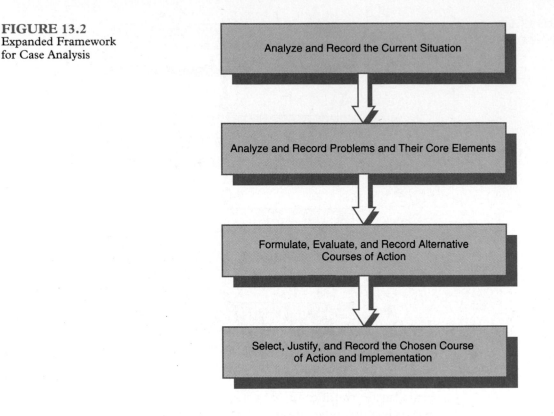

all elements of the current situation, the analyst clarifies those problems and amasses evidence that they are the central issues.

Third, this stage is useful for delineating the level of analysis for a specific case. "Level of analysis" means the overall scope of the problem. For example, some cases emphasize issues that arise at the industry level, whereas others focus on particular organizations, certain departments, individual executives, or particular strategic decisions. Clearly, determining the appropriate level of analysis is a very important aspect of case analysis.

In an effort to pinpoint case problems, it is useful to analyze sequentially each component or aspect of the general, operating, and internal environments. Table 13.2 lists these elements and the types of questions that should be asked in analyzing them.

In very few cases are all of these components or aspects crucial for the analysis. However, until each component or aspect is considered, there is no way to judge its relative importance. The analyst who considers each component and aspect in detail avoids missing critical issues. In other words, the key task at this stage of the analysis is to consider every possible environmental element in order to assess problems and opportunities in the case situation.

An analysis of any of the components or aspects of the environment may have important implications for defining case problems and for supporting appropriate solutions to the problems. Thus, keeping a detailed record of all of the relevant information uncovered in the environmental analysis is crucial. Table 13.3 presents a **worksheet** for recording this information and for further investigating its impact on the case.

TABLE 13.2

Study Areas in Environmental Analysis

GENERAL ENVIRONMENT

1. *Economic component*   What is the state of such economic variables as inflation, unemployment, and interest rates? What are the trends in these variables, and how are they relevant to the case?
2. *Social component*   What is the state of such social variables as education levels, customs, beliefs, and values? What are the trends in these variables, and how are they relevant to the case?
3. *Political component*   What is the state of such political variables as lobbying activities and government attitudes toward business? What are the trends in these variables and how are they relevant to the case?
4. *Legal component*   What is the level of such legal variables as federal, state, and local legislation? What are the trends in these variables and how are they relevant to the case?
5. *Technological component*   What is the level of technology in the industry? What technological trends are relevant to the case?
6. *Ethical component*   Does the case or problem involve ethical issues?

OPERATING ENVIRONMENT

1. *Customer component*   What are the target markets and customer profiles, and how are they relevant to the case?
2. *Competition component*   What are the major barriers to entry in this industry? What are the strengths, weaknesses, strategies, and market shares of major competitors, and how are they relevant to the case?
3. *Labor component*   What factors influence the supply of labor, and how are they relevant to the case?
4. *Supplier component*   What factors influence relationships between suppliers of resources and the firm, and how are they relevant to the case?
5. *International component*   What is the state of international factors? What international trends are relevant to the case?

INTERNAL ENVIRONMENT

1. *Organizational aspects*   What organizational or managerial issues, concepts, and analyses are relevant to the case?
2. *Marketing aspects*   What marketing issues, concepts, and analyses are relevant to the case?
3. *Financial aspects*   What financial issues, concepts, and analyses are relevant to the case?
4. *Personnel aspects*   What personnel issues, concepts, and analyses are relevant to the case?
5. *Production aspects*   What production issues, concepts, and analyses are relevant to the case?

In completing an environmental analysis, the analyst should keep six major points in mind:

1. Careful analysis is often required to separate relevant information from superfluous information. Just like the situations facing a practicing manager, cases often include information that is irrelevant to the major issues.

TABLE 13.3

General Worksheet for Analyzing the Current Situation

Environment	Relevant Issues (Specific to Case)	Case Impact (Favorable/ Unfavorable)	Case Importance (Important/ Unimportant)
GENERAL ENVIRONMENT			
Economic component	_____		
Social component	_____		
Political component	_____		
Legal component	_____		
Technological component	_____		
Ethical component	_____		
OPERATING ENVIRONMENT			
Customer component	_____		
Competition component	_____		
Labor component	_____		
Supplier component	_____		
International component	_____		
INTERNAL ENVIRONMENT			
Organizational aspects	_____		
Marketing aspects	_____		
Financial aspects	_____		
Personnel aspects	_____		

In order to get a clear understanding of the case problems, the analyst must decide what information is important and what to ignore.

2. It is important to determine the difference between symptoms of problems and current and potential problems themselves. Symptoms of problems are indicators of problems but are not problems per se. For example, a decline in sales in a particular sales territory is a symptom of a problem. The problem is the root cause of the decline in sales—perhaps the field representative stopped making sales calls on minor accounts in response to dissatisfaction with the firm's compensation plan.

3. In recording the current situation, the analyst must recognize the difference between facts and opinions. Facts are objective statements or accounts of information such as financial data reported in a balance sheet or income statement. Opinions are subjective interpretations of facts or situations. For example, when a particular executive expresses the belief that sales will increase by 20 percent next year, this is an opinion. The analyst must not place too much emphasis on unsupported opinions and must carefully consider any factors that may bias people's opinions.

4. It is often useful to collect additional information from outside the case when performing a situational analysis. Appendix 13A offers a summary of sources of secondary data from which additional information can be obtained. This information can be very useful for putting the problem in

context and for supporting an analysis. Remember, though, that the major problems are contained in the case, and the analyst should not need outside information to recognize them.

5. Regardless of how much information is contained in the case and how much additional information is collected, the analyst usually finds it impossible to characterize the current situation completely. At this point assumptions must be made. Clearly, because different analysts might make widely differing assumptions, assumptions must be stated explicitly. Doing so avoids confusion about how the analyst perceives the current situation and enables other analysts to evaluate the reasonableness and necessity of the assumptions.

6. When an analyst concludes that a certain aspect of an environmental analysis has no bearing on the case, he or she should say so explicitly. Moreover, analysts should avoid trying to force or stretch information to fit into each of the environmental components. Indeed some aspects are likely to be irrelevant to any specific case, although each must be evaluated to determine whether it is relevant.

Analyze and Record Problems and Their Core Elements

The environmental analysis just described is useful for developing a general understanding of the current situation. However, its primary purpose is to help the analyst recognize the major problems or issues. In other words, comparing the case situation with an optimal situation should highlight the inconsistencies between them. By an optimal situation, we mean a situation in which activities are performed in a manner consistent with sound managerial principles and logic.

For example, suppose analysis of a particular case revealed that although an organization had done an excellent job of setting objectives, its current strategy was not designed appropriately to accomplish these objectives. Because management principles strongly recommend that strategies flow from objectives, this inconsistency and the reasons for it should be carefully considered. The deviation in strategy is probably symptomatic of a deeper managerial problem.

Recognizing and recording problems and their core elements is crucial for a meaningful case analysis. Obviously, if the root problems are not determined and explicitly stated and understood, the remainder of the case analysis has little merit because it does not focus on the key issues.

Table 13.4 presents a worksheet to help analysts recognize and record problems. This table emphasizes the importance of providing evidence that a particular problem is a critical one. Simply stating that a particular issue is the major problem is not sufficient; analysts must also provide the reasoning by which they reached this conclusion.

Formulate, Evaluate, and Record Alternative Courses of Action

At this stage, the analyst addresses the question of what can be done to resolve the problems defined in the previous part of the analysis. Generally, several alternative courses of action that might help alleviate the problem are available. One approach to developing alternatives is to brainstorm as many as possible and then reduce the list to a workable number of the most feasible. Another

TABLE 13.4

**General Worksheet for Defining Problems
and Their Core Elements**

MAJOR PROBLEM OR ISSUE

Description of problem or issue:

_____

_____

_____

_____

Evidence that this is a major problem or issue:

1. Facts _____

_____

2. Symptoms or other effects of the problem _____

_____

3. Opinions _____

_____

4. Assumptions _____

_____

(Repeat as necessary for cases involving several problems or issues.)

approach is to screen each alternative as it is developed, saving for further evaluation and comparison only those that meet predetermined feasibility criteria. Regardless of the method used to develop alternatives, the final list should usually include only three or four of the better solutions.

After listing a number of feasible alternatives, the analyst evaluates their strengths and weaknesses. Strengths include anything favorable about the alternative (such as increased efficiency, increased productivity, cost savings, or increased sales and profits). Weaknesses include anything unfavorable about the alternative (such as its costs in time, money, and other resources or its relative ineffectiveness at solving the problem). Table 13.5 offers a worksheet for evaluating alternative courses of action.

Sound logic and the application of managerial principles are particularly important at this stage. It is essential to avoid alternatives that might alleviate the problem but could at the same time spawn a new, more serious problem or require a greater investment of resources than solving the problem warrants. Similarly, analysts must be as objective as possible in their evaluation of alternatives. For example, it is not uncommon for analysts to ignore important weaknesses of an alternative that they favor.

Select, Justify, and Record the Chosen Course of Action and Implementation

It is now time to select the alternative that best solves the problem, while creating a minimum of new problems. This alternative is selected via careful analysis of the strengths and weaknesses of each alternative scrutinized in the previous stage. Recording the logic and reasoning that precipitated the selection of a particular alternative is very important. Regardless of what alternative is selected, the analyst must justify the choice.

TABLE 13.5

General Worksheet for Evaluating Alternative Courses of Action

ALTERNATIVE 1

Description of alternative: _____

_____

_____

Strengths of alternative: _____

_____

Weaknesses of alternative: _____

_____

Overall evaluation of alternative: _____

_____

_____

ALTERNATIVE 2

Description of alternative: _____

_____

_____

Strengths of alternative: _____

_____

Weaknesses of alternative: _____

_____

Overall evaluation of alternative: _____

_____

(Repeat as necessary for each feasible alternative.)

At this stage in the analysis, an alternative has been selected, and the analyst has explained why she or he feels it is the appropriate course of action. The final phase in case analysis is to devise an action-oriented implementation plan. Analysts should describe their proposed implementation plans in as much detail as possible.

Table 13.6 offers a worksheet to use in considering implementation issues. Although cases do not always contain enough information for the analyst to answer all of these questions in detail, reasonable recommendations for implementation should be formulated. In doing so, the analyst may have to make certain assumptions about commonly used and effective methods of implementing strategic alternatives.

PITFALLS TO AVOID IN CASE ANALYSIS

Analysts commonly make a variety of errors in the process of case study. Below we discuss some of the mistakes analysts make most frequently. When evaluating your analyses or those of others, use this list as a guide to spotting potential shortcomings.

TABLE 13.6

General Worksheet for Implementing the Chosen Alternative

---

1. What should be done to implement the chosen alternative effectively?
Specific recommendation: _____
_____
_____

Justification: _____
_____

2. Who should be responsible for implementing the chosen alternative?
Specific recommendation: _____
_____

Justification: _____
_____

3. When and where should the chosen alternative be implemented?
Specific recommendation: _____
_____

Justification: _____
_____

4. How should the chosen alternative be evaluated for success or failure?
Specific recommendation: _____
_____

Justification: _____
_____

Inadequately Defining Problems

Analysts often recommend courses of action without adequately understanding or defining the problems that characterize the case. This sometimes occurs because analysts jump to premature conclusions upon first reading a case and then proceed to interpret everything in the case as justifying those conclusions—even factors that they should realize argue against them. Closely related is the error of analyzing symptoms without determining the root problems. A sound case analysis absolutely depends on a clear understanding of major case problems.

Searching for "The Answer"

Analysts sometimes spend a great deal of time searching through secondary sources to find out what an organization actually did in a particular case and then present this alternative as the one, right answer. However, this approach ignores the objective of undertaking a case study: to learn through exploration and discussion. There is no one official or correct answer to a case. Rather, many good analyses and solutions, as well as many poor ones, usually exist.

Assuming the Case Away

Analysts sometimes make such sweeping assumptions that the case problem is essentially assumed away. For example, suppose a case concerns a firm that has lost a major share of its market. Simply concluding that the firm will increase its market share by 10 percent per year for the next five years is an example of assuming the case away.

Not Having Enough Information

Analysts often complain that a case does not give enough information to support a good decision. However, there is good reason for not presenting all of the information in a case. In real business situations, managers and consultants seldom have all the information they would need to make an optimal decision. Reasonable assumptions and predictions have to be made, and the challenge is to arrive at intelligent solutions in spite of uncertainty and limited information.

Relying on Generalizations

Analysts sometimes discuss case problems and recommendations at such a general level that their work has little value. Case analysis calls for specific problems and recommendations, not sweeping generalizations. For example, to recommend that the structure of the firm be changed is to generalize. However, to provide a detailed plan for changing the organizational structure, to explain just what the structure should be, and to give one's reasons for this solution is to make a specific recommendation.

Postulating a Different Situation

Analysts sometimes exert considerable time and effort contending that "if the situation were different, I'd know what course of action to take" or "if the manager hadn't already fouled things up so badly, the firm wouldn't have any problems." Such reasoning ignores the fact that the events in the case have already happened and cannot be changed. Even though analysis or criticism of past events may be necessary in diagnosing problems, the situation as it exists must be addressed in the end, and decisions must be based on it.

Focusing Too Narrowly

Too often, analysts ignore the effects that a change in one area has on the rest of the situation. Although cases are sometimes labeled as concerning specific types of issues, this does not mean that other variables can be ignored. For example, changing the price of a product may well influence the appropriate methods of promotion and distribution.

Abandoning Realism

In many cases, analysts get so obsessed with solving a particular problem that their solutions become totally unrealistic. For example, designing and recommending a sound $1 million advertising program for a firm with a capital structure of $50,000 is totally unrealistic, even though, if it were possible to implement, it might solve the given problem.

Setting Up Straw Man Alternatives

Analysts sometimes offer a single viable alternative and several others that are extremely weak and untenable. The analysts then proceed with the evaluation and selection of an alternative (predictably enough) by discrediting the **straw man alternatives** and accepting the single viable solution. Such an approach to case analysis is inappropriate, because what is desired is a *set* of alternatives that it is worthwhile to evaluate. Case analysis can enhance the development of decision-making skills only when each alternative has some important strengths and analysts must make an informed choice.

Recommending Research or Consultants

Analysts sometimes offer unsatisfactory solutions to case problems by recommending either that some research be conducted to uncover problems or that a consultant be hired to do so. Although engaging in further research and hiring consultants may occasionally be useful recommendations as auxiliary steps in an analysis, it is still the analyst's job to identify the problems and decide how to solve them. When research or consultants are recommended in a case analysis, the rationale, costs, and potential benefits should be fully specified in the case report.

Rehashing Case Material

Analysts sometimes go to great lengths rewriting a history of an organization as presented in the case. This is unnecessary and wasteful: the instructor and other analysts are already familiar with this information. Similarly, student analysts sometimes copy case tables and figures and include them in written reports. This too is unnecessary. However, developing original graphs, pie charts, or other visual aids based on the case material is often a useful way to make a particular point.

Table 13.7 offers some further guidelines on approaching cases and gives an example of an effective student analysis.

Not Thinking!

By far the worst mistake analysts make is not thinking. Often analysts mistakenly assume that, having simply organized the case material in a logical format, they have done a case analysis! Similarly, although analysts usually have some general knowledge of a firm or situation, they often ignore it when working on a case. For example, suppose that a case involves a major automobile manufacturer. Although the case may say nothing about foreign imports, they may well have an important impact on the firm and should be considered. Analyzing cases requires that knowledge of management principles and sound logic from outside the case be applied.

After attempting unsuccessfully to analyze the first case or two, analysts sometimes give up and assure themselves that they cannot do case analyses. Such a conclusion is almost always unwarranted and ignores the fact that performing case analyses is a *learned* skill. To be sure, some students master case analysis much more quickly than others. Yet most students can become skillful analysts of cases and problems if they continue working hard on the cases and learning from class discussions.

COMMUNICATION OF THE CASE ANALYSIS

The final task in case analysis that we will consider here is to communicate the results of the analysis. The most comprehensive and insightful analysis has little value if it is not communicated effectively. Communication includes not only organizing the information in a logical manner but also using proper grammar and spelling. In addition, the overall appearance of a written report

TABLE 13.7

What Does Case "Analysis" Mean?

A common criticism of prepared cases goes something like this: "You repeated an awful lot of case material, but you really didn't analyze the case." At the same time, it is difficult to verbalize exactly what *analysis* means: Critics may say, "I can't explain exactly what it is, but I know it when I see it!"

It is not surprising that confusion arises, because the term *analysis* has many definitions and means different things in different contexts. In terms of case analysis, *analysis* means going beyond simply describing the case information. It includes determining the implications of the case information for developing strategy. This may involve careful mathematical analysis of sales and profit data or thoughtful interpretation of the text of the case.

One way of approaching analysis involves taking a series of three steps: synthesis, generalizations, and implications. A brief example of this process follows:

Case Material   The high growth rate of frozen pizza sales has attracted a number of large food processing firms, including Pillsbury (Totino's), Quaker Oats (Celeste), American Home Products (Chef Boy-ar-dee), Nestlé (Stouffer's), General Mills (Saluto), and H. J. Heinz (La Pizzeria). The major independents are Jeno's, Tony's, and John's. Jeno's and Totino's are the market leaders, with market shares of about 19 percent each. Celeste and Tony's have about 8 to 9 percent each, and the others have about 5 percent or less. [Excerpted from "The Pillsbury Company—Totino's Pizza," in Philip Kotler, *Principles of Marketing* (Englewood Cliffs, N.J.: Prentice-Hall, Inc., 1980), pp. 192–195.]

Synthesis   The frozen pizza market is a highly competitive and highly fragmented market.

Generalizations   In markets such as this, attempts to gain market share through lower consumer prices or heavy advertising are likely to be quickly copied by competitors and thus not be very effective.

Implications   Lowering consumer prices and spending more on advertising are likely to be poor strategies. Perhaps increasing freezer space in retail outlets could be effective; this objective might be obtained through trade discounts. Developing a superior product (such as better tasting pizza or microwave pizza) or increasing geographic coverage of the market might be better strategies for obtaining market share.

Note that none of these three steps includes any repetition of the case material. Rather, they all involve extracting the meaning of the information and, by pairing it with strategic management principles, coming up with its strategic implications.

---

and that of the presenters and visual aids in an oral report are often used by evaluators as an indication of the effort put into a project and of its overall quality.

Written Report

Good written reports usually start with outlines. We offer the framework in Table 13.8 as one useful format. This outline is fully consistent with the approach suggested in this chapter and, with a few exceptions, involves writing out in prose form the information in the various worksheets.

TABLE 13.8

Outline for Written Case Reports

1. Title page
2. Table of contents
3. Introduction
4. Environmental analysis
   A. General environment
   B. Operating environment
   C. Internal environment
   D. Assumptions
5. Problem definition
   A. Major problem 1 and evidence
   B. Major problem 2 (if applicable) and evidence
   C. Major problem 3 (if applicable) and evidence
6. Alternative courses of action
   A. Description of alternative 1
     a. Strengths
     b. Weaknesses

   B. Description of alternative 2
     a. Strengths
     b. Weaknesses
   C. Description of alternative 3
     a. Strengths
     b. Weaknesses
7. Chosen alternative and implementation
   A. Justification for alternative chosen
   B. Implementation specifics and justification
8. Summary of analysis
9. References
10. Technical appendices
   A. Financial analyses
   B. Other technical information

Elements of a Written Report

Title Page   The title page includes the title of the case and the names of all persons who were involved in preparing the report. It is also useful to include the name and number of the course for which the case was prepared and the date the project was submitted.

Table of Contents   The table of contents lists every heading in the report and the number of the page on which that particular section begins. If a variety of exhibits are included in a case report, it may be useful to include a table of exhibits listing every exhibit and the page number on which it is located.

Introduction   The introduction of a case analysis is not a summary of the case. It is a statement of the purpose of the report and a brief description of each of its major sections.

Environmental Analysis   This section reports the results of the analysis of each environmental component. Subheadings should be used for each of the three major environments and for each relevant component or aspect listed in Table 13.3. Again, if any of the environments or categories has no relevance to a particular case, simply report that the analysis revealed nothing crucial for this particular situational element. Any assumptions made concerning the current situation should also be reported in this section.

Problem Definition   This section offers a concise statement of the major problems in the case and reviews the evidence that led to the conclusion that these are the major issues. Problems should be listed in order of their importance and should be accompanied by an account of the evidence.

Alternative Courses of Action   This section describes each of the alternatives devised for solving the major problems in the case. The strengths and weaknesses of each alternative should be clearly delineated.

Chosen Alternative and Implementation   This section reveals which alternative has been selected and explains why it is the appropriate course of action. In addition, it should include a detailed description of how the alternative will be implemented and why this method of implementation is best.

Summary of Analysis   This brief section simply restates what the report has been about. It describes what was done in preparing the report, the basic problems, and the alternative selected for solving them. It is also useful in this section to offer any additional information that supports the quality of the analysis and the value of the alternative chosen.

References   Any outside materials used in the report should be listed alphabetically in an acceptable reference style, such as that used in articles in *The Academy of Management Journal*. (Such information should also be appropriately cited in footnotes throughout the report.)

Technical Appendices   Some cases require considerable financial analysis. Typically key financial analysis is reported in the text of the report, but detailed analysis and calculations are placed here. Any other types of analysis that are too long or too detailed for the body of the report can also be placed here.

Oral Presentation

Case analyses are often presented orally in class by individuals or teams of analysts. As is true for the written report, a good outline is critical, and it is often a good idea to provide each class member with a copy of the outline and a list of any assumptions that are made. Although there is no single best way to present a case or to divide responsibility among team members, simply reading a written report is unacceptable. (It encourages boredom and interferes with all-important class discussion.) It is important to emphasize the major points of the analysis and not get bogged down in unnecessary detail. If the instructor or a class member asks for more details on a specific point, of course, the presenter must supply them.

The use of visual aids can be very helpful in presenting case analyses in class. However, simply presenting financial statements or other detailed data contained in the case is a poor use of visual media. On the other hand, taking these statements or figures and recasting them in easy-to-understand pie charts or graphs can be very effective in making specific points. Remember that any type of visual aid should be large enough so that even people sitting in the rear of the classroom can see the information clearly.

Oral presentation of case analyses is particularly helpful to students who are learning the skill of speaking to a group, a common activity in many managerial positions. In particular, the ability to handle objections and disagreements without antagonizing others is a valuable skill to develop.

SUMMARY

This chapter presented a framework for case analysis and offered some suggestions for developing and communicating high-quality case reports. Case analysis begins with analysis and recording of the current situation, including all relevant aspects of the environment, followed by analysis and recording of the problems or issues on which the case hinges. The next step is to formulate, evaluate, and record alternative courses of action in order to narrow the field to the best feasible alternatives. Then it is necessary to select one of the proposed courses of action, explain this choice, and describe how it is to be implemented.

We cautioned against several pitfalls that can plague the student (or the ill-prepared manager) engaged in case analysis, and we offered some guidelines for communicating case analyses in a written report and in an oral presentation.

Performing good case analyses takes a lot of time and effort. Analysts must be highly motivated and willing to get involved in the case and in class discussion if they expect to learn effectively and succeed in a course where cases are utilized. Analysts with only passive interest who perform "night before" analyses cheat themselves of valuable learning experiences that are critical in preparing for a successful management career.

KEY TERMS

case, p. 317
worksheet, p. 320

straw man alternative, p. 327

CHECKLIST   An Operational Approach to Case and Problem Analysis

___   1. Read the case quickly to get an overview of the situation.

___   2. Read the case again thoroughly, underlining relevant information and taking notes on potential areas of concern.

___   3. Reread and study the case until it is well-understood.

___   4. Review outside sources of information that are relevant to the case, and record important information.

___   5. Complete the General Worksheet for Analyzing the Current Situation.

___   6. Review this worksheet in search of potential problems.

___   7. List all potential problems on the General Worksheet for Defining Problems and Their Core Elements

___   8. Review this worksheet and list the major problems in order of priority.

___   9. Complete the Worksheet for Defining Problems and Their Core Elements.

___   10. Develop several feasible solutions for dealing with the major problems.

___   11. Complete the General Worksheet for Evaluating Alternative Courses of Action.

___   12. Review this worksheet and ensure that all relevant strengths and weaknesses have been considered.

—   13. Decide which alternative solves the problems most effectively.

—   14. Complete the General Worksheet for Implementing the Chosen Alternative.

—   15. Prepare a written or oral report based on the worksheets.

APPENDIX 13A   *Selected Sources of Secondary Information*

Secondary sources of data are often useful in case analysis. They provide more thorough environmental analyses and can be used to support one's recommendations and conclusions. Many of the data sources listed below can be found in business libraries. Here they are grouped under five headings: General Business and Industry Sources, Basic U.S. Statistical Sources, Financial Information Sources, Marketing Information Sources, and Indexes and Abstracts.

General Business and Industry Sources

Aerospace Facts and Figures. Aerospace Industries Association of America.

Annual Statistical Report. American Iron and Steel Institute.

Chemical Marketing Reporter. Schnell Publishing. Includes lengthy, continuing list of "Current Prices of Chemicals and Related Materials."

Computerworld. Computerworld, Inc. Last December's issue includes "Review and Forecast," an analysis of computer industry's past year and the outlook for the next year.

Construction Review. Department of Commerce. Current statistics on construction put in place, costs, and employment.

Distribution Worldwide. Chilton Co. Special annual issue, *Distribution Guide*, compiles information on transportation methods and wages.

Drugs and Cosmetic Industry. Drug Markets, Inc. Separate publication in July, *Drug and Cosmetic Catalog*, provides list of manufacturers of drugs and cosmetics and their respective products.

Electrical World. January and February issues include two-part statistical report on expenditures, construction, and other categories by region, capacity, sales, and financial statistics for the electrical industry.

Encyclopedia of Business Information Sources. Paul Wasserman et al., eds., Gale Research Company. A detailed listing of primary subjects of interest to managerial personnel, with a record of sourcebooks, periodicals, organizations, directories, handbooks, bibliographies, and other sources of information on each topic. Two vols., nearly 17,000 entries in over 1,600 subject areas.

Forest Industries. Miller Freeman Publications, Inc. The March issue includes "Forest Industries Wood-Based Panel," a review of production and sales figures for selected wood products; extra issue in May includes a statistical review of the lumber industry.

Implement and Tractor. Intertec Publishing Corporation. January issue includes equipment specifications and operating data for farm and industrial equipment. November issue includes statistics and information on the farm industry.

Industry Surveys. Standard & Poor's Corp. Continuously revised analysis of leading industries (40 industries made up of 1,300 companies). Basic analysis features company ratio comparisons and balance sheet statistics.

Adapted from J. Paul Peter and James H. Donnelly, Jr., *Marketing Management: Knowledge and Skills,* 2nd ed. (Homewood, Ill.: BPI/Irwin, 1989), pp. 907–919.

Middle Market Directory. Dun & Bradstreet. Inventories approximately 18,000 U.S. companies with indicated worth of $500,000 to $999,999, giving officers, products, standard industrial classification, approximate sales, and number of employees.

Million Dollar Directory. Dun & Bradstreet. Lists U.S. companies with an indicated worth of $1 million or more, giving officers and directors, products, standard industrial classification, sales, and number of employees.

Milutinovich, J. S. "Business Facts for Decision Makers: Where to Find Them." *Business Horizons,* March–April 1985, pp. 63–80.

Modern Brewery Age. Business Journals, Inc. February issue includes a review of sales and production figures for the brewery industry. A separate publication, *The Blue Book,* issued in May, compiles sales and consumption figures by state for the brewery industry.

National Petroleum News. McGraw-Hill, Inc. May issue includes statistics on sales and consumption of fuel oils, gasoline, and related products. Some figures are for ten years, along with ten-year projections.

Operating Results of Department and Specialty Stores. National Retail Merchants Association.

Petroleum Facts and Figures. American Petroleum Institute.

Poor's Register of Corporations, Directors, and Executives of the United States and Canada. Standard & Poor's Corp. Divided into two sections. The first gives officers, products, sales range, and number of employees for about 30,000 corporations. The second gives brief information on executives and directors.

Quick-Frozen Foods. Harcourt Brace Jovanovich Publications. October issue includes "Frozen Food Almanac," providing statistics on the frozen food industry by product.

Statistical Sources. Paul Wasserman et al., eds. Gale Research Corp., 4th ed., 1974. A subject guide to industrial, business, social, educational, and financial data, and other related topics.

Basic U.S. Statistical Sources

Business Service Checklist. Department of Commerce. Weekly guide to Department of Commerce publications, plus key business indicators.

Business Statistics. Department of Commerce. (Supplement to *Survey of Current Business.*) History of the statistical series appearing in the *Survey.* Also included are source references and useful explanatory notes.

Census of Agriculture. Department of Commerce. Data by state and county on livestock, farm characteristics, values.

Census of Manufacturers. Department of Commerce. Industry statistics, area statistics, subjects reports, locations of plants, industry descriptions arranged by Standard Industrial Classification, and a variety of ratios.

Census of Mineral Industries. Department of Commerce. Similar to *Census of Manufacturers.* Also includes capital expenditures and employment and payrolls.

Census of Retail Trade. Department of Commerce. Compiles data for states, SMSAs, counties, and cities with populations of 2,500 or more by kind of business. Data include number of establishments, sales, payroll, and personnel.

Census of Selected Services. Department of Commerce. Includes data on hotels, motels, beauty parlors, barber shops, and other retail service organizations.

Census of Transportation. Passenger Transportation Survey, Commodity Transportation Survey, Travel Inventory and Use Survey, Bus and Truck Carrier Survey.

Census Tract Reports. Department of Commerce, Bureau of Census. Detailed information on both population and housing subjects.

Census of Wholesale Trade. Department of Commerce. Similar to *Census of Retail Trade*— except information is for wholesale establishments.

County and City Data Book. Department of Commerce. Summary statistics for small geo-graphical areas.

Current Business Reports. Department of Commerce. Reports monthly department store sales of selected items.

Economic Report of the President. Transmitted to the Congress in January (each year), to-gether with the *Annual Report* of the Council of Economic Advisers. Statistical tables relating to income, employment, and production.

Handbook of Basic Economic Statistics. Economic Statistics Bureau of Washington, D.C. Current and historical statistics on industry, commerce, labor, and agriculture.

Statistical Abstract of the United States. Department of Commerce. Summary statistics in industrial, social, political, and economic fields in the United States. It is aug-mented by the *Cities Supplement, The County Data Book,* and *Historical Statistics of the United States.*

Statistics of Income: Corporation Income Tax Returns. Internal Revenue Service. Balance sheet and income statement statistics derived from corporate tax returns.

Statistics of Income: U.S. Business Tax Returns. Internal Revenue Service. Summarizes financial and economic data for proprietorships, partnerships, and small business corporations.

Survey of Current Business. Department of Commerce. Facts on industrial and business activity in the United States and statistical summary of national income and product accounts. A weekly supplement provides an up to date summary of business.

Financial Information Sources

Blue Line Investment Survey. Quarterly ratings and reports on 1,000 stocks; analysis of 60 industries and special situations analysis (monthly); supplements on new develop-ments and editorials on conditions affecting price trends.

Commercial and Financial Chronicle. Variety of articles and news reports on business, gov-ernment, and finance. Monday's issue lists new securities, dividends, and called bonds. Thursday's issue is devoted to business articles.

Dun's Review. Dun & Bradstreet. This monthly includes very useful annual financial ra-tios for about 125 lines of business.

Fairchild's Financial Manual of Retail Stores. Information about officers and directors, products, subsidiaries, sales, and earnings for apparel stores, mail order firms, vari-ety chains, and supermarkets.

Federal Reserve Bulletin. Board of Governors of the Federal Reserve System. The "Finan-cial and Business Statistics" section of each issue of this monthly bulletin is the best single source for current U.S. banking and monetary statistics.

Financial World. Articles on business activities of interest to investors, including invest-ment opportunities and pertinent data on firms, such as earnings and dividend records.

Moody's Bank and Finance Manual; Moody's Industrial Manual; Moody's Municipal & Gov-ernment Manual; Moody's Public Utility Manual; Moody's Transportation Manual; Moody's Directors Service. Brief histories of companies and their operations, sub-sidiaries, officers and directors, products, and balance sheet and income statements over several years.

Moody's Bond Survey. Moody's Investors Service. Weekly data on stocks and bonds, in-cluding recommendations for purchases or sale and discussions of industry trends and developments.

Moody's Handbook of Widely Held Common Stocks. Moody's Investors Service. Weekly data on stocks and bonds, including recommendations for purchases or sale and discus-sions of industry trends and developments.

Security Owner's Stock Guide. Standard & Poor's Corp. Standard & Poor's rating, stock price range, and other helpful information for about 4,200 common and preferred stocks.

Security Price Index. Standard & Poor's Corp. Price indexes, bond prices, sales, yields, Dow Jones averages, etc.

Standard Corporation Records. Standard & Poor's Corp. Published in looseleaf form, offers information similar to Moody's manuals. Use of this extensive service facilitates buying securities for both the individual and the institutional investor.

Marketing Information Sources

[Based in part on Gilbert A. Churchill, Jr., *Marketing Research: Methodological Foundations,* 6th ed. (Fort Worth, TX: Dryden Press, 1995), pp. 318–335.]

Advertising Age. This important advertising weekly publishes a number of annual surveys or features of special interest related to U.S. national advertising statistics.

Audits and Surveys National Total-Market Index. Contains information on various product types including total market size, brand market shares, retail inventory, distribution coverage, and out of stock.

Commercial Atlas and Marketing Guide. Skokie, Ill.: Rand-McNally & Co. Statistics on population, principal cities, business centers, trading areas, sales and manufacturing units, transportation data, and so forth.

Dun & Bradstreet Market Identifiers. Relevant marketing information on over 4.3 million establishments for constructing sales prospect files, sales territories, and sales territory potentials and isolating potential new customers with particular characteristics.

Editor and Publisher "Market Guide." Market information for 1,500 American and Canadian cities. Data include populations, households, gas meters, climates, retailing, and newspaper information.

Guide to Consumer Markets. New York: The Conference Board. This useful annual compilation of U.S. statistics on the consumer marketplace covers population, employment, income, expenditures, production, and prices.

Industrial Marketing. "Guide to Special Issues." This directory is included in each issue. Publications are listed within primary market classifications and are listed for up to three months prior to advertising closing date.

Marketing Communications (January 1968 to January 1972, formerly *Printer's Ink,* 1914–1967.) Pertinent market information on regional and local consumer markets as well as international markets to January 1972.

Marketing Information Guide. Department of Commerce. Annotations of selected current publications and reports, with basic information and statistics on marketing and distribution.

National Purchase Diary Panel (NPDP). Monthly purchase information based on the largest panel diary in the United States with detailed brand, frequency of purchase, characteristics of heavy buyers, and other market data.

Nielson Retail Index. Contains basic product turnover data, retail prices, store displays, promotional activity, and local advertising based on a national sample of supermarkets, drugstores, and mass merchandisers.

Nielson Television Index. Well-known index that provides estimates of the size and nature of the audience for individual television programs.

Population and Its Distribution: The United States Markets. J. Walter Thompson Co. New York: McGraw-Hill Book Co. A handbook of marketing facts selected from the U.S. *Census of Population* and the most recent census data on retail trade.

Sales and Marketing Management. (Formerly *Sales Management,* to October 1975.) This valuable semimonthly journal includes four useful annual statistical issues: *Survey of Buying Power* (July); *Survey of Buying Power, Part II* (October); *Survey of Industrial*

Purchasing Power (April); *Survey of Selling Costs* (January). These are excellent references for buying income, buying power index, cash income, merchandise line, manufacturing line, and retail sales.

Selling Areas Marketing Inc. Reports on warehouse withdrawals of various food products in each of 42 major markets covering 80 percent of national food sales.

Simmons Media/Marketing Service. Provides cross referencing of product usage and media exposure for magazine, television, newspaper, and radio based on a strict national probability sample.

Standard Rate and Data. Nine volumes on major media which include a variety of information in addition to prices for media in selected markets.

Starch Advertising Readership Service. Measures the reading of advertisements in magazines and newspapers and provides information on overall readership percentages, readers per dollar, and rank when grouped by product category.

Indexes and Abstracts

Accountants Digest. L. L. Briggs. A digest of articles appearing currently in accounting periodicals.

Accountants Index. American Institute of Certified Public Accountants. An index to books, pamphlets, and articles on accounting and finance.

Accounting Articles. Commerce Clearing House. Loose-leaf index to articles in accounting and business periodicals.

Advertising Age Editorial Index. Crain Communications, Inc. Index to articles in *Advertising Age.*

American Statistical Index. Congressional Information Service. A comprehensive two-part annual index to the statistical publications of the U.S. government.

Applied Science & Technology Index. H. W. Wilson Co. Reviews over 200 periodicals relevant to the applied sciences, many of which pertain to business.

Battelle Library Review. (Formerly *Battelle Technical Review* to 1962.) Battelle Memorial Institute. Annotated bibliography of books, reports, and articles on automation and automatic processes.

Bulletin of Public Affairs Information Service. Public Affairs Information Service, Inc. (Since 1915—annual index.) A selective list of the latest books, pamphlets, government publications, reports of public and private agencies, and periodicals related to economic conditions, public administration, and international relations.

Business Education Index. McGraw-Hill Book Co. (Since 1940—annual index.) Annual author and subject index of books, articles, and theses on business education.

Business Periodicals Index. H. W. Wilson Co. A subject index to the disciplines of accounting, advertising, banking, general business, insurance, labor, management, and marketing.

Catalog of United States Census Publication. Department of Commerce, Bureau of Census. Indexes all available Census Bureau data. Main divisions are agriculture, business, construction, foreign trade, government, guide to locating U.S. census information.

Computer and Information Systems. (Formerly *Information Processing Journal* to 1969.) Cambridge Communications Corporation.

Cumulative Index of NICB Publications. The National Industrial Conferences Board. Annual index of NICB books, pamphlets, and articles in the area of management of personnel.

Funk and Scott Index International. Investment Index Company. Indexes articles on foreign companies and industries from over 1,000 foreign and domestic periodicals and documents.

Guide to U.S. Government Publications. McLean, Va.: Documents Index. Annotated guide to publications of various U.S. government agencies.

International Abstracts in Operations Research. Operations Research Society of America.

International Journal of Abstracts of Statistical Methods in Industry. The Hague, Netherlands: International Statistical Institute.

Management Information Guides. Gale Research Company. Bibliographical references to information sources for various business subjects.

Management Review. American Management Association.

Monthly Catalog of U.S. Government Publications. U.S. Government Printing Office. Continuing list of federal government publications.

Monthly Checklist of State Publications. U.S. Library of Congress, Exchange and Gift Division. Record of state documents received by Library of Congress.

New York Times Index. Very detailed index of all articles in the *Times,* arranged alphabetically with many cross-references.

Psychological Abstracts. American Psychological Association.

Public Affairs Information Service. Public Affairs Information Service, Inc. A selective subject list of books, pamphlets, and government publications covering business, banking, and economics as well as subjects in the area of public affairs.

Reader's Guide to Periodical Literature. H. W. Wilson Co. Index by author and subject to selected U.S. general and nontechnical periodicals.

Sociological Abstracts. American Sociological Association.

The Wall Street Journal Index. Dow Jones & Company, Inc. An index of all articles in *The WSJ* grouped in two sections: corporate news and general news.

Index

Mazis, Michael B., 228n
MCI Communications, 287
Mercedes, 107
Merck and Company, 95
MERCOSUR, 176
Mesch, Allen H., 43n
Mezias, Stephen, 133
Miaoulis, G., 33n
Middaugh, J. K., 138n
Miles, Raymond, 119n, 120, 121
Milkovich, G. T., 95n
Miller, Michael, 58n
Ministry of International Trade and Industry (MITI), 177. *See also* Japan
Mintzberg, Henry, 7, 8n, 9n, 24, 39–40, 111, 133, 154n
Missions, 16, 58–63, 69. *See also* **Direction, organizational**
and implementation, 128
international, 182
and long-term objectives, 67
and marketing function, 283
and social responsibility, 235
Total Quality Management (TQM) in, 208
Mission statements, 59–61
Mitchell, Russell, 115n
Mitroff, Ian I., 73
Modicon, 209
Monitoring skills, 130. *See also* **Implementation**
Morgenson, Gretchen, 305
Moseley, Ray, 232n
Motivation. *See also* Workers
and implementation approaches, 125, 127
and organizational objectives, 65–66
and vision, 56
Motorola, 254
Multifactor portfolio matrix, 101–104. *See also* **Corporate-level strategies**
Multinational corporations, 179. *See also* **International management**
Murdoch, Rupert, 232
Mustang, 133–134
Myers, Stewart C., 279

Nadler, David, 9n, 51
Nalebuff, Barry, 80n, 106
Navratilova, Martina, 305
Neff, R., 210n
Nelson, Kent, 124
Nelson, M. M., 174n
Net cash flows, 275–277. *See also* Costs

Net present value analysis, 275–278
Network organizational structures, 120–121
Neubauer, Fred, 11n
Nevin, John R., 227n
New entrants, 78. *See also* Competitors
Newly industrialized countries (NICs), 175. *See also* **International management**
New products. *See* **Product life cycle**
News International, 232
New United Motor Manufacturing Inc. (NUMMI), 184
Niche strategies. *See* **Focus strategies**
Nichols, Nancy A., 238
Nike Corporation, 121, 147
Nissan, 212
Nomani, A. Q., 170n
Nonmanufacturing operations. *See* **Service operations**
Nonprofit organizations, 283
Norgundkar, Rajendra, 158
Normann, Richard, 106
North American Free Trade Agreement (NAFTA), 170–172
Norton, David P., 66n
Nulty, Peter, 42n
Nutt, Paul C., 125n

Obermeyer, Walter R., 248n
Objectives, organizational, 16, 64–69. *See also* **Direction, organizational**
in case analysis, 323
international, 182
and marketing function, 283
in mission statements, 60
operational. *See* **Operational objectives**
and strategic control, 147–148, 156
Objective and task method of promotion budgeting. *See* **Task method** of promotion budgeting
O'Brian, Bridget, 4n
O'Brien, William, 56
Ocean Spray, 229
Ohmae, K., 181n
Olson, Jerry C., 219n, 283n
O'Neill, William J., 167
Operating environments, 34–36, 180, 321. *See also* **Environments, organizational**
Operational objectives, 66–67.

See also **Objectives, organizational**
Operations function, 21, 243–251
financial analysis for, 265
functional-level strategies for, 93
and strategic management process, 252–256
Opinions, in case analysis, 322
Opportunities. *See* **SWOT (strengths, weaknesses, opportunities, and threats) analysis**
Oral presentations, 331. *See also* Reports
Organizational Change implementation approach, 127. *See also* Change, strategic
Organizational structures, 115–121, 123, 156
Organization charts, 121
Organization of Petroleum Exporting Countries (OPEC), 181
Organizing skills, 130. *See also* **Implementation**
Oster, P., 174n
Ottensmeyer, Edward, 32n, 41n, 56n
Outlines, 329. *See also* Reports
Outputs, 246, 258. *See also* Products
Outsourcing, 92, 121, 158. *See also* **Value chain analysis**
Overall cost leadership strategy, 81–82, 86. *See also* **Formulation, strategy**
Ovitz, Michael, 147

Pacific Rim, 175–176
Pareja, P. E., 203n
Parent companies, 179, 183–184
Parkin, David, 85
Pascale, Richard, 51
Patterson, Gregory A., 26n, 167
Pearce, John A., II, 59n
Pearsall, A. E., 238
Pendleton, S., 177n
Penetration pricing strategies, 300. *See also* **Marketing** function
Pentium microprocessor, 73
Pepsi-Co, 78–79
Percentage-of-sales method of promotion budgeting, 304. *See also* **Promotion**
Pereira, Joseph, 4n, 239n
Performance. *See also* Profits
of management information systems, 154
measures of, 138, 140–148,